T0214402

Lecture Notes in Computer Science   11278

Commenced Publication in 1973
Founding and Former Series Editors:
Gerhard Goos, Juris Hartmanis, and Jan van Leeuwen

More information about this series at http://www.springer.com/series/7409

Uma Shanker Tiwary (Ed.)

Intelligent Human Computer Interaction

10th International Conference, IHCI 2018
Allahabad, India, December 7–9, 2018
Proceedings

 Springer

Editor
Uma Shanker Tiwary
Indian Institute of Information Technology
Allahabad, India

ISSN 0302-9743   ISSN 1611-3349 (electronic)
Lecture Notes in Computer Science
ISBN 978-3-030-04020-8   ISBN 978-3-030-04021-5 (eBook)
https://doi.org/10.1007/978-3-030-04021-5

Library of Congress Control Number: 2018960863

LNCS Sublibrary: SL3 – Information Systems and Applications, incl. Internet/Web, and HCI

This Springer imprint is published by the registered company Springer Nature Switzerland AG
The registered company address is: Gewerbestrasse 11, 6330 Cham, Switzerland

Preface

It is indeed a great privilege to present the proceedings of the 10th International Conference on Intelligent Human Computer Interaction (IHCI 2018) organized by the Indian Institute of Information Technology, Allahabad during December 07–09, 2018. This is one of the rare conferences focusing on human–computer interaction (HCI). The conference aims to explore new dimensions of HCI science and technologies instead of confining HCI only to various types of interfaces.

In total, 89 papers were submitted. The review committee had a very challenging task of selecting high-quality submissions. Each paper was peer-reviewed by at least three reviewers. On the recommendation of the Program Committee, 28 papers were accepted for presentation at the main conference.

The proceedings are organized in five chapters corresponding to each track of the conference as described below:

The 'ECG/EEG-Based and Other Multimodal Interactions' track was related to enabling technology that encompasses brain–computer interfaces, body sensors and communication multimodal interfaces, ECG/EEG-based feedback and control for HCI, ECG/EEG-based emotion, affect analysis and detection. In this track, eight papers were accepted. The 'Natural Language, Speech and Dialogue Processing' track was dedicated to exploring the area of natural language processing, e.g., natural language generation; dialog systems; speech-based applications; discourse, semantics, syntax, grammar, and lexicon; lexical semantics, ontologies, etc. Six papers were accepted for presentation in this track.

The 'Modeling Human Cognitive Processes and Simulation' track covered papers on modeling perceptual processes; modeling of learning and thinking; modeling of memory; brain–computer integration; collaborative learning systems; and computer supported-assistive technology. Finally, four papers were selected for this track.

The 'Image and Vision-Based Interactions' track consisted of five papers covering the area of interactive generation of textual and visual works; vision-based face, motion, and gesture capture; scene understanding; vision-based medical imaging and diagnosis; biometric interactive technologies; vision and languages; and vision for robotics.

The 'Applications of HCI' track also comprised of five papers specifically representing the area of natural user interfaces; human-robot interaction; remote and face-to-face collaboration; embodied conversational agents; mobile interfaces; technology for differently abled persons; health, multi-modal interfaces (speech, vision, eye gaze, face, physiological information etc.) and intelligent visualization tools.

We would like to thank the Organizing Committee for their efforts and time spent to ensure the success of the conference. We would also like to express our gratitude to the Program Committee members for their timely and helpful reviews. And last but not least, We thank all the invited speakers, authors, and members of the Program

Committee for their contribution in making IHCI 2018 a stimulating and productive conference; and hope to get their continued support in the future.

December 2018   Uma Shanker Tiwary

Organization

General Chair

Mriganka Sur   MIT, USA

Steering Committee

Uma Shanker Tiwary	IIIT Allahabad, India
Tom D. Gedeon	Australian National University, Australia
Debasis Samanta	IIT Kharagpur, India
Atanendu Sekhar Mandal	CSIR-CEERI, Pilani, India
Tanveer Siddiqui	University of Allahabad, India
Jaroslav Pokorny	Charles University, Czech Republic
Sukhendu Das	IIT Madras, India
Samit Bhattacharya	IIT Guwahati, India

Program Committee

P. Nagabhushan	IIIT Allahabad, India
A. G. Ramakrishnan	Indian Institute of Science, India
Achard Catherine	Sorbonne University, France
Aditya Nigam	IIT Mandi, India
Akki B. Channappa	IIIT Allahabad, India
Alexander Gelbukh	Mexican Academy of Science, Mexico
Alexandre Vervisch-Picois	Telecom SudParis, France
Alok Kanti Deb	IIT Delhi, India
Amine Chellali	Evry Val d'Essonne University, France
Amrita Basu	JU, India
Anupam Agarwal	IIIT Allahabad, India
Anupam Basu	IIT Kharagpur, India
Ashutosh Mishra	IIIT Allahabad, India
Atanendu Sekhar Mandal	CSIR-CEERI, Pilani, India
Bernadette Dorizzi	Telecom SudParis, France
Bibhas Ghoshal	IIIT Allahabad, India
Catherine Achard	Pierre et Marie Curie University, France
Daniel Wesierski	Gdansk University of Technology, Poland
Daoudi Mohamed	IMT Lille Douai, France
David Antonio Gomez Jauregui	ESTIA, France
David Griol Barres	Carlos III University of Madrid, Spain
Debasis Samanta	IIT Kharagpur, India
Dijana Petrovska	Telecom SudParis, France

Ekram Khan   AMU, India
G. C. Nandi   IIIT Allahabad, India
Geehyuk Lee   KAIST, South Korea
Geoffrey Vaquette   Commissariat à l'énergie atomique et aux énergies
                            alternatives, France
Gérard Chollet   CNRS, France
Jan Platoš   VŠB-TU Ostrava, Czech Republic
Jaroslav Pokorny   Charles University, Czech Republic
Jérôme Boudy   Telecom SudParis, France
José Marques Soares   Universidade Federal do Ceará, Brazil
K. P. Singh   IIIT Allahabad, India
Kavita Vemury   IIIT Hyderabad, India
Keith Cheverst   Lancaster University, UK
Laurence Devillers   LIMSI, University ParisSud, Paris Saclay University,
                            France
Lopamudra Choudhury   Jadavpur University, Kolkata, India
Malik Mallem   Evry Val d'Essonne University, France
Manish Kumar   IIIT Allahabad, India
Maria Stylianou Korsnes   University of Oslo, Norway
Marion Morel   Pierre et Marie Curie University, France
Martin A. Giese   CIN/HIH University Clinic Tübingen, Germany
Michele Gouiffes   LIMSI, ParisSud University, Paris Saclay University,
                            France
Mohamed Chetouani   Pierre et Marie Curie University, France
Mriganka Sur   MIT, USA
Nesma Houmani   Telecom SudParis, France
Partha Pratim Das   IIT KGP, India
Patrick Horain   Telecom SudParis, France
Plaban Kumar Bhowmick   IIT KGP, India
Pradipta Biswas   CPDM-IISC, India
Pritish K. Varadwaj   IIIT Allahabad, India
Harish Karnick   IIT Kanpur, India
Somnath Biswas   IIT Kanpur, India
Rahul Banerjee   BITS Pilani, India
Richard Chebeir   Pau et des Pays de l'Adour University, France
Samit Bhattacharya   IIT Guwahati, India
San Murugesan   BRITE Professional Services, Australia
Santanu Chaudhury   CSIR-CEERI, Pilani, India
Satish K. Singh   IIIT Allahabad, India
Shekhar Verma   IIIT Allahabad, India
Shen Fang   Pierre et Marie Curie University, France
Sukhendu Das   IIT Madras, India
Suneel Yadav   IIIT Allahabad, India
Tanveer J. Siddiqui   University of Allahabad, India
Thierry Chaminade   Institut de Neurosciences de la Timone, France
Tom D. Gedeon   Australian National University, Australia

Uma Shanker Tiwary	IIIT Allahabad, India
Vijay K. Chaurasiya	IIIT Allahabad, India
Vijayshri Tiwary	IIIT Allahabad, India
Ydalia Garcia	Telecom SudParis, France

Additional Reviewers

Ramesh Kumar Agrawal	JNU, India
Sukumar Nandi	IITG, India
Karmeshu	JNU, India
Asif Ekbal	IITP, India
Sriparna Saha	IITP, India
Jaidhar C. D.	NITK, India
Pinaki Mitra	IITG, India
Sowmya Kamath S.	NITK, India
Tirthankar Gayen	JNU, India
Rajiv Singh	Banasthali Vidyapith, India
Shiv Ram Dubey	IIITS, India
Jean-Yves Didier	Evry Val d'Essonne University, France
Mohammed Javed	IIITA, India
Triloki Pant	IIITA, India

Local Organizing Committee

Uma Shanker Tiwary	IIITA, India
Shekhar Verma	IIITA, India
Akki B. Channappa	IIITA, India
Pritish K. Varadwaj	IIITA, India
Vijayshri Tiwary	IIITA, India
Ashutosh Mishra	IIITA, India
Satish K. Singh	IIITA, India
K. P. Singh	IIITA, India
Vijay K. Chaurasiya	IIITA, India
Bibhas Ghoshal	IIITA, India
Manish Kumar	IIITA, India
Suneel Yadav	IIITA, India
Ajay Tiwary	IIITA, India
Punit Singh	IIITA, India
Rohit Mishra	IIITA, India
Sudhakar Mishra	IIITA, India
Shrikant Malviya	IIITA, India
Santosh K. Baranwal	IIITA, India
Pankaj Tyagi	IIITA, India

Contents

Modeling Human Cognitive Processes and Simulation

Image and Vision Based Interactions

Applications of HCI

ECG, EEG-Based and Other Multimodal Interactions

Single Trial P300 Classification Using Convolutional LSTM and Deep Learning Ensembles Method

Raviraj Joshi[1]($\boxtimes$), Purvi Goel[1], Mriganka Sur[2], and Hema A. Murthy[1]

[1] Indian Institute of Technology Madras, Chennai, India
{rjoshi,purvi,hema}@cse.iitm.ac.in
[2] Department of Brain and Cognitive Sciences,
Massachusetts Institute of Technology, Cambridge, USA
msur@mit.edu

Abstract. The odd ball paradigm is a commonly used approach to develop Brain Computer Interfaces (BCIs). EEG signals have shown to elicit a positive deflection known as the P300 event related potential during odd ball experiments. BCIs based on these experiments rely on detection of the P300 potential. EEG signals are noisy, and therefore P300 detection is performed on an average of multiple trials, thus making them inappropriate for BCI applications. We propose a neural network model based on Convolutional Long Short Term Memory (ConvLSTM) for single trial P300 classification. EEG data encodes both spatial and temporal information using multiple EEG sensors. Convolutional neural networks (CNNs) have been known to capture spatial information whereas LSTMs are known to capture temporal information. Our experiments show that the proposed method outperforms previous CNN based approaches on raw EEG signals. The approaches were evaluated on publicly available dataset II of BCI competition III. Another dataset was recorded locally using audio beeps as stimuli to validate these approaches. The ensemble models based on CNNs and ConvLSTM are also proposed. These models perform better than individual architectures.

Keywords: Brain-computer interface · Event related potential P300 · Convolutional neural networks · Convolutional long short term memory

1 Introduction

Brain computer interfaces have made it possible to communicate our thoughts without vocalizing or performing actions. It relies on the neural activity of the brain to interface with the external world. BCIs are useful for the speech challenged since they enable such persons with a medium of communication. Electroencephalography (EEG) is a widely used technique to develop BCI applications. EEGs are non invasive and provides a comparatively low cost solution to build BCI devices.

© Springer Nature Switzerland AG 2018
U. S. Tiwary (Ed.): IHCI 2018, LNCS 11278, pp. 3–15, 2018.
https://doi.org/10.1007/978-3-030-04021-5_1

EEGs have a high temporal resolution as compared to other brain imaging techniques. It is therefore capable of capturing very short cognitive processes in the brain, which is elicited in the form of an Event Related Potential (ERP). ERPs are the positive or negative potentials seen in the EEG signals in response to external meaningful stimuli. These potentials are time locked and can be reliably detected to build practical BCI. However, EEG signals have low signal to noise ratio, which makes it difficult to detect these potentials in individual trials. Traditionally, multiple trials are averaged together in the time domain so that noise gets canceled and ERPs can be visualized. The focus of this work is the ERP elicited during odd ball experiment known as P300 event related potential and its single trial detection. In the odd ball experiment, a series of stimuli are presented to the subject. Two types of stimuli are presented, one which is frequent, while another that is infrequent. Infrequent stimuli cause ERP.

P300 signals have been mainly studied in the context of clinical diagnostics and psychoanalysis. Recently P300 is being considered as a possible BCI. A very popular program based on P300 is the P300 speller program [10]. P300 speller is a tool used to efficiently communicate symbols of interest, by arranging them in a 6×6 grid. There are other examples of P300 being used for cursor control [14] and wheelchair control [21].

Detecting these P300 potentials in single trials has gained a lot of attention. The speed of communication will greatly improve if P300 can be reliably detected from individual trials. Previous works have used conventional machine learning techniques and neural network based classifiers for P300 classification tasks. EEG data has both spatial and temporal characteristics. The spatial structure is attributed to different EEG sensors placed on the subject's scalp and the temporal structure is implicit as it picks up the voltage value at each time instant. Moreover, P300 has timing characteristics and has different signature across the spatial structure of the brain. Thus, the spatio-temporal information is associated with P300 potential as well. In this work, we propose a neural network model based on Convolutional Long Short Term Memory (ConvLSTM) that naturally exploits both spatial and temporal characteristics [24]. As P300 potential is seen around 300 ms after the onset of stimulus for a short duration, an LSTM based architecture was chosen to model this sequential information. The convolution units of ConvLSTM encodes the spatial information captured by electrodes placed on the scalp. This is the first work to employ ConvLSTM for EEG data analysis. ConvLSTM also requires relatively less number of parameters. Thus, ConvLSTM is easy to train given the scarcity of training data in EEG experiments.

We propose an architecture that uses a 3D representation of EEG data [6]. Although ConvLSTM has fewer parameters, it performs better than CNN architectures as it provides better modeling of EEG data. Finally, we evaluate the performance of ensemble architectures based on the individual models discussed in this paper. These ensemble models perform better than individual models. The results of these experiments are better than the previous benchmarks on publicly available BCI competition III dataset.

The rest of the paper is organized as follows: Sect. 2 describes related work done in this field. The experimental setup, pre-processing methods and the models used for P300 detection are explained in Sect. 3. The results are discussed in Sect. 4 and Sect. 5 is dedicated to Conclusion.

2   Related Work

Convolutional neural network (CNN) based approach for P300 detection was first proposed by Cecotti and Graser [7]. The proposed model with two convolutional and two fully connected layers could achieve comparable P300 detection results on raw EEG signals. The two convolutional layers were designed in such a way that the first layer captured the spatial information and the second layer captured the temporal information. They proposed seven CNN architectures including three ensemble models. This work was extended by Liu *et al.* to demonstrate the importance of batch normalization in the classification process [15]. They proposed BN3 which coupled the existing CNN models with batch normalization to prevent overfitting. BN3 could achieve the state of the art character recognition rates. In these works, the EEG data was represented in a 2D matrix of dimension channels × time, thus forming an image like structure. The convolution operations were performed along the spatial and temporal axis. A more relevant EEG data representation was proposed by Carabez *et al.* [6]. In their work, a single trial EEG was represented in 3 dimensions. The first two dimensions encode the spatial structure of EEG while the third dimension is the temporal axis. The work described in this paper uses the same technique to represent the EEG signals.

Recently, Bashivan *et al.* in their work used stacked convolutional and LSTM layers to process EEG data [5]. However, their work was based on spectral features extracted in theta, alpha, and beta frequency bands. For each time instant, EEG data was represented in (r,g,b) image like structure. The first two dimensions encoded the spatial structure of channels while the third dimension was reserved for the three frequency bands. Similar approach for EEG data representation was employed by Maddula *et al.* for classifying P300 signals [16]. They proposed different stacked CNN and LSTM architectures based on the same spectral features. Their results were evaluated on P300 speller experiment which was different from BCI competition III experiment and hence the results cannot be compared. Our work is different from these works as we do not use stacked architectures and our work is completely based on processing raw EEG signals. Various other studies of using recurrent neural networks on EEG data have been proposed over time [11,18,19], but these works fail to take advantage of spatial characteristics of EEG data.

An ensemble of multiple machine learning models has been commonly used in the classification of EEG signals [23]. Previously, to account for signal variability, an ensemble of 17 support vector machines was used by Rakotomamonjy and Guigue [20]. They also proposed a recursive channel elimination algorithm to select discriminative channels. Deep learning ensemble models based on CNNs were proposed in [4,7].

3   Methodology

Two different datasets are used in this work, one of which was collected in the EEG Lab set up at Computer Science and Engineering Department, IIT Madras and other was publicly available BCI Competition dataset [13].

3.1   BCI Competition Dataset

The dataset II from BCI competition III is used in our experiments. The data consists of P300 evoked potentials generated using the P300 Speller paradigm proposed by Farwell and Dochin [10].

The data was collected from 2 subjects in 3 sessions using a 64 channel EEG sensor net. The sampling rate was 240 Hz and the signals were bandpass filtered between 0.1 to 60 Hz. The odd ball paradigm results in unbalanced data for the two classes, so the target P300 trials are replicated four times so as to get an equal number of trials for both the classes. This is a classical oversampling approach to counter data imbalance problem [17]. The number of samples for both the classes during training and testing is shown in Table 1. A detailed description of the dataset can be found in [13].

Table 1. Training and testing trials

Subject	Train		Test	
	Target	Non-Target	Target	Non-Target
A	2550	12750	3000	15000
B	2550	12750	3000	15000

3.2   Odd Beep Experiment

The EEG data was collected using the Geodesic Sensor net comprising of 128 channels [2]. Subjects were students from different department in an age group of 20 to 30 years. A written consent was given by participants before the experiment. The subjects were seated in a comfortable chair to avoid fatigue inside an acoustically and electromagnetically shielded testing chamber. The subjects were asked to keep the eyes closed and do minimal muscle movement during the recording.

The subjects are presented with a series of audio beeps with two different frequencies. One of the beep also known as odd beep or target beep is presented less frequently than the other non target beeps. The frequencies for two beeps were chosen to be 1000 Hz (non target tone) and 2000 Hz (target tone). The participant was supposed to gently tap on the mobile screen when a rare target stimulus is presented and the other stimulus did not require any response. A train of 150 beeps is presented to the subject. These 150 beeps are divided across 25 trials. Each trial, therefore, consists of 6 beeps. Out of these 6 beeps, 1 of the beep is the target beep, while the others are non-target beeps. The target beep is chosen randomly. Four extra non-target beeps were added at the start of the experiment to make the subject familiar with non-target tone. The inter-stimulus gap is set to 800 ms. A baseline of 60 s is recorded at the start and end of the experiment. The experiment timeline is shown in Fig. 1.

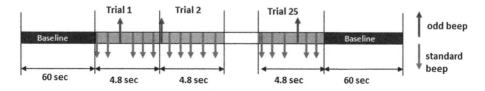

Fig. 1. Single Oddbeep experiment timeline

The performance of a neural network is defined by the availability of enough training samples. So multiple sessions of the experiment were performed on two subjects. For each subject recording was done on 5 consecutive days and 3 sessions were recorded on each day. A total of 15 sessions were recorded out of which 10 sessions were used for training and 5 sessions were used for testing. Table 2 shows the count of the target and non-target samples used for training and testing. Target trials were replicated to match the number of non-target trials. Although the number of samples is considerably less as compared to the online dataset, it is just enough to train our shallow neural networks.

Table 2. Training and testing trials for Single Odd Beep Dataset

Subject	Train		Test	
	Target	Non-Target	Target	Non-Target
A	250	1290	125	645
B	250	1290	125	645

3.3 Pre-processing

BCI Competition Dataset. The EEG data is highly dominated by noise, so the data is bandpass filtered in the range 0.1–20 Hz. Moreover, the P300 wave is characterized by a low frequency component which is captured well by the filtered signal. The P300 potential is seen in EEG signals as a positive deflection around 300 ms after the onset of the stimulus, so we consider a 667 ms time window after the onset of the stimulus [15]. As the data is sampled at 240 Hz, 667 ms corresponds to 160 samples for each trial. The data segments are downsampled and the length of segment is reduced to 80 samples. Thus, each target and non-target trial is represented by a 64×80 matrix, where 64 defines the number of channels.

In order to retain the spatial correlation of the electrodes, the 64 electrodes are mapped to a 10×11 2D map as defined in [6]. Thus, each time instant is represented by a 2D matrix and each trial is now 3 dimensional. Each column vector of the 2D matrix in the original data corresponds to a 2D frame in the 3D map. The depth of the 3D map represents the time axis (80 in this case). This 3D representation, similar to video frames is given as an input to our models.

Single Odd Beep Dataset. The pre-processing steps used for single odd beep dataset are similar to the steps used for BCI competition dataset. Two major changes are induced by the fact that this data is sampled at 250 Hz and is captured using a 128 channel EEG net. The data is band passed filtered in the range 0.1–20 Hz and a window of 640 ms after the onset of stimulus is extracted for each trial. As the sampling rate is 250 Hz, 640 ms corresponds to 160 samples.

To preserve the spatial structure, the 128 electrodes are mapped to a 14×13 2D map. Some peripheral electrodes are dropped to create a dense matrix of size 10×11 as shown in Fig. 2. The 3-dimensional structure of electrodes is converted into a 2D map using software provided by EEGLAB [9].

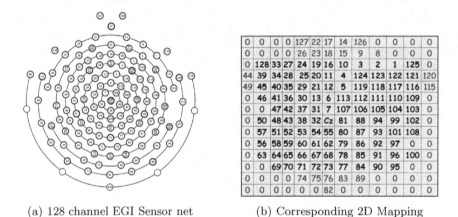

0	0	0	0	127	22	17	14	126	0	0	0	0
0	0	0	0	26	23	18	15	9	8	0	0	0
0	128	33	27	24	19	16	10	3	2	1	125	0
44	39	34	28	25	20	11	4	124	123	122	121	120
49	45	40	35	29	21	12	5	119	118	117	116	115
0	46	41	36	30	13	6	113	112	111	110	109	0
0	0	47	42	37	31	7	107	106	105	104	103	0
0	50	48	43	38	32	Cz	81	88	94	99	102	0
0	57	51	52	53	54	55	80	87	93	101	108	0
0	56	58	59	60	61	62	79	86	92	97	0	0
0	63	64	65	66	67	68	78	85	91	96	100	0
0	0	69	70	71	72	73	77	84	90	95	0	0
0	0	0	0	74	75	76	83	89	0	0	0	0
0	0	0	0	0	0	82	0	0	0	0	0	0

(a) 128 channel EGI Sensor net   (b) Corresponding 2D Mapping

Fig. 2. Mapping of 128 electrodes to 2D matrix

4 Model Description

4.1 CNN Model for 3D Data (CNN-3D)

Convolutional neural networks have been widely used in classification tasks involving images and videos. They are good at capturing spatial information

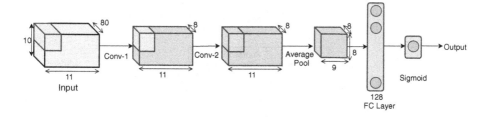

Fig. 3. Model 1: Architecture of CNN-3D

and can be used to process 3D data. CNNs are especially suited to EEG because of their translation invariance property. The EEG electrodes may be slightly misplaced across recordings. This shift of electrodes is easily accounted by convolution and pooling layers. Our model uses average pooling instead of the standard max pooling based on the fact that nearby electrodes have similar signatures. The model architecture is shown in Fig. 3 and the details of the proposed model are listed below

- The input data is batch normalized and passed to the next layer. The importance of batch normalization for EEG data is already studied in [15]. The batch size is set to 64 samples.
- The data of size $10 \times 11 \times 80$ is passed through a convolutional layer. This layer has a filter of size 3×3 which spans across the depth of input. Eight such filters are applied and appropriate padding is done to retain the input dimension. After this operation, the output is reduced to $10 \times 11 \times 8$ which is passed through *relu* non-linearity. This output is further batch normalized and a dropout of 0.2 probability is applied. The dropout operation is performed only during the training phase.
- The next layer performs a similar convolution operation with the same number of filters.
- The output is then average pooled with a filter of size 2×2 and a stride of 1. This reduces the output dimension to $8 \times 9 \times 8$. This is followed by a batch normalization layer and the 3D output is reshaped to a 1D vector.
- The flattened input is passed through a dense layer with 128 neurons and *sigmoid* activation. This is followed by a dropout of 0.2 probability.
- Since this is a binary classification problem, the final layer is a dense layer with one neuron and *sigmoid* activation. Binary cross entropy is used as a loss function with *Adam* optimizer [12]. Learning rate is kept at 0.001.

4.2   Convolutional Long Short Term Memory (ConvLSTM)

ConvLSTMs are similar to LSTMs with the dense operations replaced by convolution operations. As convolution operations use parameter sharing, the number of parameters is greatly reduced in ConvLSTM. Moreover, ConvLSTM allows

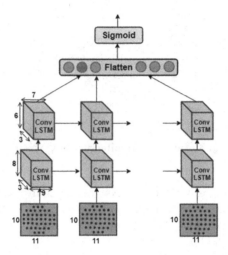

Fig. 4. Model 2: Architecture of ConvLstm

simultaneous learning of spatio-temporal features. Therefore, ConvLSTM is preferred over stacked convolution and LSTM architecture [22]. The 3D EEG data is passed as a sequence of 2D frames to the ConvLSTM. This is equivalent to passing a series of images to ConvLSTM. Although CNNs are capable of capturing temporal information, the number of parameters increases exponentially as the depth of input increases. This makes it difficult to capture long term relationships. We, therefore, explore the usage of ConvLSTM to model spatial and temporal structure of EEG. The placement of electrodes on the scalp, the mental state of the subject across sessions and trials can lead to variability. This is accounted by the convolutional operations of ConvLSTM. The temporal characteristics of EEG are captured by the LSTM structure. The model architecture is shown in Fig. 4 and the details of the proposed model is described below

- The input data is first batch normalized and passed to the next layer. The batch size is set to 64 samples.
- The sequence of inputs in the form of 2D map is passed through recurrent convolutions of filter size 3 × 3. Three such filters are used and the output is passed through *tanh* non-linearity. A dropout of 0.2 is used along with recurrent dropout of 0.1. This is followed by a batch normalization layer.
- A similar recurrent convolution is again applied on the output of the previous layer followed by batch normalization.
- The sequence returned is flattened and a dropout of 0.5 is applied. The final layer is a dense layer having only one neuron with *sigmoid* activation function. Binary cross entropy loss is used along with *Adam* optimizer for training. Learning rate is kept at 0.001.

4.3 Ensemble Models

The individual models proposed in this paper along with BN3 proposed in [15] were used to build ensemble classifiers. The individual classifiers were trained on the entire dataset and best models were picked using 10% validation data for ensemble testing. Scores from individual models were fused using simple averaging. Four ensemble models were evaluated using combinations of CNN-3D, BN3, and ConvLSTM.

5 Results and Discussion

The performance of single trial P300 detection is measured for BN3, CNN-3D, ConvLSTM and their ensembles. Several metrics that are used to evaluate the performance of the models are true positive (TP), false positive (FP), true negative (TN), false negative (FN) and others mentioned below

$$\text{Precision} = \frac{TP}{TP + FP} \qquad \qquad \text{Recall} = \frac{TP}{TP + FN}$$

$$\text{Recognition} = \frac{TP + TN}{TP + TN + FP + FN} \qquad \text{F-measure} = 2\frac{\text{Precision}.\text{Recall}}{\text{Precision} + \text{Recall}}$$

The number of trainable parameters for each of the models under consideration is shown in Table 3. Along with CNN-3D and ConvLSTM, the BN3 model is used in our analysis for comparison of the results [15]. ConvLSTM model has one-third parameters as compared to BN3 and CNN-3D. This allows the model to learn representations even with less data. These models were implemented using Keras library [8] with tensorflow backend [3]. AWS p2.xlarge instances were used for evaluation of models [1]. The results of BN3 were obtained under this environment, original results can be seen in [15]. Ensemble models use individual models having similar performance.

Table 3. Number of model parameters

BN3	CNN-3D	ConvLSTM
39,649	32,593	**11,213**

5.1 Analysis of BCI Competition Dataset

The complete results are shown in Table 4. Models CNN-1, MCNN-1 and MCNN-3 were proposed by Cecotti and Graser [7]. Their results are listed here for comparative analysis. CNN-3D gives better performance than the existing models as it takes into consideration the spatial positioning of electrodes. It classifies

Table 4. Performance of different models for Online Dataset.

Data Set	Model	TP	TN	FP	FN	Recog.	Recall	Precision	F1-score
III A	BN3 + CNN3D + CONVLSTM	1926	11,748	3252	1074	0.7597	0.6420	0.3720	0.4710
	CNN3D + CONVLSTM	1963	11,592	3408	1037	0.7531	0.6543	0.3655	0.4690
	BN3 + CONVLSTM	1919	11,701	3299	1081	0.7567	0.6397	0.3678	0.4670
	BN3 + CNN3D	1952	11,573	3427	1048	0.7513	0.6507	0.3629	0.4659
	CONVLSTM	1928	11,582	3418	1072	0.7505	0.6426	0.3606	0.4620
	CNN3D	1938	11,536	3464	1062	0.7486	0.6460	0.3588	0.4613
	BN3*	1910	11,229	3771	1090	0.7299	0.6367	0.3362	0.4400
	CNN-1	2021	10,645	4355	979	0.7037	0.6737	0.3170	0.4311
	MCNN-1	2071	10,348	4652	929	0.6899	0.6903	0.3080	0.4260
	MCNN-3	2023	10,645	4355	977	0.7038	0.6743	0.3172	0.4314
III B	BN3 + CNN3D + CONVLSTM	2003	12,810	2190	997	0.8229	0.6677	0.4777	0.5569
	CNN3D + CONVLSTM	2115	12,371	2629	885	0.8048	0.7050	0.4458	0.5462
	BN3 + CONVLSTM	1956	12,864	2136	1044	0.8233	0.6520	0.4780	0.5516
	BN3 + CNN3D	1990	12,762	2238	1010	0.8196	0.6633	0.4707	0.5506
	CONVLSTM	2099	12,330	2670	901	0.8016	0.6997	0.4401	0.5404
	CNN3D	2139	12,099	2901	861	0.7910	0.7130	0.4244	0.5321
	BN3*	2009	12,329	2671	991	0.7966	0.6697	0.4293	0.5232
	CNN-1	2035	12,039	2961	965	0.7819	0.6783	0.4073	0.5090
	MCNN-1	2202	11,453	3547	798	0.6899	0.7340	0.3830	0.5034
	MCNN-3	2077	11,997	3003	923	0.7038	0.6923	0.4089	0.5141

the examples of both the classes more accurately than the existing models. The proposed CNN-3D model has a high recognition rate as well as high precision and recall.

Results show that ConvLSTM models the spatio-temporal information well and performs better than other architectures. Table 4 shows that CNN-3D performs well for the target class whereas ConvLSTM performs better for the non-target class. Therefore, in order to retain the properties of both the models,

Table 5. Performance of different models for Single Odd Beep Dataset.

Data Set	Model	TP	TN	FP	FN	Recog.	Recall	Precision	F1-score
A	BN3 + CNN3D + CONVLSTM	88	603	42	37	0.8974	0.7040	0.6769	0.6902
	CNN3D + CONVLSTM	90	599	46	35	0.8948	0.7200	0.6618	0.6897
	BN3 + CONVLSTM	84	599	46	41	0.8870	0.6720	0.6462	0.6588
	BN3 + CNN3D	88	604	41	37	**0.8987**	0.7040	0.6822	**0.6929**
	CONVLSTM	82	596	49	43	0.8805	0.6560	0.6259	0.6406
	CNN3D	91	595	50	34	0.8909	0.7280	0.6454	0.6842
	BN3	84	588	57	41	0.8727	0.6720	0.5957	0.6316
B	BN3 + CNN3D + CONVLSTM	74	606	39	51	0.8831	0.5920	0.6549	0.6218
	CNN3D + CONVLSTM	74	592	53	51	0.8649	0.5920	0.5827	0.5873
	BN3 + CONVLSTM	75	607	38	50	**0.8857**	0.6000	0.6637	**0.6302**
	BN3 + CNN3D	77	598	47	48	0.8766	0.6160	0.6210	0.6185
	CONVLSTM	72	590	55	53	0.8597	0.5760	0.5669	0.5714
	CNN3D	78	573	72	47	0.8454	0.6240	0.5200	0.5673
	BN3	74	572	73	51	0.8389	0.5920	0.5034	0.5441

we propose ensemble models consisting of the existing BN3 architecture, the proposed CNN-3D, and ConvLSTM architectures.

The ensemble models consisting of BN3 + CNN-3D architectures and BN3 + ConvLSTM architectures have a very high recognition rate since they classify the non-target class examples with a very high precision whereas the model consisting of CNN-3D + ConvLSTM architectures have a very high recall.

5.2 Analysis of Single Odd Beep Dataset

Table 5 shows the results for different models. The results are similar to previous analysis, CNN-3D and ConvLSTM based models perform better than BN3. However, the recognition rates for odd beep dataset is better than BCI competition dataset. This can be due to the better spatial resolution provided by 128 channel EEG net. Although its scalability to more number of trials still needs to be validated.

6   Conclusions

The results obtained in this work show that the 3D input for single trial P300 classification works better than the 2D input. The reason can attributed to the fact that 3D input capture spatial surroundings of the data very well. CNNs based on 3D input captures the information well but may lack the temporal information. Spatio-temporal characteristics of EEG are captured well by ConvLSTM, and hence give better results using less parameters. Ensemble approaches that take into account the properties of both models perform significantly better.

References

1. Amazon ec2 - p2 instances. https://aws.amazon.com/ec2/instance-types/p2/. Accessed 09 Jan 2018
2. The geodesic sensor net. https://www.egi.com/research-division/geodesic-sensor-net. Accessed 9 Jan 2018
3. Abadi, M., et al.: Tensorflow: a system for large-scale machine learning. OSDI **16**, 265–283 (2016)
4. Barsim, K.S., Zheng, W., Yang, B.: Ensemble learning to EEG-based brain computer interfaces with applications on P300-spellers
5. Bashivan, P., Rish, I., Yeasin, M., Codella, N.: Learning representations from EEG with deep recurrent-convolutional neural networks (2015). arXiv preprint. arXiv:1511.06448
6. Carabez, E., Sugi, M., Nambu, I., Wada, Y.: Convolutional neural networks with 3D input for P300 identification in auditory brain-computer interfaces. Comput. Intell. Neurosci. **2017** (2017)
7. Cecotti, H., Graser, A.: Convolutional neural networks for P300 detection with application to brain-computer interfaces. IEEE Trans. Pattern Anal. Mach. Intell. **33**(3), 433–445 (2011)
8. Chollet, F., et al.: Keras (2015). https://github.com/fchollet/keras
9. Delorme, A., Makeig, S.: Eeglab: an open source toolbox for analysis of single-trial eeg dynamics including independent component analysis. J. Neurosci. Methods **134**(1), 9–21 (2004)
10. Farwell, L.A., Donchin, E.: Talking off the top of your head: toward a mental prosthesis utilizing event-related brain potentials. Electroencephalogr. Clin. Neurophysiol. **70**(6), 510–523 (1988)
11. Fedjaev, J.: Decoding EEG brain signals using recurrent neural networks (2017)
12. Kingma, D.P., Ba, J.: Adam: a method for stochastic optimization (2014). arXiv preprint arXiv:1412.6980
13. Krusienski, D., Schalk, G.: Wadsworth BCI dataset (P300 evoked potentials), BCI competition III challenge (2004). http://www.bbci.de/competition/iii/
14. Li, Y., Long, J., Yu, T., Yu, Z., Wang, C., Zhang, H., Guan, C.: An EEG-based BCI system for 2-D cursor control by combining mu/beta rhythm and P300 potential. IEEE Trans. Biomed. Eng. **57**(10), 2495–2505 (2010)
15. Liu, M., Wu, W., Gu, Z., Yu, Z., Qi, F., Li, Y.: Deep learning based on batch normalization for P300 signal detection. Neurocomputing **275**, 288–297 (2018)
16. Maddula, R., Stivers, J., Mousavi, M., Ravindran, S., de Sa, V.: Deep recurrent convolutional neural networks for classifying P300 BCI signals. In: Proceedings of the Graz BCI Conference (2017)
17. Mazurowski, M.A., Habas, P.A., Zurada, J.M., Lo, J.Y., Baker, J.A., Tourassi, G.D.: Training neural network classifiers for medical decision making: the effects of imbalanced datasets on classification performance. Neural Netw. **21**(2–3), 427–436 (2008)
18. Naderi, M.A., Mahdavi-Nasab, H.: Analysis and classification of EEG signals using spectral analysis and recurrent neural networks. In: 17th Iranian Conference of Biomedical Engineering (ICBME), pp. 1–4. IEEE (2010)
19. Petrosian, A., Prokhorov, D., Homan, R., Dasheiff, R., Wunsch II, D.: Recurrent neural network based prediction of epileptic seizures in intra-and extracranial EEG. Neurocomputing **30**(1–4), 201–218 (2000)

20. Rakotomamonjy, A., Guigue, V.: BCI competition III: dataset II-ensemble of SVMs for BCI P300 speller. IEEE Trans. Biomed. Eng. **55**(3), 1147–1154 (2008)
21. Rebsamen, B., Guan, C., Zhang, H., Wang, C., Teo, C., Ang, M.H., Burdet, E.: A brain controlled wheelchair to navigate in familiar environments. IEEE Trans. Neural Syst. Rehabil. Eng. **18**(6), 590–598 (2010)
22. Sainath, T.N., Vinyals, O., Senior, A., Sak, H.: Convolutional, long short-term memory, fully connected deep neural networks. In: IEEE International Conference on Acoustics, Speech and Signal Processing (ICASSP), pp. 4580–4584. IEEE (2015)
23. Sun, S., Zhang, C., Zhang, D.: An experimental evaluation of ensemble methods for eeg signal classification. Pattern Recognit. Lett. **28**(15), 2157–2163 (2007)
24. Xingjian, S., Chen, Z., Wang, H., Yeung, D.Y., Wong, W.K., Woo, W.c.: Convolutional LSTM network: a machine learning approach for precipitation nowcasting. In: Advances in neural information processing systems, pp. 802–810 (2015)

An Orthonormalized Partial Least Squares Based Spatial Filter for SSVEP Extraction

G. R. Kiran Kumar$^{(\boxtimes)}$ (iD) and M. Ramasubba Reddy (iD)

Indian Institute of Technology Madras, Chennai 600036, India
kirankumar.g.r@hotmail.com, rsreddy@iitm.ac.in

Abstract. In this study, a novel orthonormalized partial least squares (OPLS) spatial filter is proposed for the extraction of the steady-state visual evoked potential (SSVEP) components buried in the electroencephalogram (EEG) data. The proposed method avoids over-fitting of the EEG data to the ideal SSVEP reference signals by reducing the over-emphasis of the target (pure sine-cosine) space. The paper presents the comparison of the detection accuracy of the proposed method with other existing spatial filters and discusses the shortcomings of these algorithms. The OPLS was tested across ten healthy subjects and its classification performance was examined. Further, statistical tests were performed to show the significant improvements in obtained detection accuracies. The result shows that the OPLS provides a significant improvement in detection accuracy across subjects compared to spatial filters under comparison. Hence, OPLS would act as a reliable and efficient spatial filter for separation of SSVEP components in brain-computer interface (BCI) applications.

Keywords: Steady-state visual evoked potential (SSVEP)
Electroencephalogram (EEG) · Brain-computer interface (BCI)
Orthonormalized partial least squares (OPLS)

1 Introduction

Steady-state visual evoked potentials (SSVEP) are electroencephalogram (EEG) components that are generated over the visual cortex in response to periodically flicking visual stimuli. They are elicited in response to flicker frequencies greater than 4 Hz [9] and the SSVEP amplitude is modulated by visual spatial attention provided by the user [11]. Further, the SSVEP response is in-phase with the target frequencies and contains other harmonics. Due to its properties, relatively high signal to noise ratio (SNR) and ease of implementation, SSVEP has been studied increasingly for application in non-invasive brain-computer interfaces (BCI) [6].

This work was supported by Indian Institute of Technology Madras.

U. S. Tiwary (Ed.): IHCI 2018, LNCS 11278, pp. 16–25, 2018.
https://doi.org/10.1007/978-3-030-04021-5_2

SSVEP based brain-computer interfaces requires very low training and exhibits high information transfer rates (ITR) compared to other BCI modalities [13]. A classical SSVEP-BCI system consists of flickering target stimuli placed at different locations. The user selects the target by gazing over it and intended target is extracted by analysing the acquired EEG for components corresponding to the flicker frequency [12]. Extracting low noise SSVEP components from a given EEG data segment is a basic and crucial step in SSVEP detection methods. The band limiting of the acquired data is useful in eliminating noise outside the desired SSVEP frequency range. But, the filtering does not remove the noise embedded in the desired range. Hence, to achieve higher SSVEP SNR, a number of spatial filtering techniques employing linear signal models have been proposed.

Common spatial filtering techniques used in SSVEP based BCIs include hardware-based methods like best bipolar combination (BCC) and multivariate data analysis (MVA) algorithms like principal component analysis (PCA), minimum energy combination (MEC), maximum contrast combination (MCC), and partial least squares (PLS) spatial filter [7]. Even though BCC provides considerable improvement in SNR, the selection of the optimal electrode pair need to be done through an exhaustive search for every individual user. The PCA is an unsupervised method that exploits the common information between the input EEG channels to maximize the variance of the reconstructed data and disregards the SSVEP source model [4].

Other MVA methods are supervised linear signal models that use a simple SSVEP model consisting of sine-cosine signals as target data for improving the EEG signal components. The MEC and MCC spatial filters try to minimise the SSVEP noise or maximise SNR by computing the signal and noise components using ordinary least squares (OLS) regression method. The OLS has several shortcomings as it fails when the inter-channel correlation increases (multicollinearity) and it further assumes that the target SSVEP model as fixed [3]. Recently, a PLS spatial filter has been proposed that overcomes the disadvantages of MEC and MCC by efficiently dealing with highly correlated channels. The PLS tries to maximise the covariance between the EEG and SSVEP model and considers the target SSVEP model to contain error, thus providing a robust estimate. Among the reported spatial filters in the literature, MCC and PLS have been shown to achieve the highest performance [8].

In this study, we propose an orthonormalized partial least squares (OPLS) spatial filter that rewards the channels that better model the information contained in the features of the SSVEP target space. In PLS spatial filter, the input and output spaces with very high variance are overemphasized even if the correlation between them in the projected data is not significant. The OPLS is a variant of PLS which overcomes this disadvantage by minimizing the mean squares error (MSE) instead of the covariance and not considering the variance of the target (pure sine-cosine) space. The proposed method is evaluated by comparing its SSVEP detection performance in terms of accuracy with classical SSVEP spatial filters such as PLS and MCC using EEG data collected from ten subjects. Further, statistical tests are performed to depict the improvement achieved using OPLS method.

2   Methods

2.1   Spatial Filtering

Spatial filters for SSVEP based BCI try to find projections of the EEG data that are "maximally aligned" with the SSVEP model. Consider the EEG data ($Y \in \mathbb{R}^{N \times N_y}$) obtained using '$N_y$' electrodes and each channel contains data of length 'N'. Given the EEG data segment of small time window ('l_w'), the different filters maximize a particular objective function to preserve the SSVEP components with improved SNR. The solution to these problems in general consists of finding the transformation matrix ($W \in \mathbb{R}^{N_y \times N_l}$ where $N_l < N_y$) that acts as a linear operator and is given by,

$$\widehat{Y} = YW \tag{1}$$

Here, N_l is the number of reconstructed channels in the resulting signal, $\widehat{Y}$. The SSVEP model that is used commonly across all the spatial filters consists of sine and cosine components of a target frequency and its harmonics. The reference signal ($X \in \mathbb{R}^{N \times (2 \times N_h)}$) obtained from SSVEP model with columns equal to twice the number of harmonics ($2 \times N_h$) is given by,

$$X = \begin{pmatrix} \sin(2\pi f_m t) \\ \cos(2\pi f_m t) \\ \cdot \\ \cdot \\ \sin(2 N_h \pi f_m t) \\ \cos(2 N_h \pi f_m t) \end{pmatrix} \tag{2}$$

Here, 'f_m' is the target frequency 'm' and 't' is the time vector of length 'N'. The PSDA is used as the common feature extractor across all the methods in this study. Once the filtered signals are obtained, the detection score (feature) is computed for all the target frequencies, f_m and is given by,

$$T(f_m) = \left(\frac{1}{N_l N_h} \right) \sum_{l=1}^{N_l} \sum_{h=1}^{N_h} \widehat{P}_{h,l} \tag{3}$$

where $\widehat{P}_{h,l} = \| X_h^t \widehat{Y}_l \|^2$ is the signal power of the target frequency, 'N_h' and 'N_l' filtered channel. The following sections describe the PLS spatial filter followed by the proposed OPLS and MCC and in all the descriptions the EEG data ('Y') is assumed to be mean centred.

2.2   Partial Least Squares (PLS)

Partial least squares (PLS) is a MVA technique that allows comparison of multivariate explanatory (input) and response (output) variables, to establish a linear relationship between them. Here, the EEG data ('Y') is considered as the input variable and the SSVEP reference ('X') as the output variable. This regression model is as given in (1). The PLS extracts the latent variables that accounts for the maximum covariance between the EEG data and SSVEP model signals [8]. This is achieved by obtaining projections with orthonormality constraint that maximize the objective function given by,

$$maximize : Tr\{W_y^T C_{yx} W_x\}$$
$$subject\ to : W_y^T W_y = W_x^T W_x = I \tag{4}$$

where, W_y and W_x are the projection vectors of input and output space respectively. The solution to the above objective function is achieved via an iterative procedure known as SIMPLS [3]. Here the variables are decomposed into the form,

$$Y = TP^T + E$$
$$X = UQ^T + F \tag{5}$$

where, T and U are score vectors, P and Q are loading vectors and E and F are residuals respectively. Here the score matrices T and U are the latent variables that maximize the covariance and are obtained by computing the linear transformation of the explanatory and response variables. Each column of the score vectors known as the factors are computed one after another iteratively by minimizing the residuals E and F (via SIMPLS algorithm). The dimension of the score matrices dictates the dimension of the reconstructed data. The linear relationship between the input and the output variables is given by the transformation vector in-terms of T and U as,

$$B_{pls} = Y^T U (T^T Y Y^T U)^{-1} T^T X \tag{6}$$

The estimation of target variable via the PLS regression is given by,

$$\widehat{X} = Y B_{pls} \tag{7}$$

Once $\widehat{X}$, the reconstructed EEG data, is obtained, the detection score, T_{pls} is found via power spectral density analysis (PSDA). The target frequency (F_{pls}) is detected as,

$$F_{pls} = \max_m (T_{pls}(f_m)) \tag{8}$$

2.3   Orthonormalized Partial Least Squares (OPLS)

The orthonormalized PLS algorithm [15] is a variant of PLS method which tries to minimize the mean square error (MSE) by maximizing the objective function given by,

$$maximize : Tr\{W_y^T C_{yx} C_{yx}^T W_x\}$$
$$subject\ to : W_y^T W_y = I \tag{9}$$

where W_y corresponds to optimal regression parameters. Unlike PLS, the OPLS method does not take into account the variance of the SSVEP references [2].

A novel property of OPLS is that the optimal projections obtained are such that the it rewards the EEG latent variables that better predict the variance of the target SSVEP model. Intuitively, this means that we are more interested in approximating the actual SSVEP response signals instead of a projection of it (namely the reference signals). Due to this, the OPLS can be seen as a potential alternative to other SSVEP spatial filters. The projection matrix B_{opls} is obtained similar to PLS procedure [3]. Similarly, the detection scores (T_{opls}) are computed and target frequency (F_{opls}) is identified as depicted in (8).

2.4   Maximum Contrast Combination (MCC)

MCC algorithm is designed to find the linear combination of the EEG channels that maximizes the SNR of the desired signals [1,5]. The noise component is obtained by projecting the EEG data orthogonal to the SSVEP reference signals and is given by,

$$\tilde{Y} = Y - XA_{LS} = Y - XC_{xx}^{-1}C_{xy}^{-1} \tag{10}$$

where, $A_{LS} = P_{opt} = \left(X^T X\right)^{-1} X^T Y$. The weight matrix ($W_{mcc}$) that maximizes the SNR is obtained by minimizing the constrained optimization problem given by,

$$\min_{W_{mcc}} \frac{\|Y W_{mcc}\|^2}{\|\tilde{Y} W_{mcc}\|^2} = \min_{W_{mcc}} \frac{W_{mcc}^T Y^T Y W_{mcc}}{W_{mcc}^T \tilde{Y}^T \tilde{Y} W_{mcc}} \tag{11}$$

The solution to the above problem is obtained by decomposing the matrix, $(\tilde{Y}^T \tilde{Y})^{-1} Y^T Y$. The resulting eigenvectors corresponding to 'n' largest eigenvalues make up the columns of the weight matrix W_{mcc} (contributing to 90% of total data variance). Once the detection score (T_{mcc}) is computed from the reconstructed channels, the frequency of interest (F_{mcc}) is detected as,

$$F_{mcc} = \max_m \left(T_{mcc}(f_m)\right) \tag{12}$$

2.5   Data Acquisition

The EEG data for the study was obtained from ten subjects (denoted as S1 to S10) with normal vision using a eight electrode (Oz, Pz, O1, O2, PO3, PO4, PO7 and PO8) setup based on extended 10–20 electrode configuration (shown in Fig. 1a). An analog front end with ADS1299 and Arduino Uno based on OpenBCI system was employed to sample the EEG data at 250 Hz and transmit in real time to PC [14]. The visual stimuli and EEG data storage was managed using Processing® language. The recorded data was filtered between 2 to 40 Hz and Offline analysis was performed using MATLAB®.

The visual stimuli consisted of four on-off stimulus targets (8.57, 10, 12, and 15 Hz respectively) presented against a dark background with a centeral fixation point using a LCD screen (shown in Fig. 1b). The screen had a 60 Hz refresh rate and was placed 50 cm from the subject. Each session consisting of five trails begins with the subject at rest and looking at the fixation point. At the start,

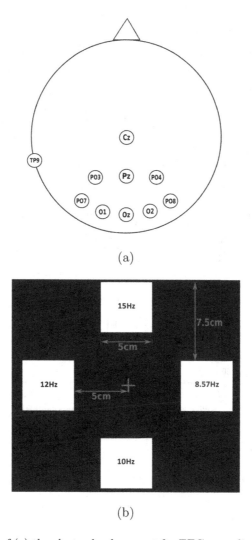

(a)

(b)

Fig. 1. Illustration of (a) the electrode placement for EEG recording and (b) the on-off stimulus design.

a visual cue is presented to the subject to gaze at a target stimuli for 10 s. Once the highlight is removed the subject is advised to move to the central fixation point for 5 s. Likewise, all the target frequencies are cued one after another which depicts a single trial. Each session of recording consists of five continuous trials. A single low artifact session (devoid of avoidable artifacts such as electrode displacements, prolonged eye closure and high levels of power line interferences) was selected and used for analysis of the detection performance of the algorithms.

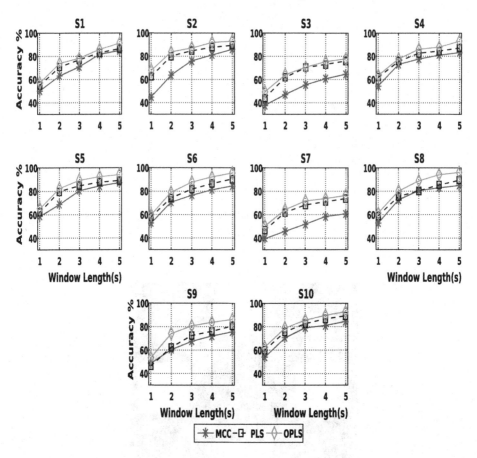

Fig. 2. Accuracies obtained for MCC, PLS and Orthonormalized PLS (represented as OPLS) spatial filters with PSDA as the feature extractor across window lengths of 1 s to 5 s for all ten subjects (S1 to S10).

3   Results and Discussion

The detection metrics for each of the algorithms discussed in the Methods section were computed from the selected EEG data for each subject across the window length of 1 s to 5 s in steps of 1 s with a 25% overlap. The EEG data is mean centred and the classification accuracies were calculated by creating a confusion matrix. Since the target frequencies were mainly in the lower frequency range ($<25\,$Hz), the algorithms were evaluated for two harmonic case only [8].

The accuracy across all ten subjects for MCC, PLS and OPLS spatial filters with PSDA as the feature extractor across window lengths of 1 s to 5 s is depicted in Fig. 2. PSDA was used across all the methods under comparison as a common feature extractor to analyse them uniformly. Overall, the detection accuracies was seen to improve as the window length increased. The OPLS provided a more

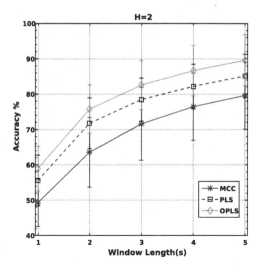

Fig. 3. Averaged accuracies obtained from MCC, PLS and OPLS spatial filters for two harmonic case, H = 2 (f_m and $2f_m$) and window lengths of 1 s to 5 s. The standard deviation from mean accuracy is depicted using error bars.

efficient and improved detection performance in terms of accuracy compared to both MCC and PLS across all the subjects. The Averaged accuracy across the ten subjects depicted in Fig. 3 which provides a insight into the stability of the algorithms to inter-subject variability. The standard deviation from mean accuracy is depicted using error bars. Similar to Fig. 2, the mean detection accuracy of OPLS was highest across the methods. The figures also confirms that OPLS can achieve consistent and stable higher detection accuracies compared classical spatial filters such as MCC and PLS.

Two way repeated measures ANOVA was used to examine the differences in accuracies depending on detection method used and window lengths. The Greenhouse Geisser correction was made if the data did not conform to the sphericity assumption. The post-hoc paired t-tests (Bonferroni corrected) were used to compare the significance of difference accuracies across detection methods for various window lengths [10,13]. The Two way ANOVA found significant differences in accuracies due to both methods factor (F(2,18) = 62.98, p < 0.001) and window length (F(4,36) = 462.98, p < 0.001) but there was no significant interaction effects. The results of the post-hoc tests can be seen in Table 1 which depicts the consistent performance of OPLS compared to PLS and MCC.

By designing a spatial filter that minimizes the MSE instead of maximizing the covariance between EEG and SSVEP model, higher detection accuracy has been achieved. The OPLS is shown to provide statistically significant improvement in the detection performance compared to conventional SSVEP spatial filters such as MCC and PLS. Further, the orthonormalized PLS improves upon the advantages of PLS algorithms such as tolerance to multicollinearity and uniquely weighs the features that provide better approximation of the SSVEP model.

Table 1. Post-hoc paired t-test (Bonferroni's corrected) of differences in detection accuracies between MCC, OPLS and PLS for window lengths from 1 s to 5 s

Methods	Time window length				
	1.0	2.0	3.0	4.0	5.0
OPLS vs. PLS	* * *	**	**	* * *	* * *
OPLS vs. MCC	* * *	* * *	* * *	* * *	* * *
PLS vs. MCC	**	**	**	**	**

Note *: $p < 0.05$, **: $p < 0.01$, * * *: $p < 0.001$,

4   Conclusion

We have proposed, orthonormalized PLS (OPLS) as a novel spatial filter for extracting SSVEP from the noisy EEG data. To demonstrate the superior performance of the proposed method, MCC and PLS were used for comparison using a common feature extractor (PSDA). The result showed that minimizing the MSE between the EEG data and SSVEP references rather than maximizing covariance improves the detection accuracy significantly. The method provides efficient performance across subjects and statistically significant improvement in accuracies across window lengths relative to the methods under comparison. Hence, the OPLS can be considered for a robust and calibration less way of extracting SSVEP features with high SNR.

References

1. Abu-Alqumsan, M., Peer, A.: Advancing the detection of steady-state visual evoked potentials in braincomputer interfaces. J. Neural Eng. **13**(3), 036005 (2016). https://doi.org/10.1088/1741-2560/13/3/036005
2. Arenas-Garcia, J., Camps-Valls, G.: Efficient kernel orthonormalized PLS for remote sensing applications. IEEE Trans. Geosci. Remote. Sens. **46**(10), 2872–2881 (2008). https://doi.org/10.1109/TGRS.2008.918765
3. Arenas-Garcia, J., Petersen, K.B., Camps-Valls, G., Hansen, L.K.: Kernel multivariate analysis framework for supervised subspace learning: a tutorial on linear and kernel multivariate methods. IEEE Signal Process. Mag. **30**, 16–29 (2013). https://doi.org/10.1109/MSP.2013.2250591
4. Bashashati, A., Fatourechi, M., Ward, R.K., Birch, G.E.: A survey of signal processing algorithms in braincomputer interfaces based on electrical brain signals. J. Neural Eng. **4**(2), 32–57 (2007). https://doi.org/10.1088/1741-2560/4/2/R03
5. Friman, O., Volosyak, I., Gräser, A.: Multiple channel detection of steady-state visual evoked potentials for brain-computer interfaces. IEEE Trans. Bio-Med. Eng. **54**(4), 742–50 (2007). https://doi.org/10.1109/TBME.2006.889160
6. Gao, X., Xu, D., Cheng, M., Gao, S.: A BCI-based environmental controller for the motion-disabled. IEEE Trans. Neural Syst. Rehabil. Eng. **11**(2), 137–40 (2003). https://doi.org/10.1109/TNSRE.2003.814449

7. Garcia-Molina, G., Zhu, D.: Optimal spatial filtering for the steady state visual evoked potential: BCI application. In: 5th International IEEE/EMBS Conference on Neural Engineering, pp. 156–160 (2011). https://doi.org/10.1109/NER.2011.5910512

8. Ge, S., Wang, R., Leng, Y., Wang, H., Lin, P., Iramina, K.: A double-partial least-squares model for the detection of steady-state visual evoked potentials. IEEE J. Biomed. Health Inform. **21**, 897–903 (2017). https://doi.org/10.1109/JBHI.2016.2546311

9. Herrmann, C.S.: Human EEG responses to 1–100 Hz flicker: resonance phenomena in visual cortex and their potential correlation to cognitive phenomena. Exp. Brain Res. **137**(3–4), 346–353 (2001). https://doi.org/10.1007/s002210100682

10. Japkowicz, N., Shah, M.: Evaluating Learning Algorithms: A Classification Perspective. Cambridge University Press, New York (2011). https://doi.org/10.1017/CBO9780511921803

11. Lalor, E.C., et al.: Steady-state VEP-based brain-computer interface control in an immersive 3D gaming environment. EURASIP J. Adv. Signal Process. **2005**, 3156–3164 (2005)

12. Müller-Putz, G.R., Pfurtscheller, G.: Control of an electrical prosthesis with an SSVEP-based BCI. IEEE Trans. Bio-Med. Eng. **55**(1), 361–4 (2008). https://doi.org/10.1109/TBME.2007.897815

13. Nakanishi, M., Wang, Y., Chen, X., Wang, Y.T., Gao, X., Jung, T.P.: Enhancing detection of SSVEPs for a high-speed brain speller using task-related component analysis **9294**, 1 (2017)

14. Nathan, V., Jafari, R.: Design principles and dynamic front end reconfiguration for low noise EEG acquisition with finger based dry electrodes. IEEE Trans. Biomed. Circuits Syst. **9**(5), 631–640 (2015). https://doi.org/10.1109/TBCAS.2015.2471080

15. Worsley, K., Poline, J.B., Friston, K., Evans, A.: Characterizing the response of PET and fMRI data using multivariate linear models. NeuroImage **6**(4), 305–319 (1997). https://doi.org/10.1006/nimg.1997.0294

A Common Spatial Pattern Approach for Classification of Mental Counting and Motor Execution EEG

Purvi Goel[1], Raviraj Joshi[1]($\boxtimes$), Mriganka Sur[2], and Hema A. Murthy[1]

[1] Department of Computer Science and Engineering,
Indian Institute of Technology Madras, Chennai, India
{purvi,rjoshi,hema}@cse.iitm.ac.in
[2] Department of Brain and Cognitive Sciences,
Massachusetts Institute of Technology, Cambridge, USA
msur@mit.edu

Abstract. A Brain Computer Interface (BCI) as a medium of communication is convenient for people with severe motor disabilities. Although there are a number of different BCIs, the focus of this paper is on Electroencephalography (EEG) as a means of human computer interaction. Motor imagery and mental arithmetic are the most popular techniques used to modulate brain waves that can be used to control devices. We show that it is possible to define different mental states using *real* fist rotation and imagined reverse counting. While people have already investigated left fist rotation and right fist rotation for dual state BCI, we intend to define a new state using mental reverse counting. We use Common Spatial Pattern (CSP) approach for feature extraction to distinguish between these states. CSP has been prominently used in the context of motor imagery task, we define its applicability for the distinction between motor execution and mental counting. CSP features are evaluated using classifiers like GMM, SVM, and GMM-UBM. GMM-UBM using data filtered through the beta band (13–30 Hz) gives the best performance.

Keywords: Brain computer interface · Electroencephalography
Motor execution · Mental counting · Common spatial pattern
Gaussian mixture model · Support vector machine

1 Introduction

Brain Computer Interface (BCI) can be seen as a link between the human brain and external devices. Development of BCIs is mainly driven by the fact that BCIs can be used by people with disabilities to communicate their thoughts or control external devices. BCIs are based on neural activity which can be recorded using different invasive and non-invasive techniques such as the Electroencephalography (EEG), Magnetoencephalography (MEG), functional Magnetic Resonance Imaging (fMRI), Electrocorticography (ECoG), etc. In this work, we use EEG

© Springer Nature Switzerland AG 2018
U. S. Tiwary (Ed.): IHCI 2018, LNCS 11278, pp. 26–35, 2018.
https://doi.org/10.1007/978-3-030-04021-5_3

to capture the neural activity. EEG is a non-invasive brain imaging technique used to record the response of the brain to various stimuli with electrodes placed on the scalp.

EEG has been used in a wide range of applications ranging from cursor control to wheel chair control [5, 10–12, 20]. The underlying principle is to modulate the brain waves to produce distinct signatures that can be used to control devices. Some techniques used for modulating the brain waves are motor imagery, real motor execution, and mental calculation [2, 12]. It is well established that motor imagination or execution affect the mu rhythms (8–13 Hz) and beta rhythms (13–30 Hz) known as Event Related Desynchronization (ERD) [12]. Similarly left hand and right hand motor movement although similar have different spatial extent [21]. A number of research efforts on the classification of left and right hand motor imagery can be found in the literature [4, 16, 21]. Previous works have also demonstrated their use in two state applications like 1D cursor control and wheel chair control [5, 12]. Another technique used to modulate brain waves is the mental calculation, where the subject is asked to perform some complex mental calculations [17].

Previous efforts have primarily focused on *imagined* motor imagery owing to its applicability for use by disabled persons, while imagining motor activity is a difficult task for normal persons. Imagined motor movement is also preferred because they inherently avoid movement related artifacts in EEG [19]. Previous studies on mental tasks also involved some non trivial mental calculations which are difficult to use in real time scenarios [17]. In this work, we focus on *real motor movement* which is easy and more natural as compared to imaginary motor movement. On similar lines, we use the covert reverse counting as a mental task because of its simplicity, ability to keep the subject engaged and attentive. The reverse counting can be considered equivalent to mental calculation followed by a covert speech of the number. Left fist and right fist rotation are the tasks considered for motor movement. These motor movements can be used to define different states, we propose reverse counting as a way to define a new state. We do so by showing that fist rotation EEG can be distinguished from reverse counting EEG using common spatial patterns (CSP) [9]. The proposed BCI system is developed for normal humans as subjects.

Gursel and Gumuel in their work tried to distinguish between motor imagery and mental task [18]. However, in their experiment, the subject was asked to solve a binary digit number multiplication problem without vocalizing. This is a discrete non trivial task of 8 s time as opposed to our continuous task of reverse counting. Using power spectral density as features, they were able to distinguish between the resting and the mental states with high accuracy but were not able to distinguish between the motor and mental activity. Keiron proposed a popular set of mental activities that invoke hemispheric brainwave asymmetry [8]. These activities include composing a letter without vocalizing, solving non-trivial multiplication problems, visualizing numbers being written on a blackboard sequentially and imagining a 3D block figure being rotated about its axis. Many works have attempted to classify these mental activities from each other [2, 6, 13, 17, 25].

In this paper, we also show that common spatial pattern based feature extraction works for classification of the motor and mental task. A 128 channel EGI sensor net [1] is used to collect the data. Although it provides a good spatial resolution the data obtained is considerably high dimensional. It, therefore, becomes necessary to select optimal channels for the classification task. CSP provides an efficient way to reduce the dimensionality of data by projecting the channels into low dimensional spatial subspace. The linear transformation is such that variance of the new time series data thus obtained has the most discriminative information for the two classes. Details of the CSP will be discussed in the next section. Earlier, CSP has mainly been used to discriminate between left and right motor imagery. A number of modifications have been proposed over a period of time [3, 9, 15, 21, 23, 24].

Major contributions of this paper are:

– Simple reverse counting can be used as a paradigm to continuously modulate the brain waves which are distinct from motor EEG.
– Application of CSP based feature extraction works well for classification of motor action and mental counting EEG.

2   Methodology

2.1   Experimental Setup

The EEG data was recorded in an acoustically shielded an-echoic room. The subjects were seated in a comfortable chair and instructions were given using audio stimuli. Eyes were closed throughout the experiment so as to avoid the eye blink artifacts. The EEG data was collected using 128 channel Geodesic Sensor net [1] distributed according to the international 10–20 system and Cz electrode was used as the reference. The data was acquired at 250 Hz sampling rate and the impedance was kept low during the recording.

The experiment was performed on healthy subjects without any disabilities. The subjects were students in an age group of 20–24 years. A written consent was given by the participants before the experiment and they were rewarded for their participation. The recordings were done on 5 consecutive days and 2 sessions were recorded on each day. A total of 10 sessions were recorded for each subject.

The timeline of one session of the experiment is shown in the Fig. 1. The subjects were provided with instructions to be in one of the following five states according to the timeline.

– **Baseline State:** This is the resting state of the subject. The subject was asked to relax for 60 s at the start and end of the experiment.
– **Left fist rotation:** The subject rotated his left fist for a period of 15 s twice in a session.

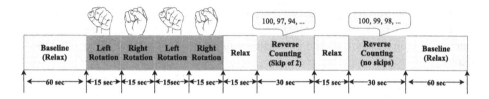

Fig. 1. Experiment timeline

- **Right fist rotation:** The subject rotated his right fist for a period of 15 s twice in a session. Right fist rotation followed the left fist rotation.
- **Reverse counting with a skip of two:** The subject was asked to perform mental reverse counting with a skip of two numbers, for example, 100, 97, 94, etc. A random seed(starting point) was communicated to the subject via headphones. The counting was done for a period of 30 s. Reverse counting was chosen in favor of simple counting to keep the subject attentive.
- **Normal reverse counting:** The subject was asked to perform normal reverse counting, for example, 100, 99, 98, etc. A random seed was provided to the subject again, and counting was done for a period of 30 s. We choose two different types of reverse counting as there are two types of fist rotation.

2.2   Pre-processing

EEG signals are very noisy and have a low signal to noise ratio. So we filter the data to remove unwanted frequencies and only retain frequencies of interest. The EEG data was band pass filtered in alpha (8–13 Hz), beta (13–30 Hz) frequency bands and performance was evaluated in each of these bands. A notch at 50 Hz was applied during filtering to avoid AC interference. Data recordings corresponding to the five mental states were segregated. Recordings corresponding to the left and right fist rotation were taken together and collectively termed as a motor execution state. Whereas the two reverse counting states were taken together as a mental counting state. These were further divided into 4 second segments with an overlap of 3 s. We consider each of these segments as a single trial and use it for classification. Thus each trial will have a size of $N \times T$, where $N = 128$ is the number of channels and $T = 1000$ corresponds to 4 s segment sampled at 250 Hz.

2.3   Feature Extraction

In order to train a machine learning model, features were extracted from the raw data. Since each trial is of size 128×1000 which is quite high dimensional, we use common spatial patterns method to reduce the dimensionality of data. The variance of this reduced data set is used for training the model. CSP method extracts the spatial components that are common to both the classes but the data projected onto these components differ in variances for the two classes.

The projection matrix provides weights for each channel that will be utilized to generate a new time series in the spatial space. This method is based on simultaneous diagonalization of the co-variance matrices for two classes as described below.

Suppose each trial is of size $N \times T$ where N is the number of channels and T is the sample length. Then the spatial co-variance matrices for the two classes are given by,

$$C_m = \frac{X_m X_m^T}{trace(X_m X_m^T)} \tag{1}$$

$$C_r = \frac{X_r X_r^T}{trace(X_r X_r^T)} \tag{2}$$

where C_m and C_r are the co-variance matrices for motor execution trial (X_m) and mental counting trial (X_r) respectively. These matrices are normalized using trace to account for the variability in the amplitude of individual trials. The co-variance matrices of individual trials are averaged to obtain the averaged normalized co-variance matrices $\bar{C}_m$ and $\bar{C}_r$. The two matrices are then added to form the composite co-variance matrix C.

$$C = \bar{C}_m + \bar{C}_r \tag{3}$$

C is then factorized as,

$$C = U\Sigma U^T \tag{4}$$

where U is the matrix of eigen vectors and Σ is the diagonal matrix containing the eigen values. Next the whitening transformation matrix P is computed

$$P = \Sigma^{-1/2} U^T \tag{5}$$

This whitening transformation matrix P equalizes the variance in the space spanned by the eigen vectors in U. P is then applied on the average co-variance matrix $\bar{C}_m$ and $\bar{C}_r$ as

$$S_m = P\bar{C}_m P^T \tag{6}$$

$$S_r = P\bar{C}_r P^T \tag{7}$$

such that S_m and S_r share common eigen vectors and the sum of the corresponding eigen values will always be 1. In other words,

$$S_m = V\Sigma_m V^T \tag{8}$$

$$S_r = V\Sigma_r V^T \tag{9}$$

and

$$\Sigma_m + \Sigma_r = 1 \tag{10}$$

The projection matrix W is then obtained by

$$W = V^T P \tag{11}$$

When sorted in descending order of the eigen values of S_r, top m eigen vectors account for the maximum variance for the first class but they also account for minimal variance in second class due to the constraint in Eq. 10. Similarly, last m eigen vectors account for minimum variance in first class but maximal variance in the second class. So, we only keep first m and last m columns of W in order to retain discriminative patterns and form a new projection matrix W_{2m}. The EEG data is converted as

$$Z = W_{2m}^T \left(\frac{X}{\sqrt{trace(XX^T)}} \right) \tag{12}$$

Z now represents the new time series in projected space that contains common and specific components in different tasks. For each trial, we compute a $2m$ dimensional feature vector which contains the variance of the rows of Z as

$$F = (f_1, f_2, .., f_{2m}) \tag{13}$$

and f can be computed as

$$f_q = log(var(z_q)) \tag{14}$$

where q denotes the row number of the matrix Z and z_q denotes the corresponding row vector.

2.4   Classification

Variance features obtained using CSP were classified using the Gaussian Mixture Model (GMM), Support Vector Machine (SVM) and Gaussian Mixture Model-Universal Background Model (GMM-UBM). GMM has been widely used in the speaker recognition and verification applications [22]. GMM is a weighted sum of multiple Gaussian functions and it captures multimodal data distribution very well. The motivation of using GMM comes from the fact that GMMs have performed extremely well for text-independent speaker verification and identification where there are different speakers, speaking on various channels. In our case, the task of classifying the two activities recorded for multiple subjects across multiple sessions bears a considerable analogy to investigate the performance of GMM.

We also evaluate the performance of a GMM-UBM system, which is known to work better when the training set is limited. We first build a background model which captures the characteristics common to the motor and mental activities using an EM algorithm. The background model which serves as a better initialization is adapted to create an activity specific model. These activity specific models are created using maximum a posteriori (MAP) estimate [22]. Data recordings from eight subjects were used to create a background model, for each subject we had 3 sessions on average. Then the data from four different subjects were used to adapt the model and test the same. For these four subjects, we had 10 sessions each. The same four subjects were also used to evaluate other classifiers. The CSP projection matrix created using train data of these subjects is used for feature extraction.

The third classifier we used is support vector machines. SVMs are very popular for classification, regression tasks and they have been extensively used in EEG classification tasks [14]. SVMs have high generalization capability and despite being a linear classifier in parameter space, it models non-linearities by transforming the data into high dimensional feature space. An appropriate kernel function is applied to transform the data into feature space. We use the radial basis function kernel (gaussian kernel) to perform the classification task [7].

3   Results and Discussion

Data from four subjects was used to evaluate our approach. For each, subject 10 sessions were recorded, 2 sessions per day. The data was pooled from all the subjects together to find a common CSP projection matrix. This was done with an objective to build cross subject BCI. To show the robustness of our model training was done using 4 days of recording i.e. 8 sessions and testing was done on remaining 2 sessions of a day. Five fold cross validation was performed on these sessions and average classification accuracy is reported in Table 1. The performance was measured by bandpass filtering the data (alpha (8–13 Hz), beta bands (13–30 Hz)). The number of CSP patterns were varied to find an optimal number of patterns for each classifier under consideration. Clearly, a single pattern doesn't work well, more than one pair of pattern is needed to achieve considerable accuracy. Figure 2 shows the average of top 12 and bottom 12 CSP

Table 1. Classification performance for different classifiers and frequency bands.

Band	CSP patterns	GMM	SVM	GMM-UBM
8–13 Hz	m = 1	74.70%	62.79%	75.89%
	m = 7	84.97%	81.39%	85.41%
	m = 10	77.82%	77.52%	79.01%
	m = 12	77.82%	77.82%	79.16%
	m = 14	76.33%	80.35%	83.33%
	m = 17	76.78%	86.45%	86.16%
	m = 19	72.02%	87.05%	85.71%
13–30 Hz	m = 1	80.39%	75.14%	77.08%
	m = 7	81.10%	84.375%	69.19%
	m = 10	86.60%	**90.77%**	84.07%
	m = 12	**88.24%**	85.71%	**91.07%**
	m = 14	84.52%	84.67%	85.41%
	m = 17	84.52%	84.82%	84.86%
	m = 19	83.48%	82.29%	84.86%

Fig. 2. Projection of averaged top 12 and bottom 12 source weights (CSP) on the scalp.

patterns. Each individual pattern corresponds to an eigen vector that shows contribution of original channels in the new space. It can be seen that two different regions account for high variance in the EEG of two activities. Figure 3 shows original signals and CSP projected signals for a single mental and motor trial. The original signals bandpassed in beta range are projected using a pair of eigen vectors. Motor trial shows high variance for one eigen vector and mental trial shows high variance for the other vector in the pair. Table 1 shows the classification accuracy for different bands, classifiers, and patterns. A pattern count m indicates first and last m eigen vectors from the projection matrix. Overall, beta band is more discriminative than alpha band and GMM-UBM classifier works better as compared to SVM and GMM.

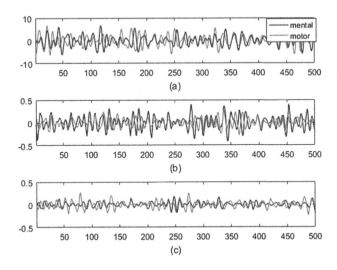

Fig. 3. Examples of CSP analysis: Figure (a) represents original signal of a trial for mental and motor activity (2 s), Figure (b) shows the projection of the original signals on one of the CSP pattern (high variance for mental activity trial) and Figure (c) shows its projection on the other pattern (high variance for motor activity trial).

4   Conclusions

In this work, we investigate the possibility of using mental counting along with actual motor activity for practical BCI systems. Reverse counting provides a continuous mental activity as compared to discrete nature of complex arithmetic calculations and can be compared with continuous motor EEG. We show that CSP approach of feature extraction provides discriminative features that can be used to distinguish between these two activities. This work evaluates the performance of GMM, SVM and GMM-UBM classifiers using different frequency band. We demonstrate that GMM-UBM classifier works best when EEG is band passed in beta frequency range. Although the performance of SVM is comparable to GMM-UBM system. Availability of extra background data helps GMM-UBM to perform slightly better than other classifiers. Moreover, previous works have shown motor activities to affect the beta rhythm, our results follow the same behavior.

References

1. The geodesic sensor net. https://www.egi.com/research-division/geodesic-sensor-net. Accessed 09 Jan 2018
2. Anderson, C.W., Sijercic, Z.: Classification of EEG signals from four subjects during five mental tasks. In: Solving Engineering Problems with Neural Networks: Proceedings of the Conference on Engineering Applications in Neural Networks (EANN 1996), Turkey, pp. 407–414 (1996)
3. Ang, K.K., Chin, Z.Y., Zhang, H., Guan, C.: Filter bank common spatial pattern (FBCSP) in brain-computer interface. In: IEEE International Joint Conference on Neural Networks, IJCNN 2008, (IEEE World Congress on Computational Intelligence), pp. 2390–2397. IEEE (2008)
4. Belhadj, S.A., Benmoussat, N., Della Krachai, M.: CSP features extraction and FLDA classification of EEG-based motor imagery for brain-computer interaction. In: 2015 4th International Conference on Electrical Engineering (ICEE), pp. 1–6. IEEE (2015)
5. Choi, K., Cichocki, A.: Control of a wheelchair by motor imagery in real time. In: Intelligent Data Engineering and Automated Learning - IDEAL 2008, 9th International Conference, Daejeon, South Korea, 2–5 November 2008, Proceedings, pp. 330–337 (2008). https://doi.org/10.1007/978-3-540-88906-9-42
6. Guo, L., Wu, Y., Zhao, L., Cao, T., Yan, W., Shen, X.: Classification of mental task from EEG signals using immune feature weighted support vector machines. IEEE Trans. Magn. **47**(5), 866–869 (2011)
7. Keerthi, S.S., Lin, C.J.: Asymptotic behaviors of support vector machines with Gaussian kernel. Neural Comput. **15**(7), 1667–1689 (2003)
8. Keirn, Z.A., Aunon, J.I.: A new mode of communication between man and his surroundings. IEEE Trans. Biomed. Eng. **37**(12), 1209–1214 (1990)
9. Koles, Z.J., Lazar, M.S., Zhou, S.Z.: Spatial patterns underlying population differences in the background EEG. Brain Topogr. **2**(4), 275–284 (1990)
10. LaFleur, K., Cassady, K., Doud, A., Shades, K., Rogin, E., He, B.: Quadcopter control in three-dimensional space using a noninvasive motor imagery-based brain-computer interface. J. Neural Eng. **10**(4), 046003 (2013)

11. Leeb, R., Friedman, D., Müller-Putz, G.R., Scherer, R., Slater, M., Pfurtscheller, G.: Self-paced (asynchronous) BCI control of a wheelchair in virtual environments: a case study with a tetraplegic. Comp. Int. Neurosci. (2007). https://doi.org/10.1155/2007/79642

12. Li, Y., et al.: An EEG-based BCI system for 2-D cursor control by combining mu/beta rhythm and P300 potential. IEEE Trans. Biomed. Eng. **57**(10), 2495–2505 (2010). https://doi.org/10.1109/TBME.2010.2055564

13. Liang, N., Saratchandran, P., Huang, G., Sundararajan, N.: Classification of mental tasks from EEG signals using extreme learning machine. Int. J. Neural Syst. **16**(1), 29–38 (2006). https://doi.org/10.1142/S0129065706000482

14. Lotte, F., Congedo, M., Lécuyer, A., Lamarche, F., Arnaldi, B.: A review of classification algorithms for EEG-based brain-computer interfaces. J. Neural Eng. **4**(2), R1 (2007)

15. Lotte, F., Guan, C.: Regularizing common spatial patterns to improve BCI designs: unified theory and new algorithms. IEEE Trans. Biomed. Eng. **58**(2), 355–362 (2011)

16. Mahmood, A., Zainab, R., Ahmad, R.B., Saeed, M., Kamboh, A.M.: Classification of multi-class motor imagery EEG using four band common spatial pattern. In: 2017 39th Annual International Conference of the IEEE Engineering in Medicine and Biology Society (EMBC), Jeju Island, South Korea, 11–15 July 2017, pp. 1034–1037 (2017). https://doi.org/10.1109/EMBC.2017.8037003

17. Osaka, M.: Peak alpha frequency of EEG during a mental task: task difficulty and hemispheric differences. Psychophysiology **21**(1), 101–105 (1984)

18. Özmen, N.G., Ktü, L.G.: Discrimination between mental and motor tasks of EEG signals using different classification methods. In: 2011 International Symposium on Innovations in Intelligent Systems and Applications (INISTA), pp. 143–147. IEEE (2011)

19. Ozmen, N.G., Gumusel, L.: Classification of real and imaginary hand movements for a BCI design. In: 2013 36th International Conference on Telecommunications and Signal Processing (TSP), pp. 607–611. IEEE (2013)

20. Pfurtscheller, G., Kalcher, J., Neuper, C., Flotzinger, D., Pregenzer, M.: On-line EEG classification during externally-paced hand movements using a neural network-based classifier. Electroencephalogr. Clin. Neurophysiol. **99**(5), 416–425 (1996)

21. Ramoser, H., Muller-Gerking, J., Pfurtscheller, G.: Optimal spatial filtering of single trial EEG during imagined hand movement. IEEE Trans. Rehabil. Eng. **8**(4), 441–446 (2000)

22. Reynolds, D.A., Quatieri, T.F., Dunn, R.B.: Speaker verification using adapted Gaussian mixture models. Digit. Signal Process. **10**(1–3), 19–41 (2000)

23. Wang, J., Feng, Z., Lu, N.: Feature extraction by common spatial pattern in frequency domain for motor imagery tasks classification. In: 2017 29th Chinese Control and Decision Conference (CCDC), pp. 5883–5888. IEEE (2017)

24. Wang, Y., Gao, S., Gao, X.: Common spatial pattern method for channel selection in motor imagery based brain-computer interface. In: 27th Annual International Conference of the Engineering in Medicine and Biology Society, IEEE-EMBS 2005, pp. 5392–5395. IEEE (2006)

25. Zhiwei, L., Minfen, S.: Classification of mental task EEG signals using wavelet packet entropy and SVM. In: 8th International Conference on Electronic Measurement and Instruments, ICEMI 2007, pp. 3–906. IEEE (2007)

A Real Time Human Emotion Recognition System Using Respiration Parameters and ECG

C. M. Naveen Kumar[(✉)] and G. Shivakumar[(✉)]

Department of E&I Engineering, Malnad College of Engineering,
Hassan, Karnataka, India
{cmn, gs}@mcehassan.ac.in

Abstract. In the field of research on computer identification of emotion, physiological signals play an important role. The selection of the specific physiological input is dependent on its contribution to the emotion. In this research paper, light has been thrown on fusion of paramount physiological signals. The four types of physiological signals taken into account are: Electrocardiogram (ECG), Respiratory Rate (RR), Blood Pressure and Inhale-Exhale temperature of respiration. The research work done on this area is found to be minimal For first three signals, time domain features were extracted with a sensor system and an Intelligent processor. The system was trained using a feedback neural network and tested with unknown class inputs. To elicit emotion, short video sequences of 180 s are used. The videos were played in a laptop and kept at a distance of 1 m away from the subject under investigation. The results obtained are encouraging with the highest accuracy of 96.6% for happy and lowest of 70.38% for disgust with an average accuracy of 80.28%.

Keywords: Emotions · Respiration inhale exhale temperature
Respiration rate · Electrocardiogram · Stimuli · Autonomous nervous system

1 Introduction

In the potential domain of human-computer interaction, emotion identification has become key issue in the research. Continuous research is under way and systems are being that can respond to the emotions. Various methods have been introduced to immediately identify the emotions. However, most of the research in this area is focused on the channels of audio-visual to identify the emotions. They include expressions in face, gestures and speech [1]. A boundary of these approaches is that expressions in face, gestures and speech can be purposefully controlled to hide states of emotion or pretend to be in different states of emotion. In order to solve this issue, some methods have been designed to identify emotions by analysing physiological signals obtained by the autonomous nervous system (ANS) performance. Physiological signals are suddenly affected by the changes in emotion, which is the main advantage of these signals that visually it cannot be assessed [2]. Therefore, several studies [3–5] have finally decided that the more precise methods in identifying emotions is by using physiological signals. Various feature generation ways have been introduced, usually

© Springer Nature Switzerland AG 2018
U. S. Tiwary (Ed.): IHCI 2018, LNCS 11278, pp. 36–45, 2018.
https://doi.org/10.1007/978-3-030-04021-5_4

by the time domain that generate statistical information, or by using the Fourier transform to generate the information in frequency domain.

The six elementary emotions can be identified by analysing patterns of ECG. The features generated from ECG are extracted then categorized to the respective state of emotion with neural networks or support vector machine (SVM) [7–9]. Compared to other modalities like pulse rate or Galvanic Skin Response (GSR), ECG has been less reactive to emotions [9]. Distinct state of emotion can also be identified by using breathing signals alone [10]. Mixing of various physiological modalities have been introduced as well and were advocated as being superior to a single modality alone [6, 11, 12]. Studies mentioned above which are not always in the order of random emotion and use stimuli of image. Therefore, large effect in the performance of the given system is done by the type of stimuli and the presentation order [7, 9]. Personalized contents to users are recommended by the several services of diffusion by maximizing the available multimedia volume especially for video clips or music [13].

These recommendations can be dependent on the user emotion i.e., the valence and arousal. For a moment, a user might seek content of pleasant and/or exciting. Moreover, the recommender can consider the contents which are liked by subject. Indeed it is happen that contents liked by the user with negative valence and/or low arousal. By keeping this possible application in mind, stimuli of video clip/music have only reached minimum success in identification emotion [6]. The purpose of this study is to research automatic emotion identification from the signals of respiratory, cardiac as well as their combination and interaction when using video clips/music as stimuli of emotion. Furthermore, it is hypothesized that as both the functions of respiration and heart are affected by the ANS, one more revealing aspects is synchronization of the above two. ECG patterns and the respiration, correlation between them are generated and classified as related to a particular state of emotion with the design of suitable ANN.

2 Emotions and Physiological Variables

2.1 Emotions

Emotion recognition is a process of recognising the excited mental state of human from visual, auditory and physiological output. This is spontaneous in human being and methodologies for detection have been built over the years. There is a universal consistency exhibited by humans in displaying emotions but also a great deal of variability showed between individuals in their capacities. This has been a main study topic in human psychology. These process techniques of leverages by many regions such as vision of computer, signal processing and machine learning. Among several emotion units, to model feelings the affective and discrete dimensional units are two usual approaches, and they are not exclusive of each other. Prescribed list of words label by label are chosen by human in discrete units and the feelings in discrete type to recognize their feeling. For example, sadness, fear, joy, anger, tension, etc. Therefore, the stimuli may blended emotions are elicit that cannot be perfectly represented in words meaning of the selected words dependent on the culture. To describe the combined feelings, discrete units need more than one word. In dividing the feelings in affective dimensional units, human requires to measure the feelings in many dimensions. Now a days, arousal and valence are the two common measures used in feeling division. In the plane of emotion of two dimensions, all the feelings are mapped onto the arousal and valence axes. For example, joy has high arousal and positive valence, whereas sadness has low arousal and negative valence. By using the expression in face, we can imitate the feelings. The user can be asked to feel or express some of them. The results sometimes are better but sometimes they are distant from the original feelings. There are several ways for elicitation of feelings. The most popular use sounds, images, video clippings, music, games and films. Use of these stimuli provides, as a result, the truthful, authentic feelings. Figure 1 shows Six Basic Emotions.

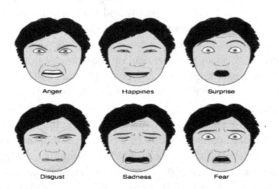

Fig. 1. Images representing six basic emotions

2.2 Physiological Variables

Psychophysiology is defined as a branch of psychology that deals with the basics of physiological and psychological process. Activation of sympathetic nerves of the ANS can inevitable or identifiable of variations in physiological pattern, even when human do not express their movement through speech, gestures and expressions in face. This activation of sympathetic expression increases pressure of blood, reduces variability in heart rate, increases heart rate and raises breathing rate. Some studies involve psycho physiological measures which are used in the interaction study of the human robot are as follows:

1. System of cardiovascular – ECG, Heart Rate Variability (HRV), BP, Cardiac Output, Inter Beat Interval (IBI), Respiratory Sinus Arrhythmia (RSA).
2. Activity in Electro dermal – Galvanic Skin Response (GSR), Skin Conductance (SC).
3. System of Respiration –Respiration per minute, Volume of Breath, Inhale-Exhale temperature.
4. System of Muscular–Electromyography (EMG).
5. Activity of Brain –Brain imaging and Electroencephalography (EEG) methods like emission tomography of positron.

Electrocardiogram (ECG): ECG denotes the electrical performance of the heart which is collected by the electrodes placed on the surface of the body and this is most representative feature of the heart performance. Lot of information is provided by distinctive morphology of the ECG signals to observer who is clinically trained and provides the information of the recorded individual heart; for the recognition of the broad range of various disorders of the heart these visually recorded ECG signals used by the cardiologists. By placing the electrodes of skin on the body surface, ECG electrodes collect electrical potential variations in the prescribed regions. During the period of the cycle of the heart these variations are occurred. To pump blood, muscles of the heart expand and contract around the system of circulation. Throughout the heart muscle conducts electrical impulses and also it extracts electrical impulses, to pump blood heart is stimulated. A typical ECG signal is shown in Fig. 2.

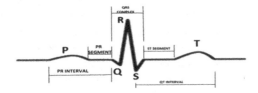

Fig. 2. ECG signal

Respiration Rate: Oxygen permeation ensured into the human body by respiration. To register breathing features special medical equipment is necessary, and is known as parameters of the respiratory system.

Those parameters characterizing state of the human health and can be classified into three groups:

- Gas metathesis Parameters within the lungs
- Parameters of volume
- Physical parameters of respiratory system.

Gas metathesis is applicable to penetration of gas into human body and while breathing exhausting from it. Parameters of volume (total lungs ability, tidal breath, remaining functional ability and others) characterize functional and potentiality of the parts of human body that answers for functions of respiration. Physical parameters are applicable to system of respiration in the mechanical unit. Table 1 shows the range of respiration rates.

Table 1. Rates of breathing range

Group	Age	Breaths/min
New-born to 6 weeks	New-born to 6 weeks	30–60
Infant	6 weeks to 6 months	25–40
Toddler	1 to 3 years	20–30
Young children	3 to 6 years	20–25
Older children	10 to 14 years	15–20
Adults	Adults	12–25

Inhale and Exhale Temperature: The process of exchanging of air which means bringing oxygen in and flushing out carbon dioxide to the lungs to facilitate the exchange of gas with the internal atmosphere is called the respiration (breathing or ventilation). To monitor and detect pathological processes a new method which is measurement of the exhaled breath temperature (EBT) in the system of respiration. In this approach the mechanism of putative is based on variations in the flow of blood in the conducting airways that are features of various disease states, the temperature of the exhaled gases influenced by this. To prove this concept in first attempts were made in conjunction with measurement of exhaled nitric oxide fraction (f_{eno}) about a decade ago. They made using open-circuit, single-breath method in a closed indoor environment, and demonstrated associations between EBT on the one hand, and bronchial blood flow, f_{eno} and sputum cellular content on the other.

Blood Pressure (BP): Across the vessel of the blood wall, the pressure of the circulation of blood is called blood pressure. Pressure in the large arteries of the heart for the circulation of the blood is called blood pressure. It is denoted as a pressure of systolic (high during single heart beat) over pressure of diastolic (low in between two heart beats) and is calculated in millimetres of mercury (mmHg), upper pressure of the surrounding environment (for comfort ability taking as zero). Here blood pressure is the sign, along with rate of respiration, oxygen saturation, heart rate, and temperature of body. In an adult, blood pressure rate is 80 millimetres of mercury (11 kPa) diastolic, and approximately 120 millimetres of Mercury (16 kPa) systolic abbreviated 120/80 mm Hg.

3 Proposed Method

Figure 3 shows the block diagram of the proposed system.

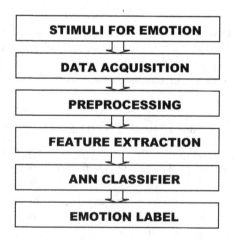

Fig. 3. Block diagram of the proposed system

3.1 Data Acquisition

There are two stages in data acquisition: Hardware and software. The physiological signals are captured using suitable sensors and signal conditioning. With a data acquisition card the information is fed to the laptop/PC. The MATLAB software package helps in storage, processing and display of necessary information. The block diagram representation of the data acquisition system is depicted in Fig. 4.

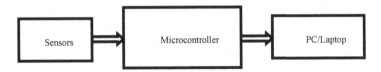

Fig. 4. Data acquisition unit

Identification of feelings from voice and the expressions in face are small in comparison to other domain like bio signals which are accompanied with the feelings. To identify particular signals earlier the system can being trained hence, it is initially needed to elicit feelings and then note the several bio-signals that accompany them. Feelings must be original to calculate the physiological signals. Elicitation of feelings has several ways; the most popular method uses pictures, music, voices, games and films. The authentic, truthful feelings are resulted by using these stimuli. Here we have used video as stimuli to elicit emotion. The video used is of length 180 s and data capture time 60 s. The videos were played in a laptop and kept at a distance of 1 m away from the subject. Figure 5 shows signal acquisition from subjects.

Fig. 5. Signal acquisition from subjects.

3.2 Pre-processing

The raw physiological contained signals with external interferences and noises in all the time. Raw signals which are affected by the addition of disturbances and artefacts because of muscular motion and devices of electrostatic energy are eliminated using moving average filter. Before processing the artefacts and disturbances are eliminated by the raw signals of physiology. We have used Low-pass filter to the raw ECG preprocessing and respiration rate signals. Segmentation of the physiological signals (Rate of breathing and ECG) into each samples and taking the mid portion of the signal by neglecting the starting and the last of every collected those are largely prone to artefacts. Re-sampled the signal at 4 Hz and baseline is subtracted.

3.3   Extraction of Features

It is required to extract the statistical features or characteristics from the signal and those are utilized to identify the content of feelings in the signals after signals are pre-processed. A high count of domain of time, statistical, domain of frequency and features of domain of time frequency can be generated by e several signals of physiology. By utilizing two signals of physiology (Breathing signal and ECG) a count of 19 features are generated. In case of ECG, to determine the features corresponding to statistical parameters the following in built MATLAB functions have been incorporated they are - 'rms', 'emd', 'mean', 'max', 'find peaks' etc. For respiratory signal feature extraction, the above mentioned built-in MATLAB functions are further utilized.

3.4   Feature Selection

The generation of information by several bio-signals may not or may be correlated with the feelings. Therefore, those information might not consist of any correlation between the various states of feelings must be erased. That information which is uncorrelated decreases the classifiers action. For the effective division of feelings, relevant information is chosen. Information selection from the extracted signal is done as represented in flowchart shown in Fig. 6.

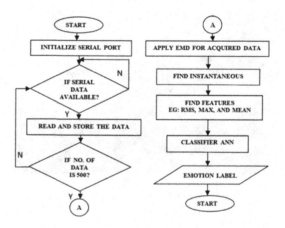

Fig. 6. Flow chart

3.5   Classification

After choosing the information which is similar to the states of feelings, they should be utilized for classifier training. The resultant classifier can classify the input to several states of feelings. so that by utilizing presented information it can divide the several states of feelings. An Artificial Neural Network (ANN) with Feed forward Back Propagation (BP) training method has been used in our work. ANN with three layers having six input neurons, 200 hidden layer neurons and 3 output layer neurons is chosen. It is difficult to compare various algorithms of the division as the devices utilize various testing/training sets of data, and elicited method of feelings is vary. When the information by all the signals of physiology are utilized for dividing the several feelings and the accuracy division is larger for the similar base of the data. A data base from 200 subjects was created and ANN has been trained with this data base.

By a single subject experiment data was gathered on various times of the day and various days. The input dataset is partitioned into training, validation and testing. The following information is included in the dataset such as Heart rate, respiration amplitude and respiration rate. Here we used the feedback neural network structure for signal training and classification of emotions. In this network structure, the signals travel in two directions, forward and backward, from the nodes of input, through the nodes of output and to the concealed node.

4   Experimental Results

The proposed system is implemented for the following emotions: Happy, Sad, Fear, Disgust, Anger and Surprise. The self-determining patterns of the test were accepted through the network structure which is trained and the outcomes were examined with

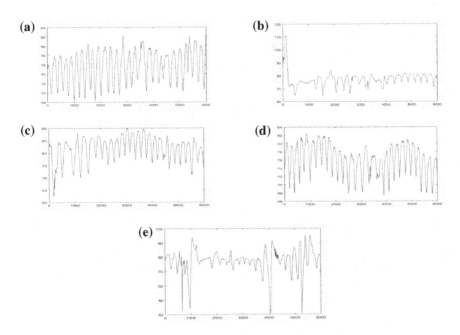

Fig. 7. (a) Happy. (b) Sad. (c) Fear. (d) Disgust. (e) Anger

the function of band which counts the correct patterns if the value of the objective and the projected lie in a specified range of distance which is bandwidth referred and shows the specific emotion of the person. The ECG patterns are as shown in Fig. 7a–e. Percentage accuracy is shown in Fig. 8a–c.

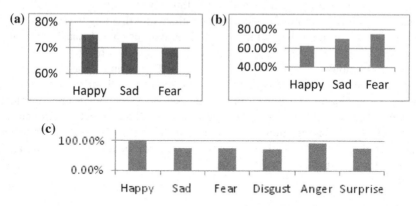

Fig. 8. (a) Percentage accuracy (ECG + inhale exhale temperature) for Adults. (b) Percentage accuracy (ECG + inhale exhale temperature) for Aged. 2 (c) Percentage accuracy (ECG + inhale exhale temperature + respiration rate + BP + pulse rate) for Adults

5   Conclusions

By utilizing the signals of the physiology we have presented and reviewed various stages of the identification of feelings of the human. Identification of feelings in its real time is still in its infantry state. As feelings are largely progressive, a general scheme for dividing all the elementary feelings rests a task. The date of the development of the system is dependent on the user and the systems which are independent of user which surpluses correctness. Therefore, large scale data of physiological signal is necessary to obtain a reliable and robust scheme of feeling identification which is independent of user. Therefore, for a little range of time variations in the physiological signals corresponding to feelings are observed. Therefore to provide good outcomes, generation of data at the instant elicitation of feelings is paramount. In addition of, for the employment of a novel and robust information generation, techniques of division and choosing information supports in growing a scheme of identification of feelings which is independent of user, and is having better accuracy of classification. An android application can be developed to sense and recognize emotions to track the health of human beings.

Acknowledgements. Authors take this opportunity to thank the authorities of Malnad College of Engineering, Hassan and Technical Education Quality Improvement Programme for supporting this research work.

References

1. Jonghwa, K., Elisabeth, A.: Emotion recognition based on physiological changes in music listening. IEEE Trans. Pattern Anal. Mach. Intell. **30**, 2067–2083 (2008)
2. Selvaraj, J., Murugappan, M., Wan, K., Yaacob, S.: Classification of emotional states from electrocardiogram signals: a non-linear approach based on hurst. Biomed. Eng. Online **12**, 3481–3499 (2013)
3. Nasoz, F., Alvarez, K., Lisetti, C.L., Finkelstein, N.: Emotion recognition from physiological signals using wireless sensors for presence technologies. Cogn. Technol. Work **6**, 4–14 (2004)
4. Vyzas, E., Picard, R.W.: Affective pattern classification. In: Emotional and Intelligent the Tangled Knot of Cognition, pp. 176–182 (2010)
5. D'Mello, S., Graesser, A., Schuller, B., Martin, J.-C. (eds.): ACII 2011. LNCS, vol. 6974. Springer, Heidelberg (2011). https://doi.org/10.1007/978-3-642-24600-5
6. Koelstra, S., et al.: DEAP: a database for emotion analysis; using physiological signals. IEEE Trans. Affect. Comput. **3**(1), 18–31 (2012)
7. Agrafioti, F., Hatzinakos, D., Anderson, A.: ECG pattern analysis for emotion detection. IEEE Trans. Affect. Comput. **3**(1), 102–115 (2012)
8. Valenza, G., Citi, L., Lanatá, A., Scilingo, E.P., Barbieri, R.: Revealing real-time emotional responses: a personalized assessment based on heart beat dynamics. Sci. Rep. **4**, 4998 (2014)
9. Goshvarpour, A., Abbasi, A., Goshvarpour, A.: Affective visual stimuli: characterization of the picture sequences impacts by means of nonlinear approaches. Basic Clin. Neurosci. **6**(4), 209–222 (2015)
10. Wu, C.-K., Chung, P.-C., Wang, C.-J.: Representative segment-based emotion analysis and classification with automatic respiration signal segmentation. IEEE Trans. Affect. Comput. **3**(4), 482–495 (2012)
11. Valenza, G., Lanatá, A., Scilingo, E.P.: Improving emotion recognition systems by embedding cardio respiratory coupling. Physiol. Meas. **34**(4), 449 (2013)
12. Betella, A., et al.: Inference of human affective states from psycho physiological measurements extracted under ecologically valid conditions. Front. Neurosci. **8**, 286 (2014). https://doi.org/10.3389/fnins.2014.00286
13. Whitman, B.: How music recommendation works - and doesn't work (2012). http://notes.variogr.am/

Analysis of Action Oriented Effects on Perceptual Process of Object Recognition Using Physiological Responses

Shanu Sharma[1]([⊠]), Anju Mishra[2], Sanjay Kumar[3], Priya Ranjan[4], and Amit Ujlayan[5]

[1] Department of CSE, ASET, Amity University, Noida, Uttar Pradesh, India
shanu.sharma16@gmail.com
[2] Department of IT, ASET, Amity University, Noida, Uttar Pradesh, India
amishra1@amity.edu
[3] Department of Psychology, Oxford Brookes University, Oxford, UK
skumar@brookes.ac.uk
[4] Department of EEE, ASET, Amity University, Noida, Uttar Pradesh, India
pranjan@amity.edu
[5] School of Vocational Studies and Applied Sciences, GBU, Greater Noida, India
amitujlayan@gbu.ac.in

Abstract. Action on any objects provides perceptual information about the environment. There is substantial evidence that human visual system responds to action possibilities in an image as perceiving any one's action stimulates human motor system. However very limited studies have been done to analyze the effect of object affordance during action perception and execution. To study the effect of object affordance on human perception, in this paper we have analyzed the human brain signals using EEG based oscillatory activity of brain. EEG responses corresponding to images of objects shown with correct, incorrect and without grips are examined. Exploration of different gripping effects has been done by extracting Alpha and Beta frequency bands using Discrete Wavelet Transform based band extraction method, then baseline normalized power of Alpha and Beta frequency bands at 24 positions of motor area of left and right side of brain are examined. The result shows that twelve pooled electrodes at central and central parietal region provides a clear discrimination among the three gripping cases in terms of calculated power. The presented research explores new applicabilities of object affordance to develop a variety of Brain Computer Interface (BCI) based devices and to improve motor imagery ability among motor disorder related patients.

Keywords: Visual perception · Action recognition
Congruent-Incongruent grip · EEG signals · DWT

© Springer Nature Switzerland AG 2018
U. S. Tiwary (Ed.): IHCI 2018, LNCS 11278, pp. 46–58, 2018.
https://doi.org/10.1007/978-3-030-04021-5_5

1   Introduction

"Perception is not something that happens to us, or in us. It is something we do: Noe [1]". Action is a way of obtaining perceptual knowledge about the environment. According to Gibson 1979 Visual affordance theory [2], any movement of body either active or passive can provide useful information. Norman [3] explained affordance in context of human computer interaction as "how an object may be interacted with". It indicates that not only the object's properties but the way we interact with the objects also affects our motor system [4,11]. So, Perception is instrumentally dependent on action and movement can alter sensory inputs and so results in different perceptions [2]. There is substantial indication that execution and observation of action both activates the same brain area and results in the same cognitive process. During planning, controlling or execution of movement, the motor cortex region of cerebral cortex is usually active. Thus, any activity related to movement or imagined movement generates brain signals that are dominant in the motor cortex of the brain [9,10]. Movement related oscillating process in these regions is usually visible in Alpha (8–12 Hz) and Beta (12–30 Hz) frequency bands [13,14].

To study the brain activity now a days brain computer interfaces (BCI's) is the most effective way. It detects and interprets signals and can generate commands to control external devices [5]. There are numerous applications of BCI's including medical, industrial, experimental psychology and neuro-rehabilitation etc., which are working on analyzing the sensory inputs [5,7]. Brain signals can be detected by capturing the electrical activity of the brain. The most effective way to understand the functioning of brain is by EEG-based oscillatory activity [8,9]. The EEG recordings contain cortical potentials which occur during various mental processes [10]. The main issue with BCI devices is to capture the human mental activities by analyzing EEG based brain waves. The development of BCI based applications is challenging task as brain waves must respond to surrounding environment in real time [5].

It is widely known phenomenon that EEG rhythmic activities occurs over motor related areas of brain while performing or imaging any movement related work [13,22]. Different spatio-temporal pattern of EEG can be predicted depending on the type of imagery performed as imagining motor actions can moderate the motor related rhythm and result in power changes [23,24]. Over the past years a lot of work has been done in the field of motor imagery based development of BCI devices [18]. In [7] a general architecture for the motor imagery signal classification for BCI devices is presented. An efficient EEG classification technique is proposed in [15] to address the issue of inter-subject variability. Similar work in the field of hand movement classification using motor imagery based EEG signals also exists [17,19–21].

According to the perceptual studies it is observed that humans are more attentive towards target oriented stimuli [11]. Thus imaging an action oriented object recognition task can provide better performance in various BCI or rehabilitation related applications. Some studies exists which explored effect of object affordance on human perception. In [4] authors explained theoretical concept behind the role of way of interaction with object while observing the action, whereas analysis of the effects is missing. EEG based grip strength classification is done using SVM classifier in [6]. Authors claimed higher classification accuracy for strong grip signals due to the higher change in EEG responses in comparison to other types of grips. Similar study is done in [16] where authors used time domain features for classification of power of hand grasps. Li et al. [14] have performed object oriented motor imagery (OI) analysis using EEG data in four different cases of object, non-object (NI), simple imagery (SI) and visual observation (VO), authors claimed that there is significant suppression in mu rhythm for OI and NI. Kumar et al. [12] have performed an ERP based analysis to examine the EEG based responses to hand actions on objects. Four types of cases have been considered for action analysis-Object with Congruent Grip, Object with In-Congruent Grip and Non-object with Congruent and In-Congruent Grip. Authors study shows that even the grip responses were unrelated to the task, ERP responses were sensitive to the type of grip congruency over posterior and motor areas of brain. This work was continued in [13] where Kumar et al. presented a study on mu rhythm de-synchronization over motor areas for different object gripping conditions.

In this paper we are working on the dataset presented by Kumar et al. in [12,13], in which further analysis of strongly effected electrodes on motor area has been done to analyze the effects of action related information on brain signals by examining the participants decisions to objects with different gripping options. The aim of further analysis is to extract certain effective features and electrodes which can be used for the development of more effective action oriented BCI based devices. We analyzed EEG responses to objects shown with congruent grips, in-congruent grips and without grips. EEG signals are decomposed into frequency bands using DWT and the alpha and beta rhythms are analyzed over both left and right hemisphere electrodes. Further central parietal electrode sites of interest are used for power calculation in all the three cases. It is hoped that the presented study will provide awareness into the role of object affordance during action perception. Further sections of paper are organized as: Sect. 1 discussed background and related work done with motor related datasets. Section 2 explains the proposed work starting from experimental paradigm, data acquisition to computational analysis of the data. Then Sect. 3 discusses the results obtained using computation procedure followed by Sect. 4 which concludes the paper.

2   Experimental Paradigms and Computational Analysis

2.1   Dataset Description

Participants and EEG Recordings: The presented analysis has been done on EEG dataset by Kumar et al. [12,13] which was recorded continuously with Ag/AgCl electrodes placed on 128 scalp locations using nylon electrode cap. The electrodes were placed according to 10-5 electrode system and eight extra electrodes were also used as references, ground, Left and Right Mastoid and for monitoring vertical and horizontal eye movement. The signals were amplified and sampled at a rate of 1024 Hz using BioSemi Active-Two amplifiers. Dataset was collected by group of 14 people (3 male, 11 female).

Stimuli and Capturing Procedure: For analyzing the effect of action of objects 2D images of 30 objects and non-objects have been used as stimuli. Images of non-objects are generated using Photoshop by combining the part of two objects. Then action based sensory inputs were measured by showing images of object with congruent grip, incongruent grip and no grip. Similarly, participants were shown images for non-objects with congruent, incongruent and no grip as shown in Fig. 1. The participants received a total of 180 stimuli of which 30 stimuli pertaining to objects and 30 were for non-object categories.

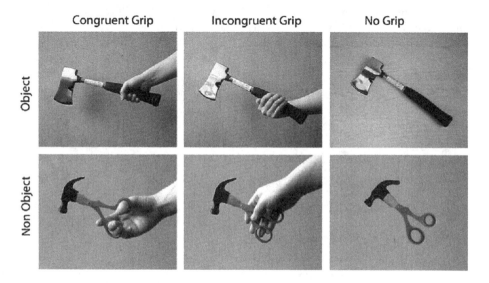

Fig. 1. Images of objects and non-objects stimuli used in experiment [12]

Before each task, the participants received twelve practice trials each of which began with the presentation of a fixation point(x) for 1000 ms followed by a target stimulus for 1000 ms. Pictorial representation of trials structure is shown in Fig. 2. Participants were asked to make a response within 4000 ms after stimulus onset. In our work for the perceptual analysis of actions on objects, we have selected the dataset corresponding to 90 stimuli with objects having congruent and in-congruent grip and no grips only. The task was to decide quickly whether the object was a real one or a non-object.

2.2   Computational Analysis

The EEG data of 7 participants corresponding to 90 stimuli with objects in three gripping conditions were selected for the analysis. For extracting the distinguishable feature, EEG data was first pre-processed, then alpha and beta

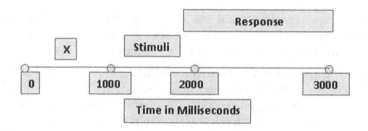

Fig. 2. Trial structure of each stimulus

band of signals were extracted using DWT based band extraction method. Then baseline normalized power of each band was extracted at different channels of motor area for each gripping conditions. These computational steps are shown in Fig. 3 and are discussed below in detail.

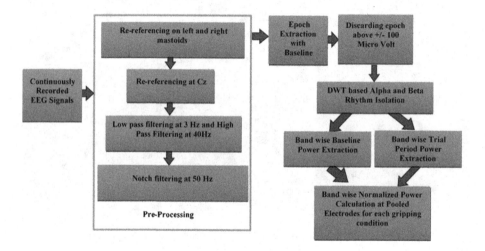

Fig. 3. Procedure for computational analysis

Raw EEG Signal: EEG data was recorded continuously using 128 electrodes positions. Original data contains 360 events corresponding to 30 events each for object and non object stimuli and response in three different gripping conditions. Data was sampled at 1024 Hz and is stored in Biosemi Data (bdf) format.

Pre-Processing: EEG signals are of very poor spatial resolution, have low voltage variations and noise thus requires a lot of pre-processing efforts. Pre-processing procedure of our work is presented in Fig. 3. Initial pre-processing of data was done using EEGLAB software. First data was offline referenced at left (M1) and right mastoid (M2) electrodes to achieve full CMRR, then re-referencing at Cz position was done to remove CM signal from the data. EEG signals were then band pass filtered from 3 to 40 Hz and notch filtered at 50 Hz to remove low frequency and power line noise.

Data Selection: As discussed in Sect. 2, that movement related EEG signals are more dominant in motor cortex region of the brain, EEG data corresponding to 24 electrodes as shown in Fig. 4 from each left and right hemisphere of motor area are selected for studying the perceptual changes of effects of different types of gripping.

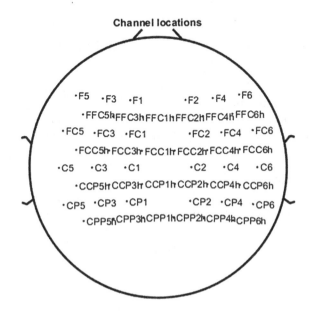

Fig. 4. Distribution of electrodes used for analyzing the motor area

Epoch Extraction: Continuous selected EEG data is then segmented into epochs of duration 2 s (1000 ms before stimuli onset and 1000 ms after stimuli onset). Epochs were extracted related to 3 different types of events corresponding to Object Congruent, Object In-Congruent and Object No Grip. Further to remove noisy epochs, epochs having values above 100 Micro Volt and below −100 Micro Volt were discarded. 1000 ms pre-stimuli period is taken as baseline period and 1000 ms post stimuli period is taken as trial period for each gripping case.

Discrete Wavelet Transform based Alpha, Beta Band Extraction: DWT performs decomposition of time series signals using high pass and low pass filtering with down sampling ratio of 2 [25,27], in which high pass filter [HP] and low pass filters are discrete "mother" and its mirror version respectively. At each level DWT outputs approximate and detailed coefficients. The approximation coefficients are then further decomposed as shown in Fig. 5 to extract localized information from the sub-band of detail coefficients.

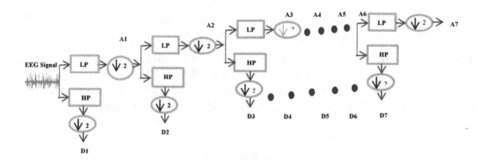

Fig. 5. DWT based signal decomposition into detailed and approximate coefficients

In DWT decomposition level is determined using the dominant frequency component of the signal. In this work EEG data used was sampled at 1024 Hz, thus we have performed 7 level DWT decomposition with Daubechies-eight (db8) mother wavelet [28]. Among extracted sub-bands as given in Table 1 Alpha and Beta bands were used for study of hand grip actions.

Table 1. DWT coefficients and frequency bands

DWT coefficients	Frequency range	Frequency bands
D1	256–512 Hz	-
D2	128–256 Hz	-
D3	64–128 Hz	-
D4	32–64 Hz	Gamma
D5	16–32 Hz	Beta
D6	8–16 Hz	Alpha
D7	4–8 Hz	Theta
A7	0–4 Hz	Delta

Baseline Normalized Power Calculation (BNP): For statistical analysis of different gripping effects on objects, baseline normalized power is calculated using Eq. 1 at each channel location and for each gripping condition [19,26]. This normalized power calculates the % change in power with respect to baseline, the purpose of normalizing the power with respect to baseline is to remove any activity in the signal that was constant over time (i.e. baseline) [29].

$$BNP = 100 * (BaselinePower - TrialPeriodPower)/BaselinePower \quad (1)$$

3   Results and Discussion

Step wise results of various steps mentioned in Fig. 3 are discussed in detail as: After re-referencing, EEG data was filtered to reduce noise. This step is necessary so that meaningful epoch should not be discarded at the time of epoch discarding. After Band pass filtering, EEG data corresponding to 24 electrodes in Fig. 4 was selected for epoch extraction. DWT based band extraction method was then applied on epoch data to extract different frequency bands. Figure 6(a), (b) and (c) shows the sample of extracted bands extracted for Congruent, Incongruent and No Grip activity at channel F1. Similar process was done for all the channels, and as any movement related activity over motor area is usually visible in Alpha (8–12 Hz) and Beta (12–30 Hz) frequency bands, these bands were chosen for further analysis. For analyzing the effect in Alpha and Beta bands over three gripping cases, baseline normalized power (BNP) was calculated. The effects were visible on all the mentioned 24 electrodes over motor area, but after analysis it was found there is a significant difference over central parietal area as shown in Fig. 7. Since we have considered the data with right hand reaches only, we have taken left side electrodes for further analysis. To find the suitable feature for differentiating three gripping cases BNP using Eq. (1) was calculated over following pooled electrodes on Left Hemisphere.

CP1 CP3 CP5 CCP1H CCP3H CCP5H CPP1H CPP3H CPP5H C1 C3 C5

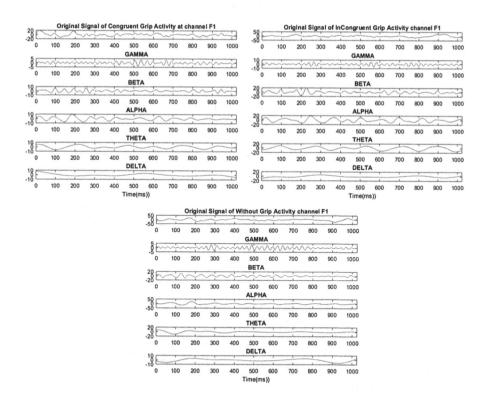

Fig. 6. DWT based extracted bands (a) Congruent (b) In-Congruent and (c) No grip activity

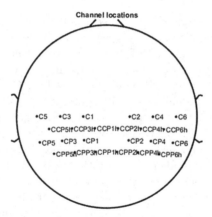

Fig. 7. Distribution of electrodes selected for pooling

Figures 8 and 9 represents the pooled baseline normalized power (BNP) of all trials of Object with Congruent and In-Congruent grip activity in Alpha and Beta Band respectively. It can be seen from Fig. 8 that BNP for Incongruent Grip is greater than Congruent grip in Alpha Band whereas in beta band (Fig. 9) BNP for Congruent Grip is greater than In-Congruent Grip.

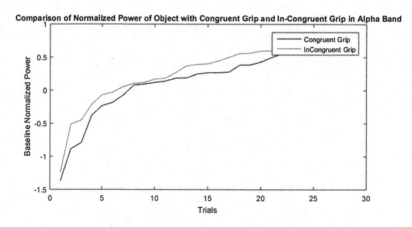

Fig. 8. Comparison of BNP of Congruent and Incongruent grip activity in Alpha Band

Similar analysis was done for Object with Congruent and Without grip activity. Results presented in Fig. 10 shows there BNP is high in Beta Band for Congruent grip activity than without grip activity, whereas little difference can be seen in Alpha Band (Fig. 11).

The average Alpha and Beta band baseline normalized power of pooled electrodes for subject 1 across all trails in Congruent, Incongruent and without grip activity is given in Table 2. Mentioned analysis on the basis of these results is summarized Table 3.

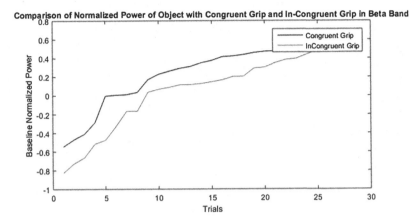

Fig. 9. Comparison of BNP of Congruent and Incongruent grip activity in Beta Band

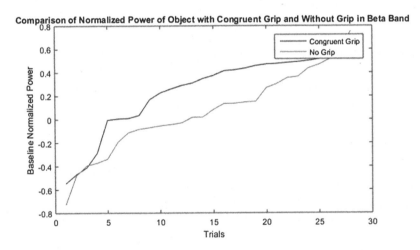

Fig. 10. Comparison of BNP of Congruent and Without grip activity in Beta Band

Table 2. Average BNP over pooled electrodes in three different gripping cases

Average BNP	Congruent grip	In-Congruent grip	No grip
Alpha power	23.4520	43.3371	28.7069
Beta Power	28.7648	12.3537	15.7364

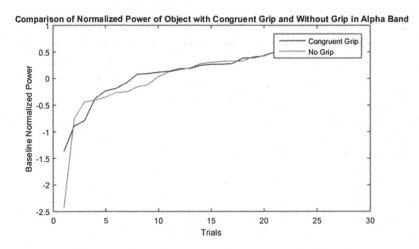

Fig. 11. Comparison of BNP of Congruent and Without grip activity in Alpha Band

Table 3. Analysis of effect of different gripping cases

Power at pooled electrodes	Congruent Grip (C) and In-Congruent Grip (IC)	Congruent Grip (CG) and No Grip (NG)
Alpha power (Baseline normalized)	C < IC	A little difference which cannot be differentiated
Beta power (Baseline normalized)	C > IC	C > NG

4   Conclusion

In this work EEG based analysis has been done to analyse the effect of object affordance on object perception and recognition. Baseline normalized power in Alpha and Beta bands were examined in three different object gripping cases i.e. Congruent, In-Congruent gripping No gripping over motor areas. Further to find the distinguishable feature 12 electrodes over central parietal areas were selected. The result shows that the effect of object with correct grip and without grip is clearly visible in Alpha band, whereas difference between object with correct grip and incorrect grip can be seen in both Alpha and Beta band. The presented study and features can be used for the development of automatically classifying EEG signals, which can be used to develop various brain machine interfaces for neurorehabilitation purpose. It is hoped that the presented study will provide awareness into the role of object affordance during action perception.

References

1. Noe, A.: Action in Perception. A Bradford Book (2006)
2. Gibson, J.J.: The Theory of Affordances-The Ecological Approach to Visual Perception. Houghton Mifflin, Boston (1979)
3. Norman, D.A.: The Psychology of Everyday Things. Basic Books, New York (1988)
4. Hailperin-Lausch, R.: A proposed EEG study: the role of object affordance during action observation. IU J. Undergrad. Res. **3**(1), 44–47 (2017)
5. Hassanien, A.E., Azar, A.T. (eds.): Brain-Computer Interfaces: Current Trends and Applications. ISRL, vol. 74. Springer, Cham (2015). https://doi.org/10.1007/978-3-319-10978-7
6. Kim, D.-E., Yu, J.-H., Sim, K.-B.: EEG feature classification based on grip strength for BCI applications. Int. J. Fuzzy Log. Intell. Syst. **15**(4), 277–282 (2015)
7. Chaudhari, R., Galiyawala, H.J.: A review on motor imagery signal classification for BCI. Signal Process. Int. J. (SPIJ) **11**(2), 16 (2017)
8. Amin, H.U., Mumtaz, W., Subhani, A.R., Saad, M.N.M., Malik, A.S.: Classification of EEG signals based on pattern recognition approach. Front. Comput. Neurosci. **11** (2017). https://doi.org/10.3389/fncom.2017.00103
9. Choi, S.H., Lee, M., Wang, Y., Hong, B.: Estimation of optimal location of EEG reference electrode for motor imagery based BCI using fMRI. In: International Conference of the IEEE Engineering in Medicine and Biology Society, New York, NY, pp. 1193–1196. IEEE (2006)
10. Schuch, S., Bayliss, A.P., Klein, C., Tipper, S.P.: Attention modulates motor system activation during action observation: evidence for inhibitory rebound. Exp. Brain Res. **205**(2), 235–249 (2010). https://doi.org/10.1007/s00221-010-2358-4
11. Oberman, L.M., Pineda, J.A., Ramachandran, V.S.: The human mirror neuron system: a link between action observation and social skills. Soc. Cogn. Affect. Neurosci. **2**(1), 62–66 (2007). https://doi.org/10.1093/scan/nsl022
12. Kumar, S., Yoon, E.Y., Humphreys, G.W.: Perceptual and motor-based responses to hand actions on objects: evidence from ERPs. Exp. Brain Res. **220**(2), 153–164 (2012)
13. Kumar, S., Riddoch, M.J., Humphreys, G.: Mu rhythm desynchronization reveals motoric influences of hand action on object recognition. Front. Hum. Neurosci. **7**(66) (2013). https://doi.org/10.3389/fnhum.2013.00066
14. Li, L., Wang, J., Xu, G., Li, M., Xie, J.: The study of object-oriented motor imagery based on EEG suppression. PLoS ONE **10**(12) (2015). https://doi.org/10.1371/journal.pone.0144256
15. Sreeja, S.R., Rabha, J., Samanta, D., Mitra, P., Sarma, M.: Classification of motor imagery based EEG signals using sparsity approach. In: Horain, P., Achard, C., Mallem, M. (eds.) IHCI 2017. LNCS, vol. 10688, pp. 47–59. Springer, Cham (2017). https://doi.org/10.1007/978-3-319-72038-8_5
16. Roy, R., Sikdar, D., Mahadevappa, M., Kumar, C.: EEG based motor imagery study of time domain features for classification of power and precision hand grasps. In: 8th International IEEE EMBS Conference on Neural Engineering Shanghai, China, 25–28 May 2017
17. Sivakami, A., Shenbaga Devi, S.: Analysis of EEG for motor imagery based classification of hand activities. Int. J. Biomed. Eng. Sci. (IJBES) **2**(3), 11–22 (2015)
18. Lange, G., Low, C.Y., Johar, K., Hanapiah, F.A., Kamaruzaman, F.: Classification of electroencephalogram data from hand grasp and release movements for BCI controlled prosthesis. Procedia Technol. **26**, 374–381 (2016)

19. Mohammad, H.A., Samaha, A., AlKamha, K.: Automated classification of L/R hand movement EEG signals using advanced feature extraction and machine learning. Int. J. Adv. Comput. Sci. Appl. (IJACSA) 4(6), 207–212 (2013)
20. Holler, Y., et al.: Comparison of EEG-features and classification methods for motor imagery in patients with disorders of consciousness. PLoS ONE 8(11) (2013). https://doi.org/10.1371/journal.pone.0080479
21. Gupta, S.S., Agarwal, S.: Classification and analysis of EEG signals for imagined motor movements. In: IEEE Workshop on Computational Intelligence: Theories, Applications and Future Directions (WCI), pp. 1–7. IEEE (2015)
22. Matsumoto, J., Fujiwara, T., Takahashi, O., Liu, M., Kimura, A., Ushiba, J.: Modulation of mu rhythm desynchronization during motor imagery by transcranial direct current stimulation. J. NeuroEngineering Rehabil. 7(27) (2010). https://doi.org/10.1186/1743-0003-7-27
23. Batres-Mendoza, P., et al.: Improving EEG-based motor imagery classification for real-time applications using the QSA method. Comput. Intell. Neurosci. (2017). https://doi.org/10.1155/2017/9817305
24. Hari Krishna, D., Pasha, I.A., Savithri, T.S.: Classification of EEG motor imagery multi class signals based on cross correlation. Procedia Comput. Sci. 85, 490–495 (2016). https://doi.org/10.1016/j.procs.2016.05.198
25. Vivas, E.L.A., García-González, A., Figueroa, I., Fuentes, R.Q.: Discrete wavelet transform and ANFIS classifier for brain-machine interface based on EEG. In: 6th International Conference on Human System Interactions (HSI), Sopot, Poland, pp. 137–144. IEEE (2013)
26. Shedeed, H.A., Issa, M.F.: Brain-EEG signal classification based on data normalization for controlling a robotic arm. Int. J. Tomogr. Simul. 29, 72–85 (2016)
27. Subasi, A.: EEG signal classification using wavelet feature extraction and a mixture of expert model. Expert Syst. Appl. 32, 1084–1093 (2007). https://doi.org/10.1016/j.eswa.2006.02.005
28. Article on Wavelet db8. http://wavelets.pybytes.com/wavelet/db8/. Accessed 20 Mar 2018
29. Cohen, M.X.: Chapter 18-Analyzing neural time series data: theory and practice. MIT Press (2014)

Classification of EEG Signals for Cognitive Load Estimation Using Deep Learning Architectures

Anushri Saha[1(✉)], Vikash Minz[1], Sanjith Bonela[1], S. R. Sreeja[1], Ritwika Chowdhury[2], and Debasis Samanta[1]

[1] Department of Computer Science and Engineering,
Indian Institute of Technology Kharagpur, Kharagpur, West Bengal, India
AnushriSaha@sit.iitkgp.ernet.in
[2] Department of Electronics and Electrical Communication Engineering,
Indian Institute of Technology Kharagpur, Kharagpur, West Bengal, India

Abstract. Measuring cognitive load is crucial for many applications such as information personalization, adaptive intelligent tutoring systems, etc. Cognitive load estimation using Electroencephalogram (EEG) signals is widespread as it produces clear indications of cognitive activities by measuring changes of neural activation in the brain. However, the existing cognitive load estimation techniques are based on machine learning algorithms, which follow signal denoising and hand-crafted feature extraction to classify different loads. There is a need to find a better alternative to the machine learning approach. Of late, deep learning approach has been successfully applied to many applications namely, computer vision, pattern recognition, speech processing, etc. However, deep learning has not been extensively studied for the classification of cognitive load data captured by an EEG. In this work, two deep learning models are studied, namely stacked denoising autoencoder (SDAE) followed by a multilayer perceptron (MLP) and long short term memory (LSTM) followed by an MLP to classify cognitive load data. SDAE and LSTM are used for feature extraction and MLP for classification. It is observed that deep learning models perform significantly better than the conventional machine learning classifiers such as support vector machine (SVM), k-nearest neighbors (KNN), and linear discriminant analysis (LDA).

Keywords: Cognitive load · Stacked denoising autoencoder
Long short term memory · Multilayer perceptron

1 Introduction

Online documents play an important role in student's education and learning. Every student has a different curiosity, learning speed and preferences. If the reading content is dull, a student may feel boring and avert their concentration

© Springer Nature Switzerland AG 2018
U. S. Tiwary (Ed.): IHCI 2018, LNCS 11278, pp. 59–68, 2018.
https://doi.org/10.1007/978-3-030-04021-5_6

from reading. Therefore, there is a need to make the learning content attractive and easier to understand. By learning the cognitive load (CL) of the person, one can estimate whether he/she is interested in the particular topic or not. To develop such a system, it is important to distinguish the learners' CLs. Moreover, CL can be defined as the amount of psychological load experienced by working memory when performing tasks [6].

Work on classifying CL using electroencephalogram (EEG) signal is advocated as EEGs are less bulky, portable and produce clear indications of cognitive processes by monitoring changes in the neural activation. Sufficient works on predicting CL from EEG signals using machine learning (ML) algorithms have been reported. Authors in [17] extracted different features and used support vector machine (SVM) to estimate different cognitive states. Das et al. [3] used a fuzzy c-means unsupervised clustering approach and Zarjam et al. [18] used multi-layer perceptron (MLP) to measure CL from EEG signals. The main drawback with ML technique is that it cannot work on noisy data, and feature extraction is necessary which is a non-trivial task.

Recently, Deep learning (DL) architectures such as deep belief networks (DBN), recurrent neural networks (RNN) and convolutional neural networks (CNN) have been applied in various fields such as computer vision, speech and audio recognition, natural language processing and brain-computer-interface (BCI). Particularly in BCI field, it has been applied for classifying motor imagery signals [9], emotion classification [14], sleep stage classification [4], affect states classification [15], epilepsy detection [12] and P300 detection [8]. Despite the growing interest of this topic, the study on DL architectures for classifying CL is scarcely reported [16]. DL approaches do not need data denoising phase. It can work efficiently on noisy data and extracts features needed for classification using its own non-linear hidden structures which can be classified using a discriminative deep network. Hence, the aim of this study is to investigate two different DL models, namely stacked denoising autoencoder (SDAE) followed by MLP and long short term memory (LSTM) followed by MLP, for classifying CL EEG signals, for the subjects who undergone the learning task.

2   Work Done

An overview of this work is shown in Fig. 1. The different tasks involved in this work is discussed in the following sub-sections:

2.1   Data Acquisition

The experimental setup was done at the BCI-HCI LAB facility at IIT Kharagpur. The EEG dataset was recorded using a 64-channel EEG device from RMS India. From the literature, it is evident that increase in difficulty level in tasks will increase CL. Thus the experiment design aims to generate three different levels of CLs in the users. A user wearing EEG device is asked to sit in a relaxing chair with armrests. The user has to read a paragraph written in English language

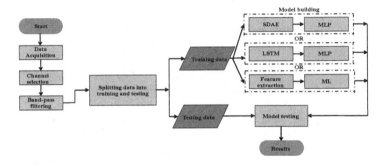

Fig. 1. Flowchart for cognitive load classification using deep neural networks.

appearing on the screen in front of him or her. Each user has undergone 2 trials and each trial consists of three different paragraphs with a varying difficulty level of understanding. Level 1 text is easy to understand with simple words and sentences, Level 2 text is difficult than Level 1 with more difficult words and complex sentences and Level 3 is the most difficult one to understand with rare English words and complicated sentences. The readability indices of the texts used in this experiment are measured using Flesch Kincaid Reading Ease and Flesch Kincaid Grade level [5]. These measures prove that Level 1 text is easy to understand, Level 2 is moderate to understand and Level 3 is difficult to understand. Three sample paragraphs of each level with their readability indices are shown in Fig. 2. Each trial includes the following timing sequence as shown in Fig. 3.

Fig. 2. Three sample texts with three different levels of difficulty

Participants: Two healthy male and two healthy female volunteers engaged in their graduate study participated in the experiment with age ranging from 25 to 30 years. All subjects were given adequate practice and idea of the experiments.

2.2   Channel Selection and Band-Pass Filtering

Working with all the channels makes the BCI system slower and moreover all the channels are not related to CL. Hence, it is better to consider the most

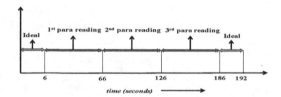

Fig. 3. Experimental template

appropriate channels responsible for capturing CL activity. From literature, it is evident that the frontal and temporal lobes of the human brain are responsible for performing cognitive task [2] and hence the 11 channels placed over these lobes are considered for further processing. The frequency of the neural potentials for the cognitive tasks mostly lie in the range 2–32 Hz [11]. Hence, Butterworth band-pass filtering with order 4 is applied on the data with a pass-band 2–32 Hz.

2.3 Data Splitting for Training and Testing

BCI systems should be designed in such a way that it should work for any subject. In order to accomplish this, the entire collected dataset are considered. This dataset is further divided into training and testing data using Monte Carlo cross validation with four splits. Monte Carlo cross-validation technique is used because of its higher optimisation over K-fold and holdout cross-validation. Using this cross validation technique, each split is separated randomly as 60:40 training and testing datasets. Using this method, predictive accuracy is obtained and then the splits are averaged to get the final results.

2.4 Classification Using SDAE

A semi-supervised approach is followed for classifying CL EEG signals. Unlabelled training data is fed as input to the unsupervised DL models namely, SDAE and LSTM. These generative DL models map the unlabelled input to the feature space and preserve all the needed information of the input. Finally, to achieve classification, the extracted features are fed as input to the discriminative DL model namely, MLP. The proposed framework of SDAE followed by MLP for CL classification is shown in Fig. 4.

Stacked Denoising Autoencoder (SDAE): The basic building block of a SDAE is Denoising Autoencoder (DAE). An Autoencoder takes an input x, and through a nonlinearity function maps it to a feature representation z as $z = f(Wx + b)$. This part is known as the encoder. This feature representation z is then mapped back into a reconstruction y in the same shape of x as $y = f(W'z + b')$. The main intention of using autoencoder is to learn the latent features from the raw input data and if necessary to reproduce the raw input back from the latent features. Generally, the weight matrix of reverse mapping

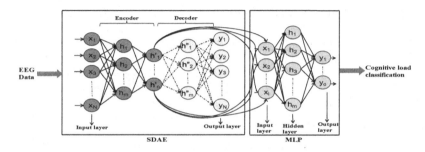

Fig. 4. SDAE architecture for classification

W', is set as $W' = W^T$, known as tied weights. The parameters of this model
are optimized such that the reconstruction error is minimized. This error can
be measured using squared error. DAE is a stochastic version of Autoencoder.
The objective of DAE is to preserve the information of the input, avoiding the
influence of the noise. If two or more DAEs are stacked, then it gives a deep
neural network, known as SDAE [1], and it is shown in Fig. 4.

Multilayer Perceptron: The DL models (SDAE and LSTM) gives the robust
and high-level features as output. These features are then fed as input to the
supervised deep MLP [7] for classification. The second block in Fig. 4, graphically
represents an MLP with a single hidden layer. The parameters of MLP model is
calculated by Backpropagation algorithm [13].

Experimental Results: The characteristics of SDAE on training and the best
5 accuracies obtained using the SDAE-MLP DL architecture is listed in Tables 1
and 2, respectively. Finally, the best explored SDAE-MLP deep network for
CL classification is shown in Fig. 5. Low learning rate is preferred so that the
network can converge to a useful and reliable structure without trapping to a
local optimum.

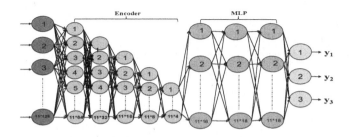

Fig. 5. Final architecture of SDAE classifier

Table 1. Characteristics of SDAE architecture

Window size = 128, Batch size = 10, Epoch = 150, Activation fn. = tanh							
Learning rate	Nodes in hidden layers					Weight relation between encoder and decoder	Loss
	Layer 1	Layer 2	Layer 3	Layer 4	Layer 5		
0.0003	11*64	11*32	11*16	11*8	11*4	tied	0.006402
0.0003	11*64	11*32	11*16	11*8	11*4	untied	0.008627
0.0004	11*64	11*32	11*16	11*8	11*4	tied	0.007035
0.0004	11*64	11*32	11*16	11*8	11*4	untied	0.015402
0.0005	11*64	11*32	11*16	11*8	11*4	tied	0.015225
0.0005	11*64	11*32	11*16	11*8	11*4	untied	0.006761

Table 2. Performance evaluation of SDAE classification

Window size = 128, Batch size = 10, Epoch = 200, Activation fn. in MLP = relu							
Learning rate	No. of nodes in MLP hidden layers			Precision	Recall	F1 score	Accuracy (%)
	Layer 1	Layer 2	Layer 3				
0.0005	11*18	11*18	11*18	0.8956	0.8949	0.8948	89.5104
0.0006	11*18	11*18	11*18	0.8601	0.8600	0.8597	86.0139
0.0007	11*18	11*18	11*18	0.8542	0.8532	0.8492	85.2112
0.0008	11*18	11*18	11*18	0.8500	0.8495	0.8497	84.9650
0.0009	11*18	11*18	11*18	0.8232	0.8252	0.8198	82.3943

2.5 Classification Using LSTM Followed by MLP

Long Short Term Memory (LSTM): The proposed framework of LSTM followed by MLP for CL classification is shown in Fig. 6. LSTM [10] is a special kind of Recurrent Neural Network (RNN) and it is more powerful than simple RNN due to its ability to learn long-term dependencies in a problem. A hidden layer in RNN has several nodes of same structure, which perform a single operation (e.g., tanh) on the given input. But in the hidden layer of LSTM, each node performs four operations on the given input in an interacting way as follows:

$$f_t = \sigma(W_f.[h_{t-1}, x_t] + b_f) \tag{1}$$

$$i_t = \sigma(W_i.[h_{t-1}, x_t] + b_i) \tag{2}$$

$$\tilde{C}_t = \tanh(W_C.[h_{t-1}, x_t] + b_C) \tag{3}$$

$$C_t = f_t * C_{t-1} + i_t * \tilde{C}_t \tag{4}$$

$$o_t = \sigma(W_o.[h_{t-1}, x_t] + b_o) \tag{5}$$

$$h_t = o_t * \tanh(C_t) \tag{6}$$

Here, x_t and h_t denote the input and output of the tth LSTM node, respectively. C denotes the memory lane of the LSTM layer and it gets updated at every node using the three gates, known as forget gate (f), input gate (i) and output gate (o). All the parameters of this model are learned by obtaining their gradients using Backpropagation through time (BPTT) algorithm [13].

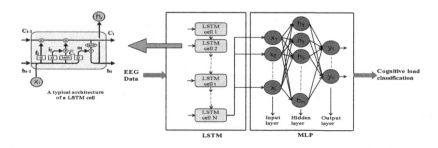

Fig. 6. LSTM architecture for classification

Experimental Results: The best 5 accuracies obtained using LSTM followed by MLP architecture and the corresponding parameters are listed in Table 3. Finally, the best explored LSTM-MLP deep network for CL classification is shown in Fig. 7. The DL network is implemented using TensorFlow library (an open source deep learning framework) in Python.

Table 3. Performance evaluation of LSTM classification

Window size = 128, Activation function = relu										
Learning rate	Epoch	Batch size	'num_units' of LSTM cells	No. of nodes in MLP hidden layers			Precision	Recall	F1 score	Accuracy (%)
				Nodes in Layer 1	Nodes in Layer 2	Nodes in Layer 3				
0.00007	500	35	900	100	100	100	0.8634	0.8603	0.8612	86.33
0.00007	300	30	850	100	100	100	0.8255	0.8202	0.8265	82.66
0.00006	250	35	850	100	100	100	0.7877	0.7805	0.7889	78.83
0.00005	250	30	900	100	100	100	0.7234	0.7201	0.7256	72.85
0.00005	200	30	850	100	100	100	0.7043	0.7008	0.7077	70.02

3   Comparison with Machine Learning Algorithms

In order to prove the efficiency of the studied DL models, they are compared with some conventional ML classifiers such as SVM, KNN and LDA. To train

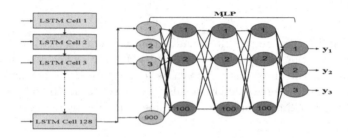

Fig. 7. Final architecture of LSTM

ML classifiers, meaningful features need to be extracted from the raw EEG data. Hence, some important features are extracted in terms of time-domain, frequency-domain and wavelet-domain, from the raw EEG data and fed as input to the classifiers.

Table 4. Comparison of machine learning and deep networks in terms of accuracy

Classifier	Parameters used	Accuracy (%)
LDA	-	72
KNN	Number of nearest neighbors (k) is set as 4 as this CL data has 3 different load levels	78
SVM	RBF kernel function used and regularization parameter C and kernel width is set as 1 and 0.00001, respectively	84
SDAE followed by MLP	5 hidden layers are there in autoencoder with the number of nodes as 11*64, 11*32, 11*16, 11*8 and 11*4 respectively. MLP constitutes with 3 hidden layers and each layer is with 20 to 18 nodes. Learning rate is varied from 0.0007 to 0.0005 with 200 epochs and batch size of 10	89.51
LSTM followed by MLP	LSTM 'num_units' is set to 900. MLP has 3 hidden layers, each with 100 nodes. Learning rate is 0.00007, batch size is 35 with 500 epochs	86.33

From Table 4, it is observed that DL models perform better than ML techniques on classifying CL. It signifies that the features extracted by DL networks has more discrimination power than the hand-crafted features in ML techniques. Conversely, in ML techniques, it might lose some valuable aspects of data due to hand-crafted features and it might lead to poor classification.

4   Conclusion

In this work, EEG-based CL data classification has been carried out using two different DL architectures. Unlike ML algorithms, DL networks do not follow signal pre-processing and feature extraction phases. Hence, in this study, two DL architectures namely, LSTM followed by MLP and SDAE followed by MLP has been exercised for cognitive load classification. It is observed that, out of the above-mentioned two DL architectures, SDAE followed by MLP outperformed the other architecture in terms of classification accuracy. Moreover, DL architectures performed better than conventional ML techniques such as SVM, KNN and LDA. Overall, DL techniques reduces the complexity by removing pre-processing steps and improves the classification accuracy by affording features concerned with the application. In the future, the work can be extended on exploring other DL architectures, to determine the best architecture for measuring the CL for real-time applications.

References

1. Introduction Auto-Encoder. https://wikidocs.net/3413. Accessed 1 June 2018
2. Baars, B.J., Gage, N.M.: Cognition, Brain, and Consciousness: Introduction to Cognitive Neuroscience. Academic Press, Burlington (2010)
3. Das, D., Chatterjee, D., Sinha, A.: Unsupervised approach for measurement of cognitive load using EEG signals. In: 2013 IEEE 13th International Conference on Bioinformatics and Bioengineering (BIBE), pp. 1–6. IEEE (2013)
4. Dong, H., Supratak, A., Pan, W., Wu, C., Matthews, P.M., Guo, Y.: Mixed neural network approach for temporal sleep stage classification. IEEE Trans. Neural Syst. Rehabil. Eng. **26**, 324–333 (2017)
5. Flesch, R.: A new readability yardstick. J. Appl. Psychol. **32**(3), 221 (1948)
6. Goldwater, B.C.: Psychological significance of pupillary movements. Psychol. Bull. **77**(5), 340 (1972)
7. Hinton, G.: Multilayer Perceptron. http://deeplearning.net/tutorial/mlp.html. Accessed 1 June 2018
8. Kawasaki, K., Yoshikawa, T., Furuhashi, T.: Visualizing extracted feature by deep learning in P300 discrimination task. In: 2015 7th International Conference of Soft Computing and Pattern Recognition (SoCPaR), pp. 149–154. IEEE (2015)
9. Lu, N., Li, T., Ren, X., Miao, H.: A deep learning scheme for motor imagery classification based on restricted boltzmann machines. IEEE Trans. Neural Syst. Rehabil. Eng. **25**(6), 566–576 (2017)
10. Olah, C.: Understanding LSTM Networks. http://colah.github.io/posts/2015-08-Understanding-LSTMs/. Accessed 1 June 2018
11. Sanei, S., Chambers, J.A.: EEG Signal Processing. John Wiley & Sons, Chichester (2013)
12. Vidyaratne, L., Glandon, A., Alam, M., Iftekharuddin, K.M.: Deep recurrent neural network for seizure detection. In: 2016 International Joint Conference on Neural Networks (IJCNN), pp. 1202–1207. IEEE (2016)
13. Werbos, P.J.: Backpropagation through time: what it does and how to do it. Proc. IEEE **78**(10), 1550–1560 (1990)
14. Xu, H., Plataniotis, K.N.: Affective states classification using EEG and semi-supervised deep learning approaches. In: 2016 IEEE 18th International Workshop on Multimedia Signal Processing (MMSP), pp. 1–6. IEEE (2016)
15. Xu, H., Plataniotis, K.N.: EEG-based affect states classification using deep belief networks. In: Digital Media Industry & Academic Forum (DMIAF), pp. 148–153. IEEE (2016)

16. Yin, Z., Zhang, J.: Recognition of cognitive task load levels using single channel EEG and stacked denoising autoencoder. In: 2016 35th Chinese Control Conference (CCC), pp. 3907–3912. IEEE (2016)
17. Zarjam, P., Epps, J., Chen, F.: Spectral EEG featuresfor evaluating cognitive load. In: 2011 Annual International Conference of the IEEE Engineering in Medicine and Biology Society, EMBC, pp. 3841–3844. IEEE (2011)
18. Zarjam, P., Epps, J., Lovell, N.H.: Beyond subjective self-rating: EEG signal classification of cognitive workload. IEEE Trans. Auton. Mental Dev. **7**(4), 301–310 (2015)

EEG Signals for Measuring Cognitive Development

A Study of EEG Signals Challenges and Prospects

Swati Aggarwal$^{(\boxtimes)}$, Prakriti Bansal, and Sameer Garg

Department of Computer Engineering, Netaji Subhas Institute of Technology,
University of Delhi, New Delhi, India
swati1178@gmail.com, prakriti.bansal98@gmail.com,
sameergarg26@gmail.com

Abstract. The use of EEG signals for measuring cognitive development is an upcoming field of research for a strong cognitive analysis to revolutionize the field of biomedical informatics and neuroscience. This paper highlights the importance of EEG signals in cognitive development experimentation and the challenges faced in conducting an EEG experiment and its intelligent analysis. Solutions to these challenges have been elaborated upon as well. Finally, the paper discusses future prospects in EEG research. A focus on these issues is essential for conducting successful EEG experimentation and choosing an accurate and precise EEG signal analysis methodology.

Keywords: Electroencephalography (EEG) · Cognitive development
Neuroscience · EEG signal analysis

1 Introduction

Various research technologies are available to study the changes in brain-behaviour and its relations [22]. Electroencephalogram (EEG) method provides an efficient, convenient and a low-cost method for measuring brain behaviour over other existing methods like ECoG (Electrocorticogram) and MEG (Magnetoencephalography) [22]. EEG is preferred as it allows the inspection of developmental changes without hampering the normal ongoing behaviours in the brain [1]. Indeed, the EEG methodology has already been used to examine the correlation between the brain electrical activity and the development of cognitive activity in infants from 5 months to 4 years [27]. "EEG experiments account for the large majority of BCI studies due to the hardware's low cost, low risk and portability" [22].

EEG is a recording of the electrical potentials of the brain from the scalp that show the electrical activity of the brain tissue [1, 6]. Researchers have experimented with EEG signals to understand the functioning of the human brain as well as for measuring the development of brain overtime [1, 6, 23]. The EEG signal is spontaneous and context-related: making it outstanding for tracking rapid shifts in brain functioning [1]. This means that the EEG generated during each specific task would generate a different signal corresponding to a different cognitive activity. The EEG signal has high

© Springer Nature Switzerland AG 2018
U. S. Tiwary (Ed.): IHCI 2018, LNCS 11278, pp. 69–77, 2018.
https://doi.org/10.1007/978-3-030-04021-5_7

temporal resolutions [22] which make the postsynaptic changes reflect in the EEG instantaneously [1]. However, the EEG signal is limited by it's low spatial resolution [12, 22], as we discuss later.

This paper discusses some of the challenges while using EEG methodology and further highlights solutions to these. Another aim of this paper is to discuss the future research prospects in the emerging field of EEG other than cognitive development. The next section discusses how EEG signals are used for measuring cognitive development, which is crucial to understanding the problems of this method.

2   EEG Signals in Measuring Cognitive Development

"Cognitive development is the construction of thought processes, including remembering, problem solving, and decision-making, from childhood through adolescence to adulthood" [2]. Cognitive analysis methodologies is uprising in the field of neuroscience and BCI applications [5]. Neural disorders aspects which can be monitored, detected through cognitive analysis include Attention Deficit Hyperactivity Disorder (ADHD) [13], cognitive development of preterm infants [10], autism [9] and alike.

The brain's cognitive activity can be measured using EEG [14]. The signal recorded by an EEG is usually a summation of multiple sine waves with varying frequencies. These waves can be decomposed into their origin sine waves using fourier analysis [23]. Once decomposed, these waves can be used for the removal of artifacts as well as investigating trends in the signals. The individual sine waves can be used for estimating the power spectral density [1, 24]. This can be used to make predictions about the cognitive activity.

Coherence is the frequency proportional to the cross correlation between two scalp electrode sites that "reflects the degree of phase synchrony between them" [1, 11]. Power and coherence are two factors for measuring the changes in the brain with development, generally associated with the function of cognitive processing [1]. The next section would now discuss the various challenges encountered in the recording and processing of EEG signals and the prevalent solutions to these challenges.

3   Challenges for EEG in Measuring Cognitive Development

Even though EEG provides a convenient and portable method for measuring brain activity, it comes with several challenges, which may overwhelm the new researchers in this field. Some of these include low spatial resolution, EEG Cap fixing, designing age-appropriate tasks and engaging EEG activities, identifying artifacts and reducing SNR and dealing with mathematical complexities of the EEG signals. We discuss several of these challenges below and how they can be minimized in the next section.

3.1   Low Spatial Resolution

The EEG signal has a very poor spatial resolution [12, 22]. This is because the skull interferes with the signal propagation to the skull and distorts the actual brain electrical activity over a large surface area of the scalp [6]. Further, it is quite possible that the recorded activity at a particular site be the sum of "multiple groupings of cortical and subcortical generators spread across a relatively wide area" [1]. Specific measures are therefore hard to obtain, since large collection of neurons are involved in brain activities and not just one [6]. Using dense electrode arrays while conducting the experimentation may reduce the problem of spatial resolution [1]. However, cost is also proportional to the number of electrodes used [6].

3.2   EEG Cap Fixing Methodology

EEG electrodes are available in many sizes from newborn to adult [1]. EEG cap fixing methodology is a task that requires expertise on the side of researchers [6]. Usually, infants are made to sit with their mother or an "entertainer" who distracts them while the cap is being placed on their head. Various means can be used to entertain the child, such as toys or games. As the toddlers grows, it becomes easier to affix the cap [1].

If the cap is not fixed properly then the EEG signal quality can reduce significantly [6]. It is essential that the affixation of the electrode to the scalp is proper to ensure high quality signal and noise free EEG signals. With gel application to the scalp it is possible to reduce these errors [6]. Brain mappings will also vary from individual to individual [4, 6]. The researchers can only try their best to map the electrodes to correct positions on scalp surface.

3.3   Designing Age-Appropriate and Engaging EEG Tasks

For the proper study of brain behaviour, it is critical that tasks be designed with proper care and the possible impact on the brain be analyzed [1, 20]. It is a challenge for researchers to identify tasks that maintain subject's visual attention and also require response from their brain. The tasks must also be age specific [1]. There is no way that a tasks that engages an adult would engage a toddler also. Usually, tasks designed for adults include instructions to be followed, processing and decision making tasks [20]. It can be said to a very large extent the success of the experiment will depend on the type of EEG task conducted for investigation. In designing age-specific tasks, movements such as eye-blinks, muscle movements must be taken into consideration as they contaminate the EEG signal.

3.4   Identifying Artifacts—SNR

Maximizing SNR in data collected is very challenging: sensitive data is hard to filter out. There are two types of undesirable artifacts - physiological and non-physiological [17]. Physiological artifacts are electric and magnetic fields generated by the human body itself like the heart, the muscles like eyes, face and the retina whereas non-physiological artifacts includes electric and magnetic fields generated by surrounding devices or wires, for e.g. power line noise or electric fields generated by electronic equipment [17].

After the data collection, pre-processing of the data must be done to remove all the artifacts from the signals containing involuntary muscle movements, eye blinks, [15] which could overpower the "actual" signal. Relevant brain activity is small compared to the interfering artifacts and compared to brain background activity [26]. Often filtering of artifacts is hard to achieve, since brain dynamics vary greatly from individual to individual. Simultaneous recording of brain activity and muscle movement can facilitate artifact detection [1]. Thus filtering artifacts from collected data before processing is crucial to the analysis and accurate results of the research.

3.5   Mathematical Complexities

"EEG signals are mathematically complicated to handle since all sensors record almost the same signal" [6], requiring sophisticated and intelligent signal processing methods. EEG signals must be properly calibrated using prior knowledge (baseline EEG) [6], repeated recordings to retain as much information as possible. Further an appropriate filtering and sampling rate must be decided for storage of signals after experimentation. Recorded EEG signals are analog in nature and must be digitized prior storage. According to the Nyquist theorem the sampling rate must at least be twice the highest frequency in the signal [17]. Both oversampling and under-sampling must be avoided and the sampling rate must be chosen to prevent aliasing or ringing [17] from occurring. Researchers must be familiar with all the common methods for analysing EEG signals before starting analysis of the data. Various algorithms should be considered and taken into account before selecting the one that fits the best.

4   Some Solutions to Improved EEG Measurement and Analysis

Having discussed the challenges to measuring EEG, we now discuss the solutions to many of these challenges. The solutions in no way provide a complete fix to the challenges but often are improvements over the naive methodologies for measuring and analyzing EEG, which result in more accurate and hence, better results. Some of these solution include using dense electrode arrays, weighted multielectrode leads, recording baseline EEG, data integrity and calibration, artifact removal, measuring ERP (Event Related Potential) rather than EEG and so on. These are discussed below.

4.1   Dense Electrode Arrays and Weighted Multielectrode Leads

Dense electrode arrays are available with the advancement in technology. Researchers using these type of electrode arrays can calculate the average of power over a region of scalp and be sure of better results as compared to those which depend on the single value of electrode obtained [6, 18, 19]. If signals from whole of brain surface need to be recorded, then dense electrode arrays are required. The number of electrodes will decide the accuracy of results, so the number of electrodes factor in EEG experimentation presents a trade-off between cost (of experiment) and the accuracy of the results.

Recently, weighted multielectrode leads have been introduced for improving SNR. In this each unipolar lead was assigned its own weight depending on the location of the brain or the electrode coordinates. The study showed an improvement in the signal amplitude of the data collected and a reduced signal-to-noise (SNR) in the same [25].

4.2   Record Baseline EEG

Recording the EEG during a resting physiology is crucial for the elimination of differences of the baseline EEG from the activity recorded data [1, 12]. Recording baseline EEG can reduce artifacts including cognitive, emotional and motor processes [6]. Further, baseline EEG can also be used draw comparisons in the two EEG recordings and highlight specific task-related [1] changes and making interpretations. The activity for recording baseline EEG for adults might include closing their eyes and relaxing or staring at a blank screen [21]. For toddlers the activity might comprise of staring at a screen with random motion of circles or a video [7]. The aim is to record a control signal that will be same for maximum participants. The baseline EEG acts as a "control variable" in the EEG method and is useful for calibrating recorded signals.

4.3   Data Integrity, Calibration and Artifact Removal

The EEG signals are significantly filled with artifacts, that vary from subject to subject. It is an important task to identify the data to be used for actual analysis. Outlier data is often not used in analysis, this could be EEG signals not recorded properly, with too many artifacts, showing no correlation with other EEG samples recorded [1, 6]. Artifact removal in essence consists of removing signals produces by body parts other than the brain, these mainly consist of ocular and muscular artifacts [8]. According to [8], ocular artifacts comprises of eye movements (such as blinks) that "prevail in the frontal and prefrontal regions of the brain" and can produce amplitudes of magnitude 10 times higher than brain signals. Muscular artifacts may consist of hand movements or facial muscle movements [8].

These artifacts can be removed manually but artifact detection can also be automated using unsupervised machine learning algorithms [8]. ICA (Independent Component Analysis) is often used for removing any artifacts or removing unwanted features during feature extraction [17]. Other machine learning techniques include SVM, Decision Trees and KNN [8]. Quality of each EEG signal must be verified to maintain the integrity of the data. Data integrity and calibration is an important factor essential to any experimentation. Like with any investigation, the data to be analysed must be cleaned and refined, similarly EEG signals must also be fine tuned and filtered for best results.

4.4   Event-Related Potential (ERP) vs. EEG

"An event-related potential (ERP) is the measured brain response that is the direct result of a specific sensory, cognitive or motor event" [3]. ERPs can be measured by the means of EE—the only difference being that instead of focusing on an EEG segment [16], ERP studies center around selection of waveform components (such as peaks) triggered as a result of a specific event [6]. The challenges discussed for EEG also apply to the ERP studies as well [1]. Often at times, the analysis of ERP signals will be easier than that of EEG, as analysis points are known. Also waveform components are easier to identify than finding meaning in patterns that are occurring with no concrete evidence.

5 Future Prospects

Measuring cognitive development using EEG is an emerging field of research in neuroscience—EEG signals are being extensively used by researchers for monitoring progress of the human brain and discovering new trends. The following section aims to discuss some of the future research areas using EEG signals other than cognitive development. This includes BCI (Brain Computer Interface), home automation, alertness monitoring, lie detection, mood assessment, sleep stage detection, thought control and many more [6]. Some of these are discussed below in greater detail.

5.1 Brain Computer Interface

Brain computer interface or BCI is a fast growing technology with the aim of building a direct channel from human brain to any computer. The commands from the human brain in such a technology control the computer and allow it to receives and send signals to the mechanical device [6, 28]. BCI applications can lead to many applications like thought-to-speech, motor control using muscle movements and many more that can be specially useful for the disabled [28]. Though-to-speech or envisioned speech is one of the uprising researches of the current times. Although many have been successful in extracting speech from thought, the accuracy continues to be considerably low. Recent researches have been able to achieve an accuracy rate of 67.03% [30], which again shines light on the scope of improvement in this particular field.

5.2 Mood Assessment

Mood assessment using EEG signals is another emerging trend in EEG research. Many researchers have studied emotion recognition using EEG signals and proposed model like Arousal-Valence dimension to detect human emotion. Further, algorithms have been designed and implemented using SVM with an accuracy of 90.72% for distinguishing between the emotion of joy, anger, sadness and pleasure [29]. Other algorithms used for EEG-based emotion recognition included Fuzzy C-Means clustering, Binary Linear Fisher's Discriminant and many more [29]. Further, another method using Fractal Dimension was proposed for improving the performance and accuracy of emotion recognition using EEG [29].

5.3 Sleep Stage Detection

"Sleep stage classification refers to identifying the various stages of sleep and is a critical step in an effort to assist physicians in the diagnosis and treatment of related sleep disorders" [31]. EEG provides a non-invasive method for measuring the sleep activity compared to other methods. The EEG waveform can be used to distinguish between different brain activities—waveform is generally divided into Delta (0–4 Hz), Theta (4–8 Hz), Alpha (8–13 Hz), Beta (13–22 Hz) and Gamma waves (>30 Hz).

Many algorithms have been used to analyze the EEG signals for sleep stage classification such as SVM, KNN (K-Nearest Neighbours), ANN (Artificial Neural Networks) and many more. In an investigation, SVM was used to distinguish between drowsy and wake state of the candidate, which resulted in a highly accurate and precise result of 98.01% and 97.91% respectively [32]. In another research, KNN was used for 2-stage classification—the first stage consisted of classifying whether the candidate was wake or sleep and the next stage classified the subject's state into a narrower classification. This resulted in accuracy of 98.32% for the first stage and 94.49% for the second stage [33]. As evident from the statistics, EEG provides a clean and efficient method for Automatic Sleep Stage Classification (ASSC) over manual scoring methods that were used previously by the physicians for analyzing sleep disorders.

6 Conclusion

This paper discussed the various considerations that the researchers must take while adopting EEG methodology for their research in particularly measuring cognitive development. Further the paper discussed the various future prospects in research using EEG signals. Five challenges while measuring and analysing these signals were discussed and four solutions were discussed to these possible challenges. Although convenient and cheap, the EEG method for measuring brain behaviour comes with its own challenges and drawbacks, which must be taken into account from the very beginning of the experimentation stage to the end of the data processing stage.

Each stage of EEG processing requires high attention and critical analysis of the design of the experiment and algorithms chosen for further analysis. Finally, we discuss in the last section the numerous applications of EEG—from understanding human thoughts to classifying the sleep stage. Therefore, despite its drawbacks EEG has opened doors to understanding the functioning of human brain.

References

1. Bell, M.A., Cuevas, K.: Using EEG to study cognitive development: issues and practices. J. Cogn. Dev. **13**(3), 281–294 (2012). https://doi.org/10.1080/15248372.2012.691143
2. Cognitive Development: Encyclopedia of Children's Health. www.healthofchildren.com/C/Cognitive-Development.html
3. Huong, N.T.M., Linh, H.Q., Khai, L.Q.: Classification of left/right hand movement EEG signals using event related potentials and advanced features. 6th International Conference on the Development of Biomedical Engineering in Vietnam (BME6). IP, vol. 63, pp. 209–215. Springer, Singapore (2018). https://doi.org/10.1007/978-981-10-4361-1_35
4. Mahajan, R., Bansal, D.: Depression diagnosis and management using EEG-based affective brain mapping in real time. Int. J. Biomed. Eng. Technol. **18**(2), 115 (2015). https://doi.org/10.1504/ijbet.2015.070033

5. Mahajan, R., Bansal, D.: Real time EEG based cognitive brain computer interface for control applications via Arduino interfacing. Procedia Comput. Sci. **115**, 812–820 (2017). https://doi.org/10.1016/j.procs.2017.09.158
6. Welcome to the Center for Functional MRI: Home - Center for Functional MRI - UC San Diego School of Medicine. cfmriweb.ucsd.edu/
7. Agyei, S.B., et al.: Longitudinal study of preterm and full-term infants: high-density EEG analyses of cortical activity in response to visual motion. Neuropsychologia **84**, 89–104 (2016). https://doi.org/10.1016/j.neuropsychologia.2016.02.001
8. Nedelcu, E., et al.: Artifact detection in EEG using machine learning. In: 2017 13th IEEE International Conference on Intelligent Computer Communication and Processing (ICCP) (2017). https://doi.org/10.1109/iccp.2017.8116986
9. Belmonte, M.K.: Autism and abnormal development of brain connectivity. J. Neurosci. **24** (42), 9228–9231 (2004). https://doi.org/10.1523/jneurosci.3340-04.2004
10. Bell, M.A., Fox, N.A.: The relations between frontal brain electrical activity and cognitive development during infancy. Child Dev. **63**(5), 1142 (1992). https://doi.org/10.2307/1131523
11. Unde, S.A., Shriram, R.: Coherence analysis of EEG signal using power spectral density. In: 2014 Fourth International Conference on Communication Systems and Network Technologies (2014). https://doi.org/10.1109/csnt.2014.181
12. Burle, B., et al.: Spatial and temporal resolutions of EEG: is it really black and white? A scalp current density view. Int. J. Psychophysiol. **97**(3), 210–220 (2015). https://doi.org/10.1016/j.ijpsycho.2015.05.004
13. Ghassemi, F., et al.: Using non-linear features of EEG for ADHD/normal participants' classification. Procedia Soc. Behav. Sci. **32**, 148–152 (2012). https://doi.org/10.1016/j.sbspro.2012.01.024
14. Sanei, S., Chambers, J.A.: EEG Signal Processing, October 2007. https://doi.org/10.1002/9780470511923
15. Valentová, H., Havlík, J.: Initial analysis of the EEG signal processing methods for studying correlations between muscle and brain activity. In: Khuri, S., Lhotská, L., Pisanti, N. (eds.) ITBAM 2010. LNCS, vol. 6266, pp. 220–225. Springer, Heidelberg (2010). https://doi.org/10.1007/978-3-642-15020-3_20
16. Jung, T.-P., et al.: Analysis and visualization of single-trial event-related potentials. Hum. Brain Mapp. **14**(3), 166–185 (2001). https://doi.org/10.1002/hbm.1050
17. Puce, A., Hämäläinen, M.: A review of issues related to data acquisition and analysis in EEG/MEG studies. Brain Sci. **7**(12), 58 (2017). https://doi.org/10.3390/brainsci7060058
18. Alizadeh-Taheri, B., et al.: An active, microfabricated, scalp electrode-array for EEG recording. In: Proceedings of the International Solid-State Sensors and Actuators Conference - TRANSDUCERS 1995 (1995). https://doi.org/10.1109/sensor.1995.717088
19. Lopez-Gordo, M., et al.: Dry EEG Electrodes. Sensors **14**(7), 12847–12870 (2014). https://doi.org/10.3390/s140712847
20. Nguyen, T.A., Zeng, Y.: Analysis of design activities using EEG signals. In: Volume 5: 22nd International Conference on Design Theory and Methodology; Special Conference on Mechanical Vibration and Noise (2010). https://doi.org/10.1115/detc2010-28477
21. Dobrea, M.-C., et al.: Spectral EEG features and tasks selection process: some considerations toward BCI applications. In: 2010 IEEE International Workshop on Multimedia Signal Processing (2010), https://doi.org/10.1109/mmsp.2010.5662010
22. Hill, N.J., et al.: Classifying event-related desynchronization in EEG, ECoG and MEG Signals. In: Franke, K., Müller, K.-R., Nickolay, B., Schäfer, R. (eds.) DAGM 2006. LNCS, vol. 4174, pp. 404–413. Springer, Heidelberg (2006). https://doi.org/10.1007/11861898_41

23. Al-Fahoum, A.S., Al-Fraihat, A.A.: Methods of EEG signal features extraction using linear analysis in frequency and time-frequency domains. ISRN Neurosci. **2014**, 1–7 (2014). https://doi.org/10.1155/2014/730218

24. Kumarahirwal, M., Londhe, N.D.: Power spectrum analysis of EEG signals for estimating visual attention. Int. J. Comput. Appl. **42**(15), 34–40 (2012). https://doi.org/10.5120/5769-7993

25. Väisänen, O., Malmivuo, J.: Improving the SNR of EEG generated by deep sources with weighted multielectrode leads. J. Physiol. Paris **103**(6), 306–314 (2009). https://doi.org/10.1016/j.jphysparis.2009.07.003

26. Ivannikov, A., et al.: Extraction of ERP from EEG data. In: 2007 9th International Symposium on Signal Processing and Its Applications (2007). https://doi.org/10.1109/isspa.2007.4555470

27. Marshall, P.J., et al.: Development of the EEG from 5 months to 4 years of age. Clin. Neurophysiol. **113**(8), 1199–1208 (2002). https://doi.org/10.1016/s1388-2457(02)00163-3

28. Ramadan, R.A., et al.: Basics of brain computer interface. Brain Comput. Interfaces Intell. Syst. Ref. Libr. 31–50 (2014). https://doi.org/10.1007/978-3-319-10978-7_2

29. Liu, Y., Sourina, O., Nguyen, M.K.: Real-time EEG-based emotion recognition and its applications. In: Gavrilova, M.L., Tan, C.J.K., Sourin, A., Sourina, O. (eds.) Transactions on Computational Science XII. LNCS, vol. 6670, pp. 256–277. Springer, Heidelberg (2011). https://doi.org/10.1007/978-3-642-22336-5_13

30. Kumar, P., et al.: Envisioned speech recognition using EEG sensors. Pers. Ubiquitous Comput. **22**(1), 185–199 (2017). https://doi.org/10.1007/s00779-017-1083-4

31. Aboalayon, K., et al.: Sleep stage classification using EEG signal analysis: a comprehensive survey and new investigation. Entropy **18**(9), 272 (2016). https://doi.org/10.3390/e18090272

32. Yu, S., et al.: Support vector machine based detection of drowsiness using minimum EEG features. In: 2013 International Conference on Social Computing (2013). https://doi.org/10.1109/socialcom.2013.124

33. Phan, H., et al.: Metric learning for automatic sleep stage classification. In: 2013 35th Annual International Conference of the IEEE Engineering in Medicine and Biology Society (EMBC) (2013). https://doi.org/10.1109/embc.2013.6610677

EEG-Based Detection of Brisk Walking Motor Imagery Using Feature Transformation Techniques

Batala Sandhya[✉] and Manjunatha Mahadevappa

School of Medical Science and Technology,
Indian Institute of Technology Kharagpur, Kharagpur, India
batalasandhya@gmail.com

Abstract. Recently motor imagery (MI) based Brain-Computer Interface (BCI) for lower limb rehabilitation is gaining attention. Feature extraction and dimensionality reduction are crucial signal processing blocks that determine the performance of a BCI system. In this work, various features, that are, band power (BP) features, autoregressive (AAR) parameters and Hjorth (HJ) parameters, widely used in BCI research are studied for their efficacy in discriminating MI brisk walking activity from the idle state. Feature transformation (FT) techniques, a type of dimensionality reduction techniques, namely Principal Component Analysis (PCA), Locality Preserving Projections (LPP) and Local Fisher Discriminant analysis (LFDA) are then applied on the extracted features to map them into a lower dimensional subspace. Ten-fold cross-validation is used to choose the dimension of the projection subspace. In a group of five novice users, it is observed that none of these features separately or all taken together represented the activity well. On using FT techniques, the discriminability of the fused features improved. Among the three techniques, LFDA performed the best showing an average increase in classification accuracy (26.9%), sensitivity (37.6%) and specificity (26.2%) over the average values obtained when no FT technique are used for the group of five subjects.

Keywords: EEG · BCI · Motor imagery · Feature transformation

1 Introduction

Electroencephalogram (EEG) based Brain-Computer Interface (BCI) noninvasively measures the electrical activity of the brain and converts them into control commands for external devices. It provides to individuals suffering from severe motor disabilities an alternate mode of control and communication with the external world like a computer cursor [1], virtual keyboards [2], movement in virtual reality [3], limb prosthetics [4, 5] etc., without using their normal neuromuscular pathway of the body.

EEG based BCI is a signal processing and pattern recognition system which decodes activities encoded in the electrical activity of the brain. It basically consists of preprocessing module, feature extraction module, dimensionality reduction module and the classifier [6]. Once EEG signals are captured they are processed to reduce noise and artifacts by the preprocessing module. Then the feature extraction module extracts

© Springer Nature Switzerland AG 2018
U. S. Tiwary (Ed.): IHCI 2018, LNCS 11278, pp. 78–89, 2018.
https://doi.org/10.1007/978-3-030-04021-5_8

representative features vectors to obtain discriminative information of each class or type. The dimension of the feature vector is reduced by the dimensionality reduction module to assure that most discriminative information is contained in a lower dimension thereby helping in improving the detection accuracy. The reduced feature vector is then fed into the classifier which translates it into control commands for the external devices. To operate on any such BCI system, the subject has to engage in active or passive mental activity. Changes in EEG corresponding to this activity is decoded by the BCI system and converted into control command for external devices [7]. One of the widely used mental strategies is motor imagery (MI) of certain tasks or activities.

MI based BCI is gaining popularity as it can be used as alternate method by the paralyzed subjects to generate changes in neuronal circuits by their motor intent rather than using their restricted ability to do physical movements [8]. While a majority of these studies are focused on classification of motor imagination of the hand movements or upper limb, only recently MI based BCI for lower limb rehabilitation is gaining attention. In [9], kinesthetic walking motor imagery of lower limb is used to control an avatar in a virtual reality environment. In [10], right and left foot motor imagery is detected from EEG signals using beta rebound. In [11], a joint channel and frequency selection method is proposed to detect the walking motor imagery of the lower limb from the idling activity. Given the smaller foot representation area in the brain [12] compared to the upper limb and subjects difficulty in using an MI based BCI, the detection rates of lower limb motor imagery is low compared to upper limb. Hence efforts have to be made to improve the classification performance to better detect the motor imagery of lower limb.

To improve the detection of motor intent from EEG, the most discriminative features have to represent different classes in the detection problem. In a classification problem, dimensionality reduction of the feature vector helps in deriving the most discriminative features for a particular task. Band power features (BP), Adaptive Autoregressive parameters (AAR) and Hjorth parameters (HJ) are successfully used in the design of BCI for classifying various motor tasks [13, 14]. The major problem in the feature based BCI system is the high dimensionality of the feature vector being fed into the classifier. This dimensionality problem indeed results in increased computational complexity and poor performance of the system. Thus dimensionality reduction techniques are used to reduce the dimension of the feature vector.

Dimensionality reduction techniques [15] are basically of two types, feature selection (FS), and feature transformation (FT) techniques respectively. In FS, best feature subset is selected from the existing set of features without changing the original representation of the features whereas, in FT techniques, the number of features is reduced by projecting the data points from higher dimensional space to a lower dimensional space. FT techniques do not neglect any features, unlike FS techniques. Since BCI systems are to be adapted to each subject differently, therefore selecting only a subset of features for designing the system does not prove beneficial for the detection problem [16].

Therefore in this work, we explore the discriminative power of different features widely used in BCI research namely BP, AAR, and HJ in representing MI of brisk walking. We also explore the role of various FT techniques mainly Principal

Component Analysis (PCA) [17], Locality Preserving Projections (LPP) [18] and Local Fisher Discriminant Analysis (LFDA) [19] in improving the detection of the features. In this study, we are evaluating the efficacy of these FT methods in improving the detection of the brisk walking motor imagery. Firstly various features were extracted from the brain signals, and then we classify these features with and without using FT techniques to test its role in improving the detection problem.

2 Materials and Methods

2.1 Subjects

Five healthy subjects (5 males: 22–28 years in age) participated in the current study. The subjects have no history of any neuromuscular disorders and have never participated in a BCI study before. The current study is approved by the Institute Ethical Committee (IEC), Indian Institute of Technology (IIT) Kharagpur, India. Informed consent is taken from the subjects prior to the study.

2.2 Experimental Setup and Data Collection

During the experiment, subjects are seated in a comfortable armchair at a distance 1.5 m from a 19 in. monitor where visual cues are shown according to which the subjects performed brisk walking motor imagery. The timing protocol of the experiment is shown in Fig. 1. The experiment begins with a cross at the center of the screen. At 2 s an auditory cue in the form of a beep acts as a marker for the visual cue of motor imagery or idle task that appears on the screen at 3 s. The cue lasts for 4 s followed by a blank screen that appears for a period of 4 s and an additional random time period of 1–2 s between trials to avoid adaptation. A total of 5 runs of 40 trials, 20 of each class (imagery and idle) respectively are collected from each subject.

EEG is recorded from 7 Ag/AgCl scalp electrodes placed over the sensorimotor region, namely at FCz, C3, C1, Cz, C2, C4, CPz. EEG is recorded using Thought Technology's Flexcomp Infinity encoder, Canada at 2048 Hz sampling frequency and notch filtered at 50 Hz to remove the power line interference.

2.3 Preprocessing and Feature Extraction

The EEG signals are then band pass filtered in the frequency range of 0.5–30 Hz to avoid artifacts and down sampled to 256 Hz for further processing. Epochs

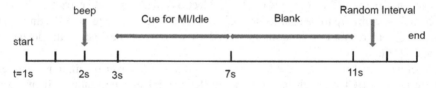

Fig. 1. The timing diagram of the experimental protocol

corresponding to the motor imagery and rest are then extracted from the data. Band powers features [20] in alpha (8–12 Hz) and beta bands (16–24 Hz), Hjorth parameters [21] and Adaptive Auto Regressive coefficients (AAR) [22] are extracted in windows of one second from each trial. The features extracted are averaged over all the windows to obtain final feature vector per trial consisting of features extracted from all channels. The flowchart of the entire methodology followed in this study is as shown in Fig. 2.

Feature Transformation. It is a type of dimensionality reduction techniques, where data points in the original feature space are projected into lower dimension feature space by combining or fusing features. Whereas in FS techniques, only a subset of features are considered from the original feature space. Since BCI systems are adapted to each subject differently, selecting only a subset of features for designing the system does not prove beneficial for the detection problem [16]. In this line of thought the utility of different FT techniques in improving detection of motor imagery of brisk walking are explored.

If $x = [x_1, x_2 \cdots x_N]$ represents the $D \times N$ feature matrix, where each column is a D dimensional feature vector x_N representing motor activity or rest, then a FT technique maps X into Z with reduced dimensionality ℓ assuming that the dataset X has an intrinsic dimensionality ℓ embedded in the original D dimensional space [3, 13].

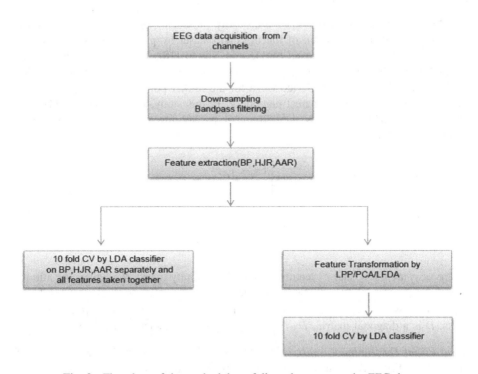

Fig. 2. Flowchart of the methodology followed to process the EEG data

The samples in the subspace are obtained by transforming the original features vectors using a projection or feature transformation matrix given by equation as under

$$Z = P^T X \tag{1}$$

where P is the projection matrix of size $D \times \ell$. The linear FT methods studied here are PCA, LPP and LFDA.

Principal Component Analysis (PCA). PCA is a popular nonparametric and an unsupervised feature reduction technique. It finds a linear lower dimensional representation for the original dataset, such that its maximal variability is preserved [17, 23]. This subspace is spanned by orthonormal unit vectors that form the new coordinate axis for the projected dataset. The feature transformation matrix for PCA is obtained by solving maximum optimization problem given as under

$$P_{PCA} = \underset{P \in \mathbb{R}^{D \times \ell}}{\arg \max} [trace(P^T C P)] \tag{2}$$

where C is the sample covariance matrix of the feature matrix X. This projection matrix P_{PCA} retains the maximal variance property of the original data set and is obtained by solving eigenvalue decomposition of the covariance matrix of the dataset.

Locality Preserving Projection (LPP). Locality preserving projections finds a linear low dimensional representation of the original dataset by preserving its local neighbourhood structure. It is proposed by He and Niyogi [18]. This transformation technique finds a subspace where data points that are close in the original dataset are also close in the reduced space and vice versa for the farther points. The adjacency of the data points is defined by k-nearest neighbour. In this study, $k = 7$ is taken [24]. The transformation matrix $\mathbf{P}_{LPP}$ is then obtained by solving a minimum optimization problem given as under

$$\begin{aligned} \mathbf{P}_{LPP} &= \underset{P \in \mathbb{R}^{D \times \ell}}{\arg \min} \left[\frac{1}{2} \sum_{i,j=1}^{N} \left\| \mathbf{P}^T \mathbf{x}_i - \mathbf{P}^T \mathbf{x}_j \right\|^2 W_{i,j} \right] \\ &= \underset{P \in \mathbb{R}^{D \times \ell}}{\arg \min} P^T X L X^T P \end{aligned} \tag{3}$$

$$\text{subject to} \quad P^T X D X^T P = 1$$

where x_i, x_j are the ith and j^{th} feature vectors. The affinity matrix $W_{i,j}$, gives the affinity between x_i, x_j. The value of the matrix elements lies in the range of $[0, 1]$. Affinity values are lower for feature vectors, x_i, x_j, that are close in the feature space and vice versa. D is a diagonal matrix, $D_{ii} = \sum_j W_{i,j}$ and L is a laplacian matrix, $L = D - A$.

Local Fisher Discriminant Analysis (LFDA). LFDA tries to combine the advantage of the LPP into Fisher Discriminant Analysis (FDA) by defining between-class covariance matrix and within-class covariance matrix in a local manner [19]. The covariance matrices are weighted or scaled by the distance between a data point and its k nearest neighbor like in LPP. Doing this it preserves within the class local structure of the data in the reduced space while ensuring maximum distance between the samples from different classes. These modified scatter matrices are used to define the Fisher ratio. Then the transformation matrix of LFDA is obtained by maximizing the Fisher ratio as done in FDA, given as under

$$P_{LFDA} = \arg \max_{P \in \mathbb{R}^{D \times \ell}} [trace((P^T \tilde{S}_w P)^{-1} (P^T \tilde{S}_B P))] \tag{4}$$

where $\tilde{S}_B$ and $\tilde{S}_w$ are between-class and within-class covariance matrices respectively. The solution is obtained by solving a generalized eigen value problem of $\tilde{S}_w$ and $\tilde{S}_B$. The transformation matrix is formed from the top ℓ eigenvectors corresponding to maximum ℓ eigenvalues.

2.4   Classification

To test the discriminating power of each individual feature, feature matrix formed from each feature type is classified separately and then classification is performed by taking all features types together. To select the reduced dimension ℓ, the feature vectors are projected sequentially, using the feature transformation technique, into the reduced space of dimension starting from first dimension till D^{th} dimension. Ten-fold cross-validation (CV) with linear discriminant classifier (LDA) [17, 23, 25] is performed in each of these subspaces. The mean accuracy, specificity and sensitivity of the 10 fold CV is computed in these subspaces. The dimension that gives maximum mean classification accuracy and minimum error rate is chosen to be the lower dimensional subspace for final projection.

3   Results

Mean classification accuracy, sensitivity and specificity values in % for 10 fold CV using LDA classifier on different features for all the subjects are given in Table 1. In this study LDA is applied to classify each feature separately and then all features are considered together. It can be inferred from these values that there is not a single feature that performs consistently well for all the subjects in detection of brisk walking motor imagery from idle state. The features perform either below, at or just above the chance level classification accuracy. HJ features performs better in case of subjects 2 and 4, AAR features in subject 1 and BP features in subject 3. The classification accuracy of the best performing feature is bold faced for each subject in Table 1. In case of subject 5, none of features perform above chance level accuracy. But the classification accuracy obtained using these FE techniques are mostly below or just above the chance level classification accuracy. Moreover, considering all the features together further decreases the classification accuracy in all the subjects. Similar observations can be drawn from the sensitivity and specificity values for the features. Using these features directly for setting up a BCI system gives poor performance. Therefore further in this study the role of FT techniques, i.e., PCA, LPP and LFDA techniques in improving the performance of the BCI system based on these features for detection of lower limb brisk walking motor intent from the idle condition is explored.

The performance of the LDA classifier post the application of FT techniques, that is, PCA, LPP and LFDA on the entire set of features taken together are given in Table 2. The FT techniques are used to project the feature matrix into reduced dimensional subspace starting from first dimension to D^{th} dimension sequentially. Mean classification accuracy, specificity and sensitivity of 10 fold cross-validation of LDA classifier is calculated in each dimension. The dimension with maximum mean classification accuracy and minimum misclassification rate is chosen as the subspace. The reduced dimension attained by each technique on the basis of above criteria is also given in the third column of Table 2. It can be clearly observed from Table 2, that classification accuracy value is improved by using the FT techniques that reduces the dimensionality of the input feature space. Among all the FT methods, LFDA performs the best in terms of accuracy, sensitivity and specificity of the classification. There is no significant difference between PCA and LPP technique on accuracy, sensitivity and specificity values except the reduced dimension attained by PCA is lower than LPP in subjects 1, 3, 4 and vice versa in subjects 2 and 5. Whereas LFDA attains significantly higher accuracy, sensitivity and specificity values compared to LPP and PCA methods. It also attains the lowest dimension for all subjects except in the case of S5 where even

Table 1. Mean classification accuracy (%), sensitivity (%) and specificity (%) of 10 fold cross-validation using LDA classifier for 5 subjects (S1–S5)

Subjects	Features	Accuracy	Sensitivity	Specificity
S1	HJR	44.50	46.00	43.00
	BP	45.00	44.00	46.00
	AAR	**50.00**	**50.00**	**50.00**
	ALL	50.00	43.00	57.00
S2	HJR	**55.00**	**51.00**	**59.00**
	BP	51.00	50.00	53.00
	AAR	50.00	49.00	51.00
	ALL	53.00	54.00	52.00
S3	HJR	51.00	51.00	51.00
	BP	**53.00**	**54.00**	**52.00**
	AAR	51.00	54.00	49.00
	ALL	48.50	50.00	47.00
S4	HJR	**55.00**	**56.00**	**54.00**
	BP	43.00	41.00	45.00
	AAR	54.50	57.00	52.00
	ALL	46.50	50.00	43.00
S5	HJR	**48.50**	**47.00**	**50.00**
	BP	45.00	50.00	40.00
	AAR	40.50	41.00	40.00
	ALL	46.50	47.00	46.00

though LPP finds a lower dimensional representation but fails in attaining better accuracy than LFDA. Similar observations can be made for subjects 1 and 3, where PCA gives lowest subspace dimension compared to LFDA but with lower values for the performance measures. To further validate the performance of the FT techniques, scatter plots of the data points in two-dimensional subspace obtained by each method for subject S2 are given in Fig. 4. It can be observed that LFDA finds two-dimensional subspace that clearly discriminates between the two classes whereas there is strong overlapping of the points in 2D subspace attained by PCA and LPP techniques.

A plot of average 10 fold CV accuracies along each reduced dimension from one to D^{th} dimensional subspace obtained by each of the FT techniques for all the subjects are given in Fig. 3. There is a great variability in the evolution of the classification accuracy for these techniques across subjects. This can be attributed to the variability of the EEG signals from subject to subject. From these plots it can be inferred that for most of the subjects the accuracy values increases with dimension or wanders about the mean value in case of PCA and LPP methods. Whereas using LFDA the accuracy is higher for lower dimensions and gradually decreases with increasing dimension. Also the mean classification accuracy for LFDA technique is higher compared to LPP and PCA technique as can be seen in the plots. But the performance of the PCA, LPP and LFDA converges in the first and at D^{th} dimension in all subjects except in S5 where they have different accuracy in the first dimension.

Table 2. Mean and standard deviation of classification accuracy (%), sensitivity (%), specificity (%) of 10 fold cross-validation and the reduced dimension attained by the FT techniques (PCA, LPP and LFDA) for subjects (S1–S5)

Subjects	DR	Red dim	Accuracy	Sensitivity	Specificity
S1	PCA	11	57.00 ± 8.88	59.00 ± 20.25	55.00 ± 9.72
	LPP	62	56.00 ± 11.50	52.00 ± 10.33	60.00 ± 15.63
	LFDA	**12**	**76.00 ± 7.38**	**76.00 ± 9.66**	**76.00 ± 6.99**
S2	PCA	64	58.50 ± 11.32	60.00 ± 16.33	57.00 ± 16.36
	LPP	43	57.50 ± 9.79	59.00 ± 17.29	56.00 ± 16.47
	LFDA	**2**	**80.00 ± 6.67**	**76.00 ± 6.99**	**84.00 ± 9.66**
S3	PCA	9	58.50 ± 11.56	59.00 ± 22.34	58.00 ± 18.14
	LPP	43	59.50 ± 13.43	57.00 ± 21.11	62.00 ± 17.51
	LFDA	**11**	**75.50 ± 10.39**	**77.00 ± 16.36**	**74.00 ± 15.06**
S4	PCA	25	53.50 ± 8.83	54.00 ± 16.47	53.00 ± 14.94
	LPP	56	53.50 ± 15.64	57.00 ± 14.94	50.00 ± 23.09
	LFDA	**2**	**75.50 ± 9.26**	**80.00 ± 9.43**	**71.00 ± 17.29**
S5	PCA	26	51.50 ± 9.44	53.00 ± 12.52	50.00 ± 17.00
	LPP	2	55.00 ± 10.8	57.00 ± 12.52	53.00 ± 17.03
	LFDA	**4**	**72.00 ± 13.37**	**73.00 ± 17.67**	**71.00 ± 15.24**

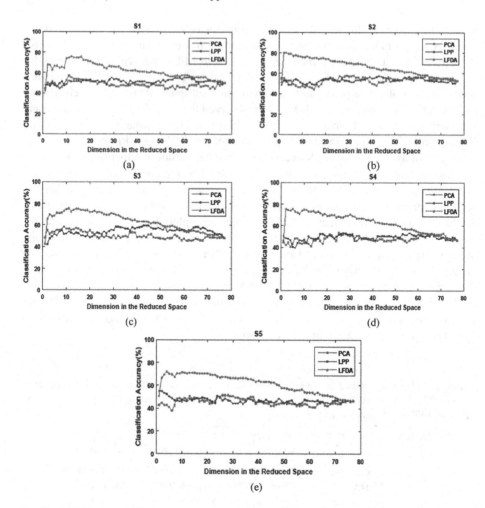

Fig. 3. 10 fold cross-validation accuracy versus reduced dimension for subjects 1 to 5 as shown in subplots (a)–(e) respectively

The results obtained by this study are in accordance with the results obtained in [16] where LFDA performs the best in identifying the motor imagery of the hand. Therefore LFDA is a promising technique which can be used for detecting motor imagery tasks. This concept is verified by testing the FT techniques in detecting brisk walking MI task in this study and thereby giving a supporting evidence of its usefulness in lower limb MI task in addition to upper limb imagery tasks performed in [16].

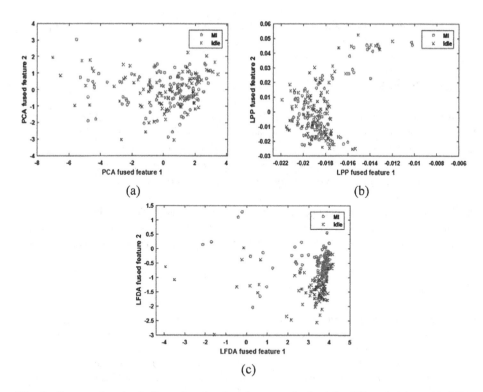

Fig. 4. Scatter plots in 2 dimensional reduced space obtained by FT techniques, (a) PCA (b) LPP (c) LFDA for subject 2

4 Discussions

In this current study, the combination of features and FT techniques in detecting the brisk walking motor intent are explored. Standard EEG features for the motor imagery are extracted and the role of the FT methods in improving the discriminative information of the features in representing the lower limb brisk walking motor imagery is explored in this study. The BP, HJ and AAR features are not able to discriminate the imagery trials from rest trials. This could be possibly because of the low signal to noise characteristics of EEG signals. Advanced artifact rejection algorithm can be applied prior to feature extraction technique to improve the signal to noise ratio. Since in the experiment, only the electrodes placed over the sensorimotor region are considered, the effects of artifacts are less pronounced and hence bandpass filtering is used to remove noise corresponding to low and high frequency.

On applying FT techniques on the complete set of poorly performing features, the classification accuracy of the detection problem is significantly improved. Among the FT techniques, best improvement is obtained using the LFDA. The detection rate of the lower limb could be further improved by considering other representative features for lower limb motor imagery task and using the capabilities of LFDA in projecting the features into a lower dimension. Channel selection methods can be explored in addition to FT techniques to select the most informative channels which would further improve the classification accuracy.

5 Conclusions

From this study it can be inferred that among various FT techniques, LFDA performs best in improving the detection of brisk walking motor imagery compared to other FT techniques or without using any FT technique. Hence LFDA can be used as a potential dimensionality reduction method in the design of feature based BCI system for detection of brisk walking motor intent from idle condition.

Acknowledgments. We would like to thank all the subjects who participated in this study. We are thankful to Professor N.K. Kishore of IIT Kharagpur for valuable discussions and authorities of IIT Kharagpur for encouragement in the work and permission to publish the paper.

References

1. Wolpaw, J.R., McFarland, D.J.: Control of a two-dimensional movement signal by a noninvasive brain-computer interface in humans. Proc. Natl. Acad. Sci. U.S.A. **101**(51), 17849–17854 (2004)
2. Townsend, G., et al.: A novel P300-based brain–computer interface stimulus presentation paradigm: moving beyond rows and columns. Clin. Neurophysiol. **121**(7), 1109–1120 (2010)
3. Leeb, R., Friedman, D., Müller-Putz, G.R., Scherer, R., Slater, M., Pfurtscheller, G.: Self-paced (asynchronous) BCI control of a wheelchair in virtual environments: a case study with a tetraplegic. Comput. Intell. Neurosci. **2007**, 7 (2007)
4. Müller-Putz, G.R., Scherer, R., Pfurtscheller, G., Rupp, R.: EEG-based neuroprosthesis control: a step towards clinical practice. Neurosci. Lett. **382**(1–2), 169–174 (2005)
5. Pfurtscheller, G., Müller, G.R., Pfurtscheller, J., Gerner, H.J., Rupp, R.: 'Thought'–control of functional electrical stimulation to restore hand grasp in a patient with tetraplegia. Neurosci. Lett. **351**(1), 33–36 (2003)
6. Bashashati, A., Fatourechi, M., Ward, R.K., Birch, G.E.: A survey of signal processing algorithms in brain–computer interfaces based on electrical brain signals. J. Neural Eng. **4**(2), R32 (2007)
7. Machado, S., et al.: EEG-based brain-computer interfaces: an overview of basic concepts and clinical applications in neurorehabilitation. Rev. Neurosci. **21**(6), 451–468 (2010)
8. Dickstein, R., Dunsky, A., Marcovitz, E.: Motor imagery for gait rehabilitation in post-stroke hemiparesis. Phys. Ther. **84**(12), 1167–1177 (2004)
9. Wang, P.T., King, C.E., Chui, L.A., Do, A.H., Nenadic, Z.: Self-paced brain–computer interface control of ambulation in a virtual reality environment. J. Neural Eng. **9**(5), 056016 (2012)
10. Hashimoto, Y., Ushiba, J.: EEG-based classification of imaginary left and right foot movements using beta rebound. Clin. Neurophysiol. **124**(11), 2153–2160 (2013)
11. Yang, H., Guan, C., Wang, C.C., Ang, K.K.: Detection of motor imagery of brisk walking from electroencephalogram. J. Neurosci. Methods **244**, 33–44 (2015)

12. Nitschke, M.F., Kleinschmidt, A., Wessel, K., Frahm, J.: Somatotopic motor representation in the human anterior cerebellum. Brain **119**, 1023–1029 (1996)
13. Lotte, F., Congedo, M., Lécuyer, A., Lamarche, F., Arnaldi, B.: A review of classification algorithms for EEG-based brain–computer interfaces. J. Neural Eng. **4**(2), R1 (2007)
14. Vidaurre, C., Krämer, N., Blankertz, B., Schlögl, A.: Time domain parameters as a feature for EEG-based brain–computer interfaces. Neural Netw. **22**(9), 1313–1319 (2009)
15. Van Der Maaten, L., Postma, E., Van den Herik, J.: Dimensionality reduction: a comparative. J. Mach. Learn. Res. **10**, 66–71 (2009)
16. García-Laencina, P.J., Rodríguez-Bermudez, G., Roca-Dorda, J.: Exploring dimensionality reduction of EEG features in motor imagery task classification. Expert Syst. Appl. **41**(11), 5285–5295 (2014)
17. Duda, R.O., Hart, P.E., Stork, D.G.: Pattern Classification. Wiley, New York (2012)
18. He, X., Niyogi, P.: Locality preserving projections. In: Advances in Neural Information Processing Systems, vol. 16, pp. 153–160 (2004)
19. Sugiyama, M.: Dimensionality reduction of multimodal labeled data by local fisher discriminant analysis. J. Mach. Learn. Res. **8**(May), 1027–1061 (2007)
20. Neuper, C., Müller-Putz, G.R., Scherer, R., Pfurtscheller, G.: Motor imagery and EEG-based control of spelling devices and neuroprostheses. Prog. Brain Res. **159**, 393–4099 (2006)
21. Hjorth, B.: EEG analysis based on time domain properties. Electroencephalogr. Clin. Neurophysiol. **29**(3), 306–310 (1970)
22. Schlögl, A.: The electroencephalogram and the adaptive autoregressive model: theory and applications. Shaker, Aachen (2000)
23. Alpaydin, E.: Introduction to Machine Learning. MIT Press, Cambridge (2014)
24. Zelnik-Manor, L., Perona, P.: Self-tuning spectral clustering. In: Advances in Neural Information Processing Systems, pp. 1601–1608 (2004)
25. Christopher, M.B.: Pattern Recognition and Machine Learning. Springer, New York (2016)

Natural Language, Speech and Dialogue Processing

Cumulative Impulse Strength Based Epoch Extraction from Singing Voice

Prigish George Abraham[1(✉)], M. S. Sinith[1(✉)], and A. R. Jayan[2(✉)]

[1] Department of Electronics and Communication Engineering,
Rajiv Gandhi Institute of Technology, Kottayam, India
`prigish92@gmail.com`, `sinithms@rit.ac.in`
[2] Department of Electronics and Communication Engineering,
Government Engineering College, Palakkad, India
`arjayan71@gmail.com`

Abstract. The instant of significant excitation of the vocal-tract system is known as epoch and since the most significant excitation takes place around the instant of glottal closure, it is also termed as glottal closure instant (GCI). In this paper, the concept of cumulative impulse strength is utilized for the extraction of epochs from singing voice and its performance has been compared with some established methods for epoch extraction from speech signals. The method is being applied on Indian classical music as well as on some types of western music. The analysis has been carried out on a large database named "LYRICS" which consists of singing sounds with synchronous electroglottogram (EGG) recordings, containing different types of singing techniques.

Keywords: Epochs · Glottal closure instant · Electroglottogram

1 Introduction

The speech production mechanism starts with the flow of the air from the lungs which passes through our vocal tract system to come out as voiced speech. During the flow of air from the lungs, it gets modulated by the vocal tract and produces quasi-periodic pulses which results in the production of sound. Major excitation of the vocal tract within a pitch period occurs at the glottal closure instant (GCI). This instant of excitation is referred to as instant of significant excitation or simply epoch [1]. Different types of epoch extraction algorithms such as Zero Frequency Resonance (ZFR [2]), Dynamic Programming Phase Slope Algorithm (DYPSA [3]) and various other methods and their performances have been reviewed. In [4], the applications of knowledge of epoch locations like time delay estimation, speech enhancement, multispeaker seperation and prosody modification have been discussed. There are significant variations in the characteristics shown by singing voice and speech signals. The source (vocal cord) filter (vocal tract) interactions in singing voice are very high when compared to speech, since the singer has a lot of control over the vocal cord while singing. There is a vast

U. S. Tiwary (Ed.): IHCI 2018, LNCS 11278, pp. 93–100, 2018.
https://doi.org/10.1007/978-3-030-04021-5_9

difference in the dynamic pitch range of singing voice (80–1400 Hz) and normal speech (80–400 Hz). Apart from the above said main characteristics, other features like controlled variations in pitch, prolonged voice sounds, prosody, etc. also make the processing of singing voices a tough task. Finally a large variety of singing techniques makes it a difficult task to accomplish since there would be a lot of variations in different singing techniques.

A lot of work related to epoch extraction has been done in the field of speech but not a lot has happened in the field of singing voices. In Babacan et al. [5], a comparison of different GCI estimation algorithms done on singing voice of different varieties of voice types has been done whereas in [6], a detailed comparison has been done on the basis of Indian classical music. These works have been the base for this paper and the former one even speaks of a good application of epochs in singing voice which is a wide range synthesizer that can be used for multiple singer categories and multiple singing techniques. The concept of cumulative impulse strength (CIS) has been previously used for extraction of epochs from speech signals in [7] and was found to be quite impressive when its performance was compared with other epoch extraction algorithms. In this paper, the work is going to be extended to singing voice of different types. The structure of the paper is as follows: Sect. 2 gives details about the epoch detection methods used and special emphasis is given to the new method used, i.e., the CIS. Section 3 gives a detailed picture of the databases involved and the details regarding the ground truth and the evaluation parameters used for the comparison. Finally Sects. 4 and 5 deal with results of comparison done on different methods and the conclusion respectively.

2   Epoch Detection Algorithms

In this section, a brief review is given about the epoch detection algorithms which have been used in this paper and their performance has been compared with CIS.

2.1   DYPSA

Dynamic Programming Phase Slope Algorithm (DYPSA) is an automatic epoch estimation algorithm which estimates GCIs by determining the crests from the Linear Prediction Residual (LPR) signal of speech. It processes the potential GCI competitors by choosing the positive to negative zero intersections of group delay function of the above calculated LPR signal. After that N-best dynamic programming is employed for the selection of most likely GCI locations among many erroneous GCI candidates. For the evaluation of this technique, the MAT-LAB execution of the DYPSA accessible in [8] has been utilized.

2.2   ZFR

Zero Frequency Resonance is one of the state-of-the-art techniques used for extracting epochs from speech signals. Zero frequency filtering method is preferred over others because the attributes of the time differing vocal tract system are independent of the attributes of the discontinuities in the yield of the resonator. It utilizes zero frequency resonators to limit the impact of vocal tract resonances and isolate the excitation pulses.

The steps involved in extracting the zero frequency filtered signal from the speech signal are as follows:-

- The samples of speech signal are differenced to remove the unwanted very low frequency components.
- Then the differenced speech signal samples are passed twice through an ideal resonator at zero frequency.
- The trends present in the signal are removed by subtracting the average over 10 ms at each sample.

The signal obtained after trend removal is called the zero-frequency filtered signal, or the filtered signal. The positive zero crossings of the filtered signal gives the location of the epochs in the speech signal.

2.3 CIS

Cumulative Impulse Strength (CIS) is one of the latest approaches used for estimation of GCIs from speech. This concept is based on the temporal quasi-periodicity property of voiced signals. This method uses both the LPR signal and a-priori calculated average pitch period for the detection of GCIs. In [7], CIS has been used on speech signals and it can be seen that the performance of this method is comparable to state-of-art algorithms used for epoch extraction from speech signals.

Concept. In [9], it is mentioned that "the position of GCIs coincide with local negative peaks of voice source signal". The above fact implies that an algorithm which uses voice source signal would require two main steps:-(i) conversion of the speech signal into a space where the voice source signal is optimally characterized (eg. LPR),(ii) reliably picking the peaks analogous to GCIs from the converted signal. This method takes into account not only the neighbourhood properties of signal around the instant of impulse-like behavior but also significance to the global behavior of the signal around all the previous postions of impulse.

Let $p[n]$ be an amplitude-perturbed, quasi-periodic train consisting of N impulses expressed as follows:-

$$p[n] = \sum_{k=1}^{N} A_k \delta[n - n_k] \tag{1}$$

where n_k is the location of the k-th impulse with amplitude A_k, N_0 is the average period of p[n] and Δ_k is the deviation of $n_k - n_{k-1}$ from N_0 and ρ is the maximum deviation.

CIS is defined recursively at each position n, by joining the impact of the signal $p[n]$ and the CIS $C[n]$ around the previous positions of impulse. Then the CIS at the n-th sample is defined as follows:

$$C[n] = \max_{n-N_0-\rho \leq m \leq n-N_0+\rho} (C[m] + p[m]) \tag{2}$$

Then a new function $V[n]$ is defined to locate impulses from $C[n]$ as follows:-

$$V[n] = \arg\max_{n-N_0-\rho \leq m \leq n-N_0+\rho} (C[m] + p[m]) \tag{3}$$

Another function $V[n]$ is defined for storing the position of impulse that maximizes the value of $C[n]$ within the interval defined in Eq. (2) for each sample. After the position of the final impulse has been determined, a back tracking procedure is utilized to find all the impulses from $V[n]$ as follows: if n_k corresponds to the position of kth impulse, the position of $(k-1)^{th}$ impulse is given by $V[n_k]$. The position of the last impulse is defined to be that which maximizes $p[m]$, $N'-1-N_0 + \rho \leq m \leq N'-1$, where N' is the span of $p[m]$. This is because the position of the maximum of the $p[m]$ within the final periodic interim corresponds to the last impulse.

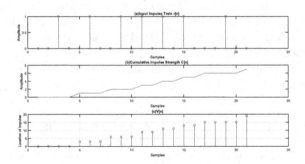

Fig. 1. Illustration of concept of CIS

Figure 1 shows an illustration of CIS. In (a), a randomly distributed impulse train $p[n]$ is shown and (b) shows the CIS applied on $p[n]$ and (c) shows the location of impulses extracted from $p[n]$.

Steps involved in GCI detection using CIS are as follows:-

- Pre-processing (pre-emphasis and windowing)
- Computation of Integrated Linear Prediction Residual (ILPR)
- CIS is computed using ILPR signal to locate the GCIs or epochs

The average pitch period needed for the algorithms (ZFR and CIS) has been calculated using SWIPE and SHR algorithm for pitch estimation but the former one gave better results.

3   Experiment Protocol

3.1   Databases

For Indian Classical music, the Hindustani classical singing database established by Deepak et al. for their work [10] was utilized. The database contains 4 songs out of which 2 songs are sung by female and the remaining 2 songs are sung by male. Song lyrics consists of Indian (Hindi and Bengali) languages. The electroglottographic (EGG) signals were captured by EGG electrodes while the acoustic signals were captured by a headphone and the sampling frequency was set to 48 kHz. Both singing voice and EGG signals were recorded at the same time.

For western music, the database created by Henrich N. et al. for their work [11] was used. Samples of 13 trained singers were taken from the LYRICS database recorded by [11,12]. The selection consists of 7 bass baritones (B1 to B7), 3 countertenors (CT1 to CT3), and 3 sopranos (S1 to S3), 2 tenors (T1 and T2) and a mezzo-sporano (MS1). The sessions were recorded in a soundproof booth and the signals were sampled at a sampling frequency of 48 kHz. Acoustic and electroglottographic signals were recorded at the same time on two channels of a DAT (Digital Audio Tape) recorder. The acoustic signal was recorded using a condenser microphone (Bruel & Kjaer 4165) placed at a distance of 5 cm from the singer's mouth, a preamplifier (Bruel & Kjaer 2669), and a conditioning amplifier (Bruel & Kjaer NEXUS 2690). The electroglottographic signal was recorded using an electroglottograph that consists of two channels (EG2). The selected samples have different types of songs, such as continuous vowels, crescendos-decrescendos, arpeggios and climbing and descending glissandos.

3.2   Ground Truth

The GCI locations obtained from differenced EGG (dEGG) signal act as the ground truth. GCIs were extracted from dEGG signal using simple peak detection above a pre-set threshold (1/6 of maximum value). GCIs were also extracted from dEGG using an algorithm named "SIGMA" but the results were found to be inaccurate, so it was ignored. The reliability of the basic truth was evaluated by visual comparisons between the dEGG signals and the positions marked using various GCI algorithms.

3.3   Evaluation Parameters

The performance of the epoch detection techniques was assessed utilizing the measures characterized in [3]. Figure 2 shows the characteristics of epoch estimates showing each of the possible choices from the epoch detection algorithms. To understand the measures, laryngeal cycle has to be know which is defined as the range of samples $(1/2)(l_{r-1}+l_r) \leq n \leq (1/2)(l_{r+1}+l_r)$, given an epoch reference at sample l_r with preceding and succeeding epoch references at samples l_{r-1} and l_{r+1} respectively. The following measures were used to evaluate the reliability and accuracy:-

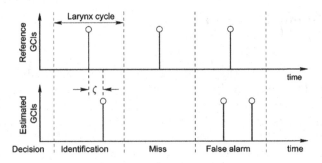

Fig. 2. Concept of parameters used for evaluation [2]

- Identification rate (IDR): The percentage of laryngeal cycles for which unique epoch is detected.
- Miss rate (MR): The percentage of laryngeal cycles for which epoch is not detected.
- False alarm rate (FAR): The percentage of laryngeal cycles for which more than one epochs are detected.
- Identification accuracy (IDA): The standard deviation of the identification error (ζ). Small values of IDA indicate high accuracy of identification.

Table 1. Performance of Different Methods on Indian Classical Music

Methods	IDR (%)	MR (%)	FAR (%)	IDA (ms)
ZFR	65.30	31.75	2.95	0.319
DYPSA	61.85	35.11	3.04	0.453
CIS	75	23.46	1.54	0.651

4   Results

The performance of all epoch detection algorithms applied on the database containing Indian classical music has been tabulated in Table 1. CIS provides the highest identification rate in comparison with other methods. Identification accuracy is best for ZFR and DYPSA can be said to be the worst performer due to its high missing rate.

Table 2 shows the results of different epoch extraction algorithms applied on the subset of LYRICS database. It can be seen that CIS outperforms the other methods in almost all types of singer categories and performs reliably across different singer types. ZFR and DYPSA perform better for lower pitch singers and a pattern of diminishing reliability can be seen with increase in pitch of the singer. In terms of identification accuracy, none of the methods reach the level that was seen in case of speech signals. It is observed that all the methods have

Table 2. Performance of Different methods By singer type

Singing type	Method	IDR (%)	MR (%)	FAR (%)	IDA (ms)
Baritone	ZFR	85.8025	11.7284	2.4691	0.4536
	DYPSA	83.3333	11.1111	5.5556	0.0813
	CIS	87.6543	11.7284	0.6173	0.3912
Tenor	ZFR	55.7500	42.0833	2.1667	0.4662
	DYPSA	77.0000	22.9167	0.0833	0.4022
	CIS	81.3333	18.6667	0	0.5671
Countertenor	ZFR	78.9971	20.5669	0.4360	0.4549
	DYPSA	82.4855	12.4273	5.0872	0.3408
	CIS	90.8430	9.0843	0.0727	0.5778
Mezzo-soprano	ZFR	76.7148	23.2852	0	0.1786
	DYPSA	56.4621	43.5018	0.0361	0.3735
	CIS	90.0361	9.9278	0.0361	0.2283
Soprano	ZFR	34.0955	57.5203	8.3841	0.2843
	DYPSA	38.2622	61.7378	0	0.1855
	CIS	80.5894	19.4106	0	0.1659

a decrease in accuracy as the pitch of the singer increases. For baritones, all the methods give good identification rate and miss rate is almost constant for all of them. For tenor and countertenor, CIS performs better than ZFR and DYPSA but miss rate is very high for ZFR in comparison to DYPSA. For mezzo-soprano, DYPSA is the worst performer but in terms of identification accuracy, ZFR seems to be better. For soprano, both ZFR and DYPSA have a poor performance and CIS is the best both in terms of both identification rate and accuracy.

5   Conclusion

A comparison of performances of different epoch extraction algorithms with Cumulative Impulse Strength is performed on Indian singing voice as well as based on a variety of other singing voices. It can be seen that CIS performs better than other methods for almost all types of singing voices irrespective of whether they are Indian or western music. But still there is scope for improvement since in some cases it is noticed that miss rate is high and accuracy can also be improved by doing alterations in the method in the future works.

Acknowledgement. The authors would like to express their sincere gratitude towards Nathalie Henrich and Onur Babacan for providing the LYRICS database.

References

1. Ananthapadmanabha, T.V., Yegnanarayana, B.: Epoch extraction of voiced speech. IEEE Trans. Acoust. Speech Signal Process. **23**(6), 562–570 (1975)
2. Murty, K.S.R., Yegnanarayana, B.: Epoch extraction from speech signals. IEEE Trans. Audio Speech Lang. Process. **16**(8), 1602–1613 (2008)
3. Naylor, P.A., Kounoudes, A., Gudnason, J., Brookes, M.: Estimation of glottal closure instants in voiced speech using DYPSA algorithm. IEEE Trans. Audio Speech Lang. Process. **15**(1), 34–43 (2007)
4. Yegnanarayana, B., Gangashetty, S.V.: Epoch-based analysis of speech signals. Sadhana **36**(5), 651–697 (2011)
5. Babacan, O., Drugman, T., d'Alessandro, N., Henrich, N., Dutoit, T.: A quantitative comparison of glottal closure instant estimation algorithmson a large variety of singing sounds. In: Proceedings of INTERSPEECH, pp. 1–5 (2013)
6. Gokul Krishnan, K.S., Govind, D.: Comparison of glottal closure instant estimation algorithms for singing voices in indian context. In: ICACCI 2017, pp. 1447–1453 (2017)
7. Prathosh, A.P., Sujith, P., Ramakrishnan, A.G.: Cumulative impulse strength for epoch extraction. IEEE Signal Process. Lett. **23**(4), 424–428 (2016)
8. Brookes, M.: Voicebox: A Speech Processing Toolbox for MATLAB (2006). http://www.ee.imperial.ac.uk/hp/staff/dmb/voicebox/voicebox.html
9. Miller, R.L.: Nature of the vocal cord wave. J. Acoust. Soc. Amer. **31**, 667–677 (1959)
10. Deepak, K.T., Prasanna, S.R.M.: Epoch extraction using zero band filtering from speech signal. Circ. Syst. Signal Process. **34**(7), 2309–2333 (2015)
11. Henrich, N., d'Alessandro, C., Castellengo, M., Doval, B.: Glottal open quotient in singing: measurements and correlation with laryngeal mechanisms, vocal intensity, and fundamental frequency. J. Acoust. Soc. Amer. **117**(3), 1417–1430 (2005)
12. Henrich, N.: Etude de la source glottique en voix parlée etchantée: modélisation et estimation, mesures acoustiques et électroglottographiques, perception (study of the glottal source in speech and singing: Modeling and estimation, acoustic and electroglottographic measurements, perception), Ph.D. dissertation, Université Paris 6 (2001)

Chaos Analysis of Speech Imagery of IPA Vowels

Debdeep Sikdar[1]([✉])[iD], Rinku Roy[2][iD], and Manjunatha Mahadevappa[1][iD]

[1] School of Medical Science and Technology,
Indian Institute of Technology Kharagpur, Kharagpur, India
deep@iitkgp.ac.in
[2] Advanced Technology Development Centre,
Indian Institute of Technology Kharagpur, Kharagpur, India

Abstract. In Brain Computer Interfacing (BCI), speech imagery is still at nascent stage of development. There are few studies reported considering mostly vowels or monosyllabic words. However, language specific vowels or words made it harder to standardise the whole analysis of electroencephalography (EEG) while distinguishing between them. Through this study, we have explored significance of chaos parameters for different imagined vowels chosen from International Phonetic Alphabets (IPA). The vowels were categorised into two categories, namely, soft vowels and diphthongs. Chaos analysis at EEG subband levels were evaluated. We have also reported significant contrasts between spatiotemporal distributions with chaos analysis for activation of different brain regions in imagining vowels.

Keywords: Speech imagery · Vowel imagery · Chaos analysis

1 Introduction

Verbal communication is the most convenient way of interacting with one another for humans. However, due to different ailments, some individuals are unable to produce speech. Assistive technologies as alternate interpreters will be highly beneficial for them in order to communicate through speech.

Classical brain-language model as proposed by Broca, Wernicke, Lichtheim, Geschwind, and others have been very useful for the researchers to locate the brain area responsible for speech imagery as well as production. While Broca's area is responsible for language production, Wernicke's area processes words. Oro-pharyngeal-laryngeal muscle groups are coordinated by premotor cortex area for proper generation of speech. However, this classic 'Wernicke-Lichtheim-Geschwind' has been challenged by recent studies for their relevancy. Rather, new concept of whole brain theory for language production is emerging.

Several studies have been conducted to decode speech imagery with different approaches. Majority of the researchers concentrated on the brain regions responsible for speech production according to classical brain language model. DaSalla et al. proposed spatial filtering based EEG classification between imagined

© Springer Nature Switzerland AG 2018
U. S. Tiwary (Ed.): IHCI 2018, LNCS 11278, pp. 101–110, 2018.
https://doi.org/10.1007/978-3-030-04021-5_10

vowels /a/ and /u/ [3]. D'Zmura et al. have considered two syllables /ba/ and /ku/ while classifying the motor imagery with matched filter for Hilbert envelope of the EEG signals [4]. Rojas et al. have utilised Blackman-Tukey transform with SVM to achieve high accuracy in order to separate spanish vowels /a/ and /e/ [9]. Mel Frequency Cepstral Coefficients of 5 vowels were classified with different classifiers by Riaz et al. [8].

In this study, we have analysed the chaos parameters of soft vowels and diphthongs in speech imagery. These were chosen from standardised International Phonetic Alphabets (IPA) to avoid language specific dependancy. Vowel sounds solely depend on the structure of mouth aperture while speaking. Diphthongs are combination of two soft vowels. As there are hardly any meaning of isolated vowels, artefacts due to associated cognitive or comprehensive imagery are very minimal. Thus, regions extending to whole brain were considered for exploring speech imagery. To further extend our analysis, we have decomposed the EEG signals into α, β, and γ subbands to explore the effect of chaos in frequency band specific level for different brain regions during vowel motor imagery. Statistical significance analysis revealed more insight on the contribution of different brain regions at different frequency levels towards imagining soft vowels and diphthongs.

2   Materials and Methods

Chaos based features were extracted from the EEGs to investigate changes in total 15 different vowels in imagined speech. These vowels were selected from IPA table. They were categorised into two categories, namely, soft vowels and diphthongs. Diphthongs are two soft vowels pronounced successively. These vowels have been standardised based on their usage in constructing words.

Each dataset were applied with chaos analysis to get CD, LLE, and ApEn. In order to distinguish between imagining soft vowels and diphthongs, significance of each parameters were evaluated for each sub-bands as well as *full*band EEGs separately for each channel through ANOVA. The Flowchart of this study is given in Fig. 1.

Ten non-impaired subjects, aged between 20 and 27 years old were chosen. The subjects had no history of speech related ailments. They were asked to perform vowel imagery according to the visual cues. None of the subjects were informed about the experimental procedure in prior to minimise biasness. Written consents were taken from the subject before participating.

2.1   Task

The subjects were seated on an armchair in front of a table. A screen was placed on the table for visual cues. Initially there was a blank screen with a crosshair at the centre. The subjects were asked to relax and concentrate on the instruction followed. Different soft vowels and diphthongs as in Table 1 were shown randomly in the screen for 2 s. Between two successive vowels, a blank screen was shown

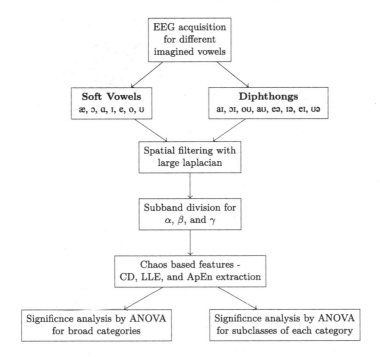

Fig. 1. Flowchart of the overall process for imagined speech.

for 2 s. The subjects were needed to imagine the letters shown. There were 20 trials for each case. Figure 2b shows the timing of the stimulus. Some stressed vowels were excluded for inconsistency in isolated pronunciation. Devnagri script was used for the vowels due to their distinct inherent pronunciation capability and also the subjects were native to the scripture.

2.2 Signal Acquisition

EEG data were recorded at a sampling rate of 1200 Hz from positions FP1, FP2, F7, F5, F3, Fz, F4, F8, FT7, FC5, FC3, FC1, FC2, FC6, T7, C5, C3, C1, Cz, C4, T8, TP9, TP7, CP5, CP3, CP1, CPz, CP2, CP6, TP10, P7, P5, P3, P1, Pz, P4, P8, O1, and O2 by scalp electrodes placed according to the International 10–20 system as shown in Fig. 2a. The reference electrode was placed to the right earlobe and the ground electrode (GND) was placed on the forehead (AFz) to form a feedback loop. The loop also drives down the common mode potential and effective impedance of ground. The EEG recording was carried out using g.Hiamp (g.tec, Graz, Austria) hardware with 39 monopolar channels. 8th order butterworth bandpass filter with 0.01–60 Hz range and 50 Hz Notch filter were added at the recording time to remove linear trends and electrical noise.

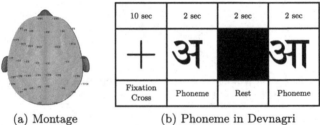

(a) Montage	(b) Phoneme in Devnagri

Fig. 2. Experiment protocol

Table 1. Vowels according to IPA

(a) Soft Vowels

Type	IPA	Devnagri	As in
Open Front	/æ/	/ऐ/	cat
Open-mid Back	/ɔ/	/अ/	saw
Open Back	/ɑ/	/आ/	dark
Close Front	/ɪ/	/इ/	grip
Close-mid Front	/e/	/ए/	bed
Close-mid Back	/o/	/ओ/	cold
Close Back	/u/	/उ/	put

(b) Diphthongs

IPA	Devnagri	As in
/ɪə/	/या/	ear
/eə/	/एया/	hair
/ʊə/	/वा/	tour
/eɪ/	/एइ/	wait
/aɪ/	/आई/	tide
/ɔɪ/	/अय/	void
/ou/	/औ/	bowl
/au/	/आउ/	house

2.3   EEG Preprocessing

After referencing, the signals were detrended. The resulting signals were further processed for EOG and EMG artefact removal. The signals were segmented according to the stimulus timing of 2 s length. For imagined dataset, α (8–12 Hz), β (13–30 Hz) and γ (30–60 Hz) frequency subbands were extracted from the preprocessed EEG data. FIR filters were used to these sub bands. For each subbands along with *full*band EEG were processed with Chaos Analysis.

3   Chaos Analysis

EEG is a nonlinear dynamic system. Different vowel imagery have high similarities across domains, however, their chaotic features may differ considerably. In this study, we have explored the variation between the chaotic behaviour of different vowel imagery. Evolution in time of a nonlinear dynamic system could remain in the close neighbourhood of attractors. Complexity is the geometric property of attractors. Correlation Dimension (CD) is used to characterise the attractor complexity. We have followed the methodology as described in our earlier works [10,11]. The chaoticity of the attractor is a measure of the convergence or divergence of nearby trajectories in phase space. The "butterfly effect" theory of chaos states that in a chaotic system, two points close together in phase space have completely different outcomes. This implies that a divergence in the trajectories suggests chaos in a system and vice versa. In this research, the Largest Lyapunov Exponent (LLE) is employed to quantify the attractor chaoticity. The Approximate Entropy (ApEn) computes the value of regularity in the attractor. Smaller value indicates more regular behaviour and higher value of it indicates less regularity on the dataset.

Time delay vectors were initially formed considering a time series $x_1, x_2, x_3, ..., x_N$, and reconstructed with total number of N points as follows:

$$y_i(d) = (x_i, x_{i+\tau}, ..., x_{i+(d-1)\tau})$$
$$i = 1, 2, ..., N - (d-1)\tau \tag{1}$$

where d is the embedding dimension and τ is the time lag.

Optimum Lag. Optimum lag is the measure of relative shift of two different portions of a time series. Here Auto Mutual Information Function (AMIF) is used to calculate optimum lag [13].

Minimum Embedding Dimension (MED). After finding optimum lag m_0, embedding dimension is needed to be calculated. Cao [2] has proposed a method for calculating true embedding dimension. As in Eq. 1, some random embedding dimension, d, is used to form time delay vector $y_i(d)$ from d. Cao has defined true embedding dimension, d_j, such that two neighbouring time delay vectors, $y_i(d_j)$ and $y_{i+1}(d_j)$ in d_j-dimensional space would lie in proximity in $(d_j + 1)$-dimensional space.

d_0 will be called MED if the mean of the ratio of distance between two neighbouring time delay vectors settles around embedding dimension larger than $(d_0 + 1)$.

Correlation Dimension (CD). For practical computations, to overcome limited number of elements in phase space, Cao has proposed neighbourhood condition $E^*(d)$,

$$E^*(d) = \frac{1}{N - dm_0} \sum_{i=1}^{N - dm_0} \left| x_{i+dm_0} - x_{n(i,d)_d m_0} \right| \tag{2}$$

where, $n(i, d)(1 \leq n(i, d) \leq N - dm_0)$ is an integer to suffice $y_{n(i,d)}(d)$ and $y_i(d)$ as the nearest neighbours in d-dimensional reconstructed phase space.

Another metric $E2(d)$ has also been proposed as follows,

$$E2(d) = \frac{E^*(d+1)}{E^*(d)} \tag{3}$$

$E2(d)$ will tend to unity for a random series, while a chaotic series will have $E2(d)$ less than unity for all values of d. The dimension d_0 corresponding saturation of $E2(d)$, gives the MED.

CD values, however fractional, are always less than or equal to embedding dimension. Thus in lagged phase space, one of the most precise measure of complexity of signal attractor is characterised by CD.

Considering optimum lag of m_0 and MED as d_0 of a signal, a finite series has been constructed as $y_1(d_0), ..., y_{N_c}(d_0)$, containing $N_c = N - m_0 d_0$, points. N_c is the total number of pairwise distances. The Correlation Dimension (CD), d_{corr}, is estimated as [12, 13]:

$$d_{corr} = - \left[\frac{2}{N_c(N_c - 1)} \sum_{i=1, j=1}^{N_c} log \left(\frac{|y_i(d_0) - y_j(d_0)|}{\epsilon} \right) \right]^{-1} \tag{4}$$

where $y_i(d_0)$ and $y_j(d_0)$ are i^{th} and j^{th} lagged phase locations with a sphere centred at any one of them with radius ϵ.

Following determination of optimum lag and MED, CD was computed by Taken's estimator considering radius (ϵ) as 10% of the size of lagged phase space [5].

Largest Lyapunov Exponent (LLE). The number of standard Lyapunov exponents is equal to the embedding dimension of the attractor. For the system to be chaotic, at least one of these exponents should be positive which implies that the LLE (λ_{max}) has to be greater than zero. The LLE characterises the rate of divergence of two neighbouring trajectories in the phase space. Trajectory divergence is defined as the distance between two neighbouring points in lagged phase space after a given time (known as prediction length). The average trajectory divergence, D_T, of the attractor for a given prediction length, T, is expressed mathematically according to Wolf's method as

$$D_T = \frac{1}{N_S} \sum_{i=1}^{N_S} \left| \frac{Y_{i+T}(d) - Y'_{i+T}(d)}{Y_i(d) - Y'_i(d)_i} \right| \tag{5}$$

where $Y_i(d)$ and $Y'_i(d)$ are neighbouring points on separate trajectories in the phase space, and $Y_{i+T}(d)$ is the location of the point that evolved from $Y_i(d)$ along the trajectory. The prediction length, T, is measured in increments of time used for the EEG signal. The LLE (λ_{max}) is then computed as the slope of the graph of the natural logarithm of trajectory divergence, D_T, versus the prediction length, T. This relationship is expressed mathematically as $D_T = D_0 e^{T\lambda_{max}}$ where D_0 is the initial divergence [14]. In this research, a modification of Wolf's method reported in Iasemidis et al. is implemented in which the parameters are adaptively estimated to better account for the nonstationary nature of the signals [1, 6].

Approximate Entropy (ApEn). This was proposed by Pincus [7]. This measure can be estimated as follows:

$$C_i^m = \sum_{j=1}^{N\nu} \frac{\Theta(r - ||y_i - y_j||)}{N_\nu} \tag{6}$$

where N_ν is the number of vectors in state space, r is the tolerance of the comparison, y_i and y_j are vectors reconstructed in state space $||.||$ represents the Euclidean distance between vectors and $\Theta(x)$ is the heaviside function such that $\Theta(x) = 1$ if $x > 0$ and $\Theta(x) = 0$ if $x < 0$. The ApEn is obtained by:

$$ApEn = \Phi^m(r) - \Phi^{m+1}(r) \tag{7}$$

$$\Phi^m(r) = \frac{1}{N - (m - 1)} \sum_{i=1}^{N-(m-1)} ln\left[C_i^m(r)\right] \tag{8}$$

where N is the length of time series and m is the embedding dimension.

To identify the internal nonlinear dynamics of EEG, chaos analysis was performed in this study. The parameters extracted as features from EEG are CD (C), LLE (L), and ApEn (A).

4   Results

Chaos parameters for each subbands and $full$band EEGs for each channels were computed. Table 2 lists the significant chaos parameters for distinguishability between soft vowels and diphthongs for different channels at different frequency band levels based on ANOVA of the parameter values with 95% confidence interval ($p < 0.05$). It was also extended with the significant parameters for separating individual soft vowels and diphthongs. It can be seen that in $full$band EEG, all the regions of the brain exhibited significantly distinct chaotic behaviour between imagining soft vowels and diphthongs but in case of distinguishing between soft vowels or diphthong, $full$band EEG has lesser effect. The lower the frequency levels, the lower are the regional distinct chaoticity. C being the most significant parameter among all the brain regions, it can be inferred that there are considerable difference in correlated processes while imagining soft vowels and diphthongs. In fact, it was found that diphthongs contained more correlation than soft vowels as diphthongs shared common soft vowels among themselves. Furthermore, it can also been seen that β band exhibited major spatial distribution of significant chaos parameters for diphthongs. α band have significant chaos in frontal regions whereas chaos parameters of posterior regions have significant distinguishability in β.

Figure 3 shows the brain region activation plots for the subbands and $full$band EEGs for soft vowels and diphthongs. The channel locations with at least one significant chaos parameter for distinguishability, as depicted from Table 2, are marked with larger dots. $Full$band EEG can be be seen to have contrasting activated Broca's area with respect to subband levels. But in case of diphthongs, they are similarly activated excepting for γ subband. Moreover, in case of diphthongs, γ subband showed highly activated motor cortical region than the other bands. This has close similarity with β subband in soft vowels. It can be seen that γ subband exhibited diffused activation of brain regions for

Table 2. Significant chaos parameters ($p < 0.05$) for each subbands and band limited EEG for each channels in distinguishing between soft vowels and diphthongs

Chan.	Soft Vowels & Diphthongs				Soft Vowels				Diphthongs			
	α	β	γ	Full	α	β	γ	Full	α	β	γ	Full
FP1				A								
FP2				C,A								
F7				C,A								
F5			L,A	C,A								
F3			A							L		
FZ		L			C,L,A		C		A			
F4			L		C	C,A				L,A		
F8		C,L		A	L				L,A	A		
FT7				C,L,A								
FC5				C,L,A	L					C		
FC3				C,A								
FC1		L		A	C,L,A	L						
FC2								C,L,A		L		L
FC6												
T7			L	C,A								
C5				C,L,A			A					
C3					C					C,L,A		
C1												
CZ			A								C,L	
C4												
T8				C					A			
TP9												
TP7				C,L,A		L	C					
CP5				C		C						
CP3	C			C		C,A				C,L,A		
CP1		L				C				L		
CPZ						C						
CP2			L							C,L,A		
CP6			L,A	C	C,L,A				C,L			
TP10							C,L,A				C	
P7												
P5										A		
P3			L									
P1										C,A		C,A
PZ											L	C,L,A
P4												C
P8		C,L,A		C					L	A		
O1												
O2				A								

soft vowels. Although whole brain participated in speech imagery, from the spatial distribution it can also be inferred that contribution of regions related to classical brain language model is significant.

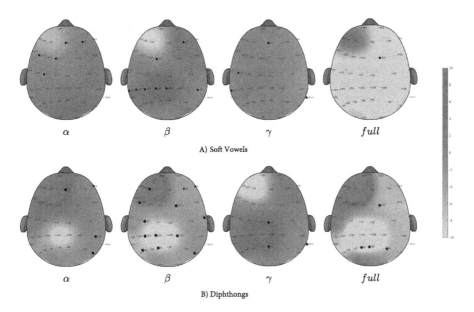

Fig. 3. EEG channel contribution on scalp

5   Conclusion

We have found although spatiotemporally different vowel imageries were indistinguishable, they are significantly distinct in non-linearity domain even in sub-band levels. We can further explore to understand the formation of diphthongs from multiple soft vowels. Moreover, similar analysis will also be evaluated on consonants and word formations to decode imagined speech using EEG.

References

1. Adeli, H., Ghosh-Dastidar, S., Dadmehr, N.: A wavelet-chaos methodology for analysis of EEGs and EEG subbands to detect seizure and epilepsy. IEEE Trans. Biomed. Eng. **54**(2), 205–211 (2007)
2. Cao, L.: Pratical method for determining the minimum embedding dimension of a scalar time series. Phys. D Nonlinear Phenom. **110**(1–2), 43–50 (1997)
3. DaSalla, C.S., Kambara, H., Sato, M., Koike, Y.: Single-trial classification of vowel speech imagery using common spatial patterns. Neural Netw. **22**(9), 1334–1339 (2009)
4. D'Zmura, M., Deng, S., Lappas, T., Thorpe, S., Srinivasan, R.: Toward EEG sensing of imagined speech. In: Jacko, J.A. (ed.) HCI 2009. LNCS, vol. 5610, pp. 40–48. Springer, Heidelberg (2009). https://doi.org/10.1007/978-3-642-02574-7_5
5. Iasemidis, L.D., Olson, L.D., Savit, R.S., Sackellares, J.C.: Time dependencies in the occurrences of epileptic seizures. Epilepsy Res. **17**(1), 81–94 (1994)
6. Iasemidis, L.D., Sackellares, J.C., Zaveri, H.P., Williams, W.J.: Phase space topography and the Lyapunov exponent of electrocorticograms in partial seizures. Brain Topogr. **2**(3), 187–201 (1990)

7. Pincus, S.M.: Approximate entropy as a measure of system complexity. Proc. Natl. Acad. Sci. **88**(6), 2297–2301 (1991)
8. Riaz, A., Akhtar, S., Iftikhar, S., Khan, A.A., Salman, A.: Inter comparison of classification techniques for vowel speech imagery using EEG sensors. In: 2nd International Conference on Systems and Informatics (ICSAI) 2014, pp. 712–717 (2014)
9. Rojas, D.A., Ramos, O.L., Saby, J.E.: Recognition of spanish vowels through imagined speech by using spectral analysis and SVM. J. Inf. Hiding Multimed. Sig. Process **7**(4), 889–897 (2016)
10. Roy, R., Sikdar, D., Mahadevappa, M., Kumar, C.: A fingertip force prediction model for grasp patterns characterised from the chaotic behaviour of EEG. Med. Biol. Eng. Comput. **56**, 2095–2107 (2018)
11. Roy, R., Sikdar, D., Mahadevappa, M., Kumar, C.: EEG based motor imagery study of time domain features for classification of power and precision hand grasps. In: 8th International IEEE/EMBS Conference on Neural Engineering (NER) 2017, pp. 440–443 (2017)
12. Takens, F.: Dynamical systems and turbulence. Lect. Notes Math. **898**(9), 366 (1981)
13. Williams, G.P.: Chaos Theory Tamed. Joseph Henry Press, Washington (1997)
14. Wolf, A., Swift, J.B., Swinney, H.L., Vastano, J.A.: Determining Lyapunov exponents from a time series. Phys. D Nonlinear Phenom. **16**(3), 285–317 (1985)

Generation of GMM Weights by Dirichlet Distribution and Model Selection Using Information Criterion for Malayalam Speech Recognition

Lekshmi Krishna Ramachandran[1,2][✉] [iD] and Sherly Elizabeth[2] [iD]

[1] Bharathiar University, Coimbatore, Tamil Nadu, India
lekshmi.kr@iiitmk.ac.in
[2] Indian Institute of Information Technology and Management-Kerala,
Thiruvananthapuram, India
sherly@iiitmk.ac.in

Abstract. Automatic Speech Recognition is a computer-driven transcription of spoken-language into human-readable text. This paper is focused on the development of an acoustic model for medium vocabulary, context independent, isolated Malayalam Speech Recognizer using Hidden Markov Model (HMM). In this work, the emission probabilities of syllables, based on HMMs are estimated from the Gaussian Mixture Model (GMM). Mel Frequency Cepstral Coefficient (MFCC) technique is used for feature extraction from the input speech. The generation of mixture weights for GMMs is done by implementing Dirichlet Distribution. The efficiency of thus generated Gaussian Mixture Model is verified with different Information Criteria namely Akaike Information Criterion, Bayes Information Criterion, Corrected AIC, Kullback Linear Information Criterion, corrected KIC and Approximated KIC (KICc, AKICc). The accuracy of medium vocabulary, speaker dependent and isolated Malayalam speech corpus for a single Gaussian is 90.91% and Word Error Rate (WER) is 11.9%. The word accuracy and WER of the system are calculated based on the experiments conducted for multivariate Gaussians. For Gaussian mixture five, a better word accuracy of 95.24% along with a WER of 4.76% is attained and the same is verified using Information Criteria.

Keywords: Acoustic model · Akaike information criterion
Bayes information criterion · HMM · GMM · Dirichlet distribution
ASR · MFCC · Kullback information criterion
Bias correction of Kullback information criterion
Approximation of Kullback information criterion · Word error rate

Kerala State Council of Science Technology and Environment-KSCSTE.
L. Krishna Ramachandran—Research Scholar
S. Elizabeth—Professor

© Springer Nature Switzerland AG 2018
U. S. Tiwary (Ed.): IHCI 2018, LNCS 11278, pp. 111–122, 2018.
https://doi.org/10.1007/978-3-030-04021-5_11

1   Introduction

The Realisation of a message encoded as one or more symbols with speech signal is the general assumption of Speech Recognition. Speech is the predominant communication technique with humans. The coordinated movement of speech is produced by articulation. The spectral characteristics of speech are influenced by the vocal tract shape, length and resonance/vibration characteristics. Speech articulation is characterized by manner and place such as Vowels, Fricatives, Nasals, Stops, Labial, Dental, Alveolar etc. Speech Recognition (SR) technology is at its growing stage. This technology has tremendous application in daily life of common man and that of 'Divyaang' people. Speech Recognition is a useful technique but a complex task.

Statistically based modern speech recognition system mainly consists of two parts- Acoustic modeling and Language modeling. In acoustic modeling basically there are two types of variability in speech recognition namely acoustic variability and temporal variability. Temporal variability deals with the rate of speech, fast or slow [1] and acoustic variability handles different pronunciation, volume and accents. The acoustic modeling can be best described by HMM [2].

Malayalam is cognominated as among the Classical Languages in India since 2013 [3] and is one of the 22 scheduled languages. In Indian language orthographic, Malayalam has the largest number of letters. It has 52 letters consisting of 36 consonants and 16 vowels. Like other Dravidian languages, Malayalam also has a canonical word order of Subject-Object-Verb (SOV). Another highlight of Malayalam is that it has different accents throughout the state.

In this work, a syllable-based GMM-HMM is proposed for a new set of Malayalam words. Each syllable is represented by 5 state HMM with simple left-to-right topology. HMM have a capability to model the variability in speech statistically. The parameter re-estimation is done using the Baum-Welch algorithm. To find the most likelihood state sequence, the Viterbi algorithm is used. The feature extraction technique is carried out with MFCC. An attempt has been made to verify that the best performance is obtained for which Gaussian mixture by model selection methods.

The rest of the paper is structured as follows. Literature Review is discussed in Sect. 2. In Sect. 3 the methodology of acoustic modeling is introduced with an architectural diagram. Preprocessing, feature extraction and acoustic modeling steps are explained with diagrams. The GMM mixture weight is generated using Dirichlet distribution [4] and different model selection methods are discussed. Section 4 describes the implementation of the technique. The WER and word accuracy for multivariate Gaussians are derived. Section 5 concludes the paper.

2   Literature Survey

Abusharisha et al. [5] developed a speech recognition system for English digits from Zero to Nine. They conducted experiments for isolated word and continuous word speech recognition. They adapted MFCC and HMM for developing the system. The authors achieved 99.5% and 79.5% accuracy for multi-speaker mode and speaker-independent mode for isolated words. In the case of continuous speech recognition, they attained an accuracy of 72.5% for multi-speaker mode and 56.25% for a speaker-independent mode.

Al-Qatab and Ainon [6] discussed the development of Arabic automatic speech recognition engine. The system is developed using the Hidden Markov Model Toolkit. The features are extracted using Mel Frequency Cepstral Coefficient (MFCC) and parameters are estimated using HMM. They obtained an overall performance of 90.62%, 98.01% and 97.99% for sentence correction, word correction and word accuracy respectively.

A good amount of research has been made in many Indian languages. Saini et al. [7] conducted an experiment for Hindi using HTK. The system recognized 113 isolated Hindi words collected from nine speakers. They obtained an overall accuracy of 96.61% and 95.49% for 10 state HMM. Kumar et al. [8] extensively studied continuous Hindi speech recognition system as an extension of previous work. They also adapted MFCC as the feature extraction method. They tried for a different number of Gaussian Mixtures and obtained a 97.04% accuracy for the SR system. A few attempts are made in Punjabi by Dua et al. [9] and in Telugu by Bhaskar et al. [10] with HTK for few selected words. An accuracy of 95.63% for Punjabi Speech Recognizer.

Only a few attempts have been made so far for Malayalam SR. The main contributions are by Kurian and Balakrishnan [11]. They developed a Malayalam digit speech recognition for speaker independent model. The system employed Mel frequency cepstrum coefficient (MFCC) as the feature for signal processing and Hidden Markov model (HMM) for recognition. They trained the system with 21 male and female voices in the age group of 20 to 40 years and there was 98.5% word recognition accuracy. Kurian and Balakrishnan [12] employed an optimum speaker-independent connected digit recognizer for the Malayalam language. The system employed Perceptual Linear Predictive (PLP) cepstral coefficient for speech parameterization and continuous density Hidden Markov Model (HMM) in the recognition process. Viterbi algorithm is used for decoding. The system obtained an accuracy of 99.5%. They [13] also developed and evaluated different acoustic models for few Malayalam words. Another work reported in Malayalam is based on wavelet-based feature extraction by Krishnan et al. [14] with an artificial neural network technique and obtained a recognition rate of 89%.

Yu [15] gave an insight into model selection methods to determine better mixture component numbers by evaluating Akaike Information Criterion (AIC), Bayes Information Criterion (BIC) and modified Bayes Information Criterion (mBIC). The model they generated with 4-mixture component GMM gave minimum value for mBIC. The author also calculated Accuracy and WER of the ASR system.

Akogul et al. [16] done a comparison of Information criteria in clustering based on a mixture of Multivariate Normal Distribution. The author studied the efficiency of information criteria that are commonly used in model selection methods like AIC, BIC, KullBack Information Criterion (KIC) etc. The information criterion technique which gives minimum score is selected as the best model. They got better results for KIC on the determination of the number of mixtures in multivariate normal distribution.

3   Methodology

In this paper, an acoustic model for speech recognition is proposed. The proposed architecture is encapsulated with a training phase and testing phase. A model is generated as the result of training and the same is used for testing. The steps involved in training is shown in Fig. 1.

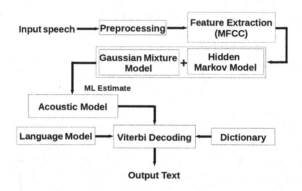

Fig. 1. Architecture of speech recognizer

3.1   Preprocessing

Speech and non-speech segmentation is an important perplexity step in speech recognition. The background noise sometimes resembles the parameters of syllables than that of silence model. So we have to remove such parts from the speech. Pre-emphasis is a step involved in preprocessing. Pre-emphasis will increase the magnitude of higher frequencies with respect to the magnitude of lower frequencies. Then the speech signals are divided into frames with frame size ranging from 10–25 ms and an overlap of 50–70% between the consecutive frames.

3.2   Feature Extraction

Feature extraction finds the properties of an utterance. This can be computed or estimated through processing the speech signal. The features include only relevant information like energy, formant frequencies, zeroth energy and avoid irrelevant information. The most commonly used feature extraction technique is MFCC.

3.3   Acoustic Modeling/HMM creation for Speech Recognition

HMM is a simple and effective method for SR, but it requires refinements to achieve better performance. HMM represents output distribution by Gaussian Mixture Densities [17]. It is a combination of a set of states, transition probability matrix a_{ij}, observation sequences $o_1, o_2, \ldots\ldots o_t$ and emission probability output distribution $b_j(o_t)$ given by,

$$b_j(o_t) = \prod_{s=1}^{S} \left[\sum_{m=1}^{M_s} c_{jsm} N \left(o_{st}; \mu_{jsm}, \sum_{jsm} \right) \right]^{\gamma_s} \tag{1}$$

where M_s is the number of mixture components in stream s, c_{jsm} is the weight of the mth component with the property,

$$\sum_{i=0}^{K} c_i = 1, c_i \in (0,1) \tag{2}$$

and

$$\mathcal{N}(.,\mu,\Sigma)$$

is a multivariate Gaussian with mean vector μ and covariance matrix Σ given by,

$$\mathcal{N}(o,\mu,\Sigma) = \frac{1}{\sqrt{(2\pi)^n |\Sigma|}} e^{-\frac{1}{2}(o-\mu)^T \Sigma^{-1}(o-\mu)} \tag{3}$$

n is the dimensionality of o, γ_s is a stream weight. This model is shown in Fig. 2.

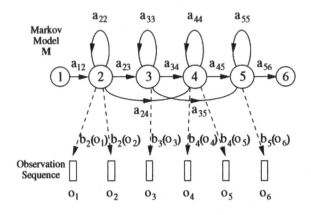

Fig. 2. The Markov generation process

3.4 Mixture Weight Calculation by Dirichlet Distribution

In most of the ASR works discussed earlier single state Gaussian Mixture Model is used. If the number of Gaussian mixture components is increased, a better accuracy (better performance) can be achieved [18]. The parameters of HMM can be re-estimated by applying the Baum - Welch re-estimation algorithm. Initial values for the parameters namely the mean, variance and component weights are assigned. More accurate values of the parameters (Maximum Likelihood Estimate) can be obtained by pruning until the values of the parameters converge [19].

The choice of initial values of component weights has a high influence on the achievement of the global minimum. The accuracy of the speech recognizer will be higher if an appropriate initial value for mixture weights are chosen. It is not easy to generate appropriate weights for GMM mixtures to attain a reliable performance. In this section, use of Dirichlet distribution to generate Gaussian mixture weights is proposed [20].

Dirichlet distribution is a continuous multivariate probability model with pdf,

$$f(x_1, x_2, ...x_K, \alpha_1, \alpha_2, ...\alpha_K) = \frac{1}{B(\alpha)} \prod_{i=1}^{K} x_i^{\alpha_i - 1} \tag{4}$$

where

$$\sum_{i=0}^{K} x_i = 1, \quad x_{i \geq 0}, \quad \text{and} \quad x_i \in (0, 1), \alpha \text{ is a normalizing constant} \tag{5}$$

4 Information Criteria for Model Selection

Model Selection is one of the fundamental tasks in scientific inquiry. The goodness of fit will be balanced if the model selection method is good. The likelihood ratio approach is generally used to determine the goodness of fit. The complexity of the model is determined by the number of parameters of the model.

The accuracy of SR depends on an appropriate model selection. This includes the determination of the number of components in the model. In order to derive the best model we use Information Criteria (IC) and is generally computed as

$$IC = 2d - plog(L) \tag{6}$$

where $log(L)$ is the Log-Likelihood, d is the number of Parameters in the model and p is a penalty factor [21]. The model which gives minimum value for IC is selected as best model. Various Information Criteria are listed below.

- The most commonly used information criteria is Akaike Information Criteria (AIC). If the number of parameters in a model is d, then AIC is defined as

$$AIC = -2logp(X|\theta) + 2d \tag{7}$$

The model that gives AIC score minimum is selected [22].

– However in some cases, the number of observations n is small relative to d, a correction to AIC is calculated

$$AIC_c = -2logp(X|\theta) + 2d\left(\frac{n}{n-d-1}\right) \tag{8}$$

The model that generates minimum value is selected as best [23].
– As described earlier, d is the number of parameters and n is number of observations, Bayesian Information Criterion is calculated as

$$BIC = -2logp(X|\theta) + dlog(n) \tag{9}$$

The model that gives the score minimum is the best model [24].
– Kullback Information Criterion (KIC) proposed by Cavanaugh [25] is defined as

$$KIC = -2logp(X|\theta) + 3(d+1) \tag{10}$$

– Bias Correction and Approximation of Kullback Information Criterion (AICc, AKICc) are given below [26, 27]

$$
\begin{aligned}
KIC_c = \ & -2logp(X|\theta) + nlog\left(\frac{n}{n-d}\right) \\
& + \frac{n((n-d)(2d+3)-2)}{(n-d-2)(n-d)}
\end{aligned} \tag{11}
$$

$$
\begin{aligned}
AKIC_c = \ & -2logp(X|\theta) \\
& + \frac{(d+1)(3n-d-2)}{n-d-2} + \frac{d}{n-d}
\end{aligned} \tag{12}
$$

5   Results and Discussions

A speaker dependent, isolated Malayalam speech recognizer is trained and consecutively experiments are conducted to test its performance. This is implemented with HTK [28]. A speech corpus is created with consonants in Malayalam as shown in Fig. 3.

കരം	കാലം	കിണ്ണം
കുവളം	കേരളം	ഗഗനം
ചവണ	ചേരണം	ജലം
ജീവനം	താലം	തോടണം
ധാര	പണം	മണം
മായം	വനം	സമയം

Fig. 3. Example of words used for speech corpus creation

A speech corpus is created with 100 words that consist of 10 speakers including male and female. Each word in the speech corpus is uttered 3 times by each speaker. It is repeated 3 more times. Thus a total of 3000 .*wav* files (100×3×10) of speech corpus is created.

The system has taken 12 MFCC feature vector plus delta (Δ) coefficients and delta-delta (Δ^2) coefficients to make a total of 39 features (MFCC_0_D_A) along with 0th coefficient energy. The pre-emphasis coefficient is set to 0.97 and the Hamming window is set as TRUE in HTK configuration parameters. The window size is 25 ms with a frame period of 10 ms. The Baum - Welch algorithm is implemented with HERest tool and recognition by the Viterbi algorithm with HVite tool in HTK. Other tools used in HTK are HRest, HInit, HCompV, HResults etc...

The mixture weights of Gaussian mixtures are derived from Dirichlet distribution using a python code. Experiments are conducted for single Gaussian and also for gaussian values 2, 3, 4, ... 8. The word accuracy of the recognizer is attained its best values for the Gaussian mixture five. Word Error Rate (WER) is used as a measure to evaluate the recognizer denoted by,

$$WER = \frac{(S + D + I)}{N} * 100 \tag{13}$$

where S is the number of substitutions, D is the number of deletions, I is the number of Insertions and N is the number of words in the transcript.

The results of different Gaussian mixtures, its mixture weights, Word accuracy (% correct) and WER is presented in Table 1. A Graph is plotted by the number of Gaussians with Word Error Rate is shown in Fig. 4.

Table 1. Word Accuracy and WER for Gaussians mixtures 1 to 8 for isolated Malayalam words

Number of Gaussians	Mixture weight	Word Accuracy (% correct)	WER (%)
Single Gaussian	—	90.91	9.40
2	0.98, 0.02	88.10	11.90
3	0.1, 0.76, 0.14	90.47	9.52
4	0.46, 0.35, 0.08, 0.11	92.85	7.14
5	**0.03, 0.17, 0.59, 0.13, 0.08**	**95.24**	**4.76**
6	0.02, 0.59, 0.19, 0.13, 0.01, 0.06	92.85	7.14
7	0.05, 0.21, 0.35, 0.07, 0.08, 0.13, 0.12	92.85	7.14
8	0.05, 0.46, 0.08, 0.08, 0.22, 0.09, 0.02, 0.08	92.85	7.14

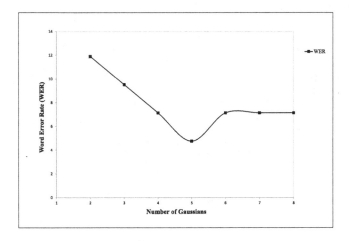

Fig. 4. Number of Gaussian mixture Vs Percentage of WER

Table 2. Number of Gaussians and corresponding AIC, BIC, AICc values and Accuracy of the ASR system

Number of Gaussians	AIC	BIC	AICc	Accuracy
2	167.5826	167.2802	168.3233	88.1
3	167.0246	166.5408	168.8708	90.47
4	162.8604	162.1951	166.3804	92.85
5	**159.847**	**159.0003**	**165.6803**	**95.24**
6	169.6254	168.5972	178.495	92.85
7	179.6254	178.4158	192.3527	92.85
8	187.3424	185.9513	204.8662	92.85

The performance of the speech system in terms of word accuracy is given by

$$WordAccuracy = \frac{(N - D - S)}{N} * 100 = \frac{H}{N} * 100 \tag{14}$$

The Information Criteria AIC, BIC, AICc and Accuracy of the ASR system (the performance of the SR system) is presented in Table 2 and also shown in Fig. 5.

Similarly the Information Criteria KIC, KICc, AKICc and Accuracy are calculated and presented in Table 3. The corresponding graph is shown in Fig. 6. The model that gives minimum value is selected as the best model.

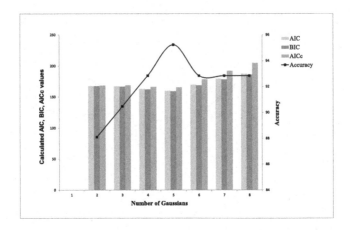

Fig. 5. Number of Gaussian mixtures Vs AIC, BIC, AICc and accuracy

Table 3. Number of Gaussians and corresponding KIC, KICc, AKICc values and Accuracy of the ASR system

Number of Gaussians	KIC	KICc	AKICc	Accuracy
2	176.847	176.4284	183.7994	88.1
3	178.0246	176.1081	180.4636	90.47
4	176.8604	175.3287	181.2213	92.85
5	**175.5826**	**173.9299**	**176.6936**	**95.24**
6	189.6254	191.1417	199.9271	92.85
7	202.6254	207.009	217.1393	92.85
8	213.3424	221.6571	233.0526	92.85

6   Conclusion

This paper proposes a better architecture for acoustic modeling of the speech recognizer for a new set of Malayalam words. The system is trained for 10 different speakers including male and female in the age group of 20–35 years. The features are extracted with MFCC along with zeroth energy, delta and Acceleration coefficient. The use of multivariate Gaussian distribution is a key factor that contributes to the improved performance of many speech recognition systems. Dirichlet distribution is used for the successful generation of the weight values for Gaussian mixtures. The performance of a trained system is evaluated by word accuracy (% correct) and WER. The proposed system got 90.91% word accuracy with 11.9% WER for single Gaussians. The experiment is conducted for various Gaussian mixture ranging from 1 to 8 and we achieved the best result at a Gaussian mixture five. That has shown a word accuracy 95.24% and WER 4.76%. The paper concludes with a verification of the performance of multivariate Gaussian mixture by different model selection methods namely

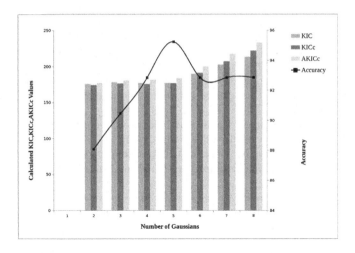

Fig. 6. Number of Gaussian mixtures Vs KIC, KICc, AKICc and accuracy

AIC, BIC, AICc, KIC, KICc, AKICc. The verification result reveals that the minimum value for Information Criterion is obtained for a 5- mixture Gaussian component model.

Acknowledgment. This research is supported by Kerala State Council for Science, Technology and Environment (KSCSTE). I thank KSCSTE for funding the project under the Back-to-lab scheme.

References

1. Benzeghiba, M., et al.: Automatic speech recognition and speech variability: a review. Speech Commun. **49**(10), 763–786 (2007)
2. Rabiner, L.R.: A tutorial on hidden markov models and selected applications in speech recognition. Proc. IEEE **77**(2), 257–286 (1989)
3. Malayalam Language (2018). https://en.wikipedia.org/wiki/Malayalam. Accessed 02 Jun 2018
4. Dirichlet   Distribution   (2018).   https://en.wikipedia.org/wiki/Dirichlet_distribution. Accessed 02 Jun 2018
5. Abushariah, A.A.M., Gunawan, T.S., Khalifa, O.O., Abushariah, M.A.M.: English digits speech recognition system based on hidden Markov models. In: 2010 International Conference on Computer and Communication Engineer (ICCCE 2010), pp. 1–5. IEEE Press (2010)
6. Al-Qatab, B.A., Ainon, R.N.: Arabic speech recognition using hidden Markov model toolkit (HTK). In: International Symposium in Information Technology (ITSim), vol. 2, pp. 557–562. IEEE (2010)
7. Saini, P., Kaur, P., Dua, M.: Hindi automatic speech recognition using HTK. Int. J. Eng. Trends Technol. (IJETT) **4**(6), 2223–2229 (2013)
8. Kumar, K., Aggarwal, R., Jain, A.: A hindi speech recognition system for connected words using HTK. Int. J. Comput. Syst. Eng. **1**(1), 25–32 (2012)

9. Dua, M., Aggarwal, R., Kadyan, V., Dua, S.: Punjabi automatic speech recognition using HTK. IJCSI Int. J. Comput. Sci. Issues **9**(4), 359 (2012)

10. Bhaskar, P.V., Rao, S.R.M., Gopi, A.: HTK based telugu speech recognition. Int. J. Adv. Res. Comput. Sci. Softw. Eng. **2**(12), 307–314 (2012)

11. Kurian, C., Balakrishnan, K.: Speech recognition of Malayalam numbers. In: World Congress on Nature & Biologically Inspired Computing, NaBIC 2009, pp. 1475–1479. IEEE (2009)

12. Kurian, C., Balakrishnan, K.: Connected digit speech recognition system for Malayalam language. Sadhana **38**(6), 1339–1346 (2013)

13. Kurian, C., Balakrishnan, K.: Development & evaluation of different acoustic models for Malayalam continuous speech recognition. Procedia Eng. **30**, 1081–1088 (2012)

14. Krishnan, V.V., Jayakumar, A., Babu, A.P.: Speech recognition of isolated Malayalam words using wavelet features and artificial neural network. In: 4th IEEE International Symposium on Electronic Design, Test and Applications, DELTA 2008, pp. 240–243. IEEE (2008)

15. Yu, K.: Generating Gaussian mixture models by model selection for speech recognition. F06 10–701 Final Project Report (2006)

16. Akogul, S., Erisoglu, M.: A comparison of information criteria in clustering based on mixture of multivariate normal distributions. Math. Comput. Appl. **21**(3), 34 (2016)

17. Young, S.: Hidden Markov model toolkit: design and philosophy. CUED/F-INFENG/TR. 152, Cambridge University Engineering Department (1994)

18. Yu, D., Deng, L.: Automatic Speech Recognition, A Deep Learning Approach. SCT. Springer, London (2015). https://doi.org/10.1007/978-1-4471-5779-3

19. Reynolds, D.A.: Gaussian mixture models. Encycl. Biom. **2009**, 659–663 (2009)

20. Karlis, D., Xekalaki, E.: Choosing initial values for the EM algorithm for finite mixtures. Comput. Stat. Data Anal. **41**(3), 577–590 (2003)

21. Steele, R.J., Raftery, A.E.: Performance of bayesian model selection criteria for gaussian mixture models. Front. Stat. Decis. Mak. Bayesian Anal. **2**, 113–130 (2010)

22. Akaike, H.: Information theory and an extension of the maximum likelihood principle. In: Parzen, E., Tanabe, K., Kitagawa, G. (eds.) Selected Papers of Hirotugu Akaike, pp. 199–213. Springer, New York (1998). https://doi.org/10.1007/978-1-4612-1694-0_15

23. Hurvich, C.M., Tsai, C.L.: Regression and time series model selection in small samples. Biometrika **76**(2), 297–307 (1989)

24. Schwarz, G., et al.: Estimating the dimension of a model. Ann. Stat. **6**(2), 461–464 (1978)

25. Cavanaugh, J.E.: A large-sample model selection criterion based on kullback's symmetric divergence. Stat. Probab. Lett. **42**(4), 333–343 (1999)

26. Seghouane, A.K., Bekara, M.: A small sample model selection criterion based on kullback's symmetric divergence. IEEE Trans. Signal Process. **52**(12), 3314–3323 (2004)

27. Seghouane, A.K., Bekara, M., Fleury, G.: A criterion for model selection in the presence of incomplete data based on kullback's symmetric divergence. Signal Process. **85**(7), 1405–1417 (2005)

28. HTK hidden Markov model toolkit (1994). http://htk.eng.cam.ac.uk

Social Choice Theory Based Domain Specific Hindi Stop Words List Construction and Its Application in Text Mining

Ruby Rani[✉] and D. K. Lobiyal

Jawaharlal Nehru University, New Delhi, India
ruby73_scs@jnu.ac.in, dkl@mail.jnu.ac.in

Abstract. In this paper, we have given an attempt to create domain specific Hindi stop words list using statistical and knowledge based techniques from prepared textual corpora of different domains. In order to remove the biased raking nature of each technique, Borda's rule of vote ranking method has been employed for unbiased stop words list construction. We also propose a novel approach called netting ranked performance evaluation (NRPE) to evaluate prepared stop words lists, in which stop words removal is done in leading and trailing fashion based on ascending and descending order of terms. Further, using combined band net (CBN) performance, we demonstrate the ability of each technique in identifying of candidate stop words followed by selection of features for text mining models. The experimental results show that a technique selects good features for classification/clustering needs not necessarily finds the good stop words. Results also show that the final Borda's lists gives normalized performance over individual technique. This approach guarantees candidate stop word removal, least information dissipation and text mining model performance enhancement.

Keywords: Hindi language · Stop words removal · Information retrieval
Borda's vote ranking method · Text classifier · Text clustering

1 Introduction

In text mining process, we come across highly frequent words with no significant semantic value, are generally known as the stop words. For e.g., "is", "and", "the" etc. in English documents. These are also known as noisy or negative dictionary words with no prediction capability, irrelevant, higher document frequency and availability in most of the labeled corpus. Some of the Hindi stop words are 'का' (of), 'में' (in), 'की' (of), 'है' (is) etc. According to the experiments in [1], larger portion of the whole text is covered by stop words only. During indexing in text mining, the absence of such words gives the tremendous performance for better information retrieval system because of dimensionality reduction of document [1–3]. Stop words vary from document to document and can be divided into two categories: generic and domain-dependent. Generic stop words are considered as standard stop words due to their high occurrence in any kind of documents [4, 5]. In reverse, domain-dependent stop words preserve

© Springer Nature Switzerland AG 2018
U. S. Tiwary (Ed.): IHCI 2018, LNCS 11278, pp. 123–135, 2018.
https://doi.org/10.1007/978-3-030-04021-5_12

higher frequency in domain specific documents only and don't have sufficient discriminating power. For example, *patient, doctor, nurse* etc. words can be stop words in medical domain, but may not be in some other domain [6].

Motivation: Stop words removal optimizes the document index size up to 40% in digital library [6]. The researchers have to be very conscious and wise while picking negative words for stop list preparation. Although, several stop words lists have already been constructed for Asian and Foreign languages but no such accepted standard Hindi stop words list is yet available [7–12]. The present researchers working in Hindi language either make use of manual stop word lists, or use pre-constructed stop word lists mentioned in [15–21]. In order to save the time and manual efforts, it is necessary to find ways to develop an almost complete stop words list for Hindi text documents. Generic stop words lists are not only sufficient for all kinds of text mining tasks, but, domain specific stop words have also shown noticeable impact. Thus, unavailability of standard stop words lists both for generic and domain specific documents [12, 16] directed us to work on this topic.

Contribution: In this paper, we have collected textual data for different domains from various online sources such as websites, news portals, blogs etc. using ILCrawler. Domain based corpus specific stop words lists are prepared using statistical and knowledge based techniques. Statistical approaches extract stop words based on word probability and distribution in the corpus while knowledge technique measures the information content carried by the word in the corpus. Fair and final lists for different domains are created using Borda's voting method [17]. Netting Ranked method has been used to extract features to feed to the text classifier/clustering. Stops lists evaluation is done using NRPE method under which different bands of stop words are removed from document and performance of classifier/clustering are analyzed.

Organization: The rest of the paper is arranged as follows. In Sect. 2, we have given the brief overview of related work of other languages and the dataset. In Sect. 3, we have given a brief overview of IL-crawler and it's working. Section 4 includes the proposed stop list construction using statistical and knowledge approaches. In Sect. 5, we analyze the experimental results and evaluate stop words lists using classification and clustering. The conclusion is given in Sect. 6.

2   Background

In this section, we briefly give the overview of data collection tools and related work about stop words for other languages.

2.1   Software Tools

Here, we briefly discuss what indian language crawler (IL-crawler) and sanitizer (IL-sanitizer).

IL-Crawler: The IL-crawler is developed by Computational linguistics R&D research group, Jawaharlal Nehru University. It extracts useful information, especially in Indian languages such as Bhojpuri, Hindi, Udia etc. from the world-wide web sites and remove the irrelevant data such as advertisements and promotion material [13].

IL-Sanitizer: The IL-sanitizer, a cleaner tool removes the unwanted data from the dataset. For e.g., it extracts the header of top web-pages and removes the news date, the author name etc. and generates systematic files with useful information [13].

2.2   Related Work

Hans Peter Luhn [14], was the first who coined the stop word concept in 1957 with informative or non-informative terms. Inspired from his idea, Francis et al. [18] and Van Rijsbergen [19] developed the stop words list for English language. Lo et al. [20] generated a stop word list using term-based random sampling method. In [7], Zou et al. prepared two lists based for Chinese language. Yao et al. prepared Chinese stop word list of 1289 words by adding stop words from different domain in traditional stop words list [8]. Hao et al. [9] developed a stop word list using statistical method for Chinese language.

Makrehchi [21, 22] have proposed a domain specific stop word list and evaluated using text classifier. White et al. have prepared domain specific stop word list and have shown their impact on ecommerce websites [6]. Since, very less work has been done in Hindi language. Some of the pioneer work in Hindi stop word removal is given in [12, 16, 23, 24] where stop words lists have shown good results. Since then, many stop word lists have been prepared for Hindi language [25–27].

3   Hindi Textual Corpora Preparation

In this section, we briefly address the online web sources, from where we have collected text data and construction methodology of textual corpora.

Data Source: We have collected the Hindi textual data from various online news portals such as *"NaiDunia"*, *"Vigyandunia"*, *"Center for Advanced Study of India"*, *"Kisanhelp"* etc. The data is aggregated from more than 11,000 online web pages.

Methodology: We crawl and collect the data on Intel(R) Core(TM) i3 3110 M CPU @ 2.4 GHz, 64-bit window 10 operating system, 8 Gb RAM using IL-crawler which is written in java. For example, we input the URLs text file of the *"NaiDunia Editorial's"* WebPages from 1 September 2015 to 31 October, 2017. These articles cover miscellaneous domains such as politics, agriculture, economy etc. To get rid from the compatibility complexities, we encode the data into UTF-8 format. Table 1 gives all the description about text corpus.

Table 1. Text corpus description

Notation	Description
Total Number of Documents	11,800+
Input Data Size	105+MB approx
Average # words in each file	i[th] word in the document
Largest document size	18 KB
Smallest Document size	4 KB
Domains Covered	Agriculture, Economy, Entertainment, Politics
# Files of Agriculture	# of Crawled Files-3284, # of Cleaned Files-2947
# Files of Economy	# of Crawled Files-3622, # of Cleaned Files-2460
# Files of Entertainment	# of Crawled Files-2359, # of Cleaned Files-1995
# Files of Politics Editorial	# of Crawled Files-2568, # of Cleaned Files-2160
# of terms in whole corpus	45,75,751
# of Unique terms	19,97,802

4 Our Work: Stop Word List Construction

Here, we construct the domain-wise stops lists for hindi language using statistical and knowledge models. Later, Unbiased Borda's vote ranked stops lists are prepared (Table 1). Notations and descriptions used in different ranking methods are given in Table 2.

Table 2. Notations and description

Notation	Description
X	Total Number of unique words
Y	Total number of documents
w_i	i[th] word in the document, $1 \leq i \leq X$
D_j	j[th] document in the dataset, $1 \leq j \leq Y$
$\|D\|$	Total number of words in document D
$MPW(w_i)$	Mean probability of ith word
TF_{ij}	Term-frequency of ith word in j[th] document
$Var(w_i)$	Variance probability of ith word
$MVR(w_i)$	Mean-variance ratio of ith word
$MAD(w_i)$	Mean absolute deviation probability of ith word
$MDR(w_i)$	Mean-deviation ratio of ith word
$STE(w_i)$	Shannon Term entropy of ith word

4.1 Statistical Models

Statistical model is important distribution measurement for each term in the dataset. Based on this distribution mechanism, we pre-process each term and arrange them.

Mean of Log-TF (MLT): Log-TF measures the logarithm value of word's frequency (TF) in every independent document. Mathematically, MLT of word w_i for all documents is the ratio of aggregate normalized frequency of word w_i in all documents D_j, where $1 \leq j \leq Y$, to the total number of documents, Y in dataset.

$$MLT(w_i) = \frac{|\sum_{j=1}^{j=Y} Log_e(TF_{ij})|}{Y} \tag{1}$$

Using Eq. 1, we observe that word of high MLT have no semantic meaning.

Variance of Log-TF (Var): In our proposed method, we computes the variance of each word w_i that tells about the squared dispersion of word's term frequency around the MLT value. Mathematically Eq. 2 gives the definition of variance for word w_i in all documents D_j, where $1 \leq j \leq Y$, to the total number of Y documents in dataset.

$$Var(w_i) = \frac{\sum_{j=1}^{j=Y}(MLT(w_i) - TF_{ij})^2}{Y} \tag{2}$$

Mean-variance ratio (MVR): The mean-variance ratio (MVR) of given word w_i is computed as the ratio of MLT value in Eq. 1 to the average variance value defines in Eq. 2 to establish a relation between two distribution methods. Mathematically, it is defined in Eq. 3, as:

$$MVR(w_i) = \frac{MLT(w_i)}{Var(w_i)} \tag{3}$$

Mean Absolute Deviation (MAD): Here, MAD is the mean of the absolute values from the data to their term-frequency. Mathematically, MAD of word w_i in Y documents is the absolute distance of each word' term- frequency TF_{ij} from the mean of word w_i.

$$MAD(w_i) = \frac{\sum_{j=1}^{j=Y}|MLT(w_i) - TF_{ij}|}{Y} \tag{4}$$

Mean Absolute Deviation Ratio (MDR): The MDR is the ratio of MLT of word w_i to the MAD of word w_i and is mathematically defined using Eq. 5 as:

$$MDR(_{wi}) = \frac{MLT(w_i)}{MAD(_{w_i})} \tag{5}$$

4.2 Entropy Based Knowledge Based Model

In 1948 [17], E. Shannon proved theory of randomness with the examples such as encoding a string by characters, spaces or punctuation marks. For example: 'क', 'म', 'ह' etc. are common while the characters 'ङ', 'ञ', 'ण' are rarely used. Therefore, due to this unpredictable behaviour of next character to be used in encoded string is measured using entropy [28].

Shannon Term Entropy (STE): The outcome of Term Entropy is explained as the word of higher entropy value is considered as the word with least knowledge and it is chosen as candidate for stop word list. For example: 'पर' (on), 'में' (in),' है' (is), 'से' (from), 'और' (and), 'भी' etc. STE of a word is calculated is computed as follows:

$$STE(w_i) = \sum_{j=1}^{j=Y} TF_{i,j} \times \log(\frac{1}{TF_{i,j}}) \tag{6}$$

4.3   Election Voting Ranked Based Fair Stop Words List Construction

Stop words lists are constructed by applying statistical and knowledge models. However, for final stops lists, election vote ranking method is applied. In Election winner selection strategy, every voter has his different preference for candidates for voting. For e.g., the voter votes 'n' to his most preferred candidate, 'n–1' to second most preferred candidate and so on. In the end, final rank of the candidate is the sum of ranks given to him by all voters and the final winner is declared as rank first [29]. Similarly, number of methods are considered as voters and rank given to words is the rank given by the particular method to the word. Finally, the sword is ranked using the sum of weights given to it in each technique and final stop word list is prepared. For e.g., word 'और' (and) is ranked '1' by statistical model's *MLT* method while ranked '2' knowledge model's *STE* method, so the final rank of the word 'और' is 3.

5   Netting Ranked Based Performance Evaluation of Stop Lists

In this section, we have used text classifier and text clustering approaches to evaluate the constructed stop words lists. The rationale behind using classifier and clustering is that performance of these techniques is affected by stop words such as K-Means clustering approach is very sensitive towards noise, while KNN is simple in implementation and requires no training. Thus, these two approaches are the better choices for stop words lists evaluation. The effect of stop words shows the impact on the performance of classifier/clustering. Further, performance of K-Means clustering results has been shown using different accuracy measures such as precision, recall and F-score while K-Fold cross validation is applied only on KNN classifier. We have constructed two kinds of stop words lists. First kind of lists contain terms into ascending order of ranks given in set $S = \{w1, w2, w3, \ldots, wn\}$ while set $S' = \{wn, wn-1, wn-2, \ldots, w2, w1\}$ carries the terms in descending order their ranks. These sets have been prepared using six different techniques as described in Sect. 4. Initially, we don't know the nature of the term whether it is rich or poor in knowledge. Thus, in first phase, we consider w_1 as the poorest in knowledge while w_n is ranked as knowledge-rich term based on the ranking approaches such as MLT. We have filtered *top-m* knowledge-poor terms from n terms such that $m \leq n$ from set S and rest of the terms are retained. These retained '$n - m$' terms from the vocabulary set S will be treated as features for classification/clustering. Manifestly, In second case, w_n is considered as the poorest-knowledge while w_1 is ranked as knowledge-rich. Similar to first phase, *top-m* terms of Vocabulary S' can be removed for stop word list evaluation and rest '$n - m$' terms are contained as features. We have considered *Net* of d' number of ranked terms where d' = a + d, d = 100, $0 \leq d' \leq m$, a = 100, m = 500 are defined. For example, in first phase worst-d' knowledge poor terms will be in the net for rejection from vocabulary set S where initial d' = a = 100. In this way, the initial net contains 100 terms and increase every stage by d number of terms. Thus it is named as Netting Ranked Performance Evaluation (NRPE). Depending on the order of stop words filtration either ascending or descending order, NRPE is termed as Leading NRPE or Trailing NRPE respectively. In case of Leading NRPE (Trailing NRPE), d_1^{th} net of words from set S (S') is enlisted knowledge-poor (knowledge-rich) if removal of words in this net yields good (poor) classification or clustering results than d_2^{th} net of ranked terms and so on until the condition is met. We can express two statements mathematically using the idea of Combined Leading Band for Netting Ranked Performance Evaluation (CLB-NRPE) and Combined Trailing Band for Netting Ranked Performance Evaluation (CTB-NRPE) is as follows:

$$CLB_{n-m} = \sum\nolimits_{100 \leq d' \leq m} P(S - d') \qquad (7)$$

$$CTB_{n-m} = \sum\nolimits_{100 \leq d' \leq m} P(S' - d') \qquad (8)$$

where d' is the net of terms to be removed from vocabulary set S (S'), m denotes maximum number of words (domain wise least informative words) under d'^{th} net. This way, after removal of knowledge-poor terms, CLB_{n-m} and CTB_{n-m} are the bands of remaining words contributing to vocabulary of features in ordered set S (S') based on CLB-NRPE (CTB-NRPE). CLB (CTB) can be compared and described through the Combined Band Net (CBN) performance results in leading (trailing) phase. $P(S - d')$ and $P(S' - d')$ are the approximate performance of classifier/cluster on $S - d'$ leading vocabulary set and $S' - d'$ trailing vocabulary set respectively.

Experimental Results

In this section, we have discussed the prepared domain specific stop lists and their evaluation using text classification and clustering results. In this process, first we preprocess the text which includes removal of non-Hindi words, punctuation marks followed by some phrases such as 'सुर्खियोंमें', 'बड़ीखबरें' etc. On this preprocessed corpus, statistical and knowledge based approaches are implemented. In both the models, the following grammatical categories are considered for stop words such as adjectives; 'सिर्फ़' (only), 'ज्यादा' (more) etc., adverbs; 'धीरे-धीरे' (slowly), 'शीघ्र' (urgently) etc., conjunctions; 'और' (and), 'या' (or) etc., auxiliaries; 'है' (is), 'चाहिए' (should), prepositions; 'पर' (on), 'में' (in) and interjections 'वाह' (wow!), 'हुर्रें' (Hurrah!) etc. These grammatically frequent words are used to prepare generic stop words list while domain specific stop words list covers subject oriented common words discussed in document.

Table 3. Top-10 ranked terms using statistical, knowledge based models and Borda's ranks

Mean	Variance	MVR	MAD	MDR	Entropy	Borda's
ही	सिक्का	के	की	को	के	की
इस	प्रियंका	की	को	की	में	को
लिए	गीता	से	में	हौसला-	की	के
तो	खेर	में	है	अफजाई	है।	में
भी	अकादेमी	को	के	हौव्वा	को	बीएचयू
हैं	चाबहार	का	सिक्का	होने	से	से
यह	डिपो	कि	प्रियंका	होतीं	कि	है
है	रोहिंग्या	पर	गीता	होती	का	कि
और	दसवीं	और	खेर	होगा	पर	का
नहीं	सुन्0ी	इस	अकादेमी	हो	ने	नौसैनिक

Table 4. Top-10 Borda's ranked terms from each domain in Leading (left) and Trailing (right) order

AG	EC	ENT	Politics	AG	EC	ENT	Politics
के	के	में	की	चोला	अक्षुण्ण	नरसिंहैया	एयरबेस
की	में	है	को	गुजरां	सेस्बेनिया	बालमणि	झेलम
हरिन्य	की	की	के	सेलेक्टर	सीएफएल	राजु	अप्रतिबंधित
संवृत	और	परन्तु	में	गुरीला	सस्ट्रेटा	काशीनाथ	अभिकरण
सदस्याँ	शिक्षावल्ली	सोरिंग	बीएचयू	गुलआरा	शिक्षाक्षेत्र	दियाँ	अवमानना
हिन्दु	हिचकी	सुधाकर	से	सूर्यकुण्ड	विन्ध्यन	जसबीर	असुविधा
मेट्रो:	हेपेटाइटिस	अस्मा	है	गिरावट	विकिफ़्राई	लाहिड़ी	इंडिया
बरखा	हरफन	आर्यभट	कि	गोदपुरा	अनुक्षिताजॉय	गुरबख्शा	आतंकवादी
वर्ष:	स्काड्न	एड्मिशन	का	गोनर्द	अचीवमेंट	चिंतामन	कौंसिल
रिपोर्ट:	सुब्रत	एलेक्जेंडर	नौसैनिक	सुखासिंह	यूरेट	जेकब	खर्चीली

For example, 'सरकार' (government), 'राष्ट्रीय' (national), 'देश' (country), 'भारतीय' (Indian) etc. are the common words in politics domain. Top-10 stop words are shown in Borda's column of Table 3 from different techniques while Table 4 shows Borda's fair stop words lists for different domains in leading and trailing manner. Figure 1 shows the behavior of different statistical and knowledge based approaches in stop-words extraction from politics corpus. In this experiment, aforementioned approaches extract the number of stop words from the band of Top-N ranked terms, where N = 500 to 10000 in whole dataset using Borda's stop words list. It is observed that each method shows similar behavior in stop-words extraction. In Fig. 2, we have seen that the first span of highest Top-500 ranked terms contains highest number of stop words, for e.g. 274 stop words in politics documents. The second band of 501–1000 top ranked terms contains lesser number of stop words than first band, for e.g., 173 stop words. The last Top-500 (9,550–10,000) terms carry average 15 terms as stop words. This also shows nearly decreasing behavior of presence of number of stop words as we move from lower band to higher band for different techniques. In this experiment, we have divided Top-10,000 terms into different spans with size of each span is 500 terms.

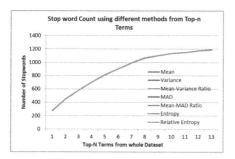

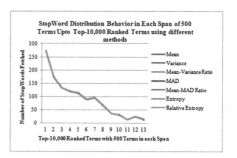

Fig. 1. Stop words count using different methods from Top-n Terms of politics corpus. Horizontal axis is divided into bands (spans) where each band have 500 terms. For e.g. '1' on x-axis denotes Top-500 terms, '2' denotes Top-1000 terms and so on.

Fig. 2. StopWords in Top-10,000 Ranked terms using different methods. X-axis is divided into different spans with size of a span = 500 Terms. e.g. '1' on x-axis is span of first Top-500 Terms, '2' denotes next span of Top-500 Terms and so on.

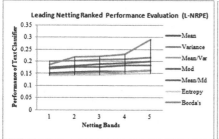

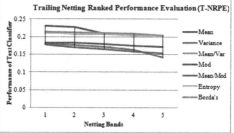

Fig. 3. Leading (left) and Trailing (right) Netting Ranked Bands performance of the ranking techniques for whole data set

Secondly, Constructed Stop words lists cannot be evaluated independently using NRPE method, an external interference is needed that is text classifier and text clustering. It uses KNN and K-Means approaches for evaluation where K-Means is computationally expensive and average accuracy of KNN is measured using K-fold cross validation where K = 5. Number of nearest neighbor in K-Nearest neighbor has been chosen through cross validation and miscellaneous error graph. On the other hand, K-Means accuracy has been measured in terms of precision, recall and f-score and elbow curve has been used to find optimal number of clusters in different net stages. Both KNN and K-Means performance against different nets is illustrated using Figs. 3 and 4 respectively. A total of 140 experiments were performed, using 7 statistical and knowledge based ranking measures on 5 different folds of training data and 10 different nets. After considering K-Means computation cost and time, only 5 net levels are used. In leading-NRPE, Fig. 6(left) shows the KNN text classification performance for Entropy and Variance where latter is more efficient in classifying document than prior. This is turn concludes that stopwords ranked by Variance are least informative and

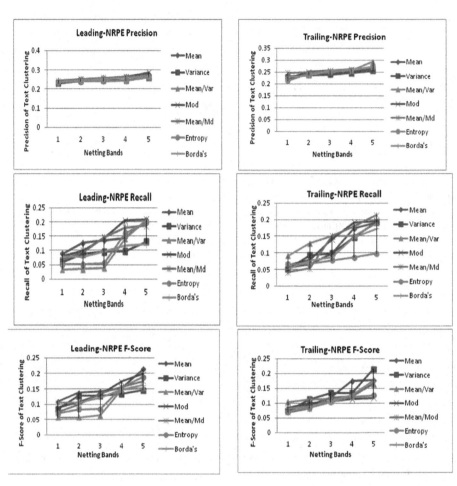

Fig. 4. Leading NRPE Precision (upper), Recall (middle) and F-Score (lower)

Fig. 5. Trailing NRPE Precision (upper), Recall (middle) and F-Score (lower)

reduction of these terms from document gives better features selection for text classification. Although, Trailing-NRPE results shown in Fig. 6(right), prove that Variance has given worst stop words ranking with respect to Shannon Term Entropy and affects text classifier performance. Moreover, we cannot rely only one stop word fetching technique, this is due to the reason that every technique ranks terms in different order as explained in Sect. 4.2. Thus, an unbiased ranked stop words list is proposed using Borda's vote ranking method as shown in results using Borda's line. Evaluation over classifier is shown in Fig. 3(left) and (right) where in both Leading and Trailing NRPE, stop words list ranked by Borda's vote ranking method shows highest classifier performance. Precision, Recall and F-score is computed for K-Means clustering, precision as shown in Fig. 4(upper), (middle) and (below) respectively. F-Score in Fig. 4(below), for leading NRPE shows highest text clustering performance by Mean and least performance by Variance. On the other hand, from Fig. 5(below), we can observe that Variance stop words reduction contributes to highest clustering performance while Mean Absolute Deviation (MAD) contributes to knowledge-poor features selection which hurts the clustering performance. Thus, NRPE method helps us to distinguish the qualitative stop words in both Leading and Trailing phases of stop words list evaluation. The proposed evaluation method is applicable for both generic and domain specific stop word lists. Leading NRPE (Trailing NRPE) will cover larger CBN performance in case of better feature selection for text classifier and text clustering after removal of both generic and domain specific stop words. For example, Fig. 6(left) demonstrates CLB(Variance) > CLB(Entropy) for better feature selection or better stopword removal by Variance method while Fig. 6(right), describes CTB (Entropy) > CTB(Variance) reverse to CLB.

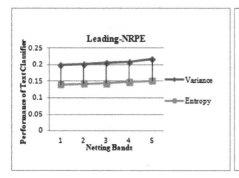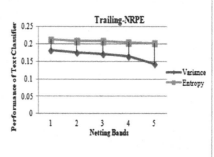

Fig. 6. Leading (left) and Trailing (right) NRPE characteristics for Entropy and Variance for Text Classifier

6   Conclusion and Future Work

In this paper, we create several domain specific Hindi stop words lists using statistical and knowledge techniques. Secondly, unbiased lists are prepared using Borda's vote ranking method. We evaluate the prepared lists using proposed NRPE approach in which CBN performance of text classifiers or text clustering is computed in leading and trailing NRPE fashion. Leading NRPE uses the prepared ascending ordered lists while trailing NRPE uses the descending ordered lists of stop words. In CBN, we observe that the filtration of adaptive Top-N ranked words from ascending ordered list gives better feature selection for one technique while the same technique fails into fetching good features when adaptive bottom-N ranked words are removed from descending ordered list. The quality of selected features and identification of good stop words is computed in terms of text classification/clustering performance. Finally, one more observation show that F-Score value in text clustering of each technique for leading netting bands stop words are nearly inversely proportional to F-Score value of each technique for trailing netting band stop words.

Acknowledgements. This work has been partially supported by the UPE-II grant received from JNU. Authors would like to thank anonymous reviewers for their kind comments.

References

1. Ricardo, B.-Y.: Modern Information Retrieval. Pearson Education, India (1999)
2. Yang, Y.: Noise reduction in a statistical approach to text categorization. In: Proceedings of the 18th Annual International ACM SIGIR Conference on Research and Development in Information Retrieval, pp. 256–263 (1995)
3. Sparck Jones, K.: A statistical interpretation of term specificity and its application in retrieval. J. Doc. **28**(1), 11–21 (1972)
4. Sinka, M.P., Corne, D.: Evolving better stoplists for document clustering and web intelligence. In: HIS, pp. 1015–1023 (2003)
5. Petras, V., Perelman, N., Gey, F.: UC Berkeley at CLEF-2003 – Russian language experiments and domain-specific retrieval. In: Peters, C., Gonzalo, J., Braschler, M., Kluck, M. (eds.) CLEF 2003. LNCS, vol. 3237, pp. 401–411. Springer, Heidelberg (2004). https://doi.org/10.1007/978-3-540-30222-3_39
6. White, B.J., Fortier, J., Clapper, D., Grabolosa, P.: The impact of domain-specific stop-word lists on ecommerce website search performance. J. Strateg. E-Commerce **5**(1/2), 83 (2007)
7. Zou, F., Wang, F.L., Deng, X., Han, S., Wang, L.S.: Automatic construction of chinese stop word list. In: Proceedings of the 5th WSEAS International Conference on Applied Computer Science, pp. 1010–1015 (2006)
8. Yao, Z., Ze-wen, C.: Research on the construction and filter method of stop-word list in text preprocessing. In: International Conference on Intelligent Computation Technology and Automation (ICICTA), 2011, vol. 1, pp. 217–221 (2011)
9. Hao, L., Hao, L.: Automatic identification of stop words in chinese text classification. In: International Conference on Computer Science and Software Engineering, 2008, vol. 1, pp. 718–722 (2008)
10. Alhadidi, B., Alwedyan, M.: Hybrid stop-word removal technique for Arabic language. Egypt. Comput. Sci. J. **30**(1), 35–38 (2008)
11. Alajmi, A., Saad, E.M., Darwish, R.R.: Toward an ARABIC stop-words list generation. Int. J. Comput. Appl. **46**(8), 8–13 (2012)
12. Jha, V., Manjunath, N., Shenoy, P.D., Venugopal, K.R.: HSRA: Hindi stopword removal algorithm. In: International Conference on Microelectronics, Computing and Communications (MicroCom), 2016, pp. 1–5 (2016)
13. Choudhary, N., Jha, G.N.: Creating multilingual parallel corpora in Indian languages. In: Vetulani, Z., Mariani, J. (eds.) LTC 2011. LNCS (LNAI), vol. 8387, pp. 527–537. Springer, Cham (2014). https://doi.org/10.1007/978-3-319-08958-4_43
14. Luhn, H.P.: A statistical approach to mechanized encoding and searching of literary information. IBM J. Res. Dev. **1**(4), 309–317 (1957)
15. Shenoy, P.D., Srinivasa, K.G., Venugopal, K.R., Patnaik, L.M.: Dynamic association rule mining using genetic algorithms. Intell. Data Anal. **9**(5), 439–453 (2005)
16. Pandey, A.K., Siddiqui, T.J.: Evaluating effect of stemming and stop-word removal on Hindi text retrieval. In: Tiwary, U.S., Siddiqui, T.J., Radhakrishna, M., Tiwari, M.D. (eds.) Proceedings of the First International Conference on Intelligent Human Computer Interaction, pp. 316–326. Springer, New Delhi (2009). https://doi.org/10.1007/978-81-8489-203-1_31

17. Shannon, C.E.: A mathematical theory of communication. Bell Syst. Tech. J. **27**(3), 379–423 (1948)
18. Kucera, H., Francis, W.N.: Frequency analysis of English usage: Lexicon and grammar. Houghton Mifflin, Boston (1982)
19. Van Rijsbergen, C.J.: A non-classical logic for information retrieval. Comput. J. **29**(6), 481–485 (1986)
20. Lo, R.T.-W., He, B., Ounis, I.: Automatically building a stopword list for an information retrieval system. J. Digit. Inf. Manage **5**, 17–24 (2005). Special Issue on the 5th Dutch-Belgian Information Retrieval Workshop (DIR)
21. Makrehchi, M., Kamel, M.S.: Extracting domain-specific stopwords for text classifiers. Intell. Data Anal. **21**(1), 39–62 (2017)
22. Makrehchi, M., Kamel, M.S.: Automatic extraction of domain-specific stopwords from labeled documents. In: Macdonald, C., Ounis, I., Plachouras, V., Ruthven, I., White, Ryen W. (eds.) ECIR 2008. LNCS, vol. 4956, pp. 222–233. Springer, Heidelberg (2008). https://doi.org/10.1007/978-3-540-78646-7_22
23. Singh, S., Siddiqui, T.J.: Evaluating effect of context window size, stemming and stop word removal on Hindi word sense disambiguation. In: International Conference on Information Retrieval & Knowledge Management (CAMP), 2012, pp. 1–5 (2012)
24. Rani, R., Lobiyal, D.K.: Automatic construction of generic stop words list for Hindi text. Procedia Comput. Sci. Elsevier J. **132**, 1–7 (2018)
25. Ranks, "Hindi stopwords". Accessed 17 Dec 2017
26. Taranjeet, "Hindi stopwords", 17 April 2017
27. GitHub, "Hindi stopword list", 29 December 2011
28. Kantor, P.B., Lee, J.J.: The maximum entropy principle in information retrieval. In: Proceedings of the 9th Annual International ACM SIGIR Conference on Research and Development in Information Retrieval, pp. 269–274 (1986)
29. Myerson, R.B.: Fundamentals of social choice theory. Quart. J. Polit. Sci. **8**(3), 305–337 (2013)

Effect of Devanagari Font Type in Reading Comprehension: An Eye Tracking Study

Chetan Ralekar[1(✉)], Punyajoy Saha[2], Tapan K. Gandhi[1], and Santanu Chaudhury[1,3]

[1] Department of Electrical Engineering, IIT Delhi, New Delhi 110016, India
chetan.ralekar@ee.iitd.ac.in, tgandhi@iitd.ac.in
[2] Department of Computer Science and Technology, IIEST, Shibpur, Howrah, India
punyajoysaha1998@gmail.com
[3] CSIR-Central Electronics Engineering Research Institute (CEERI), Pilani, India

Abstract. In this world of digitization, screen reading has grown immensely due to the availability of affordable display devices. Most of the people prefer to read on display devices as compared to the print media. To make the reading experience of the reader pleasant and comfortable, the font designers strive hard to choose suitable typographical properties of the text such as font type, font size etc. Some of the researchers suggest that the typography of the text affects the reading performance of the readers to some extent. However, the research focusing on the effect of typography on the reading behavior of the readers is limited and it is hardly touched upon for the Indian scripts. Therefore, the proposed paper aims to find out the effect of Devanagari font type on the reading performance, especially reading comprehension of the readers. In addition to this, a method to reduce the error in the gaze estimation of the eye tracker is also proposed. In order to understand the reading behavior, an eye tracking experiment is performed on 14 participants asking them to read 22 pages, in 3 different font types, presented on the screen of the eye tracker. The performance of the readers is analyzed in terms of total reading time, comprehension score, number of fixations, fixation duration and number of regressions. Our results show that there is a significant difference in the fixation duration, a number of fixations and the comprehension score, when the same document is read in different font type. Thus, there is a scope for improvement in the reading comprehension, by changing the physical properties of the document without changing its content. These findings might be useful to understand the readers' preference for the font and to design a proper font type for online reading.

Keywords: Eye tracking · Reading comprehension · Font type Devanagari script

1 Introduction

In this era of the internet, all the information we want is available on a single click on the computer. With the availability of cheaper storage and display devices, most of the people prefer to read on the display devices as compared to the printed media. Font

U. S. Tiwary (Ed.): IHCI 2018, LNCS 11278, pp. 136–147, 2018.
https://doi.org/10.1007/978-3-030-04021-5_13

designers or type designers are trying hard to choose a font type and font size which will make the readers' reading experience pleasant and joyful. Another objective of choosing a suitable font is to make the readers get involved in the reading process so that they can concentrate on the contents of the material being read. In order to achieve this objective, font designers are developing different fonts for different purposes. However, the selection of proper font type and font size remains a challenge.

During the course of reading, the readers try to take out significant meaning from the text being read and this process is called as reading comprehension. According to the literature related to reading comprehension, it has been assumed that the reading comprehension depends on the phonological skill, vocabulary, language skill, knowledge, word processing ability of the readers [1]. However, the reading comprehension also depends on the comfort level of the readers with a particular text. In other words, it depends on the font type, font size, etc. used while typing the text. However, the literature commenting on the effects of changing the properties of the documents such as font style, size, etc. on reading comprehension is very rare. However, there are some research studies carried out for Latin script. When it comes to Latin script, there is a broad categorization between font type as serif and non-serif. In serif font, there is a small decorative line attached to the basic form of the character and san serif does not have that decorative line attached [2]. Michal Bernard et al. [3] compared san serifs and serif fonts of various font sizes such as 10, 12, 14. They reported significant variation in reading time, whereas reading efficiency was not that significant across the font sizes. Serif and san serif fonts were further analyzed for differences in reading comprehension [4]. However, these studies reported the non-significant difference in reading comprehension for both serif and non-serif fonts [4, 5].

With the advancement of technology, researchers started using eye trackers to understand the cognitive processes involved during reading [6]. Eye Tracking has been used for understanding the cognitive process involved in reading comprehension [7] as the eye can be considered a window to the mind. The eye-tracking, has been used to find out the reading comprehension level of the reader [8] which in turn helped to comment on the language expertise of the readers reading the document The eye tracking features such as fixations, saccades, total fixation durations, etc. can be used as measure to understand the reading experience for the readers. Eye Fixation refers to the point where the eyes take rest during reading, and the fast movement of the eyes is termed as saccade [6]. The back and forth movement of eyes while reading is referred as regression. David Beymer et al. [5] used these eye tracking features and found that for smaller font sizes, fixation duration was longer. This longer duration resulted in longer reading time. However, the difference in reading time across font sizes was not significant.

When we look for the similar research for non-Latin script or Indian script, we rarely find it. One of the most widely used scripts in the world is the Devanagari script which is used by almost 41% people in India [2]. There are various languages such as Hindi, Marathi, Rajasthani, etc. which are written using the Devanagari script. Chetan et al. [9] have used eye tracking features to understand the recognition of distorted Devanagari letters. The Devanagari script has its unique structure for every character and there are many ways we can write those artistically. However, the effect of the various font types on reading the behavior of the readers is not given that much attention. Therefore, the proposed paper aims to understand the effect of these Devanagari font types on reading comprehension and reading behavior of the readers reading the text.

This paper has been divided into five sections wherein Sect. 1 talks about the introduction; the experimental setup has been presented in Sect. 2. The hypothesis to be tested is given in Sect. 3. Section 4 highlights the results and discussions over the results. Last section deals with concluding remarks with possible future extensions.

2   Experimental Setup

This section deals with the experiment design and experimental procedure.

2.1   Participant Screening

Total 14 (7 males, 7 females) graduate participants volunteered to perform the experiment. All participants were having normal or corrected to normal vision and mean age of 24 years (SD = 2.5). All the participants were well-versed in reading Devanagari script and spending at least an hour every day, in reading online documents written in Devanagari script. They had given their consent for participation and were offered with some refreshments at the end of the experiment.

2.2   Stimulus Design

In order to understand the effect of different font type on the reading performance of the readers, we chose 3 stories from the Grade 8, NCERT book [10]. Each story was comprised of at least 7 pages. Each participant had to read all stories, i.e. around 22 pages. In order to avoid any bias, the stories selected for the experiment were of the same genre and the same level of hardness. These documents were formatted in three different Devanagari fonts such as Nirmala, Kokila and Aparajita with the font size as 20 and line spacing as 2 as shown in Fig. 1.

Each page consisted of around 14 lines of text. Each story was formatted in 3 different font types.

Each font has its own characteristics in terms of the thickness of the stroke, character width and height, loop, curves, knots, counters etc. [2]. Figure 2 shows the letter 'क' written in three different font types with the same font size. The letters in Nirmala font is mono-linear i.e. the strokes are of uniform thickness throughout the structure of letter whereas the thickness of strokes varies for letters in Kokila and Aparajita font. When we compare the height and the width of the character, we can see that the Aparajita font has more character width as compared to the height. On the other hand, the Nirmala font has more character height as compared to the width. The height-width proportion will make the words look condensed, regular or expanded. Therefore, the number of words that can be accommodated in a line varies. This affects the reading behavior of the readers. It can be seen in Fig. 1.

In order to minimize the error between estimated gaze position by the eye tracker and the actual location where the person is gazing, we have designed the stimuli and

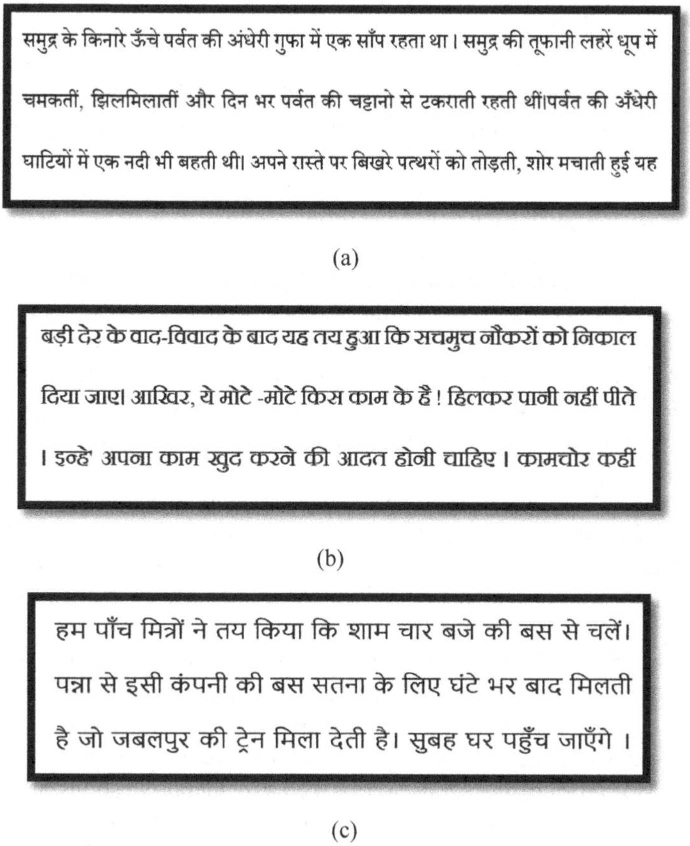

समुद्र के किनारे ऊँचे पर्वत की अंधेरी गुफा में एक साँप रहता था । समुद्र की तूफानी लहरें धूप में

चमकतीं, झिलमिलातीं और दिन भर पर्वत की चड्डानो से टकराती रहती थीं।पर्वत की अँधेरी

घाटियों में एक नदी भी बहती थी। अपने रास्ते पर बिखरे पत्थरों को तोड़ती, शोर मचाती हुई यह

(a)

बड़ी देर के वाद-विवाद के बाद यह तय हुआ कि सचमुच नौकरों को निकाल

दिया जाए। आखिर, ये मोटे -मोटे किस काम के है ! हिलकर पानी नहीं पीते

। इन्हे' अपना काम खुद करने की आदत होनी चाहिए । कामचोर कहीं

(b)

हम पाँच मित्रों ने तय किया कि शाम चार बजे की बस से चलें।

पन्ना से इसी कंपनी की बस सतना के लिए घंटे भर बाद मिलती

है जो जबलपुर की ट्रेन मिला देती है। सुबह घर पहुँच जाएँगे ।

(c)

Fig. 1. Text written in (a) Kokila Font, (b) Aparajita Font, (c) Nirmala Font

(a)   (b)   (c)   (d)

Fig. 2. Devanagari Letter 'क' written in (a) Kokila Font, (b) Aparajita Font, (c) Nirmala Font, (d) explaining different parts of letter

experimented with those stimuli before the presentation of the text. The stimuli consisted of 50 static images of size 1280×1024 pixels, with a circle of radius 10 pixels black in color on each image, against the white background as shown in the third block of Fig. 3. The circle was plotted at random locations; however we were aware of the coordinates of its location. The center of that circle was painted white so that participants could be instructed to focus at the center of the circle.

2.3   Equipment Used

The Tobii T120, a remote eye tracker, was used to capture the eye movements of the participants. In this research, Tobii Studio, a software package, was used for experiment design and data recording. The data was collected at a sampling frequency of 120 Hz.

2.4   Experiment Protocol

The experiment was performed in a quiet experimental room. Before starting the experiment, participants were given all the instructions about the experiment and their exact role in the study was explained. In order to maintain the confidentiality of the data, the participants were assigned different ID numbers. The participant was asked to sit comfortably in front of the eye tracker at a distance of 60–70 cm from the eye tracker. The experiment was carried out in 3 phases. Each phase started with the 9 point calibration of the eye tracker.

In order to have more precise and accurate data quality, the stimuli consisting of 50 images with static random points plotted on it, were presented on the screen of the eye tracker. Each image was presented for 2 s and participants were asked to gaze at the respective point and the corresponding eye tracking data of the participants was collected.

After the successful completion of the above step, the first story, consisting of around seven pages, was presented to the participant. Each participant was asked to read it carefully and comprehend it. The participant was allowed to move between the pages by pressing the arrow keys of the keyboard. In order to check the comprehension of the reader, two types of questions were asked viz. literal questions and inferential questions, after the completion of the reading of each story. The answer for the literal question could be found directly from the story, whereas inferential question requires proper understanding from the context of the story. Once the participant finished answering the questions, the participant was allowed to take a short break of 5–10 min before starting the second phase.

In phase II, 9 point calibration was performed again and the second set of documents i.e. story 2 was presented. The story 2 was presented in a different font other than the font used for story 1 and story 3. After the completion of reading, some questions were asked. Similarly, the third set of documents i.e. story 3 was presented in remaining font type. Thus, a single participant was presented with all 3 stories in 3 different font types. The same procedure was repeated for all the participants. The stories were presented to the participants in random order. The presentation of the stories was controlled in such a way that every story was presented in each font type (for example, story 1 in Nirmala, Kokila and Aparajita) and was read by at least 4 different participants (i.e. participant P1 read story 1 in Nirmala, participant P2 read the story 1 in Kokila font, participant P3 read the story 1 in Aparajita font...). The complete experimental procedure is shown in the form of a block diagram as shown in Figs. 3 and 4.

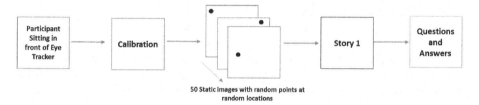

Fig. 3. Experimental Procedure for Phase I

Fig. 4. Experimental Procedure for Phase II and III

3   Hypothesis Testing

In our study, we are going to test the following hypotheses:

$H_{0,0}$ = The reading comprehension is independent of Font type i.e. there is no difference between the average comprehension score across all three Font types

$H_{0,1}$ = The reading comprehension is dependent on Font type i.e. there is a difference between an average comprehension score across Font types

$H_{1,0}$ = The average fixation duration across the font types with the same font size is same

$H_{1,1}$ = The average fixation duration across the font types with the same font size is not the same

$H_{2,0}$ = The average number of fixations across the font types with the same font size is same

$H_{2,1}$ = The average number of fixations across the font types with the same font size is not the same

$H_{3,0}$ = The average reading time is same across all font types

$H_{3,1}$ = The average reading time is different across font types

$H_{4,0}$ = The average number of regressions is same across all font types

$H_{4,1}$ = The average number of regressions is different across font types

Here, $H_{0,i}$ is null hypothesis and $H_{1,i}$ is an alternative hypothesis, where i = 1,2,3. We have performed a One-way ANOVA test on the observed data. We have computed the F-score for our data and compared with the critical value of F from f-distribution to either accept or reject the NULL hypothesis. If the observed F-value is greater than the critical F-value, then we reject the NULL hypothesis otherwise accept it.

4   Results and Discussions

We have performed the experiment on 14 participants; however the eye tracking samples for 2 participants are not sufficient for the analysis. Therefore, we have to discard them. Therefore, we are considering the eye tracking data of 12 participants for analysis based on eye tracking metrics and all 14 participants for the analysis based on reading statistics such as reading time, comprehension score.

In order to get eye tracking features such as fixations and saccades from the raw eye tracking data, a velocity based classification algorithm called as Velocity-Threshold Identification (I-VT) fixation classification algorithm [11] is used. This algorithm classifies the eye movements into fixation and saccades based on the velocity of the directional shift of the eye. A threshold is set and velocity greater than the threshold is classified as saccade and if it is less then fixation. We have set the velocity threshold at 30 degrees/seconds with eye selection in average mode and designed I-VT filter.

4.1   Minimizing the Error in the Eye Tracker

The eye tracker estimates the gaze position of the participant. This estimated gaze position may be different from the actual position, where the person is gazing. This difference introduces some error in the collected eye tracking data. The calibration process helps in minimizing this error. However, in order to minimize this error to some more extent, we have performed an additional step, wherein participants were presented with the images of random points and asked to gaze at those points. If there exists an error, then we need to shift the data point, estimated by the tracker, horizontally and/or vertically towards the actual location which in turn minimizes that error. Based on the data collected for those random points, a linear regression model is used to predict the error made by the eye tracker at different points on the screen. In each image, the x-shift and y-shift of the centroid of the raw data are measured from the known coordinates of the point to be gazed. This x-shifts and y-shifts are recorded and used to train the model. In order to make the data more precise, we have selected two neighboring data points to a reference data point and changed the reference data point to the centroid of these three data points. It helps in bringing the data points close and hence increasing the precision of the raw data. Thus, we get more precise and accurate data point as shown in Figs. 5 and 6.

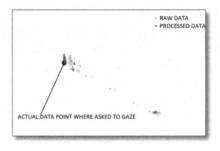

Fig. 5. Raw data and data after applying pre-processing step are shown on a sample image out of 50 static images

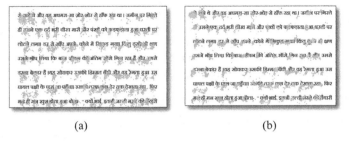

Fig. 6. (a) Raw eye gaze data points, (b) Pre-processed data points

From Fig. 6, we can see that the pre-processing step has helped to minimize the error to some extent. The gaze points recorded below the sentence line by the eye tracker have been shifted appropriately.

4.2   Effect of Font Type on Fixation Duration, Number of Fixations and Total Reading Time, Number of Regressions

We have plotted the corresponding fixations on the respective document. Each circle in the Fig. 7 denotes the respective fixation and diameter of the circle varies as a function of duration. More is the fixation duration; more is the diameter of the circle.

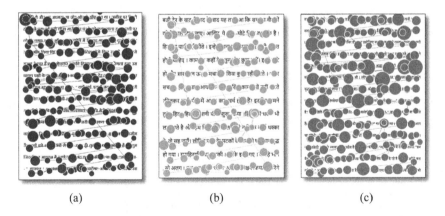

Fig. 7. Gaze Plot for text written in (a) Aparajita Font, (b) Nirmala Font, (c) Kokila Font

The fixation duration indicates the amount of time reader fixated on a particular location i.e. area of interest (AOI). In our experiment, the whole page is selected as Area of Interest. In general, fixation duration is an indication of the time taken to process the information by the brain. From the literature, [5] the fixation duration is more for a smaller font size and less for bigger font. Thus, it can be said that fixation duration varies according to font size and if the font size is same then fixation duration should be almost the same.

In our experiment, we have kept the font size constant across all the font types. The respective fixation duration and a number of fixations (i.e. the number of times readers fixated on AOI) for all the participants are plotted and shown in Figs. 8 and 9 respectively. It can be seen from Figs. 8 and 9, that the number of fixations and fixation duration is more when the text is read by the participants in Kokila font. It is comparatively lesser for the text in Aparajita font and least in Nirmala font. We have performed a one-way ANOVA test on fixation duration which has resulted $F(2,33) = 8.27$, p-value = 0.001224. Similarly, the analysis is carried out for the number of fixations which has given us $F(2,33) = 7.30181$, p-value = 0.002368. Thus, for both fixation duration and number of fixations, ANOVA gives us p-value < 0.05, this means results are significant and supports our claim that the average total fixation duration, average number of fixations is not the same across the fonts.

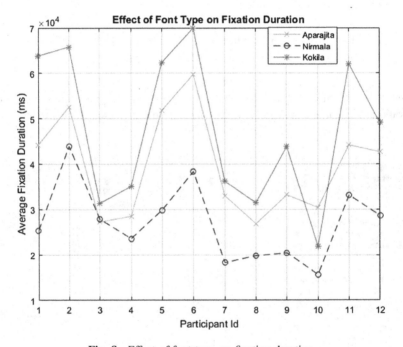

Fig. 8. Effect of font type on fixation duration

The Devanagari script is written from left to right and is being read in the similar way. When the readers are not able to comprehend a sentence, they will trace the sentence again and again. In other words, the eye movements of the readers will be recorded from right to left. This is called as a regression. This concept has been used by Utpal et al. [12] to find a difficult word in a document. In our experiment, we found that there is no significant difference in the number of regressions when the document is read in different fonts (p-value > 0.05).

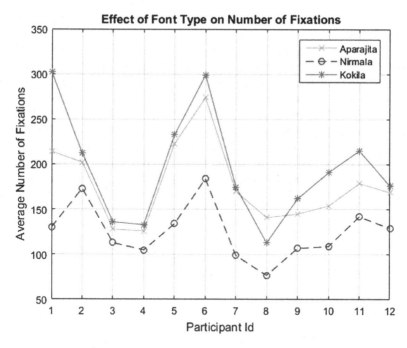

Fig. 9. Effect of font type on number of fixations

4.3   Effect of Font Type on Reading Comprehension

The comprehension process involves reading the text carefully, processing it and deriving significant meaning out of it. In order to comprehend the text being read, it is required that the readers read the text attentively. The eye fixations can be considered as a good measure to comment on the readers' attention and engagement [13]. The fixation duration gives us the idea of how the brain processes the information being read. In addition to this, the increase in fixation duration can be considered as an indication of more reader engagement with the document. Therefore, fixation duration is an important factor needed to be considered for commenting on the reader's engagement while reading the document.

In order to comment on the comprehension of the participants, the answers given by the participants are evaluated and rated by the two evaluators. The average of the scores given for each question by the two evaluators is given as the final score. For understanding the effect of font type on reading comprehension, we have considered all 14 participants. It can be seen from the box plot in Fig. 10, when the text presented in Kokila font, it is very well comprehended by almost all the participants as compared to other font types. There is a significant difference in the comprehension score when the text is read in a different font type supported by one-way ANOVA, $F(2, 39) = 8.395$, p-value $= 0.000928$.

It can be seen from Figs. 7 and 8 that the fixation duration for the text written in Kokila font is significantly more than the rest of the two fonts and comprehension score is also more. Thus, it can be claimed that readers are more involved in reading the text and processed the information very well when presented with the text in Kokila font. As a result, the comprehension score is also more. The number of fixations for Nirmala font are significantly lower which means the reading time is less, however, we found that it is not significantly less (p-value > 0.5). If we compare the comprehension score, we can see that the corresponding comprehension score for Nirmala font is lesser as compared to text when presented in Kokila font. In other words, readers find it easy to read, but not able to get engaged in the document when presented in Nirmala font. There is more variations in comprehension scores for Aparajita Font as compared to other two font types. However, when the readers were asked about their experience with these fonts, almost all the participants enjoyed reading the text in Kokila font. They rated Kokila font followed by Aparajita based on their preference to read a particular font type.

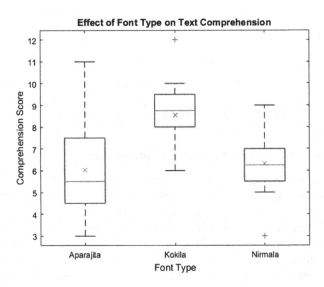

Fig. 10. Effect of font type on reading comprehension. The 'x' in the box plot denotes the average score for that respective font type

5   Conclusions

In this paper, we have tried to understand the effect of font type on the reading behavior and comprehension of the readers. The results show that there is a significant difference in the fixation duration, a number of fixations and comprehension score, when one document is read in a different font type. Therefore, we can say that reading comprehension is not only dependent on the readers' language skills, vocabulary but also depends on the typography i.e. physical properties of the text such as font type, font size to some extent. These findings will help the type designers to design the font type which will make readers more engaged in reading and make their reading experience more pleasant. We plan to experiment with more number of participants to get more insights into our findings. In the future, we are planning to perform the study for school children and try to understand their behavior for different font types. The proposed paper gives us the ray of hope in improving the reader engagement and comprehension by modifying the physical properties of the documents without changing its content.

Acknowledgements.   We would like to thank all the participants participated in our study. We would also like to thank the Visvesvaraya PhD Scheme/DIC/MeitY for providing financial assistance to the first author to carry out research.

References

1. Katzir, T., Hershko, S., Halamish, V.: The effect of font size on reading comprehension on second and fifth grade children: bigger is not always better. PLoS ONE **8**(9), e74061 (2013)
2. Dalvi, G.: Conceptual model for Devanagari typefaces. Doctoral dissertation, Ph.D. thesis, Industrial Design Centre, Indian Institute of Technology Bombay (2010)
3. Bernard, M., Lida, B., Riley, S., Hackler, T., & Janzen, K.: A comparison of popular online fonts: Which size and type is best. Usability news, 4(1). (2002)
4. Akhmadeeva, L., Tukhvatullin, I., Veytsman, B.: Do serifs help in comprehension of printed text? An experiment with Cyrillic readers. Vision Res. **65**, 21–24 (2012)
5. Beymer, D., Russell, D., Orton, P.: An eye tracking study of how font size and type influence online reading. In: Proceedings of the 22nd British HCI Group Annual Conference on People and Computers: Culture, Creativity, Interaction, vol. 2, pp. 15–18. BCS Learning & Development Ltd. (2008)
6. Rayner, K.: Eye movements in reading and information processing: 20 years of research. Psychol. Bull. **124**(3), 372 (1998)
7. Raney, G.E., Campbell, S.J., Bovee, J.C.: Using eye movements to evaluate the cognitive processes involved in text comprehension. J. Visual. Exp. JoVE, (83) (2014)
8. Yoshimura, K., Kise, K., Kunze, K.: The eye as the window of the language ability: estimation of English skills by analyzing eye movement while reading documents. In: 2015 13th International Conference on Document Analysis and Recognition (ICDAR), pp. 251–255. IEEE (2015)
9. Ralekar, C., Gandhi, T.K., Chaudhury, S.: Unlocking the mechanism of devanagari letter identification using eye tracking. In: Shankar, B.U., Ghosh, K., Mandal, D.P., Ray, S.S., Zhang, D., Pal, S.K. (eds.) PReMI 2017. LNCS, vol. 10597, pp. 219–226. Springer, Cham (2017). https://doi.org/10.1007/978-3-319-69900-4_28
10. http://ncertbooks.prashanthellina.com/class_8.Hindi.Vasant. Accessed 7 July 2017
11. Salvucci, D.D., Goldberg, J.H.: Identifying fixations and saccades in eye-tracking protocols. In: Proceedings of the 2000 Symposium on Eye Tracking Research and Applications, pp. 71–78. ACM (2000)
12. Garain, U., Pandit, O., Augereau, O., Okoso, A., Kise, K.: Identification of reader specific difficult words by analyzing eye gaze and document content. In: 2017 14th IAPR International Conference on Document Analysis and Recognition (ICDAR), pp. 1346–1351. IEEE (2017)
13. Miller, B.W.: Using reading times and eye-movements to measure cognitive engagement. Educ. Psychol. **50**(1), 31–42 (2015)

Bone Conducted Speech Signal Enhancement Using LPC and MFCC

Premjeet Singh[1](✉), Manoj Kumar Mukul[1](✉), and Rajkishore Prasad[2](✉)

[1] Birla Institute of Technology, Mesra, Ranchi 835215, India
premsingh0693@gmail.com, mkm@bitmesra.ac.in
[2] B.N. College, Patna 800004, India
profrkishore@yahoo.com

Abstract. The air microphone used in communication devices to acquire speech signal gathers highly imperceptible signal in noisy background conditions. Bone conducted speech signal appears to be a promising tool to avoid this situation and improve the quality of communication between two users because of its inherent capability of attenuating high frequency signals. Though, there is no background noise present, the quality of extracted bone conducted signal is usually quite low in terms of intelligibility and strength. The reason for this quality degradation can again be accounted to the high frequency signal repulsion nature of bones. To rectify this issue and to make the bone conducted signal useful in communication systems, some signal processing schemes are required to be developed. This paper introduces application of two signal processing schemes which are very commonly used in speech recognition systems, Linear Predictive Coding (LPC) and MFCC (Mel Frequency Cepstral Coefficient), to enhance the bone conducted signal and shows comparison between them. Results of the analysis show that slight improvement in noise reduction is possible by using the proposed techniques. However, retrieval of lost information, due to bone conduction of speech, cannot be achieved by any of the two proposed techniques and a more robust scheme has to be developed for bone conducted signal improvement.

Keywords: Bone conducted signal · Air microphone signal · LPC MFCC

1 Introduction

Bone Conducted (BC) speech signals refers to the signals which are obtained when the vibrations from the human bones are extracted and converted into electrical signal. Such vibrations appear because of speech generated in the vocal cavity, which gets dispersed over the proximity areas, e.g, collarbone, skull, muscles near voice box etc. These vibrations are basically speech signals devoid of any external background noise, since bones do not allow transmission of any high frequency vibration signals. Hence bone conducted signals can be used to enhance

© Springer Nature Switzerland AG 2018
U. S. Tiwary (Ed.): IHCI 2018, LNCS 11278, pp. 148–158, 2018.
https://doi.org/10.1007/978-3-030-04021-5_14

the quality of communication over mobile phones. The signals that are acquired by air microphone (Air Conducted or AC signals) contains undesired background noises along with desired speech signal which significantly effect the communication quality between speaker and listener in certain situations. For example, while attempting a conversation in crowded areas such as in traffic jams, public gathering, railway stations, dockyards etc. background loud sounds makes it very difficult for listener to perceive the information. Cell phone manufacturers have tried to reduce the effect of this ambient noise over communication link by introducing various noise cancellation mechanism. These mechanisms basically makes use of two different microphones placed at a distance. One microphone is placed close to the speaker and other is usually placed facing the probable noise source. From these, the signal acquired by the microphone with higher strength is considered for transmission and signal with lower strength is subtracted with the former. This helps in reduction of low frequency noise signals but does not affect high frequency noises. For HF, adaptive algorithms have to be developed. Implementation of such algorithms and processes has increased the link efficiency but has also increased cost and complexity of the devices [1].

Using Bone Conducted (BC) signals may help in avoiding this extra cost and complexity as it remains inherently devoid of any external noise. The bone acts as a low pass filter with cutoff ranging from 1 to 1.5 KHz [4]. In spite of the absence of noise, the extracted BC speech signal cannot be directly used in communication systems. BC speech signals are found to be distorted in a complex manner. Such signals are also significantly attenuated as compared to AC speech signal. This complexity arises due to the conduction of the speech generated at vocal cavity to the point of extraction on skull. Therefore, for mitigation of such factors, a signal processing scheme has to be developed. Such a scheme must be capable of enhancing the quality of BC speech signal so that the speech must sound clean and natural.

Several methods have been tried by researchers to enhance the quality of BC signal with varying improvements and complexity. Researches done by McBride [2] and Munger [3] focused on the dispersion of BC signal over the human skull and examined the differences in SNR and intelligibility of BC signals for different words (vowels, fricatives etc.) over different positions on the skull. Such studies are very helpful as the more the BC signal is enriched with desirable frequency components, less complex the processing scheme would become. The work reported that speech signal extracted form forehead is found to contain most of the speech information which improves its intelligibility. This formed the basis of extraction of BC speech from forehead in our situation. Prasad *et al.* explained how vibrations from the human skull can be extracted by making use of a PVDF polymer film and also analysed few characteristics of BC signal to estimate its similarity with air microphone signal [4]. A signal enhancement technique using Auto Regressive (AR) coefficients to improve formant frequencies were introduced by Rahman *et al.* [5]. Rahman *et al.* did significant analysis over BC signal characteristics as well [6]. Shimamura *et al.* proposed a reconstruction filter design based on neural network learning from bone and air conducted speech [7]. They also proposed an inverse filtering mechanism to remove the bone conduction parameters and introduce vocal tract parameters into BC signal [8]. Tychtl *et al.* proposed an algorithm to generate a speech signal by using the MFCC coefficients of the signal [9]. The same algorithm is used to generate the BC speech signal from MFCCs in Sect. 3. tat Vu *et al.* proposed a method of signal improvement by using LPC based model for both bone and air conduction signals [10]. Then by using inverse filtering, speech is enhanced. Prediction of Air Conducted LP coefficients was done by them to implement inverse filtering without acquiring the air conducted signal. They have also proposed another blind model for improving bone signal quality by converting LPC of the bone signal to LSF coefficients to remove limitations of LPCs [11]. They studied the sensitivity of BC speech over words that produce different formant frequencies and changes in BC speech amplitude that takes place when these formants differ for different words. Won *et al.* used LPC and Cepstral analysis to generate an average transfer function from air to bone conduction sound and then compared it with actual bone conducted sound [12].

Though different researches have resulted in different BC speech signal enhancements, none of the methods showed profound improvements. Also, among the methods involving signal enhancement, except for that proposed by tat Vu *et al.* [10], the methods made use of characteristics of AC speech signal in some manner to improve BC signal quality. This would require acquiring two signals at a time followed by its processing, making the system complex and difficult to implement in real time. Methods which included analysis of BC speech over the skull and its extraction did not address any technique for BC enhancement. In this paper, two very common signal processing schemes, LPC and MFCC which are mostly used in speech recognition, are implemented for BC speech signal enhancement with the comparison between the two. LPC is implemented along with inverse filtering as explained by [10] and MFCC is implemented by changing the DCT step in MFCC to DST and manually changing the values of coefficients.

Next section of the paper gives a description of the implementation of LPC in BC speech signal enhancement. Section 3 gives description of MFCC for the same. Section 4 describes experimental approaches followed by Sects. 5 and 6 which give the results and a brief comparison between the two techniques.

2 LPC Analysis

Linear Predictive Coding (LPC) is a very common method used in speech processing. The method includes prediction of next oncoming sample values by making use of a definite number of previous sample values. The LPC coefficients then determine the closeness of predicted sample values with original sample values. Another interesting property of these LPC coefficients is that these samples can be used to estimate the formants of the speech signal and hence can be used for modelling of vocal tract parameters, i.e., the parameters which effects the vibrations from the vocal cords and gives the speech its actual essence.

This very property of LPC coefficients has been used here to remove the effects that bone inflicts over the speech while conduction through it and introduce back the vocal tract parameters in it. Such an operation is performed with a view that it must cause some positive effect over BC speech signal quality.

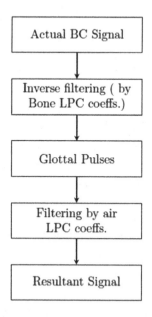

Fig. 1. Block diagram of LPC processing

By using MATLAB function 'lpc', LPC coefficients of the air conducted speech signal are first calculated. Since these coefficients can be used for modelling the vocal tract, they describe the vocal tract parameters of the speech. The transfer function is generated by using the formula,

$$H(z) = \frac{1}{1 + \sum_{k=1}^{n} a_k z^{-k}}$$

where n is the order of LPC transfer function, a_k is the kth LPC coefficient. Now, BC speech is acquired and equivalent transfer function is generated by using LPC coefficients in the same manner as before. Here, the transfer function describes the effect that bone conduction implements over speech when it moves or conducts through the bone. The acquired BC signal is then passed through a filter having the transfer function inverse of the BC LPC coefficients generated transfer function. This would remove all the bone conduction parameters introduced into the BC speech and we would be left with only the glottal pulse i.e. the vibration pulses from vocal cords. The LPC order taken for air microphone signal is 80 and that for BC signal is 130 which are much greater than generally taken values for LPC orders. Such high values were required to have a clear view of all the formants and to check whether BC signal contained same formants as air microphone signals or not.

This glottal pulse is then again passed through a filter whose transfer function is same as AC LPC coefficients generated transfer function. This would introduce all those frequency components into glottal pulse which describes the characteristics of vocal tract. Such a processing makes BC signal much like AC signal and improves its quality. Figure 1 shows a block diagram describing the above stated steps. The method was first introduced by tat Vu [10] and is used here as standard of comparison with a new method introduced in next section.

3   MFCC Analysis

Mel Frequency Cepstrum Coefficients are profoundly used in almost every automatic speech recognition (ASR) system. Here, we present a BC speech signal enhancement approach by making use of the MFC coefficients.

MFCC stands for Mel Frequency Cepstrum Coefficients. Different steps are followed to generate the MFC coefficients of a particular speech signal. First, the actual speech signal is divided or chopped into different frame segments of duration less than 20 ms. This is done such that the speech signal becomes stationary or its statistical parameters remains constant over the frame duration. The second step is to window the framed sequences by using appropriate windowing function. This helps in preventing the spectral leakage which occurs because of abrupt change in signal due to chopping off operation. Next, the frequency response of each frame is generated, showing different frequency components present in every frame. The frequency response of the whole signal is then passed through a set of non-uniformly placed triangular filters with increasing bandwidth, or Mel-scale filter bank. Such a filter bank is placed over Mel frequency scale which is designed to match the perception of sound by the human brain. The outputs generated after passing through Mel-filter bank are summed corresponding to a particular filter band followed by logarithmic operation over the outputs to generate one coefficient at the output of every filter bank. The final step in MFCC generation includes Discrete Cosine Transform operation of the generated coefficients. The DCT helps in compression of data, as first few MFC coefficients can describe most of the energy of the speech signal and also in decorrelation between different frames of the speech signal.

The basic operation of DCT in MFCC is the multiplication of integral multiple half wave cosines with the output of Mel filter bank. This results in increase or decrease in value of different coefficients of Mel filter output, as shown in Fig. 2. Since these coefficients represent the strength of different frequency bands of the speech signal, this increase or decrease in value causes amplification and attenuation of different frequency bands. Hence, if after generation of MFCC these coefficients are selectively manipulated, change in the strength of different frequency bands may take place which can help in emphasizing desirable frequency bands and de-emphasizing of undesirable bands. Because of the structure of a cosine wave, only low frequency components can be improved by such an operation and not the middle part of frequency response which mostly contains useful

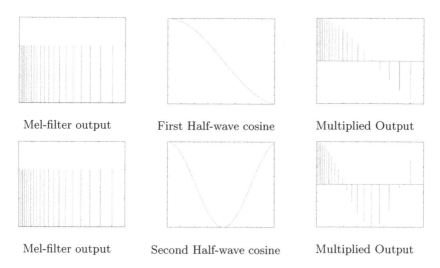

| Mel-filter output | First Half-wave cosine | Multiplied Output |

| Mel-filter output | Second Half-wave cosine | Multiplied Output |

Fig. 2. DCT operation in MFCC

frequencies as can be seen in Fig. 2. Therefore, if DCT can be replaced by Discrete Sine Transform (DST) same operation can be performed but over middle frequency ranges amplifying useful frequency components and removing high frequency parts which generally are responsible for infliction of noise in speech signal (Fig. 3). This approach may help in improving those frequency components of speech signal which gets attenuated while conduction through bone.

Regeneration of speech signal from MFCCs is done by using RASTAMAT voice box which operates over the principle described by Tychtl *et al.* [9]. Since, high frequency components of speech signals are generally attenuated by bone conduction, changing MFCCs by some empirical values must result in improvement of most of the BC speech signals.

4 Experiment

The dataset required for processing was taken from the analysis done by one of the researchers in [4] where a PVDF sensor placed over forehead was used to capture speech signal. PVDF film generates charges on its edges when mechanical force appears over it due to vibration on the forehead. The sensor was tied with belt under soft cushion to increase its sensitivity in a direction parallel to its length. A charge amplifier was used to convert the charges produced by the sensor into analog voltage, which was further converted to digital format by using an Analog to Digital Converter circuit. The sensitivity of charge amplifier as set to 500 pC/unit. Signal generated from PVDF sensor was collected through ADC circuit into LABVIEW environment. The same data from LABVIEW is fetched into MATLAB for further processing.

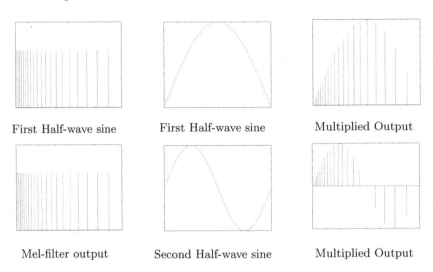

First Half-wave sine	First Half-wave sine	Multiplied Output
Mel-filter output	Second Half-wave sine	Multiplied Output

Fig. 3. DST operation in MFCC (Proposed)

Both Air Microphone and Bone Conducted speech signals of four subjects were taken from the database created by [4] and proposed processing schemes were applied. Air and Bone speech signals of 15 s duration were recorded simultaneously at a sampling rate of 16 kHz. Subjects were made to speak three vocals (Omm, Umm and Onn) and two of them spoke a sentence in the Hindi language. The reason of selecting different syllables is to obtain the affect of bone conduction over different frequencies of vibration for whole duration of speech.

5 Results

Table 1 shows the SNR values for actual BC signals. Tables 2 and 3 shows the SNR values for LPC and MFCC processed signals for different subjects and syllables. All values are in Decibel (dB) scale.

Figure 4 shows the spectrum curve generated by LPC coefficients of air microphone and bone conducted signal of OMM syllable spoken by subject 3. We can see from the figure that in the frequency range less than 1.5 kHz same formants are present in both air and bone conducted signal though these are much feeble in BC signal. Hence this proves that by using some processing scheme, speech information from BC signal can be extracted and can be improved in quality better than air microphone signal.

It is clear from tables above that the SNR values of signals after application of LPC processing scheme is much lower than actual BC signal SNR values. On the other hand, same signals enhanced by MFCC scheme shows significant improvement in SNR. Figure 5 shows the frequency response of actual BC signal. The frequency responses of signals generated by both processing techniques also show the results of processing (Figs. 6 and 7). In LPC processed signal, much

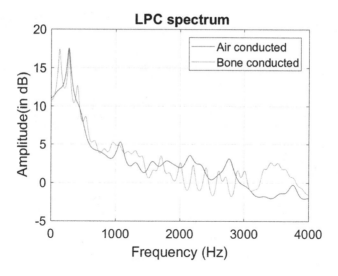

Fig. 4. Spectrum curves generated using LPC coefficients

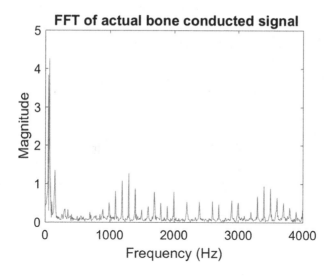

Fig. 5. Frequency response of actual BC signal (OMM spoken by subject 3)

high frequency components are present (mostly noise) whereas, in MFCC high frequency components are almost absent improving its SNR. Also, MFCC processed signal is quite attenuated in amplitude as compared to original BC signal. The improvement in intelligibility was found to be greater in LPC processing than in MFCC.

In spite of the reduction of external noises, MFCC processing does not improve the desired high frequency speech signals which get attenuated while

Table 1. SNR values of actual BC signals for different subjects (OMM spoken by subject 3)

Syllables	Subject 1	Subject 2	Subject 3	Subject 4	Avg.
OMM	16.36	5.29	13.71	15.49	12.71
ONN	18.34	5.84	1.32	15.29	10.195
UMM	17.83	9.55	10.25	13.19	12.71
Sentence	5.96	3.09	—	—	4.54

Table 2. SNR values of LPC processed signals for different subjects

Syllables	Subject 1	Subject 2	Subject 3	Subject 4	Avg.
OMM	4.84	5.68	9.87	15	8.84
ONN	11.51	10.89	13.55	7.05	10.75
UMM	7.68	9	12.05	13.07	10.45
Sentence	8.44	10.96	—	—	9.7

Table 3. SNR values of MFCC enhanced signals for different subjects

Syllables	Subject 1	Subject 2	Subject 3	Subject 4	Avg.
OMM	20.73	15.37	22.07	26.83	21.25
ONN	20.74	13.97	9.4	26.5	17.65
UMM	23.43	13.59	20.98	20.31	19.58
Sentence	19.04	16.97	—	—	18

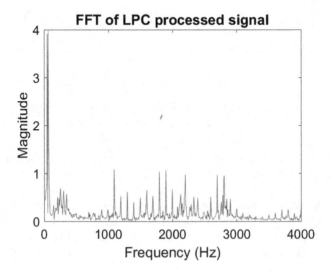

Fig. 6. Frequency response of LPC processed signal (OMM spoken by subject 3)

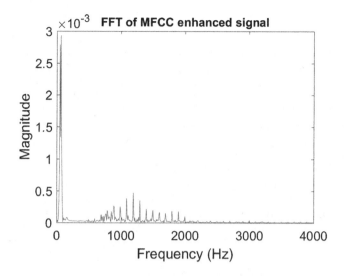

Fig. 7. Frequency response of MFCC enhanced signal (OMM spoken by subject 3)

conduction through bone. In LPC processing since glottal pulses are filtered with vocal tract parameters, it contains more high frequency components which makes the processed signal resemble much closer to original signal as compared to MFCC but this also increases high frequency noise component.

6   Conclusion

Two methods of processing were analysed in this paper to enhance the Bone Conducted speech signal quality, LPC and MFCC. Improvement in SNR was found in the signal which was processed by changing the MFC coefficients and regenerating signal using the manipulated coefficients but this lead to great reduction in the magnitude of the resultant signal. On the other hand, degradation in SNR of LPC processed signal was clear, rather slight improvement in intelligibility was observed accounting to filtering by vocal tract parameters, the magnitude is found to be attenuated though not very profoundly.

Other than small improvements, the high frequency components of the speech signal which gets attenuated while conduction through bone was not improved by any method. Hence the resultant signal lack the naturality of sound. Therefore, a much robust processing scheme needs to be developed which can enhance BC signal quality and without requiring characteristics of air microphone signal as input.

In future, more analysis would be done over the proposed methods by performing the experiments in noisy surroundings so that effect of ambient noise over processing techniques can be observed.

References

1. Hadei, S.A., et al.: A family of adaptive filter algorithms in noise cancellation for speech enhancement. Int. J. Comput. Electr. Eng. **2**(2), 307 (2010)
2. McBride, M., Tran, P., Letowski, T., Patrick, R.: The effect of bone conduction microphone locations on speech intelligibility and sound quality. Appl. Ergon. **42**(3), 495–502 (2011)
3. Munger, J.B., Thomson, S.L.: Frequency response of the skin on the head and neck during production of selected speech sounds. J. Acoust. Soc. Am. **124**(6), 4001–4012 (2008)
4. Prasad, R., Koike, T., Matsuno, F.: Speech signal captured by PVDF sensor. In: SICE Annual Conference, pp. 9–12. IEEE (2008)
5. Rahman, M.S., Shimamura, T.: Intelligibility enhancement of bone conducted speech by an analysis-synthesis method. In: 2011 IEEE 54th International Midwest Symposium on Circuits and Systems (MWSCAS), pp. 1–4. IEEE (2011)
6. Rahman, M.S., Shimamura, T.: A study on amplitude variation of bone conducted speech compared to air conducted speech. In: 2013 Asia-Pacific Signal and Information Processing Association Annual Summit and Conference (APSIPA), pp. 1–5. IEEE (2013)
7. Shimamura, T., Mamiya, J., Tamiya, T.: Improving bone-conducted speech quality via neural network. In: 2006 IEEE International Symposium on Signal Processing and Information Technology, pp. 628–632. IEEE (2006)
8. Shimamura, T., Tamiya, T.: A reconstruction filter for bone-conducted speech. In: 48th Midwest Symposium on Circuits and Systems, pp. 1847–1850. IEEE (2005)
9. Tychtl, Z., Psutka, J.: Speech production based on the mel-frequency cepstral coefficients. In: Sixth European Conference on Speech Communication and Technology (1999)
10. tat Vu, T., Unoki, M., Akagi, M.: A study on an LP-based model for restoring bone-conducted speech. In: First International Conference on Communications and Electronics, ICCE 2006, pp. 294–299. IEEE (2006)
11. tat Vu, T., Unoki, M., Akagi, M.: An LP-based blind model for restoring bone-conducted speech. In: Second International Conference on Communications and Electronics, ICCE 2008, pp. 212–217. IEEE (2008)
12. Won, S.Y., Berger, J.: Estimating transfer function from air to bone conduction using singing voice. In: ICMC (2005)

Modeling Human Cognitive Processes and Simulation

Measuring Conceptual Incongruity from Text-Based Annotations

Nisheeth Srivastava[(⊠)][iD]

Department of Computer Science, IIT Kanpur, Kanpur, India
nsrivast@cse.iitk.ac.in

Abstract. We propose a method for measuring the conceptual incongruity of a digital object using associated text meta-data. We show that this measure correlates well with empirical creativity ratings elicited from human subjects in laboratory settings. Extending our focus to online resources, we show that the predicted incongruity of a movie plot in the Movielens database is weakly correlated with users' ratings for the movie, but strongly correlated with variability in ratings. Movies with incongruous plots appear to elicit much more polarized responses. Further, in domains where cognitive theories suggest users are likely to be looking for incongruity, e.g. humor, we show, using the Youtube Comedy Slam Dataset, that user ratings for comedy pieces are considerably well-predicted by their incongruity score. These evaluations provide convergent evidence for the validity of our incongruity measurement, and immediately present several direct application possibilities. We present a case example of including incongruity as a recommender system metric to diversify the set of suggestions made in response to user queries in ways that align with users' natural curiosity.

Keywords: User modeling · Cognitive psychology · UI design

1 Introduction

Search engines, recommender systems and even the emerging Smart Devices paradigm all share the conceit that predictively anticipating users' preferences is a good thing. This assumption tends to bias such systems towards present only the most typical, relevant and/or popular suggestions in response to a query [7]. While this is a good thing when users are performing a simple lookup search, it is suboptimal in assisting exploratory search [15], which is increasingly a desideratum for contemporary information retrieval and decision support systems.

The state-of-the-art strategy to present non-obvious items, diversification, involves measuring item similarities, and reranking baseline suggestions to increase the representation of items dissimilar to the most relevant item [6], effectively simply adding noise to the existing ranking. The development of more principled ways of presenting non-obvious items requires a deeper view of user behavior than simply their revealed preferences. HCI research has benefited

© Springer Nature Switzerland AG 2018
U. S. Tiwary (Ed.): IHCI 2018, LNCS 11278, pp. 161–169, 2018.
https://doi.org/10.1007/978-3-030-04021-5_15

greatly from the psychology research of Piroll and Card, who demonstrated that humans search for information on the web could be explained in formal terms using a foraging metaphor - they concentrate their attention on items that potentially contain large amounts of useful information [9]. In this paper, we extend the information processing view of user behavior in online settings to present an alternative criterion for making user-item recommendations.

We adopt a 'Bayesian brain' view of peoples' information processing, best envisaged in terms of a hierarchy of control, where lower level controllers encode automatic, well-habituated patterns of behavior, and higher-level controllers determine which lower-level controllers to trust to perform well in a particular environmental condition [5]. The success of such a cognitive architecture is strongly dependent on the ability to detect shifts in environmental conditions quickly, the brain dividing its environment into controller-centric action *contexts*, where transitions from one context to the next may occur rapidly. Observations within a new context will appear surprising to a controller adapted to the old one, the temporally first few such data points will appear statistically *incongruous*. Thus, attending strongly to incongruous observations is a rational strategy for a Bayesian brain - they likely signal context changes.

In this paper, we use this insight - that humans likely believe incongruous items contain more information on average - in conjunction with the information foraging hypothesis [9] to study the role of incongruity in humans' evaluations of online content. We present a quantitative measurement of the conceptual incongruity of an item extracted from text-based annotations and validate it using human judgments. We then explore the effect of incongruity on users' ratings for digital content in general, and in contexts where they are likely looking for incongruous items and show that incongruity significantly affects the variance of ratings in the former and mean of ratings in the latter case. We conclude with a case-study based discussion of the possible applications of this measurement in information retrieval and decision support systems.

2   Measuring Incongruity

In essence, incongruity is characterized by the violation of context-generated expectations. For instance, the statement, 'I went to the store to buy candy' is normal, while 'I went to the store to buy a hippopotamus' is incongruous. However, the statement, 'I went to the zoo to see a hippopotamus', is entirely normal. Thus, the word 'hippopotamus' is incongruous specifically in the context of store purchases.

The major psychological assumption of our work is that this intuition about incongruity can be measured in the space of semantic word similarities. We reason that words that describe an established context are likely to co-occur frequently, e.g. {dine, food, restaurant}, thus forming clusters in word similarity space. Words that appear anomalously far away from such a cluster could be fairly assessed as violating expectations engendered by the cluster, e.g. try putting a hippo into the above cluster. Our computational goal, therefore, is to define a usable similarity space for meta-data, and then to define a way of measuring the number of violations therein.

2.1 Semantic Similarity

The first part of this task is straightforward. Semantic similarity is now a well-defined area of research in language processing [8]. Existing methods for measuring the similarity between two words include counting word co-occurrence frequencies, document hyperlinking frequencies, and measuring shortest paths between documents. Empirical evaluations show that most of these methods are approximately equivalent in performance, as measured by correlation with human similarity ratings of the same words (although some techniques that involve manual curation can outperform these entirely automated methods) [2].

Since the basic premise of our work is that word-cooccurrence predicts contextual relevance, it is natural for us to use word-cooccurrence based similarity judgments. Therefore, we used Normalized Google Distance [4]. Since Google does not permit free automated queries, we adapted the Wikipedia Search API in its stead, so that our similarity measure calculates relatedness using word (co)-occurrences across the English Wikipedia rather than the entire web, as the canonical NGD would. For any pair of words, we performed a wikipedia search, and used the number of results returned as inputs into the canonical NGD formula.

2.2 From Similarity to Incongruity

Computing Semantic Diversity. Diversity indicates the presence of some *context* in the data that is non-trivial to predict or put simply the presence of a loosely knit sense-cluster. Let S denote the similarity matrix for media object M_a. We use least absolute deviation (Eq. 1) to measure the diversity of S. The number of words varies from set to set; hence we further normalize it with the cardinality of the word set in each case.

$$D_a = min_j \left| \sum_{i=1}^{n} S(i,j) \right| \tag{1}$$

Computing Semantic Anomalousness. We deploy a simple anomaly detection algorithm. After creating the wiki distance matrix for all tags corresponding to an object, we first compute the sum of distances for each word from all the other words in a given set, by summing across rows. We then find words for whom this sum is three SD away from the median sum across all words in the tag set. Any such words are considered anomalous, and their count, divided by the total number of words in the tag set, gives us the corresponding incongruity score. The median and standard deviation of the distances between cluster members defines the length scale on which anomalousness is measured.

The cumulative divergence score d_i for the i_{th} word from all the other words in the set is given by Eq. 2. After obtaining the divergence scores; d_i for all the words, the problem reduces to finding the most deviant points from this set. We use a well-known non-parametric technique from the anomaly detection literature [3] - the inter-quartile measure, summarized in Eq. 3. $Q1$ denotes the first quartile, $Q3$ is the third quartile and IQR is the interquartile range and UB, LB denote the upper and lower bounds of the data respectively. Points lying outside the ranges specified by Eq. 3 are counted as anomalies.

$$d_i = \sum_{j=1}^{n} S(i,j) \tag{2}$$

$$LB = Q1 - 1.5 * IQR; UB = Q3 + 1.5 * IQR \tag{3}$$

Finally, we normalize the anomaly score of a set by its cardinality. If n_1 and n_2 denote the number of points (words) outside the LB and UB respectively, and n be the total number of words, then the anomalousness score will be computed as $(n1 + n2)/n$.

Measuring Semantic Incongruity. We attribute incongruity to the joint presence of diversity and anomalousness. In order to quantify the simultaneous presence of these two factors, we combine their individual scores using the Borda positional rank aggregation technique [13]. The use of rank aggregation instead of algebraic combination is preferred since it allows us to avoid concerns about parameterization and scaling affecting our analysis in any way. Given a set of ranked lists, $L = \{l_1, l_2, .., l_n\}$, the Borda method assigns a score $Score_i(k)$ to each candidate in l_i which is simply the number of candidates ranked below it in that list. The final score of every element is simply the sum of all the scores generated across the entire set of ranked lists. The scores are then sorted in decreasing order to find the highest ranking ones. For example, an object that is the 2nd most diverse (8 elements below it) and the 6th (4 elements below it) most anomalous out of 10 categories would have an incongruity score of $8 + 4 = 12$.

3   Experiments

Our strategy for empirical evaluation was to first validate our measure of conceptual incongruity against psychological assessments of related concepts. To this end, we first show how our wikipedia based semantic similarity construct corresponds well with both NGD values and with human similarity judgments elicited in the standard similarity judgment study. Absent psychological data about the incongruity of concept sets, we compare our algorithmic metric of incongruity against an existing dataset of creativity ratings assigned to concept sets by human raters [10] and show reasonable correlation just as well. We then investigate how this now psychologically validated measure of incongruity correlates with user ratings of movies and videos, and show interesting results.

3.1   Incongruity Predicts Arousal, Not Valence

We empirically tested whether the incongruity of a media object (say a video, a blog post, a movie etc.) affects reported user engagement and/or satisfaction. We used the latest full Movielens dataset, containing both ratings and personal tags for a large number of movies. Since this dataset is not yet version controlled, we have made the version we used available, along with the code used to process it[1]. Also, since every similarity computation required a call to the Wikipedia API, and we did not want to abuse this free resource, we restricted our dataset to up to the first 20 movies rated and tagged by the 8676 unique users we identified in this dataset. This truncation still gave us access to ∼73000 ratings and tag sets across 12753 movies, which is sufficient for us to draw statistically informed conclusions for our analysis.

Again, giving deference to Wikipedia's community standards, we restricted the number of queries by using only up to the first 10 tags assigned by each user to each movie. Since these tags were assigned by individual users in one go, it is reasonable to assume that there would be diminishing returns in informativeness of later tags. So, cutting off after the first N tags is rational.

For each of these users, we computed individualized per-movie tagset similarity matrices. Given each similarity matrix, we computed the corresponding incongruity measure. Using Wikipedia instead of Google as our semantic corpus, in combination with the usual noise seen in user-generated tags (misspellings, idiosyncratic term use etc.), caused significant loss of coverage. However, we were able to retrieve incongruity scores for 68% of our queries, leaving us with a final dataset of ∼50000 rating-incongruity pairs across users and movies.

We find that normalized movie rating has a weak positive correlation with incongruity 0.07, statistically significant at $p \ll 0.001$ due to the overwhelming amount of data we used, but with a vanishingly small effect size. More interestingly, the variability of the normalized rating appears to increase strongly as a function of incongruity, as is visually evident in Fig. 1. It is also statistically evident: for ratings corresponding to non-zero incongruity scores, the residual from the best fit linear model is itself best fit by a line with a positive slope 0.72 ± 0.05 with the error term reflecting a bootstrapped 95% CI.

These results jointly present compelling evidence that our incongruity measure is in fact psychologically salient, but in a subtle way, one that supports recent 2-dimensional models of emotion classification which suggest that peoples' emotions can be represented using two general dimensions of evaluation - valence and arousal [12]. Incongruity does not seem to affect users' valence, or liking, for a movie very much but strongly influences their level of arousal, thereby amplifying their reported valence. An incongruous movie that a user likes receives a higher rating than a non-incongruous movie with similar valence.

---

[1] https://www.dropbox.com/sh/9t23yh96jm9zp4s/AACdtMtAE9gLV89GylODoq7ja?dl=0.

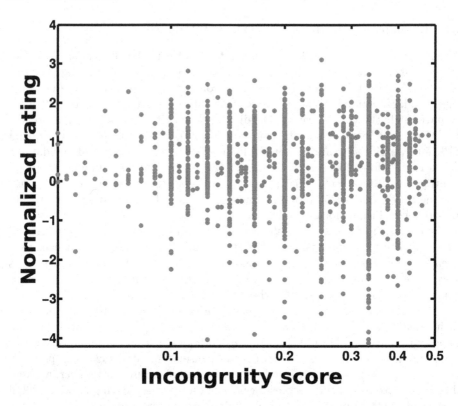

Fig. 1. This figure shows the relationship between our measure of conceptual incongruity computed using individual users' tags for a movie, and their corresponding rating of that movie. The incongruity score is shown on a log plot for clarity. Ratings were normalized across each users' overall rating pool, including movies only rated, not tagged.

3.2 Incongruity Predicts Valence in Comedy

The previous analysis suggests that incongruity affects users' arousal levels, but not choice valence, we expect this to be true for the vast majority of cases wherein users are not looking to be aroused, but are looking for high valence objects. In the special case where they are, however, the valence and arousal dimensions become correlated, and our account would predict some degree of correlation between measures of user satisfaction and incongruity.

But is it possible to characterize settings in which users are unambiguously looking to be aroused? One such possible setting could be the search for humor. Humor, as an emotion, is recognized to be linked to finding and resolving incongruities [11]. Therefore, if incongruity is positively correlated with ratings in any domain, it should be so in comedy video ratings.

To test this hypothesis, we used the binary preference data in the Youtube Comedy Slam Dataset [14]. This dataset contains responses to multiple users' responses to which of two presented videos are funnier. We restricted our analysis to the $\sim$2500 unique videos in the dataset that had more than 100 ratings. For each unique video, we tallied up the number of positive (p) and negative (n) votes, and calculated the population's preference expressed as the difference between the two counts divided by the total, i.e. $\frac{p-n}{p+n}$.

Unlike in the Movielens data, where we had personalized tags available, for this analysis, we directly scraped the corresponding videos tags. Since youtube tags are provided by the content providers, they are heavily search-engine optimized. For comedy videos, such optimization generally involves tags directly asserting that the video is funny. As a crude filter for such noise, we eliminated from consideration all videos that contained more than 6 instances of any of the following words {'funny', 'lol', 'prank', 'laugh'}. This procedure reduced our dataset considerably, leaving us with $\sim$1200 usably tagged videos.

For the remaining videos, we calculated the correlation between incongruity and the population-level preference. This turns out to be moderately positive (0.31), statistically significant at $p < 0.01$. This suggests that, in addition to generally predicting variability in ratings, there will be some specific domains within media browsing wherein people might actively seek incongruity, in which cases it will become a useful direct predictor of satisfaction. While characterizing such domains explicitly is a difficult question, in practice, it is simple to permit users to determine how much incongruity they want to add to their basic RS engine. Such a UI fix would also calibrate the optimal amount of incongruity desired, which will vary across users, time and browsing contexts.

Finally, we compared the correlations obtained using our incongruity measure with those obtained by a baseline measure of word set diversity, viz. the mean standard deviation of distance from all words. We find, expectedly, that this measure does not yield a non-zero slope for the residual of the best fit linear model of diversity vs movielens data (slope $= -0.03 \pm 0.06$), or with preference-derived ratings for the comedy data ($\rho = 0.006$, $p = 0.67$), verifying to some extent the specificity of our measure.

4   Conclusion

We report a method for quantitatively measuring the *incongruity* of an individual object given its text-based annotations. We have performed a series of corpus-based experiments exploring how the measured incongruity of movies and comic videos, respectively, influence users' perceptions. We found that, in general, greater incongruity appears to make user ratings for items more variable, whereas in domains where users are expected to be seeking out incongruity, i.e. in humor, incongruity is also substantially correlated with average user ratings. These insights can immediately guide the design of human-facing information retrieval and decision support systems in interesting ways. We have presented one such example - a search engine built around our incongruity-seeking algorithm that returns creative associations in response to user queries.

Some previous research has also investigated the value of providing 'unexpected' recommendations [1] in the context of recommender systems. However, these methods measure unexpectedness as item dissimilarity from items a baseline model would predict. In contrast, we measure conceptual incongruity *within* an item using meta-data, such that every item has a corresponding incongruity measurement independent of other items in the list of predicted items.

While the empirical correlations we report are not remarkably strong, it is important to note that our experiments were conducted using the most convenient semantic similarity measure at hand, and user-generated tags. Using a better, though more effort-intensive, semantic similarity measure, e.g. ESA and a more intensively curated tag set, could result in significant improvements above our proof-of-concept baseline. Future work could also assess the validity of using automatically generated keywords instead of user-provided meta-data, which would further generalize the applicability of this approach, so that it can be tested on more datasets to further evaluate its validity.

References

1. Adamopoulos, P., Tuzhilin, A.: On unexpectedness in recommender systems: or how to better expect the unexpected. ACM Trans. Intell. Syst. Technol. (TIST) **5**(4), 54 (2014)
2. Bollegala, D., Matsuo, Y., Ishizuka, M.: Measuring semantic similarity between words using web search engines. WWW **7**, 757–766 (2007)
3. Chandola, V., Banerjee, A., Kumar, V.: Anomaly detection: a survey. ACM Comput. Surv. (CSUR) **41**(3), 15 (2009)
4. Cilibrasi, R.L., Vitanyi, P.M.: The google similarity distance. IEEE Trans. Knowl. Data Eng. **19**(3), 370–383 (2007)
5. Clark, A.: Whatever next? predictive brains, situated agents, and the future of cognitive science. Behav. Brain Sci. **36**(3), 181–204 (2013)
6. Herlocker, J.L., Konstan, J.A., Terveen, L.G., Riedl, J.T.: Evaluating collaborative filtering recommender systems. ACM Trans. Inf. Syst. (TOIS) **22**(1), 5–53 (2004)
7. Lops, P., de Gemmis, M., Semeraro, G.: Content-based recommender systems: state of the art and trends. In: Ricci, F., Rokach, L., Shapira, B., Kantor, P.B. (eds.) Recommender Systems Handbook, pp. 73–105. Springer, Boston (2011). https://doi.org/10.1007/978-0-387-85820-3_3
8. Meng, L., Huang, R., Gu, J.: A review of semantic similarity measures in wordnet. Int. J. Hybrid Inf. Technol. **6**(1), 1–12 (2013)
9. Pirolli, P., Card, S.: Information foraging in information access environments. In: Proceedings of the SIGCHI Conference on Human factors in Computing Systems, pp. 51–58. ACM Press/Addison-Wesley Publishing Co. (1995)
10. Ranjan, A., Srinivasan, N.: Dissimilarity in creative categorization. J. Creat. Behav. **44**(2), 71–83 (2010)
11. Ritchie, G.: Current directions in computational humour. Artif. Intell. Rev. **16**(2), 119–135 (2001)
12. Russell, J.A.: Core affect and the psychological construction of emotion. Psychol. Rev. **110**(1), 145 (2003)
13. Schalekamp, F., Zuylen, A.v.: Rank aggregation: together we're strong. In: 2009 Proceedings of the Eleventh Workshop on Algorithm Engineering and Experiments (ALENEX), pp. 38–51. SIAM (2009)

14. Shetty, S.: Quantifying Comedy on Youtube: Why the Number of o's in Your LOL Matter (2012)
15. Toms, E.G.: Serendipitous information retrieval. In: DELOS Workshop: Information Seeking, Searching and Querying in Digital Libraries. Zurich (2000)

Interactive Landslide Simulator: Role of Contextual Feedback in Learning Against Landslide Risks

Pratik Chaturvedi[1,2($\boxtimes$)] and Varun Dutt[1]

[1] Applied Cognitive Science Lab, Indian Institute of Technology Mandi,
Kamand, India
prateek@dtrl.drdo.in, varun@iitmandi.ac.in
[2] Defence Terrain Research Laboratory,
Defence Research and Development Organisation, New Delhi, India

Abstract. Landslides cause extensive damages to property and life and there is an urgent need to increase community awareness against landslide risks. Interactive simulations help to provide people with experience of landslide disasters and increase community awareness. However, it would be interesting to evaluate the influence of contextual feedback via messages and images in people's decision- making in these simulations. The main objective of this paper was to evaluate the role of contextual feedback in an interactive landslide simulator (ILS) tool. ILS considers both human and environmental factors to influence landslide risks. Fifty participants randomly participated across two between-subject conditions in the experiment: feedback-rich (messages and images present) and feedback-poor (numeric feedback only; messages and images absent). Participants made repeated monetary decisions against land- slides in ILS. Investments were greater in the feedback-rich condition compared to feedback-poor condition. We highlight the implications of our results for awareness against landslide risks.

Keywords: Landslide risks · Human factors · Interactive simulation
Contextual feedback · Awareness

1 Introduction

Catastrophic and disastrous effects of landslides cause extensive damage to life, property, and public-utility services [1]. Landslides and associated debris flows are a major concern for disaster-prevention groups in regions with steep terrain, especially in Himalayan mountains [2–4]. Several physical factors like ground slope, soil depth, and rainfall may precipitate landslides. Besides these physical causes of the landslide, land development and other man-made activities also aggravate landslide disasters [2–5]. The consequences of extreme natural events like landslides are a combination of both physical factors as well as the actions taken by people before landslides occur (human factors). Indeed, Eiser et al. [6] state that risks in the context of natural hazards always involve interactions between natural (physical) and human (behavioral) factors. Eiser et al. [6] also point to a lack of research dealing with the combination of physical and

© Springer Nature Switzerland AG 2018
U. S. Tiwary (Ed.): IHCI 2018, LNCS 11278, pp. 170–179, 2018.
https://doi.org/10.1007/978-3-030-04021-5_16

behavioral aspects of such natural events and their consequences. The primary objective of this paper is to investigate the role of human decisions in influencing landslide risks in the presence of different types of contextual feedback about landslide consequences. We investigate this objective using simulation tools.

Prior research has proposed numerous empirical and process-based models for predicting landslides and associated risks [7–9]. One could use some of these models for the development of simulation tools [10, 11] that could then help people gain awareness and understanding of landslide risks. Simulation tools are computer-based interactive software that could help simulate the landslide system dynamics and let people explore the consequences of their actions against landslide risks. Simulation tools provide practical ways of experiencing landslide disasters in a controlled environment, where participants could get feedback about causes and consequences of their decisions [12, 13]. Thus, with simulation tools, it is possible to study complex interactions between variables and their effects on behavior and outcomes [14–16]. In this paper, we highlight the use of an interactive landslide model as well as an interactive landslide simulator (ILS) tool in educating the general public about landslide risks. Specifically, we provide contextual feedback involving messages and imagery in ILS and evaluate their effects on investments made against landslides. We believe contextual feedback will likely cause people to increase the activation of relevant actions in their memory [17]. This feedback also likely enables people to develop a deeper causal understanding about landslide disasters and their consequences. The central hypothesis under test is whether monetary contributions against landslide risks (which is an indicator of improved understanding) are larger when contextual feedback about financial losses is richer.

2 Background

Research shows that informative feedback delivered via simulations tools helps people understand the underlying system [17, 19, 20, 24]. For example, a game named Power House was designed to increase players' interest in energy-related issues and improve their knowledge on energy-consuming activities in the home [25].

According to Bang et al. [25], within the game environment, users can safely explore cause-and effect relations and uncover new behaviors. For example, Dutt and Gonzalez [19, 21–23] developed a Dynamic Climate Change Simulator (DCCS) tool to help participants understand basic characteristics of the climate system. The DCCS provided feedback about emissions and absorption decisions and helped reduce people's misconceptions about Earth's climate. Thus, DCCS-like tools can improve the understanding of the interplay between physical and behavioral factors in coping with risks.

In a study conducted by Lim et al. [30], negative feedback was provided using non-vivid textual messages. The textual messages induced a higher level of subsequent task performance compared to vivid (multimedia) messages. Similarly, in this paper, our aim is to understand how context-rich feedback about landslide losses helps or hurts participants' investment against landslides.

As experience and recency of events in simulation tools influences people's awareness and perception [17, 19], we expect that contextual feedback concerning numbers, messages, and imagery in a landslide simulation tool will help people increase their understanding of landslide risks. This expectation is also because of the emotional response to presented stimuli, which is likely to influence people's risk perception and decision-making against landslides.

3   Interactive Landslide Simulator (ILS) Tool

The ILS tool is an interactive dynamic system for studying people's decisions against landslide risks [2, 3]. Details about the ILS tool were already discussed by [2, 3], and here we briefly cover the tool's working. Figure 1 shows the investment screen of ILS tool, where people need to invest some part of their daily income against landslide risks. Investment against landslides could be used to mitigate its risk by building retaining wall, planting long-root plants, or building boulder catching nets.

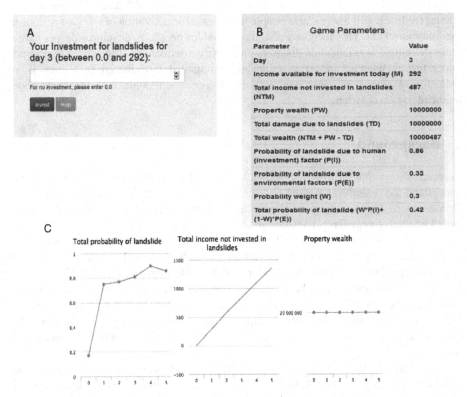

Fig. 1. The different components on the investment screen of ILS tool. (A): The text box giving choice for daily investments to reduce landslide risk. (B): Game parameters window showing values of parameters used in ILS model. (C): Dynamic plots of changing outcomes with every decision.

Feedback is shown to participants in three ways (Fig. 2A): monetary information about total wealth, text messages about different losses, and imagery corresponding to losses. There is a decrease in the daily income whenever injury and fatality due to landslides takes place. While damage to property causes a loss of property wealth. If there is non-occurrence of landslide in a certain trial, a positive feedback is presented to participant (Fig. 2B).

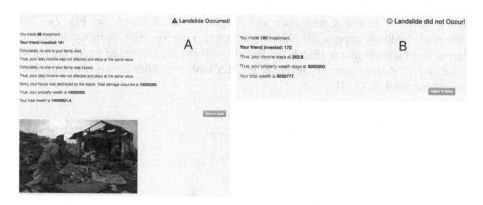

Fig. 2. Contextual feedback screen in the ILS tool showing monetary losses, messages, and associated imagery. (A) Negative feedback when a landslide occurred. (B) Positive feedback in case of non-occurrence of landslide.

In ILS, landslide risks were generated using the probability equation from Hasson's [31] study. The likelihood of landslides due to physical factors is calculated considering the combination of the effects of rainfall, slope, and soil properties. It is based on the method proposed by Matthew et al. [32]. The slope and soil characteristics are expressed as P(S), which represent the local probability of landslides, given the geological features of the location. The determination of spatial probability of landslides, P(S) is done from Landslide Susceptibility Zonation (LSZ) map of the area [33, 34]. Table 1 provides a Total Estimated Hazard (THED) based on the Landslide Hazard Map sectioning [33, 34].

Table 1. Total Estimated Hazard (THED)

Hazard zone	Range of THED	Description of zone
I	THED < 3.5	Very low hazard (VLH) zone
II	$3.5 \leq$ THED < 5.0	Low hazard (LH) zone
III	$5.0 \leq$ THED ≤ 6.5	Moderate hazard (MH) zone
IV	6.5 < THED ≤ 8.0	High Hazard (HH) zone
V	THED > 8.0	Very high hazard (VHH) zone

From this table, the spatial probability can be calculated by dividing the THED by the corrected Landslide Hazard Evaluation Factor (LHEF), which considers individual and net effect of landslide causal factors. The environmental probability of a landslide event is the product of the two probabilities, $P(S)$ and $P(R)$. Calculation of $P(R)$ is based on rainfall data collected from the NASA's TRMM project, between January 1, 2004, and April 30, 2013 (see Fig. 3); whereas, location data is derived from the Landslide Susceptibility Zonation (LSZ) map of the area [33, 34]. Once participants make investment decisions against landslide risks, they are provided contextual feedback in terms of numbers, messages, and imagery in the ILS tool (see Fig. 2). This contextual feedback represents different damages ranging from property losses to injuries and fatalities due to landslides. Data from Parkash [35] served us for the initial calculation of damage severity levels in the ILS tool. For other details about the ILS tool, please refer to [2, 3].

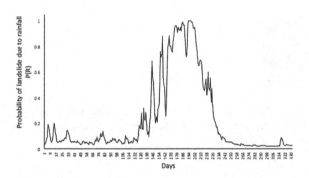

Fig. 3. Graph of probability of landslide due to rainfall over days

4 Experiment Involving Different Amounts of Feedback in the ILS Tool

The ILS tool not only considers environmental factors (spatial geology and rainfall); but, it also considers the human factors (people's investments against landslides) for calculating landslide risks. In this paper, we present results of an experiment in which human participants interacted with the ILS tool in two different damage information-feedback conditions. We expected participants' investments against landslides to be higher when the feedback was contextual in nature.

Experimental Design
Fifty participants from diverse fields of study participated across two feedback conditions (between-subjects): feedback-rich (N = 25) and feedback-poor (N = 25). Both conditions were 30-trials long and all participants were recruited from Mandi, India and adjoining areas. Before the experiments, the participants were asked about their knowledge about landslide risk. In response to this question, out of a total of 50 participants, 30 cited basic understanding, 14 cited little understanding, 5 responded as knowledgeable, and 1 did not have any idea about landslides. In feedback-rich

condition, participants were provided contextual feedback about landslide damages in terms of numeric values, text messages and images on the feedback screen (Fig. 2A). In feedback-poor condition, contextual feedback about messages, and images was absent and landslide damages were only shown via numeric values. Data were analyzed for all participants in terms of their investment ratio in both the feedback conditions. The investment ratio was defined as the ratio of total investments made by participants up to a trial divided by the total investments that could have been made up to the trial. Given the effectiveness of feedback in simulation tools [17–20, 23, 24, 26, 27, 30], we expected participant investments to be greater in the feedback-rich condition compared to the feedback-poor condition.

Participants

All participants were from Science, Technology, Engineering, and Mathematics (STEM) backgrounds and their ages ranged in between 21 and 28 years (Mean = 22 years; Standard Deviation = 2.19 years). The sample was representative of Mandi area's population because the literacy rate is quite high (81.5%) in Mandi town and surrounding areas [36]. Participants were given INR 30 as compensation for performing in the experiment. In addition, money left-over in ILS tool after 30-rounds was converted to real money and paid a performance incentive to participants (in no case, participants won more than INR 20 as performance incentive).

Procedure

Participants were invited to a landslide awareness study via a flyer advertisement in Mandi, India. Participants signed a consent form and participation was entirely voluntary. Participants were provided with instructions about the study before starting in the ILS tool and questions were answered.

5 Results

We performed a repeated-measures mixed-factorial ANOVA with contextual feedback as a between-subjects factor and investment-ratio over a 30-day period as a within-subjects factor. As per our expectation, the average investment ratio was significantly higher in the feedback-rich condition (0.48) compared to that in the feedback-poor condition (0.36) (F (1, 48) = 3.85, $p < 0.05$, $\eta^2 = 0.07$) (see Fig. 4A).

Furthermore, the trend of investment ratio in both feedback-rich and feedback-poor conditions over 30-trials was similar (F (29, 1392) = 133, $p = 0.11$, $\eta^2 = 0.03$; see Fig. 4B). Overall, the results suggest that contextual damage feedback of both kinds helped participants to increase their investments for landslide mitigation.

In the current experiment design, investing one's full income against landslides (invest-all) was the optimal strategy and use of this strategy by the participants indicated learning in the ILS tool. The proportion of participants making use of the full-invest strategy is shown in Fig. 4C. As seen in Fig. 4C, a greater proportion of participants learnt to use the invest-all strategy in feedback-rich condition compared to feedback-poor condition.

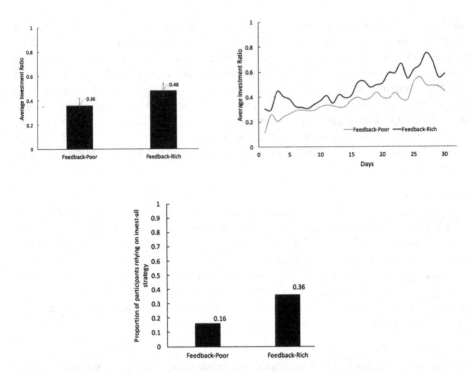

Fig. 4. Results of the experiment. **A.** Average investment ratio in feedback-rich and feedback-poor conditions. The error bars show 95% CI around the point estimate. **B.** Average investment ratio in feedback-rich and feedback-poor conditions across 30-trials. **C.** Proportion of participants relying on the full-investment strategy in feedback-poor and feedback-rich conditions.

6 Discussion and Conclusions

Recent research had proposed the use of an Interactive Landslide Simulator (ILS) tool to help people improve their understanding and awareness of landslide risks [2, 3]. The ILS tool not only considers environmental factors (spatial geology and rainfall); but, it also considers human factors (people's investments against landslides) [2, 3]. In this paper, we used the ILS tool to test the influence of differing amounts of contextual feedback. Results showed that high contextual feedback enabled people to increase their investments against landslides compared to low contextual feedback.

One likely reason for our results is due to the increase in activation of experiences in memory when people encounter richer contextual information [11, 30]. When people encounter richer contextual information, the extra information in feedback due to messages and imagery likely helps people create experiences with a rich set of attributes. These attributes likely enable participants to retrieve these experiences with ease from memory while making investment decisions. Another likely reason for our results is due to people's reliance on affect-based feedback [28, 29]. Due to the contextual messages and imagery, people likely get into different affectual states [29]. These states help them make improved decisions against landslide risks.

Our paper has several implications for the real world. First, as contextual feedback helped participants improve their contribution against landslide risks in ILS, it would be worthwhile to use contextual feedback in simulation tools to enable people to develop awareness and understanding of the underlying dynamics governing landslides. Specifically, K-12 education could benefit by introducing ILS-like tools in schools, where people are provided contextual feedback in such tools. Besides, ILS-like tools are also likely helpful to policymakers as contextual feedback would probably help these policymakers understand the cost of different consequences against landslide disasters.

Building upon this study, we plan to conduct several experiments using ILS in the near future. As part of our future research, we plan to investigate how people decide against landslide risks due to different system's response to human actions, feedback about damages, social norms governing the problem, and social dilemmas. This innovative and comprehensive approach, where we look at both individual and community levels of decision-making, could help us provide with a better understanding of the dynamics of the relevant decision processes concerning landslide risks. In the current work, invest-all was the optimal strategy; however, as part of future research, it would be worthwhile investigating how people's decision-making evolves in conditions where investments unlikely influence the landslide probability. In this paper, the experimental design involved a single region of study. In our future work, we plan to conduct experiments involving ILS with people from different regions for overcoming this limitation. We also plan to perform computational modeling of our experimental results using different cognitive algorithms. This modeling will allow us to understand the cognitive processes involved making decisions in ILS.

Acknowledgement. We thank Akshit Arora for developing the website for ILS. We thank students of IIT Mandi who have helped in collection of data in this project.

References

1. Margottini, C., Canuti, P., Sassa, K.: Landslide science and practice. In: Proceedings of the Second World Landslide Forum, Rome, Italy, vol. 2 (2011)
2. Chaturvedi, P., Arora, A., Dutt, V.: Learning in an interactive simulation tool against landslide risks: the role of amount and availability of experiential feedback. Nat. Hazards Earth Syst. Sci. Discuss. (2017, in review). https://doi.org/10.5194/nhess-2017-297
3. Chaturvedi, P., Arora, A., Dutt, V.: Interactive landslide simulator: a tool for landslide risk assessment and communication. In: Duffy, V. (ed.) Advances in Applied Digital Human Modeling and Simulation. AISC, vol. 481, pp. 231–243. Springer, Cham (2017). https://doi.org/10.1007/978-3-319-41627-4_21
4. Chaturvedi, P., et al.: Remote sensing based regional landslide risk assessment. Int. J. Emerg. Trends Electr. Electron. (IJETEE) **10**(10) (2014). ISSN 2320-9569
5. Chaturvedi, P., Dutt, V.: Evaluating the public perceptions of landslide risks in the Himalayan Mandi Town. In: Proceedings of the 2015 Human Factor & Ergonomics Society (HFES) Annual Meeting, L.A (2015)
6. Eiser, J.R., et al.: Risk interpretation and action: a conceptual framework for responses to natural hazards. Int. J. Disaster Risk Reduct. **1**, 5–16 (2012)

7. Rogers, D., Tsirkunov, V.: Implementing hazard early warning systems. Report, Global Facility for Disaster Reduction and Recovery (2011)
8. Dai, F.C., Lee, C.F., Ngai, Y.Y.: Landslide risk assessment and management: an overview. Eng. Geol. **64**(1), 65–87 (2002)
9. Montrasio, L., Valentino, R., Losi, G.L.: Towards a real-time susceptibility assessment of rainfall-induced shallow landslides on a regional scale. Nat. Hazards Earth Syst. Sci. **11**(7), 1927–1947 (2011)
10. Meissen, U., Voisard, A.: Increasing the effectiveness of early warning via context-aware alerting. In: Proceedings of the 5th International Conference, on Information Systems for Crisis Response and Management (ISCRAM), pp. 431–440 (2008)
11. Sterman, J.D.: Learning in and about complex systems. Syst. Dyn. Rev. **10**(2), 291–330 (1994)
12. Schon, D.A.: The Reflective Practitioner: How Professionals Think in Action. Basic Books, New York (1983)
13. Sterman, J.D.: Risk communication on climate: mental models and mass balance. Science **377**, 532–533 (2008)
14. Ben-Asher, N., Meyer, J., Parmet, Y., Möller, S., Englert, R.: Security and usability research using a microworld environment. In: Proceedings of MobileHCI 2009, Bonn, Germany (2009)
15. Möller, S., Ben-Asher, N., Engelbrecht, K.P., Englert, R., Meyer, J.: Modeling the behavior of users who are confronted with security mechanisms. Comput. Secur. **30**(4), 242–256 (2011)
16. Papert, S.: Mindstorms: Children, Computers, and Powerful Ideas. Basic Books, Inc., New York (1980)
17. Garson, G.: Computerized simulation in the social sciences. Simul. Gaming **40**(2), 267–279 (2009)
18. Dutt, V., Gonzalez, C.: The role of inertia in modeling decisions from experience with instance-based learning. Front. Psychol. **3**, 177 (2012)
19. Dutt, V., Gonzalez, C.: Decisions from experience reduce misconceptions about climate change. J. Environ. Psychol. **32**(1), 19–29 (2012). https://doi.org/10.1016/j.jenvp.2011.10.003
20. Dutt, V., Gonzalez, C.: Reducing the linear perception of nonlinearity: use of a physical representation. J. Behav. Decis. Mak. **26**, 51–67 (2013). https://doi.org/10.1002/bdm.759
21. Dutt, V., Gonzalez, C.: Responding linearly in nonlinear problems: application to earth's climate. In: Carpenter, M., Shelton, E.J. (eds.) Carbon Dioxide Emissions: New Research, pp. 15–30. Nova Science Publishers, Hauppauge (2013)
22. Gonzalez, C., Ben-Asher, N., Martin, J.M., Dutt, V.: A cognitive model of dynamic cooperation with varied interdependency information. Cogn. Sci. **39**(3), 457–495 (2015)
23. Meadows, D., Sweeney, L.B., Mehers, G.M.: The Climate Change Playbook. Chelsea Green Publishing, White River Junction (2016)
24. Wagner, K.: Mental models of flash floods and landslides. Risk Anal. **27**(3), 671–682 (2007)
25. Bang, M., Torstensson, C., Katzeff, C.: The PowerHhouse: a persuasive computer game designed to raise awareness of domestic energy consumption. In: IJsselsteijn, W.A., de Kort, Y.A.W., Midden, C., Eggen, B., van den Hoven, E. (eds.) PERSUASIVE 2006. LNCS, vol. 3962, pp. 123–132. Springer, Heidelberg (2006). https://doi.org/10.1007/11755494_18
26. Dutt, V., Gonzalez, C.: Why do we want to delay actions on climate change? Effects of probability and timing of climate consequences. J. Behav. Decis. Mak. **25**(2), 154–164 (2012)

27. Isenberg, P., Elmqvist, N., Scholtz, J., Cernea, D., Ma, K.-L., Hagen, H.: Collaborative visualization: definition, challenges, and research agenda. Inf. Vis. **10**(4), 310–326 (2011)
28. Knutti, R., Joos, F., Müller, S.A., Plattner, G.K., Stocker, T.F.: Probabilistic climate change projections for CO_2 stabilization profiles. Geophys. Res. Lett. **32**(20) (2005)
29. Fischer, C.: Feedback on household electricity consumption: a tool for saving energy? Energ. Effi. **1**(1), 79–104 (2008). https://doi.org/10.1007/s12053-008-9009-7
30. Lim, K.H., O'Connor, M.J., Remus, W.E.: The impact of presentation media on decision making: does multimedia improve the effectiveness of feedback? Inf. Manag. **42**(2), 305–316 (2005)
31. Hasson, R., Löfgren, Å., Visser, M.: Climate change in a public goods game: investment decision in mitigation versus adaptation. Ecol. Econ. **70**(2), 331–338 (2011)
32. Mathew, J., Babu, D.G., Kundu, S., Kumar, K.V., Pant, C.C.: Integrating intensity–duration-based rainfall threshold and antecedent rainfall-based probability estimate towards generating early warning for rainfall-induced landslides in parts of the Garhwal Himalaya, India. Landslides **11**(4), 575–588 (2014). https://doi.org/10.1007/s10346-013-0408-2
33. Anbalagan, R., Chakraborty, D., Kohali, A.: Landslide hazard zonation (LHZ) mapping on meso-scale for systematic town planning in mountainous terrain. J. Sci. Ind. Res. **67**, 486–497 (2008)
34. Clerici, A., Perego, S., Tellini, C., Vescovi, P.: A procedure for landslide susceptibility zonation by the conditional analysis method. Geomorphology **48**(4), 349–364 (2002)
35. Parkash, S.: Historical records of socio-economically significant landslides in India. J. South Asia Disaster Stud. **4**(2), 177–204 (2011)
36. Census2011.co.in: Mandi District Population Census 2011, Himachal Pradesh literacy sex ratio and density (2017). http://www.census2011.co.in/census/district/233-mandi.html. Accessed 19 Nov 2017

An Adaptive Cognitive Temporal-Causal Network Model of a Mindfulness Therapy Based on Music

S. Sahand Mohammadi Ziabari and Jan Treur[✉]

Behavioural Informatics Group, Vrije Universiteit Amsterdam,
Amsterdam, The Netherlands
sahandmohammadiziabari@gmail.com, j.treur@vu.nl

Abstract. In this paper the effect of a music therapy is modeled based on a Network-Oriented Modeling approach. Music therapy is a mindfulness therapy used since many years ago. The presented adaptive temporal-causal network model addresses music therapy for a person who in a first phase develops an extreme stressful emotion due to an ongoing stressful event. In a second phase, music therapy is considered to reduce the stress. This happens by playing memorable music first and then singing on that music. The music and the singing have a direct relaxing effect on the body. Hebbian learning is incorporated to increase the effect of the therapy.

Keywords: Cognitive temporal-causal network model · Hebbian learning Extreme emotion · Music therapy · Mindfulness

1 Introduction

Mindfulness therapies help on decreasing the level of an extreme emotion to make stressed-individual gets relaxed and became calm after some period of time after performing available therapies related to decrease the stress level [29]. Some of these therapies are currently approved to be work perfectly therapies like Music therapy and Autogenic training [30] which have started as a therapy many years ago and have been proved to have a good effect by decreasing the level of the emotion and some of them are still under investigation named Gene therapy which works with putting enzyme into the cells by using viruses as a vector. A variety of therapies working according to different mechanisms, is available, some of which have been analyzed by computational modeling; for example, see [30–33]. In [30] the two main goals in Autogenic training have been taken into account, focusing on warm and heavy limbs; the cognitive model shows how this therapy achieves reduction in the person's stress level, thereby using Hebbian learning. In [18] it is stated that music therapy uses musical interaction as a means of communication and expression. Due to the fact that lyrics demonstrate melodic verbal communication, there is an innate association between songs and relationship between different humans [2]. In [2] the elements of music therapy are stated as:

© Springer Nature Switzerland AG 2018
U. S. Tiwary (Ed.): IHCI 2018, LNCS 11278, pp. 180–193, 2018.
https://doi.org/10.1007/978-3-030-04021-5_17

'Elements of song experiences -cognitive stimulation, the building of relationships, singing, and listening- can provide frameworks for tension release, integration, and pleasure. (...)
Music therapy in the care of cancer patients and their families aims to promote comfort, develop meaningful communication, and resolve issues. The music therapist aims to soothe and energize, stimulate the expression of thoughts and feelings, help integrate families and persons into their social environments, provide sensory stimulation, and diminish pain.' [2], pp. 5–6.

Complicated Grief (CG) is a condition of ongoing firmly or obstinately in a course of action in spite of difficulty or opposition of symptoms of sorrow, which in the model introduced here is the image of a lost person considered in the mind of the person to remember the lost one for the sad music, with the thoughts of the lost person [24].

The paper is organized as follows. In Sect. 2 the neuropsychological principles of the effects of stress and the parts of the brain which deal with stress are addressed. In Sect. 3 the adaptive temporal-causal network model is introduced and illustrated by simulation of an example scenario. In Sect. 4 the simulation results of the model are discussed. Finally, Sect. 5 is a discussion.

2 Neuropsychological Principles

In [17] it was found out that music has an impact on Prefrontal cortex and also high tempo music (but not low-tempo music or low-level noise), has a considerable impact on learning and performing suppressing control. Also, in contrast to visual stimuli, they figured out that music itself has an impact on the cognitive functions: 'In contrast to images, high tempo music appeared as a salient cognitive factor that significantly attenuated learning to inhibit the inappropriate response.' In this section the neurological principles of music therapy in different areas of brains will be explained.

First the Amygdala is considered [1, 4, 10, 11] to perform an action while listening to the music. During listening to joyful music, the connectivity is increased between Nucleus Accumbens (NAcc), and between the mediodorsal thalamus and amygdala. The laterobasal amygdala which consists of the lateral, basolateral, basomedial, and paralaminar nuclei, is responsible for auditory and sensory perception and information. The amygdala is responsible for beginning, integrating, preserving and canceling emotions. In [12] results on music stimuli emotions are presented in a sense that music influences the performance of emotion processing in brain areas like Amygdala, Hippocampus, Orbitofrontal Cortex. As noted in [14] there are two types of regulation that need to be adjusted in mourning and grief: External adjustment, Internal Adjustment.

The External adjustment begins with singing of the individual who has lost somebody (deceased person) in her life and the difficulties that she has in her life without her. 'Participants sang imaginal songs with their deceased loved ones about their problems, especially if the deceased had been a person who provided deliberations and support in the individual's life. Individuals verbally acknowledged adjusting to the external world, such as sensing closer to surviving relatives since the death.' [14]. In the External adjustment individuals think about how they have improved their feeling as it has been explained in [14], p. 179.

'Data showed that all the participants reflected on their personal strength. For example, "I feel alive, actually. A sense of growth. Growing. I am stronger than I look'.

The remarkable aspect of hearing music is that it can adjust and incite perception and cognition [7]. In much literature [7, 20, 25] it has been noted that music, with using perceptual patterns, under-takes attentional networks and it was shown that music makes changes in EEG topography and coherence in alpha brain wave rhythms among frontal cortical networks. In [9] it was demonstrated that music can reduce stress and anxiety:

'music offers a comfortable, nonthreatening milieu which is an important aspect for the mood of the patient during therapy sessions.' [9], p. 11.

In [16] the emotional results have been stated as follows:

'Emotions give rise to affective experiences such as feelings of happiness, sadness, pleasure, and displeasure; activate widespread physiological adjustments to the evoking conditions; and lead to expressive behaviors that are often, but not always, goal directed and adaptive.' [16], p. 62.

There are many ways how music can stimulate emotions as brain stem responses, evaluative conditioning, emotional contagion, mental imagery, episodic memory and musical expectancy [8]. It has been stated that music has impacts in decreasing in sympathetic nervous control and eventually a reduction in heart rate and respiration rates, metabolism, oxygen consumption and muscle tension [13]. In [3] it has been stated that:

'Cerebral blood flow changes were measured in response to subject-selected music that elicited the highly pleasurable experience. As intensity of chills increased, cerebral blood flow increases and decreases were observed in brain regions thought to be involved in reward/motivation, emotion, and arousal, including ventral striatum, midbrain, amygdala, orbitofrontal cortex, and ventral medial prefrontal cortex.' [3], p. 11818.

In [6] it is mentioned;

'the Amygdala, hippocampus, fusiform gyrus, striatum, and thalamus are all implicated in emotional reactivity, whereas the OFC, vlPFC, dlPFC, and anterior insula are implicated in effortful regulation of emotion' [6], p. 2.

In [22] it has been shown that during music therapy, clients by using music experiences like free improvisation, singing, listening to, discussing and moving to achieve treatments goals that making better their affective behaviors and states. More on psychological and neuroscientific principles will be explained in Table 1.

3 The Adaptive Temporal-Causal Network Model

First the Network-Oriented Modelling approach used to model this process is briefly explained. As discussed in detail in [12, Chap. 2] this approach is based on temporal-causal network models which can be represented at two levels: by a conceptual representation and by a numerical representation. A conceptual representation of a temporal-causal network model in the first place involves representing in a declarative

Table 1. Explanation of the states in the model

X_1	ws_{ee}	World (body) state of extreme emotion ee	X_{17}	$ss_{singing1}$	Sensor state of sad singing (hearing)
X_2	ss_{ee}	Sensor state of extreme emotion ee	X_{18}	$ss_{singing2}$	Sensor state of happy singing (hearing)
X_3	ws_c	World state for context c	X_{19}	$srs_{singing1}$	Sensory representation of sad singing
X_4	ss_c	Sensor state for c (perceiving c)	X_{20}	$srs_{singing2}$	Sensory representation of happy singing
X_5	srs_{ee}	Sensory representation state of extreme emotion ee	X_{21}	srs_{m1}	Sensory representation of sad music
X_6	srs_c	Sensory representation state of context c	X_{22}	srs_{e1}	Sensory representation state of emotion of sad music
X_7	fs_{ee}	Feeling state for extreme emotion ee	X_{23}	srs_{m2}	Sensory representation of happy music
X_8	ps_{ee}	Preparation state for extreme emotion ee	X_{24}	srs_{e2}	Sensory representation state of emotion of sad music
X_9	es_{ee}	Execution state (bodily expression) of extreme emotion ee	X_{25}	bs_n	Negative belief
X_{10}	srs_b	Sensory representation of body state b	X_{26}	bs_p	Positive belief
X_{11}	$goal_b$	Goal (Relax b by music therapy)	X_{27}	ps_{sing1}	Preparation state for singing sad music
X_{12}	ps_b	Preparation state of body state b	X_{28}	ps_{sing2}	Preparation state for singing happy music
X_{13}	ws_{m1}	World state of playing sad music m_1	X_{29}	ps_{e1}	Preparation state for emotion of sad music
X_{14}	ws_{m2}	World state of playing happy music m_2	X_{30}	ps_{e2}	Preparation state for emotion of happy music
X_{15}	ss_{m1}	Sensor state of sad music (hearing)	X_{31}	$es_{singing1}$	Execution state of sad singing
X_{16}	ss_{m2}	Sensor state of happy music (hearing)	X_{32}	$es_{singing2}$	Execution state of happy singing

manner states and connections between them that represent (causal) impacts of states on each other, as assumed to hold for the application domain addressed. The states are assumed to have (activation) levels that vary over time. In reality, not all causal relations are equally strong, so some notion of *strength of a connection* is used. Furthermore, when more than one causal relation affects a state, some way to *aggregate multiple causal impacts* on a state is used. Moreover, a notion of *speed of change* of a state is used for timing of the processes. These three notions form the defining part of a conceptual representation of a temporal-causal network model:

- **Strength of a connection** $\omega_{X,Y}$. Each connection from a state X to a state Y has a *connection weight value* $\omega_{X,Y}$ representing the strength of the connection, often between 0 and 1, but sometimes also below 0 (negative effect) or above 1.
- **Combining multiple impacts on a state** $c_Y(..)$. For each state (a reference to) a *combination function* $c_Y(..)$ is chosen to combine the causal impacts of other states on state Y.
- **Speed of change of a state** η_Y. For each state Y a *speed factor* η_Y is used to represent how fast a state is changing upon causal impact.

Combination functions can have different forms, as there are many different approaches possible to address the issue of combining multiple impacts. Therefore, the Network-Oriented Modelling approach based on temporal-causal networks incorporates for each state, as a kind of label or parameter, a way to specify how multiple causal impacts on this state are aggregated by some combination function. For this aggregation a number of standard combination functions are available as options and a number of desirable properties of such combination functions have been identified; see [12, Chap. 2, Sects. 2.6 and 2.7]. In Fig. 1 the conceptual representation of the temporal-causal network model is depicted. A brief explanation of the states used is shown in Table 1, and their relation to domain literature is indicated in Table 2.

Next, the elements of the conceptual representation shown in Fig. 1 are explained in some more detail. The states ws_c, ws_{ee}, and ws_{m1}, ws_{m2} stand for world states for context c, body state of extreme emotion ee and world state of playing sad and happy music, respectively.

The states ss_c and ss_{ee} are the sensor states of the context c and of body state of extreme emotion ee. The states srs_c and srs_{ee} are the sensory representation states of the context c and the body state for the extreme emotion, respectively. The state srs_c is a trigger affecting the activation level of the preparation state ps_{ee} which is the preparation state for the extreme emotional response ee, and fs_{ee} shows the feeling state associated to this extreme emotion. The state es_{ee} represents the execution state of an extreme emotion (expression in body state). The states srs_b denotes sensory representation of the relaxed body state b. The state $goal_b$ shows the goal for the music therapy to raise body state b (relaxation). The state ps_b is the preparation state of body state b. The states $\left(ss_{singing1}, ss_{singing2}\right)$, $\left(srs_{m1}, srs_{m2}\right)$ are the sensor states of singing by the individual and sensor states of music itself for sad and happy music, respectively.

The sensory representation states $\left(srs_{m1}, srs_{m2}\right)$, $\left(srs_{singing1}, srs_{singing2}\right)$ are the sensory representation states of music and singing for sad and happy music, respectively. Two belief states bs_n and bs_p are considered here as part of (re)appraisal for the singing. The state bs_p denotes a positive belief and bs_n a negative belief. The preparation states ps_{sing1}, ps_{sing2} denote preparation states of singing of sad and happy music, respectively. The states $\left(es_{singing1}, es_{singing2}\right)$ denote the execution states of sadly and happily singing.

The connection weights ω_i shown in Fig. 1 are as follows. The sensor states ss_{ee}, ss_{cc} have connections entering from ws_{ee} and ws_c with weights ω_1, ω_2, respectively. The world state of an extreme emotion ws_{ee} has an arriving connection from es_{ee} as a body-loop with weight ω_{11}. The sensory representation state of an extreme emotion srs_{ee} has three arriving connections with weights ω_3, ω_8, ω_{14} from states called sensor

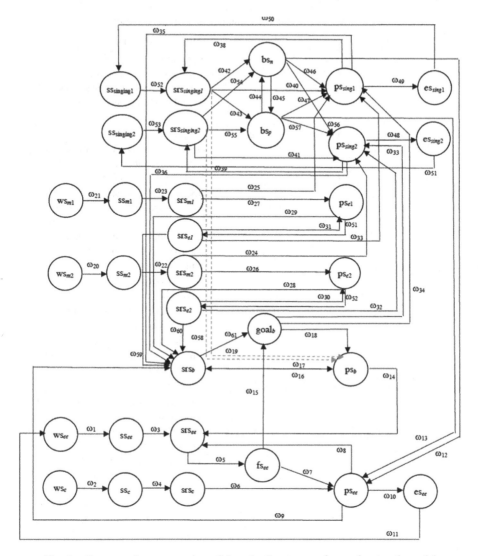

Fig. 1. Conceptual representation of the adaptive temporal-causal network model

state ss_{ee} of an extreme emotion, preparation state ps_{ee} of an extreme emotion, and preparation state ps_b of the relaxed body state b, respectively. The weight ω_5 is the incoming connection weight for the feeling state fs_{ee} from sensory representation state of an extreme emotion. The preparation state ps_{ee} of an extreme emotion has four entering connection weights ω_6, ω_7, ω_{12}, ω_{13} from states srs_c, fs_{ee}, negative belief (bs_n) and positive belief (bs_p), respectively. The incoming connection weight from ps_{ee} of the execution state es_{ee} of an extreme emotion is ω_{10}. The sensory representation state srs_b has six incoming connection weights from execution state of an extreme emotion ps_{ee} (suppression), preparation state of body state of the goal ps_b, preparation state of

Table 2. States and their relations to domain literature

States	Principles	Quotation, references
ws_{ee}	External stressor	External stress-inducing event [12]; 'Cortisol is a hormonal response to acute stress and has been measured to be higher before competition than at resting conditions.' [29], p. 71
ss_{ee}	Sensor state for perception of the stressor	'Emotions give rise to affective experiences such as feelings of happiness, sadness, pleasure, and displeasure; activate widespread physiological adjustments to the evoking conditions; and lead to expressive behaviors that are often, but not always, goal directed and adaptive.' [16], p. 62 'Human states can refer, for example, to states of body parts to see (Eyes), hear (ears) and fee (skin).' [5, 12] p. 52
srs_{ee}	Sensory and feeling representation of stressful event	'The dACC was activated during the observe condition. The dACC is associated with attention and the ability to accurately detect emotional signals.' [19], p. 18
$goal_{b1}$	Executive function and manage goal	'Appropriate use of song material promotes the achievement of therapeutic goals.' [2], p. 10
ss_{m1} ss_{m2}	Sensor state for perception of sad and happy music (hearing)	'Music therapy in the care of cancer patients and their families aims to promote comfort, develop meaningful communication, and resolve issues. The music therapist aims to soothe and energize, stimulate the expression of thoughts and feelings, help integrate families and persons into their social environments, provide sensory stimulation, and diminish pain.' [2], p. 6
$ss_{m1}ss_{m2}$	Sensory representation of sad & happy music	'Through songs, they can communicate their problems, their past or present unsatisfied needs or desires, their happiness, their loneliness.' [2], p. 9
ps_{e1} ps_{e2}	Preparation state of state of emotion of sad & happy music (Ventral striatum, ventral medial prefrontal cortex, Regional Cerebral blood flow (rCBF))	'Cerebral blood flow changes were measured in response to subject-selected music that elicited the highly pleasurable experience. As intensity of

(continued)

Table 2. (*continued*)

States	Principles	Quotation, references
		chills increased, cerebral blood flow increases and decreases were observed in brain regions thought to be involved in reward/motivation, **emotion**, and arousal, including ventral striatum, midbrain, amygdala, orbitofrontal cortex, and ventral medial prefrontal cortex.' [3], p. 11818
srs_{e1} srs_{e2}	Sensory representation of emotion of sad and happy music	'Music offers a comfortable, nonthreatening milieu which is an important aspect for the mood of the patient during therapy sessions.' [3], p. 11820
ps_{sing1} ps_{sing2}	Preparation state of singing	'The sound of the human voice provides intimate contact between the source and the listener, for the human voice is an individual's most intimate means of self-expression. The voice is the instrument through which a human communicates sounds and by which infants form the association between bodily contact and sound.' [2], p. 7 'The music therapist can use the verbal messages within the songs to promote enhanced exploration of inner thoughts and feelings.' [2], p. 6
es_{sing1} es_{sing2}	Execution state of singing (sad and happy)	'Songs are unique in that, by their nature, they need medium for the words to be expressed. This medium is most often the human voice'. [2], p. 7
ps_b	Preparation state for body states $b1$ and $b2$	'A complex mosaic of interconnected Frontal lobe areas that lie rostral to the Primary motor cortex also contributes importantly to motor functions. The medial premotor cortex, like the lateral area, mediates the selection of movements.' [23], p. 23
srs_b	Sensory representation and feeling of body states (Bilateral anterior temporal lobe)	'Bilateral anterior temporal lobe Task domain: emotion and affect. Core affect generation: engaging vicermotor control of the body to create core affective feelings of pleasure or displeasure with some degree of arousal' [21], p. 2112

singing ps_{sing1}, ps_{sing2} (sad and happy), sensory representation state of emotion of sad and happy music srs_{e1}, srs_{e2} (The feeling of singing may be positive and as such have a positive impact on a positive belief and a negative impact on a negative belief).

Two types of music are addressed: happy music makes individual sing a happy song and sad music makes her sing a sad song. The effect on the singing from the positive and the negative beliefs has connection weights named ω_{46}, ω_{47} (for sad singing) ω_{56}, ω_{57} (for happy singing) respectively. The state $goal_b$ has one incoming connection ω_{15} from srs_{ee}. The preparations state ps_b of the body state b has four incoming connection weights $(\omega_{17}, \omega_{18}, \omega_{19}, \omega_{55})$ from $(srs_b, goal_b, ss_{singing1}, ss_{singing2})$, respectively. Note that dotted lines in the model shows the Hebbian learning connections $(\omega_{19}, \omega_{55})$.

The states $ss_{singing1}$, $ss_{singing2}$ both have an entering connection weights ω_{50} and ω_{51} from execution states of es_{sing1} and es_{sing2}. The sensor state ss_{m1} and ss_{m2} both have an arriving connection weight from world state of music ws_{m1} and ws_{m2} named ω_{20} and ω_{21}. The preparation state of singing has two incoming connection weights are $(\omega_{26} \ \omega_{27})$, $(\omega_{30} \ \omega_{31})$ from ss_{m1} and ss_{m2}, respectively. The sensory representation state of emotion of sad and happy music has three incoming connection weights from sensor state of singing $ss_{singing}$, sensory representation of music srs_m and preparation state of singing $ps_{singing}$ named ω_{25}, ω_{24}, and ω_{35} respectively. The negative belief state bs_n has three connection weights from $ss_{singing1}$, $ss_{singing2}$ and for being exclusive from positive belief bs_p, ω_{42}, ω_{54} and ω_{44} respectively and similar for bs_n as ω_{43}, ω_{55} and ω_{43}. The preparation state of singing, ps_{sing1} and ps_{sing2} have six incoming connection weights from the $goal_b$, the negative belief, the positive belief, $srs_{singing1}$, and srs_{e1} with ω_{34}, ω_{46}, ω_{40}, ω_{25}, ω_{34} and ω_{47} and vice versa for ω_{56}, ω_{57}, ω_{36}, ω_{33}, ω_{32} and ω_{24}. The execution states of singing, $es_{singing1}$, $es_{singing2}$ both have an incoming connection weight ω_{49}, ω_{48} from preparation states ps_{sing1}, ps_{sing2}, respectively.

This conceptual representation was transformed into a numerical representation as follows [12, Chap. 2]:

- at each time point t each state Y in the model has a real number value in the interval [0, 1], denoted by $Y(t)$
- at each time point t each state X connected to state Y has an impact on Y defined as **impact**$_{X,Y}(t) = \omega_{X,Y} X(t)$ where $\omega_{X,Y}$ is the weight of the connection from X to Y
- The *aggregated impact* of multiple states X_i on Y at t is determined using a *combination function* $\mathbf{c}_Y(..)$:

$$\textbf{aggimpact}_Y(t) = \mathbf{c}_Y\big(\textbf{impact}_X1_{,Y}(t), \ldots, \textbf{impact}_Xk_{,Y}(t)\big)$$
$$= \mathbf{c}_Y\big(\omega_X1_{,Y}X_1(t), \ldots, \omega_Xk_{,Y}X_K(t)\big)$$

where X_i are the states with connections to state Y

- The effect of **aggimpact**$_Y(t)$ on Y is exerted over time gradually, depending on speed factor η_Y:

$$Y(t + \Delta t) = Y(t) + \eta_Y[\mathbf{aggimpact}_Y(t) - Y(t)]\Delta t$$

or $\quad \mathbf{d}Y(t)/\mathbf{d}t = \eta_Y[\mathbf{aggimpactY(t)} - Y(t)]$

- Thus, the following *difference* and *differential equation* for Y are obtained:

$$Y(t + \Delta t) = Y(t) + \eta_Y[\mathbf{c}_Y(\omega_X1_{,Y}X_1(t), \ldots, \omega_Xk_{,Y}X_k(t))]\Delta t$$
$$\mathbf{d}Y(t)/\mathbf{d}t = \eta_Y[\mathbf{c}_Y(\omega_X1_{,Y}X_1(t), \ldots, \omega_Xk_{,Y}X_k(t))] - Y(t)$$

For states the following combination functions $\mathbf{c}_Y(\ldots)$ were used, the identity function **id(.)** for states with impact from only one other state, and for states with multiple impacts the scaled sum function $\mathbf{ssum}_\lambda(\ldots)$ with scaling factor λ, and the advanced logistic sum function $\mathbf{alogistic}_{\sigma,\tau}(\ldots)$ with steepness σ and threshold τ.

$\mathbf{id}(V) = V$

$\mathbf{ssum}_\lambda(V_1, \ldots, V_k) = (V_1, \ldots, V_k)/\lambda$

$\mathbf{alogistic}_{\sigma,\tau}(V_1, \ldots, V_k) = \left[\left(1/\left(1 + e^{-\sigma(V_1 + \ldots + V_{k-\tau})}\right)\right) - 1/(1 + e^{\sigma}\tau)\right](1 + e^{-\sigma}\tau)$

Here first the general Hebbian Learning is explained which is applied to ω_{35} and ω_{36} for $(X_{19}, X_{15}$ and $X_{20}, X_{16})$. In a general example model considered it is assumed that the strength ω of such a connection between states X_1 and X_2 is adapted using the following Hebbian Learning rule, taking into account a maximal connection strength 1, a learning rate $\eta > 0$ and a persistence factor $\mu \geq 0$, and activation levels $X_1(t)$ and $X_2(t)$ (between 0 and 1) of the two states involved [10]. The first expression is in differential equation format, the second one in difference equation format:

$$d\omega(t)/dt = \eta[X_1(t) X_2(t) (1 - \omega(t) - (1 - \mu)\omega(t)]$$
$$\omega(t + \Delta t) = \omega(t) + \eta[X_1(t) X_2(t)(1 - \omega(t)) - (1 - \mu)\omega(t)]\Delta t$$

4   Example Simulation

An example simulation of this process is shown in Figs. 2 and 3. Table 3 shows the connection weights used, where the values for the Hebbian learning connections are initial values as these weights are adapted over time. The time step was $\Delta t = 1$. The scaling factors λ_i for the states with more than one incoming connection are also depicted in Table 3. In the scenario, the music is used as a therapy to decrease the level of the extreme emotion of the stressed individual. At a first step, an external world state of the stressful context c (denoted by X_1) affects the internal world state of the individual state with an extreme emotion (denoted by X_3). The stressed person senses the extreme emotion (denoted by X_2); by this the sensory representation of an extreme emotion of an individual comes to have a role (denoted by X_5), also the music comes in (The upper part of the model as the music starting by X_{17}, X_{18}). In this scenario, two types of music are considered as a therapy called sad and happy music. For simplicity, here we just simulate only one type of music, happy music and put the value of sad music to zero and without any effect on the stressed person. There is a main goal which is considered as the goal to achieve relaxation by singing with the music. The sensory representation of music has an influence on preparation state of the body state b (denoted by X_{27} and X_{12}) and decreases the preparation state of the extreme emotion to affect the sensory representation of the extreme emotion of the individual (denoted by X_5).

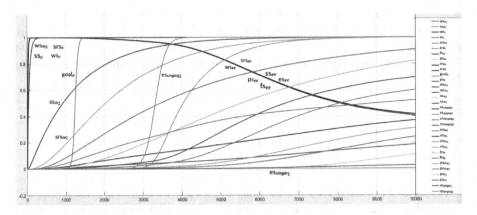

Fig. 2. Simulation results of the music therapy

There are two beliefs (denoted by X_{25} and X_{26}: positive and negative belief, respectively), and there are two sensory representations of emotion which are also considered to have impacts on sensory representation of body state, X_{10} as a sensory representation state of body state b. When the music therapy starts the stressed individual senses and hears the music (denoted by X_{15} and X_{16}). The goal gets a role from time around 1200 on. After giving some time to the stressed individual to hear and sense the music the preparation and sensory representation of emotion starts to have a role and after internally being emotional she starts singing from time around 2000 as an as-if loop from preparation state of singing (X_{22} and X_{24} as sensory representation states of emotion) so she makes it stronger and prepared to perform singing (X_{27} and X_{28}) to be more relaxed. As can be seen from the simulation of the sad singing and music, this has no effect on reducing the stress level in contrast to the reducing effect of the happy music and singing. in that case the reduction of the stress level continues until the time around 10000 to become in the equilibrium level from 1 (high-level of stress) to just 0.4 (low-level of stress). Mirroring links are considered between the sensory representation of body state and the preparation state of the body state (denoted by X_{10} and X_{12}).

As it can be seen from Fig. 3, the Hebbian learning connections which have been used from srs$_{singing1}$, srs$_{singing2}$ to ps$_b$ show increase from time 4000. The parameter setting for both Hebbian Learning connections are as follows; for both connections the speed factors η are equal to 0.5, and the persistence factors μ are equal to 0.97.

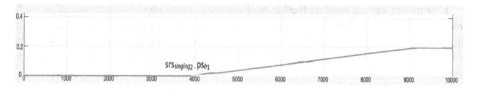

Fig. 3. Simulation results for Hebbian learning connections

Table 3. Connection weights for the example simulation

Connection weight	ω_1	ω_2	ω_3	ω_4	ω_5	ω_6	ω_7	ω_8
Value	1	1	1	1	1	1	1	1
Connection Weight	ω_9	ω_{10}	ω_{11}	ω_{12}	ω_{13}	ω_{14}	ω_{15}	ω_{16}
Value	-0.001	1	1	0.2	-1	-0.1	1	1
Connection Weight	ω_{17}	ω_{18}	ω_{19}	ω_{20}	ω_{21}	ω_{22}	ω_{23}	ω_{24}
Value	1	0.01	0.01	1	1	1	1	1
Connection Weight	ω_{25}	ω_{26}	ω_{27}	ω_{28}	ω_{29}	ω_{30}	ω_{31}	ω_{32}
Value	1	1	1	1	0.1	0.1	1	1
Connection Weight	ω_{33}	ω_{34}	ω_{35}	ω_{36}	ω_{37}	ω_{38}	ω_{39}	ω_{40}
Value	1	1	1	1	1	1	1	1
Connection Weight	ω_{41}	ω_{42}	ω_{43}	ω_{44}	ω_{45}	ω_{46}	ω_{47}	ω_{48}
Value	1	1	-0.2	-0.15	-0.15	-0.9	-0.9	1
Connection Weight	ω_{49}	ω_{50}	ω_{51}	ω_{52}	ω_{53}	ω_{54}	ω_{55}	ω_{56}
Value	1	1	1	1	1	-0.01	1	1
Connection Weight	ω_{57}	ω_{58}	ω_{59}	ω_{60}	ω_{61}			
Value	-0.9	0.01	1	1	-0.9			

state	X_5	X_8	X_{10}	X_{12}	X_{19}	X_{20}	X_{25}
λ_t	2	2	3	3	1.1	2	1
state	X_{26}	X_{27}	X_{28}	X_{29}	X_{30}		
λ_t	1	2.21	4.01	1	2		

5 Discussion

In this paper an adaptive cognitive temporal-causal network model of a mindfulness therapy based on music was presented by helping Hebbian learning to decrease the level of stress of individual with extreme stress. As far as the authors know there do not exist computational models for such a therapy. Due to Hebbian learning the model is adaptive by which the effect becomes stronger over time.

A variety of simulations were executed one of which was presented in the paper. Findings from Neuroscience were taken into account in the design of the adaptive model. This literature reports experiments and measurements of music therapy for emotion-induced conditions as addressed from a computational perspective in the current paper.

This model can be used as the basis of a virtual agent model to get insight in such processes and to consider certain support or treatment of individuals and prevent some stress-related disorders that otherwise might develop. In further research, control states in the brain can be added for more antecedent-focused and response-focused emotion regulation strategies.

References

1. Assoa, L.: On the relationship between emotion and cognition. Nat. Rev. Neurosci. **9**, 148–158 (2008). https://doi.org/10.1038/nrn2317
2. Bailey, L.M.: Use of songs in music therapy with cancer patients and their families. Music. Ther. **4**(1), 5–17 (1984)
3. Blood, A.J., Zatorre, R.J.: Intensely pleasurable responses to music correlate with activity in brain regions implicated in reward and emotion. Proc. Natl. Acad. U. S. A. **98**, 11818–11823 (2001)
4. Goldin, P.R., McRae, K., Ramel, W., Gross, J.J.: The neural bases of emotion regulations: reappraisal and suppression of negative emotions. Biol. Psychiatry **63**, 577–586 (2008). https://doi.org/10.1016/jbiopsych.2007.05.31
5. Holzel, B.K., et al.: Mindfulness practice leads to increases in regional brain gray matter density. Psychiatry Res. **191**, 36–43 (2011)
6. Hou, J., et al.: Review on neural correlates of emotion regulation and music: implications for emotion dysregulation. Front. Psychol. **8**, 501 (2017). PMID: 28421017
7. Jones, M.R., Holleran, S.: Cognitive Bases of Musical Communication. American Psychological Association Publishers, Washington, DC (1992)
8. Juslim, P.N., Vastfjall, D.: Emotional responses to music: the need to consider underlying mechanisms. Behav. Brain Sci. **31**, 559–575 (2008). https://doi.org/10.1017/S0140525X08005293
9. Kleinstauber, M., Gurr, B.: Music in brain injury rehabilitation. J. Cogn. Rehabil. **24**, 4–14 (2006)
10. Koelsch, S.: Towards a neural basis of music-evoked emotions. Trends Cogn. Sci. **14**, 131–137 (2010). https://doi.org/10.1016/j.tics.2010.01.002
11. Koelsch, S.: Brain correlates of music-evoked emotions. Nat. Rev. Neurosci. **15**, 170–180 (2014). https://doi.org/10.1038/nrn3666
12. Koelsch, S., et al.: The roles of superficial amygdala and auditory cortex in music-evoked fear and joy. Neuroimage **81**, 49–60 (2013). https://doi.org/10.1016/j.neuroimage.2013.05.008
13. Lee, O.K., Chung, Y.F., Chan, M.F., Chan, W.M.: Music and its effect on physiological and anxiety levels of patients receiving mechanical ventilation: a pilot study. J. Clin. Neurosci. **14**(5), 609–620 (2005)
14. Iliya, Y.A.: Music therapy as grief therapy for adults with mental illness and complicated grief: a pilot study. Death Stud. **39**(3), 173–184 (2015). https://doi.org/10.1080/07481187.2014.946623
15. Limb, C.J., Braun, A.R.: Neural substrates of spontaneous musical performance: an fMRI study of jazz; intensely pleasurable responses to music correlate with activity in brain regions implicated in reward and emotion. Proc. Natl. Acad. Sci. U. S. A. **98**, PloS ONE **3**(2), 11818–11823 (2008). https://doi.org/10.1073/pnas.191355898
16. Lundqvist, L.O., Carlsson, F., Hilmersson, P., Juslin, P.N.: Emotional responses to music: experience, expression, and physiology. Psychol. Music **37**(1), 61–90 (2009)

17. Mansouri, A.F., Acevedo, N., Illipparampil, R., Fehring, D.J., Fitzgerald, P.B., Jaberzadeh, S.: Interactive effects of music and Prefrontal Cortex stimulation in modulating response inhibition. Sci. Rep. **7**, 18096 (2017). https://doi.org/10.1038/s41598-017-18119-x

18. Mossler, K., Chen, X., Heldal, T.O., Gold, C.: Music therapy for people with schizophrenia and schizophrenia-like disorders. Cochrane Database Syst. Rev. **12**(12) (2011). https://doi.org/10.1002/14651858.CD004025.pub3

19. Murakami, H., et al.: Neural Networks for mindfulness and emotion suppression. PLoS ONE **10**(6), e0128005 (2015). https://doi.org/10.1371/journal.pone.0128005

20. Nayak, S., Wheeler, B.L., Shiflett, S.C., Agostinelli, S.: Effect of music therapy on mood and social interaction among individuals with acute traumatic brain injury and stroke. Rehabil. Psychol. **45**, 274–283 (2000)

21. Oosterwijk, S., Lindquist, K.A., Anderson, E., Dautoff, R., Moriguchi, Y., Barrett, L.F.: States of mind; emotions, body feelings, and thoughts shared distributed neural networks. Neuroimage **62**(3), 2110–2128 (2012). https://doi.org/10.1016/j.neuroimage.2012.05.079

22. Otto, M.W., Powers, M.B., Fischmann, D.: Emotional exposure in the treatment of substance use disorders: conceptual model, evidence, and future directions. J. Clin. Psychol. **25**, 824–839 (2005). https://doi.org/10.1016/j.cpr.2005.05.002

23. Purves, D., et al.: Neuroscience, 2nd edn. Sinauer Associates, Sunderland (2001)

24. Shear, M.K., et al.: Complicated grief and related bereavement issues for DSM-5. Depress. Anxiety **28**, 103–117 (2011). https://doi.org/10.1002/da.20780

25. Thaut, M.H., Peterson, D.A., McIntosh, G.C.: Temporal entrainment of cognitive functions: musical mnemonics induce brain plasticity and oscillatory synchrony in neural networks underlying memory. Ann. N. Y. Acad. Sci. **1060**, 243–254 (2005)

26. Thaut, M.H., et al.: Neurologic music therapy improves executive function and emotional adjustment in traumatic brain injury rehabilitation. Ann. N. Y. Acad. Sci. **16**, 1169–1406 (2009)

27. Treur, J.: Network-Oriented Modeling: Addressing Complexity of Cognitive, Affective and Social Interactions. Springer Publishers, Cham (2016). https://doi.org/10.1007/978-3-319-45213-5

28. Treur, J.: Verification of temporal-causal network models by mathematical analysis. Vietnam J. Comput. Sci. **3**, 207–221 (2016)

29. Kachanathu, S.J., Verma, S.K., Khanna, G.: The effect of music therapy and meditation on sports performance in professional shooters. J. Exerc. Sci. Physiother. **6**(2), 133–136 (2010)

30. Mohammadi Ziabari, S.S., Treur, J.: Cognitive modelling of mindfulness therapy by autogenic training. In: INDIA 2018. AISC. Springer, Heidelberg (2018)

31. Treur, J., Mohammadi Ziabari, S.S.: An adaptive temporal-causal network model for decision making under acute stress. In: Nguyen, N.T., Pimenidis, E., Khan, Z., Trawiński, B. (eds.) ICCCI 2018. LNCS (LNAI), vol. 11056, pp. 13–25. Springer, Cham (2018). https://doi.org/10.1007/978-3-319-98446-9_2

32. Mohammadi Ziabari, S.S., Treur, J.: Integrative Biological, Cognitive and affective modeling of a drug-therapy for a post-traumatic stress disorder. In: TPNC 20018. Springer, Heidelberg (2018)

33. Mohammadi Ziabari, S.S., Treur, J.: Computational analysis of gender differences in coping with extreme stressful emotions. In: Proceedings of the 9th International Conference on Biologically Inspired Cognitive Architecture (BICA 2018), Czech Republic, Elsevier (2018)

Perceptual Filling-in of Blind-Spot for Surrounding Color Gradient Stimuli

Amrita Mukherjee[1]([✉]), Avijit Paul[2], Rajarshi Roy[3], Shibsankar Roy[1], and Kuntal Ghosh[1,4]

[1] Center for Soft Computing Research, Indian Statistical Institute, 203 B T Road, Kolkata 700108, India
amrita.mukherjeepaul@gmail.com, kuntal@isical.ac.in,
shibshankarroy2014@gmail.com
[2] TATA Consultancey Services, Kolkata, India
avijit.paul05061987@gmail.com
[3] Indian Institute of Technology, Indore, India
rajarshiroy1993@gmail.com
[4] Machine Intelligence Unit, Indian Statistical Institute, Kolkata, India

Abstract. Perceptual filling-in of blind-spot is still a mystic brain mechanism for which a great deal of research work is still going on using psychophysical and computational techniques. We conduct psychophysical experiments with a large number of stimuli to examine a retinotopic rule recently proposed by a group of researchers based on Cortical Magnification Factor (CMF). In our experiment we come across a phenomenon which could not be explained by the above mentioned retinotopic rule. So, we propose a new hypothesis for blind-spot filling-in for non-homogeneous surroundings. Our hypothesis encircles the importance of Trichromatic theory, Information theory and CMF in blind-spot filling-in mechanism. We also observe that two kinds of illusions namely Simultaneous Brightness Contrast (SBC) and Brightness Assimilation (BA), till now thought of as antagonistic with respect to brightness induction, are significantly similar and it bears analogy with the blind-spot filling-in mechanism.

Keywords: Blind-spot · Cortical Magnification Factor
Trichromatic theory · Information theory · Assimilation · Contrast

1 Introduction

Photoreceptors (rod and cone cells), capable of transducing light energy to electrical signals are situated inside our retina behind the ganglion, amacrine, bipolar and horizontal cells in order to be protected from getting damaged by light

Supported by Cognitive Science Research Initiative (CSRI), Department of Science and Technology, Govt. of India.

falling directly on them. Since information is processed from the photoreceptors back towards the ganglion cells, i,e., in a direction opposite to the direction
of light, the region from where optic nerves together come out of the eye is a
photoreceptor free zone. No physical information is obtained from this location.
This area is known as blind-spot which approximately subtends 6° to 8° visual
angle and is centered about 15° in nasal retina [1]. This gap in each eye is supposed to be taken care of by the other eye and hence in monocular vision, we
should expect to perceive a hole in every object we see. Surprisingly, however
we do not see any hole in vision. In other words, our brain creates a sort of
virtual reality for the spot. Our blind-spot region is possibly filled by the surrounding colors or textures and this incident is termed as perceptual filling-in.
The perception of reality without actual physical information is still a mystery
to be solved. To this end, we perform some psychophysical experiments in the
light of the work of Li et al. [1] with our own augmentation. They recommended
that the filling-in pattern follows a retinotopic rule which suggests that blind-
spot filling-in is asymmetric from nasal to temporal side of the visual half in
case of bi-colored stimuli where the color in the nasal part highly dominates
the color belonging to the temporal part of the visual field. In our experiments,
we use black and white along with the primary colors (red, green and blue) in
the stimuli and get some interesting results that suggests an incompleteness of
Li et al.'s [1] retinotopic rule. Relevant research studies related to our experiments are described systematically in Sect. 2. We present our experimental
methodology and the obtained results in Sects. 3 and 4 respectively. In Sect. 5,
we discuss our hypothesis and observations regarding the pattern of filling-in
and compared the same with brightness contrast and brightness assimilation
phenomena. In Sect. 6 the concluding remarks are presented.

2   Related Research Works

Ramachandran [2] asserted that perceptual filling-in involves some computational mechanisms in brain and it is obtained by surface interpolation.
Ramachandran and Gregory's spatio-temporal characteristics of artificial scotoma filling-in [3], Durgin et al.'s [4] amodal filling-in with zero crossing techniques, bar-stimuli experiments of Lou et al. [5] and background-foreground
attributional denotation of Hsieh and Tse [6] are some of the earliest works.
Abadi et al. described the effect of awareness on blind-spot filling-in   [7].
Paradiso and Nakayama [8] worked on monoptic and dichoptic vision while He
and Devis [9] investigated filling-in for dichoptic vision. Li et al. [1] explained the
role of Cortical Magnification Factor (CMF) with respect to blind-spot filling-in.
As for some particular combinations of bi-colored stimuli their hypothesis did
not hold good, we have proposed a novel solution for the explanation. De Weered
et al. [10] explained that perceptual filling-in is the resultant minimization of the
difference of neurological activities of with-hole and no-hole images. Meng et al.
[11] described visual phantoms, Zur and Ullman [12] explained the virtual reality
created by filling-in mechanism, Komatsu [13] suggested that neurons in the deep

layer are activated based on the kind of stimulus in case of filling-in. According to Awater et al. [14], the filling-in at the blind-spot may occur due to the spatial propagation of signal from the periphery of the blind-spot region. Spillmann et al. [15] tried to measure the minimum width of the periphery around the blind-spot for colored and textured surroundings. Weil and Rees [16] described that activation of filling-in phenomena may be related to the real image contour. With the help of the idea of edge detection and surface interpolation in human visual system as propounded by David Marr, Ghosh et al. [17] modelled the excellent non-classical receptive field of retinal ganglion cells. Hierarchical Predictive Coding [18] devised by Rao and Ballard, dynamic predictive coding utilized by Hosoya et al. [19], Kwisthout and Rooij's [20] top-down and bottom-up predictive coding approach and Hierarchy Predictive Coding approach used by Raman and Sarkar [21] are some of the attempts in computational modelling of blind-spot.

3   Experimental Methodology

3.1   Materials and Method

Eight subjects (5 males and 3 females) participated in the experiments are from Indian Statistical Institute, Kolkata, India aged between 25 to 35 years. All have normal or correct to normal vision and they do not have any history of neurological disorders. Subjects were naive for these experiments and they practiced with demo sets of these experiments 2–3 times before participating in the final experiments. All the stimuli were presented in an eizo247 monitor, refresh rate of which is 60 Hz. Subjects observed the monitor from a distance of 0.4 m. The monitor was subtended at a visual angle of 65.88° to the subjects. A chin-forehead rest was used to stabilize the heads of the subjects. Data acquisition was accomplished by the help of MATLAB software.

3.2   Mapping of Blind-Spot and Generation of Visual Stimuli

The blind-spot of each subject was mapped using a computer-controlled procedure. This procedure was generated by the MATLAB software using Psychophysics toolbox. For mapping purpose, subjects fixated their one eye at a green cross [0 255 0] presented on a black background (0.13 cd/m^2) while the other eye was covered. A small white probe (32.34 cd/m^2) was used to move horizontally from 8° to 25° and vice versa. This process was repeated several times with a certain downward displacement to cover a predefined area. The probe also moved vertically from 7° to −9° in the same manner across the whole area. The positions where the probe disappeared and reappeared were marked digitally to keep track of them. This mapping procedure was conducted in a dark room. This process was repeated for a number of times and the best fitted results were taken into account (see Fig. 1). All the bi-colored annuli used in this study were generated by MATLAB software using psychophysics toolbox.

The experiments were conducted in mesopic condition. The width of the bi-colored stimuli was set at 3°. Also, we created an grey oval to cover the blind-spot area of the subjects throughout the experiments. During the experiment if the grey oval became visible to the subjects, the experiment was declared void. Red [255 0 0], green [0 255 0] and blue [0 0 255] colors were chosen in such a way that all of them had luminance of nearly 10 cd/m². White and black were set at a luminescence of 44.5 cd/m²and 0.67 cd/m² respectively. Luminance of all the stimuli were measured by a luminance meter (Mavospot 2). The stimuli were presented on a grey background having luminance of 14.89 cd/m². Subjects were asked to fix their right eye at the green cross while closing their left eye and were asked to mark the junction of the two colors (using the black line) by pressing a computer key (screen shot of one of the visual stimuli is shown in Fig. 2). A total of 14 such stimuli used, are presented in Table 1.

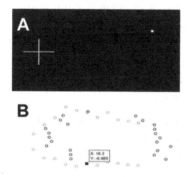

Fig. 1. Screen shots of blind-spot mapping and map of a subject's blind-spot are depicted in A and B respectively. (Color figure online)

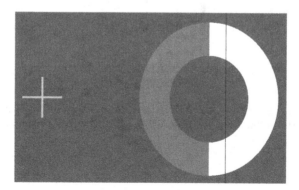

Fig. 2. A screen shot depicting one of the visual stimuli. (Color figure online)

Table 1. Classification of 14 bi-colored stimuli.

Position of Color, Black and White in the Nasal and Temporal half of visual field					
White-Primary Color		Black-Primary Color		Black-White	
Nasal	Temporal	Nasal	Temporal	Nasal	Temporal
Red	White	Red	Black	Black	White
Green	White	Green	Black	White	Black
Blue	White	Blue	Black		
White	Red	Black	Red		
White	Green	Black	Green		
White	Blue	Black	Blue		

4   Results

The color filling-in patterns of bi-colored stimuli are discussed below. By the combination m - n we indicated that color m is put in the nasal half and color n is put in the temporal half of the visual field.

4.1   Color Filling-in Pattern of Stimuli Made of White and Primary Colors

Filling-in pattern in the visual field is asymmetrical with nasal colors' dominance for primary color - white combination but it is almost symmetrical for white - primary color combination (see Fig. 3).

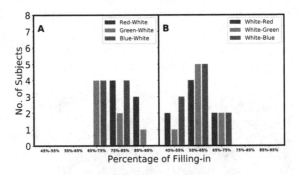

Fig. 3. Bar graph A shows the filling-in pattern for primary color - white stimuli. Bar graph B shows the filling-in pattern of white - primary color stimuli. (Color figure online)

4.2   Color Filling-in Pattern of Stimuli Made of Black and Primary Colors

Filling-in pattern in the visual field is asymmetrical with nasal colors' dominance for primary color - black combination but it is almost symmetrical for black - primary color combination (see Fig. 4).

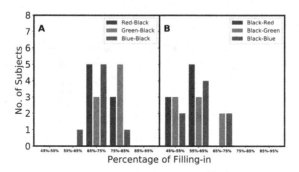

Fig. 4. Bar graph A shows the filling-in pattern for primary color - black stimuli. Bar graph B shows the filling-in pattern of black - primary color stimuli. (Color figure online)

4.3   Color Filling-in Pattern of Stimuli Made of Black and White

We found filling-in pattern inclined a bit to nasal side for both black - white and white-black stimuli (see Fig. 5).

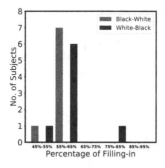

Fig. 5. A bar graph of filling-in pattern for white - black and black - white stimuli. (Color figure online)

5   Discussion

We find that the influence of primary colors in the nasal side of visual field in filling-in have the same effects as described by Li et al. However, there is a noted difference in the filling-in pattern for white - primary color/black - primary color, white - black and black - white combination. Based on the results of our experiments, we propose a hypothesis to explain the reason of asymmetrical and symmetrical filling-in at the blind-spot region with bi-colored surround.

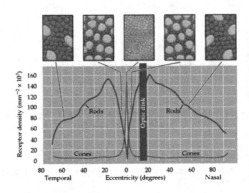

Fig. 6. Anatomical distribution of rod and cone cells throughout the retina [22].

5.1   Prerequisites to Describe Our Hypothesis

- The unequal distribution of photoreceptors (see Fig. 6) throughout the retina may have a role in blind-spot filling-in process.
- The nasal half of visual field is processed by the temporal side of the retina and vice versa.
- The Trichromatic theory (proposed by Thomas Young in 1802 and modified by Herman Von Helmholtz in 1852) states that the primary color information is processed by L/M/S cone cell and the white and black information is processed by L, M and S cone cells. All the three types of cone cells respond together as (L + M + S) for white (with the presence of all the three primary colors) and as -(L + M + S) for black (with absence of all the three primary colors). So, the processing of white or black requires more information to take into account than that for the primary colors and our brain always tries to be in a low information state. [23]. Thus in case of blind-spot filling-in brain tends to give higher priority to primary colors than white or black during any rivalry.
- CMF increases as the retinal eccentricity decreases. With higher CMF the priority of filling-in becomes higher.

5.2   Proposed Hypothesis in Light of Our Observations

The priorities of visual halves in filling-in and the compatibility of the obtained results with our proposed hypothesis which describes the roles of Trichromatic theory, Information theory and CMF are discussed in the Tables 2 and 3 respectively. We are trying to simulate over computer our proposed hypothesis as our future work.

Table 2. The priority of colors belonging to two visual halves in filling-in of blind-spot.

Different cases	I	II	III	IV
Nasal-Temporal	Primary Color-Primary Color	Primary Color-White/Black	White/Black-Primary Color	White/Black-Black/White
Priority in filling-in of blind-spot	Nasal	Nasal	Equal	Inclined a bit to Nasal

Table 3. Description of our hypothesis.

Cases as mentioned in Table 2	Probable reasons for priority of black, white and primary colors in case of blind-spot filling-in in the light of the prerequisites as described in Subsect. 5.1
I	As for processing primary colors one of the L/M/S cones is involved, the expense of energy with respect to cone related information by our brain for both the halves are same. But the higher CMF of the temporal half of retina helps the nasal half of visual field gain higher priority over the temporal half
II	More information is needed to process white or black than to process primary colors and our brain tries to keep itself in low entropy state. So, the expense of energy related to information biases our brain towards primary color. CMF of temporal part of retina is also higher than that of the nasal half. Thus both CMF and that bias provide nasal half of the visual field with higher priority over the temporal half
III	More information is needed to process white or black than to process primary colors and our brain tries to keep itself in low entropy state. So, the expense of energy related to information biases our brain towards primary color. But CMF of temporal part of retina is higher than that of the nasal half. Thus CMF neutralizes that bias and both the visual halves enjoy equal priority
IV	If white is placed in nasal and black is in temporal half of the visual field or vice versa, same amount of energy is expensed by L, M, S cone information for both the halves. CMF of temporal half of retina is also higher than that of the nasal half. But as three types of cones are involved in this case, we hypothesize that CMF will be less effective to influence like it does for any primary color (the reason being primary colors are processed by one of L/M/S cones). This causes the priority of filling-in to be inclined a bit to the nasal half of visual field

5.3   Perceptual Filling-in, Brightness Assimilation and Contrast

While analyzing the process of blind-spot filling-in, we also look into some visual illusions where we perceive some more information than that from the real images. Different illusions have different sets of logic to explain the biological plausibility of the brain functioning. But our brain works as an integrated synchronous system. So, a generic explanation for the illusions is required. Keeping that in mind, we consider two typical illusions namely Simultaneous Brightness Contrast (SBC) and Brightness Assimilation (BA) [24,25]. In case of SBC, the forepart creates a contrast with the background and in case of BA, (the left most of the three in Fig. 7), the brightness of the forepart is induced to the background. Till now we have learnt that SBC and BA are two opposite phenomena [26]. In SBC, the foreground test patch is influenced by the background colors while in BA, the opposite happens. Our observations suggest that the only difference between them is the amount of test patch which we need to concentrate for brightness change. We design SBC and BA with the same experimental setup as discussed in Sect. 3. Yellow [255 255 0] and black [0 0 0] are chosen as background for SBC and yellow as the background for BA. For both the illusions, we choose green [0 255 0] as foreground. The spatial area is 200 by 200 pixels for both the illusions. In BA, we take the dimension of each foreground rectangle as 5 by 200 pixels (i.e., the area is (5 × 200) square unit). In SBC, we consider the foreground square as 50 by 50 pixels (i.e., the area is (50 × 50) square unit). When we place only one rectangle at the front of BA, we find no influence of foreground but 3 spatially separated foreground rectangles of BA has some influence on the background (see Fig. 7). When we place 11 rectangles as foreground for BA, the full background is impacted as seen from Fig. 8. Blind-spot filling-in mechanism somewhat agrees with SBC mechanism, but in case of blind-spot filling-in the surrounding region is not influenced by the missing neural input and there is no perceptual change of color-brightness after filling-in occurs.

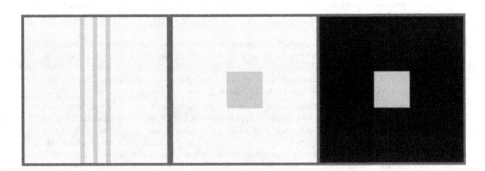

Fig. 7. A screen shot of BA and SBC where 3 rectangles are there in foreground of BA.

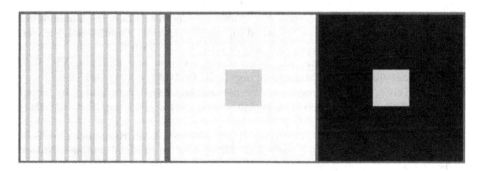

Fig. 8. A screen shot of BA and SBC with 11 rectangles as foreground of BA [25].

6   Conclusions

We observe that nasal side gains more priority over the temporal one when any primary color is present in the nasal half of visual field but when the positions of colors in the stimulus gets reversed both of the visual halves acquire equal priority in filling-in. For black and white colored stimuli, filling-in biases a bit towards nasal half irrespective of the positions of black and white in the visual halves. We notice the importance of Trichromatic theory, Information theory and CMF in explaining our hypothesis. We also observe that two kinds of illusions namely SBC and BA, till now thought of as antagonistic with respect to brightness induction, have a significant similarity. We conclude that the blind-spot filling-in mechanism has similarity with some aspects of brightness induction illusions and some disparity with the other aspects of those illusions. More experiments and simulations are presently being conducted by us towards a unified understanding of brightness illusions and blind-spot filling-in as foreseen by Ramachandran [2].

References

1. Li, H., Luo, J., Lu, Y., Kan, J., Spillmann, L., Wang, W.: Asymmetrical color filling-in from the nasal to the temporal side of the blind spot. Front. Hum. Neurosci. **8**(7), 835–840 (2014). https://doi.org/10.3389/fnhum.2014.00534
2. Ramachandran, V.S.: Blind spots. Sci. Am. **266**(5), 86–91 (1992)
3. Ramachandran, V.S., Gregory, R.L.: Perceptual filling in of artificially induced scotomas in human vision. Nature **350**(6320), 699 (1991). https://doi.org/10.1038/350699a0
4. Durgin, F.H., Tripathy, S.P., Levi, D.M.: On the filling in of the visual blind spot: Some rules of thumb. Perception **24**(7), 827–840 (1995). https://doi.org/10.1068/p240827
5. Lou, L., Chen, J., et al.: Attention and blind-spot phenomenology. PSYCHE **9**, 02 (2003)
6. Hsieh, P.J., Tse, P.: Feature mixing rather than feature replacement during perceptual filling-in. Vis. Res. **49**(4), 439–450 (2009). https://doi.org/10.1016/j.visres.2008.12.004

7. Abadi, R.V., Jeffery, G., Murphy, J.S.: Awareness and filling-in of the human blind spot: linking psychophysics with retinal topography. Investig. Ophthalmol. Vis. Sci. **52**(1), 541–548 (2011). https://doi.org/10.1167/iovs.10-5910

8. Paradiso, M.A., Nakayama, K.: Brightness perception and filling-in. Vis. Res. **31**(7), 1221–1236 (1991). https://doi.org/10.1016/0042-6989(91)90047-9

9. He, S., Davis, W.L.: Filling-in at the natural blind spot contributes to binocular rivalry. Vis. Res. **41**(7), 835–840 (2001). https://doi.org/10.1016/S0042-6989(00)00315-1

10. De Weerd, P., Gattass, R., Desimone, R., Ungerleider, L.G.: Responses of cells in monkey visual cortex during perceptual filling-in of an artificial scotoma. Nature **377**(6551), 731 (1995). https://doi.org/10.1038/377731a0

11. Meng, M., Remus, D.A., Tong, F.: Filling-in of visual phantoms in the human brain. Nature Neurosci. **8**(9), 1248–1254 (2005). https://doi.org/10.1038/nn1518

12. Zur, D., Ullman, S.: Filling-in of retinal scotomas. Vis. Res. **43**(9), 971–982 (2003). https://doi.org/10.1016/S0042-6989(03)00038-5

13. Komatsu, H.: The neural mechanisms of perceptual filling-in. Nature Rev. Neurosci. **7**(3), 220–231 (2006). https://doi.org/10.1038/nrn1869

14. Awater, H., Kerlin, J.R., Evans, K.K., Tong, F.: Cortical representation of space around the blind spot. J. Neurophysiol. **94**(5), 3314–3324 (2005). https://doi.org/10.1152/jn.01330.2004

15. Spillmann, L., Otte, T., Hamburger, K., Magnussen, S.: Perceptual filling-in from the edge of the blind spot. Vis. Res. **46**(25), 4252–4257 (2006). https://doi.org/10.1016/j.visres.2006.08.033

16. Weil, R.S., Rees, G.: A new taxonomy for perceptual filling-in. Brain Res. Rev. **67**(1), 40–55 (2011). https://doi.org/10.1016/j.brainresrev.2010.10.004

17. Ghosh, K., Sarkar, S., Bhaumik, K.: A new multi-scale gaussian interpolator that models the blind spot in human eye. In: 2006 IEEE International Conference on Engineering of Intelligent Systems, pp. 1–6. IEEE (2006). https://doi.org/10.1109/ICEIS.2006.1703166

18. Rao, R.P., Ballard, D.H.: Predictive coding in the visual cortex: a functional interpretation of some extra-classical receptive-field effects. Nature Neurosci. **2**(1), 79–87 (1999). https://doi.org/10.1038/4580

19. Hosoya, T., Baccus, S.A., Meister, M.: Dynamic predictive coding by the retina. Nature **436**(7047), 71–77 (2005). https://doi.org/10.1038/nature03689

20. Kwisthout, J., van Rooij, I.: Predictive coding and the Bayesian brain: intractability hurdles that are yet to be overcome. In: CogSci. (2013)

21. Raman, R., Sarkar, S.: Predictive coding: a possible explanation of filling-in at the blind spot. PloS one **11**(3), e0151194 (2016). https://doi.org/10.1371/journal.pone.0151194

22. Purves, D., et al.: Neuroscience. Sinauer Associates, Inc, Sunderland (2001)

23. Penrose, R., Mermin, N.D.: The Emperors New Mind: Concerning Computers, Minds, and The Laws of Physics (1990)

24. Ghosh, K., Bhaumik, K.: Complexity in human perception of brightness: a historical review on the evolution of the philosophy of visual perception. OnLine J. Biol. Sci. **10**(1), 17–35 (2010)

25. Jory, M.K., Day, R.H.: The relationship between brightness contrast and illusory contours. Perception **8**(1), 3–9 (1979). https://doi.org/10.1068/p080003

26. Shapley, R., Reid, R.C.: Contrast and assimilation in the perception of brightness. Proc. Natl. Acad. Sci. **82**(17), 5983–5986 (1985). https://doi.org/10.1073/pnas.82.17.5983

Image and Vision Based Interactions

Convolutional Neural Network Based Meitei Mayek Handwritten Character Recognition

Deena Hijam$^{(\boxtimes)}$ and Sarat Saharia$^{(\boxtimes)}$

Tezpur University, Napaam 784028, Assam, India
{deenahi,sarat}@tezu.ernet.in

Abstract. Off-line Handwritten Character Recognition (HCR) is the process of automatic conversion of images of handwritten text into a form that computers can understand and process. Several research works for HCR of different scripts are found in literature. They make use of one or more feature sets and classification tools for recognition of characters. Recently, Convolutional Neural Network (CNN) based recognition is found to show significantly better results. However, only a handful of studies are found of Meitei Mayek script and none based on CNN. Also, no dataset is available publicly for the said script. In order to study the recognition of characters for a particular script, a significantly large dataset is needed. In this paper, for the first time, a dataset consisting of 60285 handwritten characters of Meitei Mayek script is introduced which will be made publicly available to the researchers for use at http://agnigarh.tezu.ernet.in/~sarat/resources.html. A CNN architecture is also proposed for the recognition of characters in the dataset. An accuracy of 96.24% is achieved which is promising as compared to state-of-the-art works for the concerned script.

Keywords: Convolutional Neural Network · Meitei Mayek
Handwritten Character Recognition · Dataset creation
Optical Character Recognition

1 Introduction

Optical Character Recognition (OCR) is a research area which has been extensively studied for a couple of decades. However, as far as Meitei Mayek is concerned, this area of research remains least explored. One of the reasons is unavailability of a publicly available dataset for the said script. As pointed out in [15] the text data stored in printed or handwritten documents are of immense importance for the purpose of future reference and acts as a record for history, events, culture, literature, etc. It is a common practice to digitize handwritten documents so that they can be stored more compactly and can be electronically edited, searched, etc. However, the amount of such documents present today is overwhelmingly large and as such it becomes a tedious and time-consuming job to manually process them.

© Springer Nature Switzerland AG 2018
U. S. Tiwary (Ed.): IHCI 2018, LNCS 11278, pp. 207–219, 2018.
https://doi.org/10.1007/978-3-030-04021-5_19

Hence development of an automatic-reading system is the key even if their recognition accuracy is not as good as humans. With the replacement of Bengali script by Meitei Mayek script to write Manipuri language, the development of such a system will prove beneficial for the government as well as the people in general. Since now is a transition phase from Bangla to Meitei Mayek, development of a robust OCR is very important which in turn is pivotal for development of other systems such as machine transliteration system, especially one which translates Meitei Mayek script to Bangla script and vice-versa.

Studies in off-line HCR have focused mainly on major world scripts like English, Chinese, Arabic and Japanese. Several studies have also been reported in off-line HCR of some Indian scripts. Bangla, Devanagari, Gujarati, Kannada, Gurumukhi, Oriya, Telugu, Malayalam, Tamil and Nastaliq (Urdu) are the Indian scripts which have been more explored in terms of handwritten character recognition. Maximum research on off-line handwritten recognition has been done for Bangla script [16]. Commonly used classifiers include Neural Network (NN) and its variants, k-NN, SVM and HMM.

The use of CNN for pattern recognition and computer vision tasks has been popularized by the concept of gradient-based learning [10]. A simple CNN model is proven to give promising results in the studies carried out in document analysis [18]. The complexity of character recognition tasks varies among different scripts due to differences in the shapes, strokes and other script specific characteristics.

1.1   Existing Works in HCR of Meitei Mayek

An OCR system consists of five stages namely image acquisition, preprocessing, feature extraction, classification and post-processing. Of these five stages, feature extraction and classification are found to have major impact on the recognition accuracy of a system. Different techniques have been proposed for the recognition of Meitei Mayek script.

Tangkeshwar et al. [21] was one of the first researchers to work on handwritten character recognition of Meitei Mayek. In their work, the image is first binarised after which the character pattern is segmented using heuristic segmentation technique. KL-divergence technique and a neocognitron simulator was used for feature extraction and recognition of segmented characters and achieved an accuracy of 90%. In another work by them [22], probabilistic and fuzzy features were used with neural network as classifier. It was found that the accuracy achieved was 85.92% for probabilistic features alone, 88.14% for fuzzy features alone and 90.3% for the hybrid features.

HCR for handwritten Meitei Mayek numerals [8] and alphabets [9] using multilayer feed forward neural network with back propagation learning was reported by Laishram et al. The overall accuracy achieved was 85% for the numerals. In the latter work, the focus is given on the segmentation of character from a scanned whole document. Segmentation of lines and words is done using histogram based algorithm and segmentation of characters is done using connected component method. The accuracy was measured in two ways - one where input to the neural network is correct, in which case the accuracy is 85% and 80%

otherwise. Accuracy is affected by the segmentation stage because as the images are dilated, connected component analysis technique tends to consider adjacent characters as a single character during segmentation.

Maring and Dhir [12] achieved an accuracy of 89.58% for recognition of Meitei Mayek numerals using Gabor filter-based technique and SVM classifier.

For recognition of Meitei Mayek numerals, Kumar and Kalita [5] used various feature extraction techniques such as zone based diagonal, background directional distribution (BDD), Histogram Oriented Gradient (HOG) and projection histograms with SVM classifier. They concluded that HOG feature is more appropriate as compared to others and highest recognition of 95.16% is obtained for combination feature set comprising of HOG, histogram, BDD and diagonal features. Kumar et al. [7] also achieved accuracy of 94%, 92% and 98% using distance profile features (DPF) and background directional features (BDF) and hybrid (DPF+BDF) respectively on 27 consonants.

Tangkeshwar [20] reported the use of vertical and horizontal projection profiles and connected component analysis methods for segmentation of isolated digits and non-touching characters. Probabilistic features (PF) and fuzzy features (FF) were used with K-L divergence technique and feed forward back propagation neural network (MLPs) for recognition. Recognition using the hybrid feature set (PF+FF) was also performed and it was concluded that it gave better recognition rate than that using PF or FF alone. An algorithm based on the zoning information to recognize a word with isolated and overlapping characters in Meitei Mayek script was also proposed. It was done so to test the trained neural network for that word only and it was not a generalized algorithm.

A hybrid point feature based recognition using Harris corner detector, Gilles feature, Laplacian-of-Gaussian (Log) detector and Harris-Laplacian detector was reported by Kumar et al. [6]. An accuracy of 97.16% was achieved using SVM.

Nongmeikapam et al. [14] in their work used HOG features with k-NN classifier and achieved an accuracy of 94.29% on a dataset of 56 classes. Table 1 summarizes the works that have been carried out in HCR of Meitei Mayek.

Analysing the works that have been done in HCR of Meitei Mayek, it can be seen that all the works carried out used their own datasets created in the laboratory environments and there exists no publicly available dataset as far as this script is concerned. Also, sizes of the datasets used are small compared to the ones that are available for other scripts which can be used for evaluating real time applications. Some of the works reported have used data samples collected from individuals who do not use or know Meitei Mayek resulting in a drawing of characters rather than writing them naturally. This gives rise to the need for development of a benchmark dataset for Meitei Mayek script. The contributions of present work are summarized below:

- to the best of our knowledge, the dataset created will be the first publicly available dataset for handwritten Meitei Mayek character.
- for the first time, recognition of Meitei Mayek characters is carried out using CNN.

Table 1. Existing works in HCR of Meitei Mayek

Work	Dataset size	Number of classes	Classifier(s) used	Highest test accuracy
Tangkeshwar et al. [22]	594	27	NN	90.3%
Laishram et al. [8]	1000	10	NN	85%
Laishram et al. [9]	1000	43	NN	80%
Kumar et al. [5]	2000	10	SVM	95.16%
Kumar et al. [7]	14850	27	SVM	98%
Maring et al. [12]	7200	10	SVM	89.58%
Tangkeshwar et al. [20]	1000	10	MLP	96%
	3040	36	MLP	90.14%
	1890	27	MLP	92.96%
	1000	10	MLP	97.5%
	3520	43	MLP	87.95%
Nongmeikakpam et al. [14]	5600	56	k-NN	94.29%
Kumar et al. [6]	6750	-	SVM	97.16%

Rest of the paper is organized as follows: Sect. 2 discusses creation of the Meitei Mayek Handwritten Character (MMHC) dataset, Sect. 3 talks about the architecture of CNN for recognition of characters in the dataset. Sections 4 and 5 discuss the issues of overfitting in deep network and how data augmentation can be used to avoid the issue. Section 6 gives the experimental setup and results for evaluation of the proposed architecture on the developed dataset. Section 7 concludes the paper.

2   Meitei Mayek Dataset Creation

2.1   Meitei Mayek Script

Meitei Mayek script is used to write Manipuri language which is one of the 22 official (as per the Eighth Schedule of the Constitution of India) Indian languages. It is the predominant language and lingua franca in the state of Manipur and is also spoken in the Northeast Indian states of Tripura and Assam, and in countries like Bangladesh and Myanmar. It has around 1.25 million native speakers. The script was used in the ancient times from about the 11th century until the 18th century. In the early 18th century, all the documents written in Meitei Mayek were burnt down with the introduction of Vaishnavism in the princely state of Manipur. This day known as the "Puya Meithaba" marked the beginning of destruction of the script, which eventually got replaced by Bengali script. This fact tells us how important the storage of text in the digital form is for, among other reasons, the survival of a script. Nevertheless, during the year 1930–1980, there were a lot of attempts to bring back the use of Meitei Mayek script. After a lot of attempts to revive the script, it was finally approved by the government of Manipur in the year 1980. After almost 25 years since approval of the script, the Manipur government for the first time included Meitei Mayek as part of academic curriculum in the academic session 2005–2006 [4]. There are 56 letters in Meitei Mayek. They are 27 consonants (Iyek Ipee), 8 final consonants (Lonsum Iyek), 8 vowels (Cheitap Iyek), 3 punctuation marks (Khudam Iyek) and 10 numerals (Cheising Iyek).

2.2 Collection of Data Samples

The collection of data samples was carried out in two phases. The first phase consists of distributing a tabular form and asking people to write the characters five times each. Filled-in forms were collected from around 200 different individuals in the age group 12–23 years. The second phase was the collection of handwritten sheets such as answer sheets and classroom notes from students in the same age group. Example of samples collected are shown in Fig. 1. A total of 279 such pages written by 279 different individuals were collected. The reason why a particular age group is considered is because of the fact that individuals older than that do not know how to write the script as Bangla was the script which was used during their times. So in order to capture the natural handwriting and not the drawing of characters, the mentioned age range is considered. The data samples are collected from schools and colleges in different parts of Imphal.

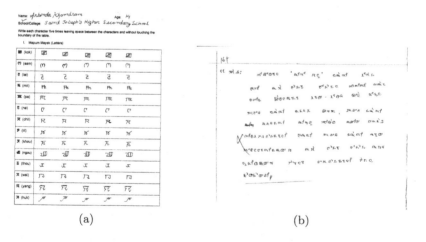

(a)   (b)

Fig. 1. Samples of data collected (a) tabular form (b) answer sheet

2.3   Dataset Creation

The forms and pages collected are scanned at 300 dpi using a canon flatbed scanner in grayscale format and saved in TIF format. The dataset consists of 37 classes (27 consonants and 10 numerals). Information and steps regarding creation of the dataset are given below:

- Step 1: Each row from the forms were manually cropped. The bounding box of each character was then considered to crop the characters. During this process, a number of unwanted connected components such as dots and small lines also get cropped. In order to get rid of these types of unwanted cropped images, any image smaller than width 10 pixels or height 10 pixels was deleted. After this step, manual checking was done to clean the dataset of any unwanted images.
- Step 2: For the answer sheets and classroom notes, each character was manually cropped and its bounding box found out and then cropped accordingly.
- Step 3: Since the occurrence of numerals and a few characters is very rare in the answer sheets and classroom notes, in order to make the number of samples in each class fairly equal, these characters were collected separately from another 60 different individuals in the tabular form. And the procedure of step 1 was carried out.
- Step 4: Characters inside the bounding box are then size normalized to fit in a box of 24 × 24 pixels. The total number of characters in the dataset is 60285. The distribution of samples over the classes is uneven. The characters are divided randomly into training samples (90%) and testing samples (10%) as shown in Table 2. Training set has 54239 images and testing set has 6046 images.

The number of training and testing samples in each class is different and vary according to the total number of samples in the respective class. Samples from the first five classes of consonants and numerals each are shown in Fig. 2.

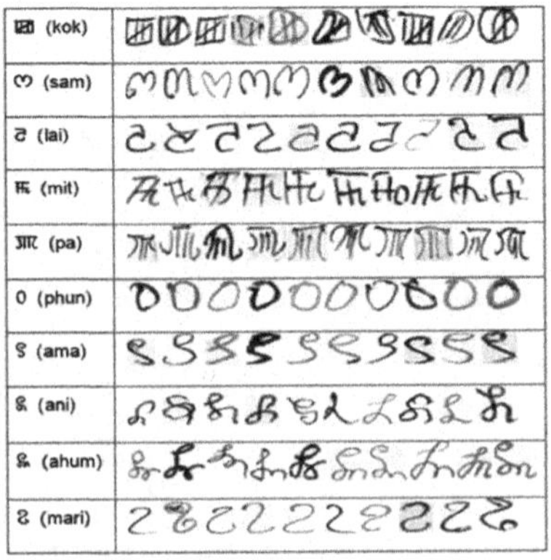

Fig. 2. Samples from some of the classes

Table 2. Number of training and testing samples in each class

Character	Training	Testing	Total	Character	Training	Testing	Total
Ama	1812	202	2014	Ngou	1368	152	1522
Ani	1737	194	1924	Thou	1391	155	1546
Ahum	1656	185	1841	Wai	1233	137	1371
Mari	1686	188	1875	Yang	1404	156	1562
Manga	1674	187	1859	Huk	1349	150	1501
Taruk	1647	183	1837	Un	1382	154	1537
Taret	1629	182	1811	Ee	1355	151	1505
Nipal	1661	185	1842	Pham	1294	144	1438
Mapal	1602	179	1781	Atiya	1363	152	1516
Phun	1762	196	1958	Gok	1340	149	1491
Kok	1364	152	1516	Jham	1558	174	1717
Sam	1373	153	1527	Rai	1370	153	1523
Lai	1382	154	1536	Baa	1363	152	1515
Mit	1377	154	1531	Jil	1382	154	1536
Paa	1354	151	1505	Dil	1379	154	1533
Naa	1401	156	1557	Ghou	1522	170	1682
Chil	1393	155	1546	Dhou	1455	162	1608
Til	1398	156	1556	Bham	1460	163	1613
Khou	1363	152	1515				

3   Character Recognition

3.1   Preprocessing

Preprocessing is employed to bring the images to a format which further stages can process. One of the advantages for using CNN as a recognition tool is that the input to such a system does not need a lot of preprocessing as compared to that needed for hand-crafted feature extraction. In the present study, the only preprocessing that has been done is normalization of the raw gray-scale images to normalize the pixel intensity values to the range [0, 1]. These normalized images are then fed into the system.

3.2   CNN Based Recognition

Convolutional Neural Network: CNN is a deep learning network whose basic architecture consists of three types of layer: convolutional, pooling and fully-connected layers stacked one above another in a manner which is a design choice.

CNN was first introduced by Fukushima et al. [2] where they proposed a NN model called "neocognitron" which is a multilayered network consisting of a cascade connection of many layers of cells where some of the connections are variable and can be updated by learning. However, it was not very popularly used because of the difficulty in the leaning algorithm. CNN, as we know today was proposed by LeCun et al. [10] where they used backpropagation and gradient-based learning to train a Neocognitron-like architecture and refined the architecture trying different variations of the model. They achieved very good results with these changes made and since then researchers have been working on many improved variants of CNN for pattern recognition tasks. CNN has shown its superiority as a recognition tool and hence is the obvious choice of many researchers due to its unique properties such as it (a) can an be used as both feature extractor and classifier (b) takes advantage of local spatial coherence of the pixels (c) uses shared parameters and hence less number of trainable parameters to deal with (d) is robust to noise and is shift-invariant.

3.3   CNN Architecture and Parameters Setup

In the present study, we have considered a CNN model to classify the characters of Meitei Mayek. The architecture used for our work is inspired by a combination of three architectures: the classic LeNet-5 [10], AlexNet [3] and VGGNet [19]. We have adopted a simple architecture similar to LeNet-5 with alternating convolutional and pooling layers; the concept of max pooling, Rectified Linear Unit (ReLU) activations as adopted in AlexNet and increasing number of filters by double fold for each convolutional layer as was done in VGGNet.

The CNN architecture consists of seven layers - one input layer, four layers of two alternating convolutional and pooling layers, one fully connected layer and one output layer (Fig. 3). In the proposed architecture, more number of filters are considered as to capture more high level features for characters. Max-pooling is employed instead of mean-pooling as it can lead to faster convergence, extract invariant features more efficiently and improve generalization [17]. ReLU activation function is adopted as it is shown to be computationally faster and reduces the likelihood of vanishing of the gradient unlike sigmoid and tangent functions [13]. Mini-batch stochastic gradient descent with momentum is used as it converges faster than the original or batch gradient descent [11]. The first convolutional layer (C_1) has an output mapping of 24 feature maps produced by convolution of the input image with filter mask size 5×5. The activation function used is ReLU (Rectified Linear Unit). The feature maps at this layer is of size $(24 - 5 + 1) = 20 \times 20$ pixels. The total number of connections at this layer is $(20 \times 20 \times 24) \times (5 \times 5 + 1) = 2,49,600$. However, the number of trainable parameters is very less compared to this figure because of the weight-sharing feature of CNN. The number of trainable parameters at this layer is $(5 \times 5 \times 24) + 24 = 624$. Next layer is the first pooling layer (P_1) which is responsible for CNN being able to achieve local-distortion and translation invariance to a certain extent and it also makes the system robust to noise. In the present architecture, max pooling is employed with sub-sample size of 2×2 pixels with stride 2. This layer produces down-sampled output of 24 feature maps with size 10×10 pixels. The number of trainable parameters is 0.

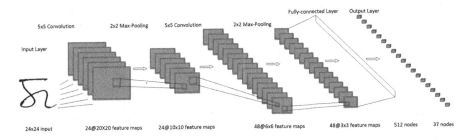

Fig. 3. The overall CNN architecture used in the present work

For the second convolutional layer (C_2), there are output mapping of 48 feature maps with filter mask of 5×5 pixels which produces an output of 48 feature maps of size 6×6 pixels. The number of trainable parameters for this layer is calculated as $(5 \times 5 \times 24 \times 48) + 48 = 28,848$. The second pooling layer (P_2) has a sub-sample size 2×2 pixels and max pooling is carried out with stride 2 to produce 48 feature maps of size 3×3. These feature maps are input to the first fully connected layer (FC_1) which has 512 nodes. Sigmoid activation function is used for the fully-connected layer. The number of parameters for this layer is $(512 \times 48 \times 3 \times 3) + 512 = 2,21,696$. The second fully-connected and last layer is the output layer (FC_2) which uses softmax function with cross entropy loss function to calculate cost. It has 37 nodes, each node indicating a character class and having number of parameters given by $(37 \times 512) + 37 = 18,981$. Thus, the total number of trainable parameters is 2,70,149 (Table 3).

Table 3. CNN Parameters Setup

Layer	Layer type	No. of feature maps	Filter size	No. of parameters
C_1	Convolution	24	5×5	624
P_1	Pooling	24	2×2	0
C_2	Convolution	48	5×5	28,848
P_2	Pooling	48	2×2	0
FC_1	Fully-connected	512	1×1	2,21,696
FC_2	Fully-connected	37	1×1	18,981

Hyperparameters Tuning: In any deep learning system, tuning hyperparameters is the most important and challenging task to be done in order to have better accuracy. It was pointed out by Bengio [1] that for a stochastic gradient descent optimization, learning rate and batch size are two most important hyper-parameters that need to be fine-tuned for achieving better accuracy. The optimal learning rate is dependent on the model architecture as well as the dataset. For our model, we start out by taking mini-batch size of 32, 64, 128, 256 and 512 by setting the initial learning rate to 0.01. Mini-batch size of 256 is chosen empirically. Once the mini-batch size is decided upon, we fine-tune the learning rate by taking values 0.3, 0.1, 0.01 and 0.001 and a learning rate annealing with the formula as follows

$$\alpha = \frac{1}{1 + decay\_rate * en} * \alpha_0 \tag{1}$$

α is the learning rate for the epoch number en, α_0 is the initial learning rate, $decay\_rate$ is set to 1. An initial learning rate of 0.1 is found to be appropriate for our model and hence it is used. The momentum for SGD is set to 0.9 which is the best default value.

4   Overfitting in Deep Network

Deep learning networks like CNN require a lot of data samples for training since it deals with a huge number of parameters and weights to generalize the system. If there are not enough amount of training data the system tends to overfit, i.e. it becomes biased to the data that it has seen during training and hence it cannot generalize the learned network to the data it has not seen before [19]. This reduces test accuracy of the system which is undesirable. One of the strategies to avoid overfitting is *data augmentation*. It is a process of incrementing the number of training data by applying techniques such as blur, rotation, translation, etc. on the original data.

5   Data Augmentation for Dataset Increment

Number of training samples in the present study was incremented by rotating the original images randomly in the range -10 to $10°$, introducing salt and pepper noise and blurring using Gaussian filter resulting in a dataset of size four times the original one. The augmented dataset thus consists of 2,16,956 training images. The original dataset will be referred to as dataset A and the augmented dataset as dataset B in the later sections.

6   Experimental Results

The system is trained with datasets A and B. The number of epochs has a significant effect on the test accuracy of a recognition system. Our system is analyzed with different number of epochs and the resulting test accuracies are observed. For dataset A, the test accuracy stabilizes after 12 epochs of training. The highest accuracy achieved is 96.24%. For dataset B, the α_0 of learning rate decay equation (Eq. 1) is replaced by α (learning rate of the previous epoch) so that the learning rate decays by greater amount after each epoch since the number of weight updates per epoch is more in this case because of a larger number of training samples. The model stabilizes much faster when trained with dataset B at 6th epoch. This augmented training set shows an improved test accuracy as was expected and achieves highest accuracy of 97.09%. Evaluation performance of the system on these two training sets is shown in Fig. 4.

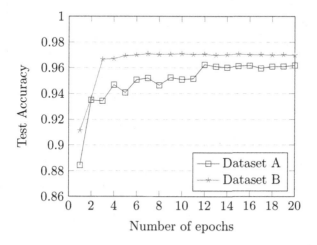

Fig. 4. Test accuracies at different epochs (Learning rate decay is different for the two datasets)

7   Conclusion

A pioneering work of developing a public dataset of Meitei Mayek handwritten characters is reported. The dataset consists of 60285 characters for 37 classes (27 consonants and 10 numerals). A CNN architecture is also proposed for recognition of characters in the developed dataset. We have analyzed the effect of data augmentation to avoid overfitting of the deep network and we were able to achieve better accuracy by training the system with augmented training set. The accuracy achieved in this work is promising considering the diversity of handwriting styles contained in the dataset and challenges due to high degree of similarity between some of the characters with one another.

References

1. Bengio, Y.: Practical recommendations for gradient-based training of deep architectures. In: Montavon, G., Orr, G.B., Müller, K.-R. (eds.) Neural Networks: Tricks of the Trade. LNCS, vol. 7700, pp. 437–478. Springer, Heidelberg (2012). https://doi.org/10.1007/978-3-642-35289-8_26

2. Fukushima, K.: Neocognitron: a hierarchical neural network capable of visual pattern recognition. Neural Netw. **1**(2), 119–130 (1988)
3. Krizhevsky, A., Sutskever, I., Hinton, G.E.: ImageNet classification with deep convolutional neural networks. In: Advances in Neural Information Processing Systems, pp. 1097–1105 (2012)
4. Kshetrimayum, N.: A comparative study of Meetei Mayek: from the inscribed letterform to the digital typeface. Unpublished Masters Dissertation. University of Reading. Reading, UK (2010)
5. Kumar, C.J., Kalita, S.K.: Recognition of handwritten numerals of Manipuri script. Int. J. Comput. Appl. **84**(17), 1–5 (2013)
6. Kumar, C.J., Kalita, S.K.: Point feature based recognition of handwritten Meetei Mayek script. In: Kalam, A., Das, S., Sharma, K. (eds.) Advances in Electronics, Communication and Computing. LNEE, vol. 443, pp. 431–439. Springer, Singapore (2018). https://doi.org/10.1007/978-981-10-4765-7_46
7. Kumar, C.J., Kalita, S.K., Sharma, U.: Recognition of Meetei Mayek characters using hybrid feature generated from distance profile and background directional distribution with support vector machine classifier. In: Communication, Control and Intelligent Systems (CCIS), pp. 186–189. IEEE (2015)
8. Laishram, R., Singh, A.U., Singh, N.C., Singh, A.S., James, H.: Simulation and modeling of handwritten Meitei Mayek digits using neural network approach. In: Proceedings of the International Conference on Advances in Electronics, Electrical and Computer Science Engineering-EEC, pp. 355–358 (2012)
9. Laishram, R., Singh, P.B., Singh, T.S.D., Anilkumar, S., Singh, A.U.: A neural network based handwritten Meitei Mayek alphabet optical character recognition system. In: 2014 IEEE International Conference on Computational Intelligence and Computing Research (ICCIC), pp. 1–5. IEEE (2014)
10. LeCun, Y., Bottou, L., Bengio, Y., Haffner, P.: Gradient-based learning applied to document recognition. Proc. IEEE **86**(11), 2278–2324 (1998)
11. Li, M., Zhang, T., Chen, Y., Smola, A.J.: Efficient mini-batch training for stochastic optimization. In: Proceedings of the 20th ACM SIGKDD International Conference on Knowledge Discovery and Data Mining, pp. 661–670. ACM (2014)
12. Maring, K.A., Dhir, R.: Recognition of cheising iyek/eeyek-Manipuri digits using support vector machines. IJCSIT **1**(2) (2014)
13. Nair, V., Hinton, G.E.: Rectified linear units improve restricted Boltzmann machines. In: Proceedings of the 27th International Conference on Machine Learning (ICML 2010), pp. 807–814 (2010)
14. Nongmeikapam, K., Manipur, I., Kumar, I.W.K., Singh, M.P.: Exploring an efficient handwritten Manipuri Meetei-Mayek character recognition using gradient feature extractor and cosine distance based multiclass k-nearest neighbor classifier. In: Proceedings of ICON-2017, Kolkata, India, pp. 328–337. NLPAI, December 2017
15. Pal, U., Jayadevan, R., Sharma, N.: Handwriting recognition in Indian regional scripts: a survey of offline techniques. ACM Trans. Asian Lang. Inf. Process. (TALIP) **11**(1), 1 (2012)
16. Pal, U., Sharma, N., Wakabayashi, T., Kimura, F.: Handwritten character recognition of popular south Indian scripts. In: Doermann, D., Jaeger, S. (eds.) SACH 2006. LNCS, vol. 4768, pp. 251–264. Springer, Heidelberg (2008). https://doi.org/10.1007/978-3-540-78199-8_15

17. Scherer, D., Müller, A., Behnke, S.: Evaluation of pooling operations in convolutional architectures for object recognition. In: Diamantaras, K., Duch, W., Iliadis, L.S. (eds.) ICANN 2010. LNCS, vol. 6354, pp. 92–101. Springer, Heidelberg (2010). https://doi.org/10.1007/978-3-642-15825-4_10
18. Simard, P.Y., Steinkraus, D., Platt, J.C., et al.: Best practices for convolutional neural networks applied to visual document analysis. In: ICDAR, vol. 3, pp. 958–962 (2003)
19. Simonyan, K., Zisserman, A.: Very deep convolutional networks for large-scale image recognition. arXiv preprint arXiv:1409.1556 (2014)
20. Singh, T., Bawa, S.G., Bansal, P., Vig, R.G., et al.: Off-line handwritten character recognition of Manipuri script. Ph.D. thesis (2017)
21. Tangkeshwar, T., Bonsai, R.: A novel approach to off-line handwritten character recognition of Manipuri script. In: Soft Computing, p. 365 (2005)
22. Thokchom, T., Bansal, P., Vig, R., Bawa, S.: Recognition of handwritten character of Manipuri script. JCP 5(10), 1570–1574 (2010)

Automated Fall Detection Using Computer Vision

Pramod Kumar Soni and Ayesha Choudhary(✉)

School of Computer and Systems Sciences, Jawaharlal Nehru University,
New Delhi 110067, India
pramod.apr10@gmail.com, ayeshac@mail.jnu.ac.in

Abstract. The population of elderly people is increasing day-by-day in the world. One of the major health issues of an old person is injury during a fall and this issue becomes compounded for elderly people living alone. In this paper, we propose a novel framework for automated fall detection of a person from videos. Background subtraction is used to detect the moving person in the video. Different features are extracted by applying rectangle and ellipse on human shape to detect the fall of a person. Experiments have been carried out on the UR Fall Dataset which is publicly available. The proposed method is compared with existing methods and significantly better results are achieved.

Keywords: Human fall detection · Computer vision
Background subtraction · Elderly care · Assisted living

1 Introduction

Caring of elderly or ailing people, who live alone, is one of the most important concerns in a family. One of the most dangerous situations is a person falling when alone at home. Approximately 60% injuries in the case for elderly in hospitals are due to falls. Falls affect the elderly people living alone because the person may not be able to call for help, such as if he or she is unconscious or paralyzed. In general, a person who is alone needs help if he or she has fallen. This is more necessary in case of ailing or elderly people. A fall at home can occur in many situations, like falling from bed, loss of balance, fall from walking and fall from a sitting or standing position.

According to the European Union Commission and the World Health Organization [1], the population of older people will increase threefold between 2008 and 2060. In this report, it is mentioned that every year approximately $28 - 35\%$ people over 60 and $32 - 42\%$ over 70 years of age, fall and these numbers are increasing. This increasing population of the elderly makes caring for old people a greater challenge. Not all falls create serious injuries but most of the time elderly people are unable to get up without help of others after falling and the time period which is spent lying on the floor can also create some health problems like dehydration, hypothermia, etc.

© Springer Nature Switzerland AG 2018
U. S. Tiwary (Ed.): IHCI 2018, LNCS 11278, pp. 220–229, 2018.
https://doi.org/10.1007/978-3-030-04021-5_20

There are many existing methods which are based on wearable devices [3–8]. These methods use an accelerometer and a gyroscope to detect a fall of a person. However, the person feels uncomfortable after wearing such devices for a long time and if the person forgets to wear it, falls can no longer be detected. Therefore, visual monitoring has greater advantages. Computer vision based approaches provide an inconspicuous and non-intruding way of observing objects, people and their activities, i.e., the person does not wear any device. Such approaches are not affected by noise, unlike other non-vision based devices which may be affected by noise. Some other advantages are as follows.

Computer vision systems use a camera that has the advantage of observing and storing vast amounts of information of the scene in its view. The other advantages are that the camera has the capability of identifying multiple events at the same time. Also, a camera is less intruding because it can be fixed in a structure and need not be worn by the person. The video recorded by the camera can be used for remote processing and verification. Moreover, a camera system may be easily installed and the user need not have any expertise in using the system.

In our framework, we process the video frame by frame. The processing step gives the contour representing the human body. We then extract features that describe a fall and use our learning based algorithm for fall detection in videos.

We continue the paper as follows. Section 2 provides discussion of similar work is presented. In Sect. 3, we describe the proposed method for detecting fall of a person. In Sect. 4 , we show our experimental results and compare the performance of our proposed method with the state of the art methods. The main findings and possible future directions are summarized in Sect. 5.

2   Related Work

The first fall detection system was proposed in the early 1970s [9]. It was designed in such a way that it can send an alert message when user pressed a remote transmitter button. Automatic fall detection method started appearing in 1990s [10] which was proposed by Lord and Calvin. This system was based on accelerometer.

Muheidat et al. [11] proposed a context-aware and real time fall detection system for elderly. The system consisted of sensors which are placed under carpet and the electronics reads the walking activity. Then smart phone is used to improve smart carpet for improving the efficiency to detect the fall. Joshi et al. [12] proposed a fall detection system using computer vision and internet of things. Single camera is used to capture the different activity of the person. Center of Mass, aspect ratio and orientation angle are calculated to detect the fall of a person and an email is sent with attached screenshot. Djelouat et al. [13] proposed a computer vision based fall detection system for elderly person. First, acceleration data is gathered for different activity of person. Then data is multiplied by a binary sensing matrix. KNN and extended nearest neighbor is used to classify fall from other activities.

In 2016, Merrouche et al. [14] proposed a fall detection method using computer vision techniques and camera. This system used human shape analysis, head tracking and center of frame detection methods. Relationship between time and distance, translated by covariance, is calculated for discriminating falls. The system achieved 92.8% accuracy. Wang et al. [15] presented a fall detection method using RGB camera. Background subtraction method is used to detect the moving object. Then contour of the body is extracted to obtain width and height of the human body. Speed of the human body is calculated using an optical flow method. Then fall of a person is detected based on magnitude and direction of body. Wang et al. [16] proposed a method for detecting fall of a person. A vision component is used to detect and extract the moving person in the video. Then histogram of oriented gradients, local Binary Pattern and feature extraction by the Deep Learning framework are used to detect the fall of a person. The system achieved 93.5% sensitivity and 92% specificity.

Rougier et al. [17] proposed a fall detection which is based on the analysing human shape in a video. A shape matching method is used to keep track of the posture of the person in the video. The shape deformation is quantified from these postures using shape analysis methods. Fall of a person is recognized using the Gaussian Mixture Model. Lazzi et al. [18] proposed a fall detection system using video. First, images are captured and then background subtraction method is used to detect the moving object in the video. They, then apply some processing method to improve the result. After that different features are extracted for detecting the fall of a person. Yajal et al. [19] proposed a fall detection method using directional bounding boxes. The method was evaluated in the video using RGB-D camera. Aspect ratio is calculated to monitor the movement of the person. Diaz et al. [20] developed a dynamic background subtraction method for detection of fall of a person using 2D camera. Background subtraction method is used to detect the moving object from the images. Then movement detection method is used to detect the fall of a person. The system achieved up to 85.37% accuracy.

Ma et al. [21] proposed a fall detection system via shape analysis using a camera. Two computer vision techniques, shape-based fall characterization and learning based classifier, are used to detect the fall form other daily living activities of a person. The system achieved 91.15% sensitivity and 77.14% specificity. Chua et al. [22] proposed a fall detection method using uncalibrated camera. The method combined human shape and human head detection together to recognize the fall of a person. Different features are extracted from fitting the ellipse to detect the fall. The head detection method is used to differentiate fall from other daily living activities of a person. Dumitrache et al. [23] presented a fall detection method which is dependent on triaxial accelerometer data. This algorithm was designed to be implemented in a mobile system that uses a micro controller for data processing and a tri-axial accelerometer for data acquisition. Xiao et al. [24] proposed for detecting fall activities by using Gaussian mixture model (GMM) and spatial temporal analysis of aspect ratio. First, GMM is used to get background and foreground part of image. Then aspect ratio feature are calculated from the minimum external rectangle of person. By using spatial temporal analysis of aspect ratio, the system output the fall behaviour more robust. Khawandi et al. [25] developed a framework of fall detection which uses different machine learning algorithm. The algorithm easily learned the data, classified the data and identified falls from data which is received by a multi sensor monitoring system. Then decision tree is used to classify fall of the person.

Yun et al. [26] developed a fall detection system based on analysing human shape by applying unified Riemannian manifold. It represented dynamic shapes as points moving on a unit of n-sphere and computed velocity corresponding to manifold points which are based on geodesic distance. The proposed system achieved 96.77% detection rate and 10.26% false alarm rate.

3   Fall Detection Method

We detect the fall of a person in a room environment. Here, we assume that a camera is mounted in the room in such a way that it can cover a large area of room and there are no major occlusions in the room. We also assume that the focal length and field of view (FOV) of the camera does not change. The camera captures the scene frame by frame and sends it to the on board computer. Again, the input image is of size 320×240. The experiment is done on UR Fall dataset [2] which is publicly available.

3.1   Background Subtraction

In a video sequence, identifying moving objects is the fundamental and critical task. The most common method to detect moving objects in the video is background subtraction. Background subtraction which is also known as foreground detection is a technique to detect moving objects in the video sequence. Here, we use the Mixture of Gaussian (MoG) method to detect moving objects (which includes the person) in the video as shown in the Fig. 1

Fig. 1. Result of background subtraction.

3.2   Morphological Operations

Morphology is a large set of image processing operations that process the image which is based on architecture. These operations take input image and then apply a structuring element to that input image and generate output image which is of similar size. In these operations, every pixel value in the resulting image is based on correlation of the related pixels for the input image with its adjoin image. Erosion and dilation are the most basic morphological operation. We have taken the output of background subtraction technique and applied dilation and erosion on those images to get the proper connected components which may be lost during foreground segmentation.

3.3   Extraction of Connected Components

This method scans the images and combines the pixels into component which is based on pixel association, i.e. all pixels in a connected component divide same pixel values and these values are connected to each other. Once all clusters are calculated, every pixel value is marked with a colour or gray level based on the component it is allowed to. Connected component trademark works by searching an image, pixel by pixel in order to find connected pixel areas. Here, we have used 8-connected component so that whole human body could appear all together. A big contour is most probably caused by a large area for human body. A small contour is also found due to some noise i.e. lighting effect, moving cutting, etc. Upon this observation, a filter is applied on the list of contours to extract those contours that fall between two limits. A suitable range of these two limits are found experimentally.

3.4   Extraction of Contours

The contour extraction stage has been able to remove a significant amount of noise and unwanted objects. A big contour is most probably caused by a large area for human body. A small contour is also found due to some noise. Upon this observation, a filter is applied on the list of contours to extract those contours that fall within a threshold. A suitable range of the thresholds are found experimentally. At this stage, we have a list of contours that are most likely to represent actual human body shape.

3.5   Our Proposed Method

We process the video frame by frame. First, we apply background subtraction method to detect the person from the video. Then we extract those contours that represent the actual human shape in the video. After recognizing the contour, we fit the ellipse and rectangle as shown in the Fig. 2 After fitting ellipse and rectangle, we calculate the area and orientation of the ellipse and the aspect ratio of the bounding rectangle frame by frame and apply incremental clustering to it. In the first frame, we create the first cluster using the aspect ratio of

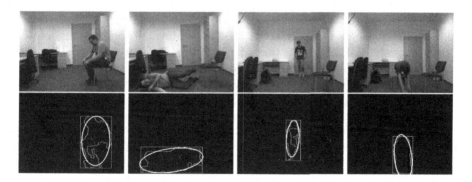

Fig. 2. Results of ellipse and rectangle fitting on the segmented foreground.

bounding rectangle, area and orientation of the ellipse as the features. When a new frame comes, we again calculate these parameters and compare it with the feature values of the existing clusters, for each feature separately. If there exists similarity with an existing cluster, we put it in the same cluster. Otherwise we create a new cluster, with these features as the first element. For more than one element in a cluster, the average of the feature values are used for comparison with the new features.

Let X_1, X_2 and X_3 are the three variables where X_1 is the angle of ellipse, X_2 is the area of the ellipse and X_3 is the aspect ratio of the rectangle. First, we find the height and weight of the ellipse and then area of the ellipse is defined as

$$X_2 = PI * (H/2.0) * (W/2.0) \tag{1}$$

Here, we divide H and W by 2.0 for maximum and minimum radii. After fitting the ellipse, now we fit the rectangle. Then, we find the aspect ratio of the rectangle, which is calculated as:

$$Aspect\ Ratio = \frac{width\ of\ the\ rectangle}{height\ of\ the\ rectangle} \tag{2}$$

Now, we take these parameters and apply clustering method to detect the fall of a person in the video. Three conditions are applied together:

1. The angle of ellipse lies between 5 to 40 or between 70 to 100 i.e. $0 \leq X_1 \leq 50$ or $70 \leq X_1 \leq 100$.
2. The area of the ellipse lies between 4000 and 12000 i.e. $4000 \leq X_2 \leq 12000$.
3. The aspect ratio is greater than 1 i.e. $X_3 > 1$.

4 Experimental Results and Discussion

The proposed algorithm has been implemented using C++ and OpenCV open source computer vision library version 3.0 on Linux operating system. In the

dataset [2], there are total 60 video segments which are taken for fall detection
and 40 video segments for daily activities like bending, sitting, walking, etc. In
this system, only RGB-dataset is taken for detection of fall of a person. There are
some healthy person and old person in the dataset and there is no large occlusion
occurs in the room. The implemented algorithm runs on Linux operating system
of type 64-bit with clock speed of 2.4 GHz, 6 GB of RAM running at 1333 MHz.
Before measuring the frame per second on each dataset, CPU scaling was turned
off to ensure that it runs at constant 2.4 GHz all the time on all these datasets.
The proposed method detect fall either from walking or from chair. When a
person falls, it shows red rectangle and write fall on the image as shown in the
Fig. 3.

Fig. 3. Fall of a person in different situations. The red box indicates that the fall is
correctly recognized. (color figure online)

For daily activities, it shows green rectangle on the image as shown in the Fig. 4.
Again, comparison is made with 3 existing methods in terms of the sensitivity
and specificity as follows:

$Sensitivity = TP/(TP + FN)\,and$
$Specificity = TN/(TN + FP)$
where TP, FN, FP and TN is defined as:
$TP(TruePositive)$: the number of falls correctly detected.
$FN(FalseNegative)$: the number of falls not correctly detected.
$FP(FalsePositive)$: the number of normal activities detected as a fall.
$TN(TrueNegative)$: the number of normal activities not detected as a fall.
Here, high sensitivity means most fall activities are detected correctly. Similarly,
high specificity means that most daily activities are not detected as fall.

The proposed system achieved 99.10% sensitivity and 97.10% specificity
(Table 1).

Fig. 4. Daily living activities of a person. The green box indicates that the activity is correctly recognized as "Not Fall".

Table 1. Comparison of different methods in terms of sensitivity and specificity.

Method	Sensitivity(%)	Specificity(%)
Rougier et al. [17]	95.40	95.80
Ma et al. [21]	99.93	91.67
Yun et al. [26]	96.77	89.74
Proposed method	**99.10**	**97.10**

5   Conclusion and Future Work

In this paper, we have proposed a novel framework for automatic fall detection of a person in the room. In our framework, first contours are extracted from video frame by frame through a series of low image processing methods. After that rectangle and ellipse are applied on human body shape and by taking three different features, falls are recognized. The experimental result shows that our algorithm gives good result. Our proposed system assumes that there is no large occlusion in the room. In the future, we will attempt to recognize fall in more challenging conditions as well as different daily living activities of a person.

References

1. World Health Organization. World Health Organization global report on falls prevention in older age, 2007 (2011)
2. UR Fall Detection Dataset. http://fenix.univ.rzeszow.pl/mkepski/ds/uf.html
3. Elfaramawy, T., Fall, C.L., Morissette, M., Lellouche, F.: Wireless respiratory monitoring and coughing detection using a wearable patch sensor network. In: 15th IEEE International New Circuits and Systems Conference (NEWCAS), pp. 197–200 (2017)
4. Chen, K., Chen, Y., Sun, Y. Liu, J.: A system of fall detection using a wearable device based on bluetooth communication. In: 13th IEEE International Conference on Solid-State and Integrated Circuit Technology (ICSICT), pp. 382–384 (2016)

5. Otanasap, N.: Pre-impact fall detection based on wearable device using dynamic threshold model. In: 17th International Conference on Parallel and Distributed Computing, Applications and Technologies (PDCAT), pp. 362–365 (2016)

6. Ozcan, K., Velipasalar, S.: Wearable camera and accelerometer based fall detection on portable devices. IEEE Embed. Syst. Lett. **8**(1), 6–9 (2016)

7. Geo, H.W., Hsieh, T.T., Huang, Y.S., Chien, J.C., Haraikawa, K., Shieh, J.S.: A threshold-based algorithm of fall detection using a wearable device with tri-axial accelerometer and gyroscope. In: International Conference on Intelligent Informatics and Biomedical Sciences (ICIIBMS), pp. 54–57 (2015)

8. Wang, C., et al.: Low-power fall detector using triaxial accelerometry and barometric pressure sensing. IEEE Trans. Ind. Inf. **13**(6), 2302–2311 (2016)

9. What's new in electronics: Emergency Dailer. Popular Science, p. 104. Bonnier Corporation, New York (1975)

10. Lord, C.J., Colvin, D.P.: Falls in the elderly: Detection and assessment. In: IEEE Proceedings of the Annual International Conference of the Engineering in Medicine and Biology Society, pp. 1938–1939 (1991)

11. Muheidat, F., Tawalbeh, L., Tyrer, H.: Context-aware, accurate, and real time fall detection system for elderly people. In: 12th IEEE International Conference on Semantic Computing (ICSC), pp. 329–333 (2018)

12. Joshi, N.B., Nalbalwar, S.L.: A fall detection and alert system for an elderly using computer vision and Internet of Things. In: 2nd IEEE International Conference on Recent Trends in Electronics, Information and Communication Technology (RTE-ICT), pp. 1276–1281 (2017)

13. Djelouat, H., Baali, H., Amira, A., Bensaali, F.: CS-based fall detection for connected health applications. In: 4th International Conference on Advances in Biomedical Engineering (ICABME), pp. 1–4 (2017)

14. Merrouche, F., Baha, N.: Depth camera based fall detection using human shape and movement. In: IEEE International Conference on Signal and Image Processing (ICSIP), pp. 586–590 (2016)

15. Wang, X., Liu, H., Liu, M.: A novel multi-cue integration system for efficient human fall detection. In: IEEE International Conference on Robotics and Biomimetics (ROBIO), pp. 1319–1324 (2016)

16. Wang, K., Cao, G., Meng, D., Chen, W., Cao, W.: Automatic fall detection of human in video using combination of features. In: IEEE International Conference on Bioinformatics and Biomedicine (BIBM), pp. 1228–1233 (2016)

17. Rougier, C., Meunier, J., St-Arnaud, A., Rousseau, J.: Robust video surveillance for fall detection based on human shape deformation. IEEE Trans. Circuits Syst. Video Technol. **21**(5), 611–622 (2011)

18. Iazzi, A., Thami, R.O.H. , Rziza, M.: A novel approach to improve background subtraction method for fall detection system. In: 12th IEEE/ACS International Conference of Computer Systems and Applications (AICCSA), pp. 1–2 (2015)

19. Yajai, A., Rodtook, A., Chinnasarn, K., Rasmequan, S.: Fall detection using directional bounding box. In: 12th International Joint Conference on Computer Science and Software Engineering (JCSSE), pp. 52–57 (2015)

20. Hernandez, S.D., DeLaHoz, Y., Labrador, M.: Dynamic background subtraction for fall detection system using a 2D camera. In: IEEE Latin-America Conference on Communications (LATINCOM), pp. 1–6 (2014)

21. Ma, X., Wang, H., Xue, B., Zhou, M., Ji, B., Li, Y.: Depth-based human fall detection via shape features and improved extreme learning machine. IEEE J. Biomed. Health Inf. **18**(6), 1915–1922 (2014)

22. Chua, J.L., Chang, Y.C., Lim, W.K.: Visual based fall detection through human shape variation and head detection. In: International Conference on Multimedia, Signal Processing and Communication Technologies (IMPACT), pp. 61–65 (2013)
23. Dumitrache, M., Pasca, S.: Fall detection algorithm based on triaxial accelerometer data. In: E-health and Bioengineering conference (EBH), pp. 1–4 (2013)
24. Xiao, H., Wang, X., Li, Q., Wang, Z.: Gaussian mixture model for background based automatic fall detection. In: International Conference on Cyberspace technology (CCT), pp. 234–237 (2013)
25. Khawandi, S., Ballit, A., Daya, B.: Applying machine learning algorithm in fall Detection Monitoring System. In: 5th International Conference on Computational Intelligence and Communication Networks (CICN), pp. 247–250 (2013)
26. Yun, Y., Gu, I.Y.: Human fall detection via shape analysis on Riemannian manifolds with applications to elderly care. In: IEEE International Conference on Image Processing (ICIP), pp. 3280–3284 (2015)

Wild Animal Detection from Highly Cluttered Forest Images Using Deep Residual Networks

Anamika Dhillon and Gyanendra K. Verma[✉]

Department of Computer Engineering, National Institute
of Technology Kurukshetra, Kurukshetra 136119, India
dhillon.anamika2390@gmail.com, gyanendra@nitkkr.ac.in

Abstract. Wild animal detection is a dynamic research field since last decades. The videos acquired from camera-trap comprises of scenes that are cluttered that poses a challenge for detection of the wild animal. In this paper, we proposed a deep learning based system to detect wild animal from highly cluttered natural forest images. We have utilized Deep Residual Network (ResNet) for features extraction from cluttered forest images. These features are feed to classification through some of the best in class machine learning techniques, to be specific Support Vector Machine, K-Nearest Neighbor and Ensemble Tree. Our outcomes demonstrate that our detection system through ResNet outperforms compare to existing systems reported in the literature.

Keywords: Wild animal detection · DCNN feature extractor
Ensemble tree · KNN · Natural scenes · SVM

1 Introduction

Presently extensive information and digital data about wild animal action and conduct could be easily acquired spanning bigger spaces and for long durations. Camera trap alongside the work of various researchers aids in observing and analyzing wild animals. With the increase in information on natural life, the researches have turned out to be more advantageous and comfortable, for example, determining the impacts of environmental changes on wild animal behavior and action and effect of human Intervention [1].

Sensor cameras deployed on trees in an area making a stationary camera trap network to observe wild animals. The camera traps actuated whenever a movement is detected, thus, make a short video or consecutive images of wild animal actions and their visual aspects alongside insights about the environment (light levels, moisture, temperature, and area). Such systems are essential for procurement of wild animal information with no unsettling influence. Likewise such systems are financially possible, simple to convey in bigger spaces and have low upkeep requirements; subsequently, broadly utilized for wild animal

© Springer Nature Switzerland AG 2018
U. S. Tiwary (Ed.): IHCI 2018, LNCS 11278, pp. 230–238, 2018.
https://doi.org/10.1007/978-3-030-04021-5_21

monitoring. Additionally, camera trap networks can be used to extract the biometric components of species along with the details of the wildlife environment and surroundings [2]. In this work, our focus is to propose a dependable and precise wild animal detection system using camera trap network.

The traditional methodologies are not capable of analyzing images with dynamic nature. Background segmentation and object detection with the movement of objects is an essential stride for automated scanning and analysis from sort videos [4]. The primary aim for wild animal recognition is to configure a model that can deal with complex backgrounds and productively identify animals in dynamic natural scenes.

Wild animal detection is a sub-field under object detection that needs to manage the issue of precision and speed because of the profound dynamic and complex nature of videos acquired from camera traps. This study is in-line with our previous work [5] on wild animal detection. The system was implemented utilizing CNN architecture along with vgg-f model [6]. We claimed 91.4% accuracy on a standard camera-trap dataset. However, in this study, we have implemented the system with ResNet model [7]. A ResNet model is relatively new model compare to vgg-f model.

The paper is sorted out as: the following section gives a short review of the current wild animal detection systems and existing research done in the field of automated wild animal detection. In Sect. 2, a concise portrayal of deep learning model provided. The methodology has given under Sect. 3, and the outcome and experimental setup discussed in Sect. 4 followed by conclusion in Sect. 5.

2   Related Work

In this section, we give a concise survey of the related work on the wild animal detection. Frame differencing is a technique used to extract information about the moving objects in an image sequence. Frame differencing generally utilizes the difference between two frames at the pixel level to acquire information about the moving object in an image sequence [8].

The temporal differencing technique is used to acquire the regions of moving objects from the background. It utilizes the pixel-level difference of consecutive frames in an image sequence [9]. It is highly adaptive to the dynamic nature of an image but fails to identify the moving object, in case the movement of the object is slow and has a consistent textural behavior. Moreover, if the object becomes stationary, its identification is not possible resulting in a high false negative rate.

The challenge faced with background subtraction is the changes of the background with input image sequence. Also, it has to handle the problems such as:

- Motion: The movement of regions such as branches of the tree, leaves, waving objects due to the wind, waves in water, etc. poses a challenge for background identification.
- Variation in illumination: A gradual difference required in background illumination and contrast over time.

– Shadows: The shadows of an object should be a background. However, the shadow of a moving object makes it difficult to identify as a background.
– Camouflage: In case, the pixel values of the foreground and background regions are similar to each other. The background regions create an illusion of foreground region.
– Bootstrapping: Even though a background model is not present for training, the background should be maintained by the model.

In the optical flow technique, optical flow of an image is calculated which involves the clustering to the distribution of the optical flow of the image. Optical flow technique extracts the entire information of an object based on its motion and uses this information for detection the object [10]. Even though it gives reasonable accuracy, the method has some limitations such as it is sensitive to noise and includes enormous calculations. Hence, it is not suitable for real-time applications. Existing studies [11,12] are based on DCNNs for object identification and recognition. For smooth and fast processing of DCNN based object detection, the regions of interest in an image are analyzed to avoid the absolute amount of analyses of the entire image. Existing studies on object recognition utilizing object proposition approach are [13–15]. Erhan et al. [13] utilize deep neural networks for region proposal and multi-class classification.

3   Methodology

The images from the camera trap database retrieved along with the dimensions of the patch. The patches defined with the help of IEC algorithm, which is specified into the camera trap database [3]. Each image in the camera trap database consists of a dimension for a patch that is cropped out from every image. The patches acquired are included in positive dataset. However, some images do not contain animals; therefore, no patch defined on such images. The images with no patch (no animal present) are used to create some patches of random size and included in the negative set. The features extracted from positive and negative set used for training and testing phase of a classifier for the animal-background model. The classifier determines the presence of a wild animal in an image by features. The input images are high-quality real-time images with both visual and infrared images depicting both day and night time. Thus the system has been trained to work for both day and night time.

The input images are real-time images for both day and night time. Hence, the input images are in visual and infrared format. Due to the difference in formats, these images are different from each other regarding quality and each image needs to be preprocessed such that each image processed through a single animal-background model. Every image has different size and aspect ratios. Therefore, the model needs to work with candidate wild animal regions that are of variable sizes and proportions since they generated through ensemble graph cuts.

The images are of varying sizes where the large-sized images contain some irrelevant information that contributes to the high computation time, therefore, each image is normalized to reduce the computational time and using only the required information. The images resized to the dimensions required by DCNN model used. Therefore, each image has the same size and aspect ratio before feature extraction.

4   Experimental Setup and Results

4.1   Datasets

A camera-trap dataset [3], a benchmark database for wild animal detection has been used to evaluate the performance of the proposed system. The available images are in both visual and infrared configuration, bringing about wild animal detection framework for both day mode and night mode. Camera trap systems give complex images with much-cluttered image sequences from the natural scene. The images acquired have the resolution ranging from 1920×1080 to 2048×1536. The quantity of image frames in each short video ranges from 10 to 300. The size of the video relies on the time of activity by a wild animal. An aggregate of 1110 patches separated from the dataset labeled as positive database. Figure 1 shows positive and negative samples of camera trap database.

4.2   Implementation Details

We utilize MatLab 2018a with equipment configuration as Intel® Core™ i7-7700 CPU @ 3.60 GHz (8 GB RAM) for wild animal detection framework. Since the deep model requires high computing time for training that is only possible with dedicated GPU, we have used pretrained model. In this manner, we have deployed a deep model as feature extractor while we have utilized diverse machine learning techniques as classifiers. We have employed different machine learning approaches as a classifier, for example, Support Vector Machines (SVM), K- Nearest Neighbour (KNN) and Ensemble tree.

The primary purpose of utilizing five-fold-cross-validation is to guarantee that outcomes stay unprejudiced to any particular set of data. Out of five-folds, four used for training and the one fold left is considered for testing. Consequently, 90% of the dataset utilized for training, 10% for testing. The procedure repeated five times such that each fold can be utilized for testing once. The average of the results obtained in five iterations considered as an outcome. The prominent features with one thousand feature dimensions are obtained after fine-tuning of pretrained model with our experimental database. These features are then fed to state-of-the-art machine learning algorithms namely SVM, KNN and Ensemble tree. We have employed linear and cubic SVM with corresponding kernel functions and automated kernel scale. Ensemble Bagged tree is used with bag ensemble technique, decision tree learner type, 30 number of learners, 20 number of splits and 0.1 learning rate. The training time and prediction speed vary for each classifier as shown in Table 1.

Fig. 1. Sample images of camera trap database (a) positive (b) negative samples

4.3   Result Analysis and Discussion

We have utilized distinctive performance measurements for evaluation of proposed system with standard evaluation measures namely accuracy, True Positive Rate (TPR), False Positive Rate (FPR) and Area Under Curve (AUC). TPR and FPR can be calculated using Eqs. 1 and 2 respectively.

$$TPR = T_P/(T_P + F_N) \tag{1}$$

$$FPR = F_P/(F_P + T_N) \tag{2}$$

We have accomplished approximate 99.9% accuracy with the machine learning technique such as SVMs, KNNs and ensemble classifiers. We observe that the proposed system obtains accurate results in cluttered images. The overall accuracy of the system is obtained to be in the range from 98.4%–99.9%. The highest accuracy is obtained using ensemble discriminant with 99.9% of accuracy. Table 2 demonstrates the system performance with the help of various performance measurements, for example, accuracy, TPR, FPR, AUC on the camera trap database. ROC curves for different algorithms are shown in Fig. 2 and confusion matrices are shown in Fig. 3.

We have obtained 99.9% accuracy with ensemble discriminant that outperform the work reported in [3,5,16]. In our previous study inline with this work, we claimed 0.9825 recall. This study is based on ResNet model and outperforms against all previous studies shown in Table 3.

Table 1. System training time for different algorithms

Classifiers	Training time (sec)	Prediction speed (obs/sec)
Ensemble discriminant	20.669	1100
Cubic SVM	1.8484	6800
Linear SVM	1.835	6800
Ensemble Bagged Trees	5.4588	3900
Ensemble KNN	31.047	180
Cosine KNN	3.549	1900

Table 2. System performance on Camera-Trap database (TPR: True Positive Rate, FPR: False Positive Rate, AUC: Area Under ROC Curve)

Algorithm	Accuracy (%)	TPR	FPR	AUC
Ensemble discreminant	99.9	1.0	0	1.0
Cubic SVM	99.6	0.99	0	1.0
Linear SVM	99.5	0.99	0	1.0
Ensemble Bagged Trees	99.3	0.98	0	1.0
Ensemble KNN	98.5	0.96	0	0.99
Cosine KNN	98.4	0.95	0	1.0

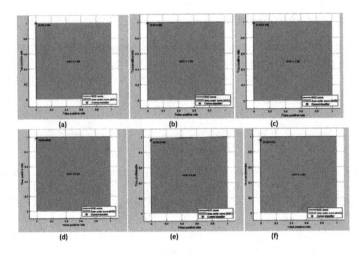

Fig. 2. ROC curves for different algorithms (a. Ensemble discriminant b. Cubic SVM c. Linear SVM d. Ensemble Bagged Trees e. Ensemble KNN f. Cosine KNN)

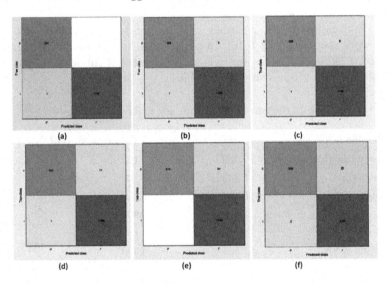

Fig. 3. Confusion matrices for different algorithms (a. Ensemble discriminant b. Cubic SVM c. Linear SVM d. Ensemble Bagged Trees e. Ensemble KNN f. Cosine KNN)

Table 3. Accuracy comparison with similar systems

Reference	Year	Features	Accuracy
Zhang et al. [16]	2015	Ensemble graph cuts	0.9137 (recall)
Zhang et al. [3]	2016	Deep learning and HOG features	0.8597 (recall)
Verma et al. [5]	2017	DCNN features with vgg-f model	0.9825 & 91.4%
This study	2018	DCNN features with ResNet model	0.9825 & 99.9%

5   Conclusion

The proposed wild animal detection system from cluttered images is an efficient approach for surveillance and monitoring purpose. An animal-background verification model is constructed through feature extraction using ResNet model, then assessing the best classification algorithm by applying different machine learning algorithms. The different machine learning algorithm used is SVM and its variants, KNN and its variants and ensemble trees.

Furthermore, in the future, we try to evaluate the system for reducing the false positive rate further, by preprocessing the images and using videos. We will also try to evaluate different CNN model as both classifier and feature extractor.

References

1. Tilak, S., et al.: Monitoring wild animal communities with arrays of motion sensitive camera. Int. J. Res. Rev. Wireless Sensor Netw. **1**, 1929 (2011)
2. Kays, R., et al.: eMammal-Citizen science camera trapping as a solution for broadscale long-term monitoring of wildlife populations. In: Proceedings of North American Conservation Biology, pp. 80–86 (2014)
3. Zhang, Z., He, Z., Cao, G., Cao, W.: Animal detection from highly cluttered natural scenes using spatiotemporal object region proposals and patch verification. IEEE Trans. Multimed. **18**(10), 2079–2092 (2016)
4. Chacon-Murguia, M.I., Gonzalez-Duarte, S.: An adaptive neural-fuzzy approach for object detection in dynamic backgrounds for surveillance systems. IEEE Trans. Ind. Electron. **59**(8), 3286–3298 (2012)
5. Verma, G.K., Gupta, P.: Wild animal detection using deep convolutional neural network. In: Chaudhuri, B., Kankanhalli, M., Raman, B. (eds.) Proceedings of 2nd International Conference on Computer Vision & Image Processing. Advances in Intelligent Systems and Computing, vol. 704, pp. 327–338. Springer, Singapore (2018). https://doi.org/10.1007/978-981-10-7898-9_27
6. Chatfield, K., Simonyan, K., Vedaldi, A., Zisserman, A.: Return of the devil in the details: delving deep into convolutional nets. In: Proceedings of the British Machine Vision Conference 2014 (2014). https://doi.org/10.5244/c.28.6
7. He, K., Zhang, X., Ren, S., Sun, J.: Deep residual learning for image recognition. In: Proceedings of the IEEE Conference on Computer Vision and Pattern Recognition, pp. 770–778 (2016)
8. Rakibe, R.S., Patil, B.D.: Background subtraction algorithm based human motion detection. Int. J. Sci. Res. Publ. **3**(5), 2250–3153 (2013)
9. Joshi, K.A., Thakore, D.G.: A survey on moving object detection and tracking in video surveillance system. Int. J. Soft Comput. Eng. **2**(3), 44–48 (2012)
10. Chauhan, A.K., Krishan, P.: Moving object tracking using Gaussian mixture model and optical flow. Int. J. Adv. Res. Comput. Sci. Softw. Eng. 3(4) (2013)
11. Sharif Razavian, A., Azizpour, H., Sullivan, J., Carlsson, S.: CNN features off-the-shelf: an astounding baseline for recognition. In: Proceedings of the IEEE Conference on Computer Vision and Pattern Recognition Workshops, pp. 806–813 (2014)
12. Oquab, M., Bottou, L., Laptev, I., Sivic, J.: Learning and transferring mid-level image representations using convolutional neural networks. In Proceedings of the IEEE Conference on Computer Vision and Pattern Recognition, pp. 1717–1724 (2014)

13. Szegedy, C., Toshev, A., Erhan, D.: Deep neural networks for object detection. In: Advances in Neural Information Processing Systems, pp. 2553–2561 (2013)
14. Sermanet, P., Eigen, D., Zhang, X., Mathieu, M., Fergus, R., LeCun, Y.: Overfeat: integrated recognition, localization and detection using convolutional networks. arXiv preprint arXiv:1312.6229 (2013)
15. Szegedy, C., Reed, S., Erhan, D., Anguelov, D., Ioffe, S.: Scalable, high-quality object detection. arXiv preprint arXiv:1412.1441 (2014)
16. Zhang, Z., Han, T. X., He, Z.: Coupled ensemble graph cuts and object verification for animal segmentation from highly cluttered videos. In: IEEE International Conference on Image Processing (ICIP) 2015, pp. 2830–2834. IEEE (2015)

A Non-deterministic Approach to Mitigate Replay Attack and Database Attack Simultaneously on Iris Recognition System

Richa Gupta$^{(\boxtimes)}$ and Priti Sehgal

University of Delhi, New Delhi, India
richie.akka@gmail.com

Abstract. Biometric authentication is associated with prevalent security related issues. They compromise with user identity and also make that user characteristic feeble for any further use. Several attack points have been identified in literature and research has been widely carried out on each of them independently. In this paper, we combine two attack points – replay attack and template-based attack. We extend our previous work on robust iris regions to mitigate both these attacks simultaneously. The proposed approach uses cancelable biometrics generation technique. The technique is based on non-invertible transform of the selected robust iris regions. This transformed or cancelable template is used for user authentication. The system attains the EER of 1.75% which is comparable to other state-of-art approaches.

Keywords: Cancelable biometrics · Iris recognition
Non-Deterministic approach · Replay attack · Template attack

1 Introduction

Biometric templates are at a high risk of being stolen and misused. This leaves the biometric useless for any further use. Ratha et al. [1] listed several attack points on biometric authentication system. This led to an evolution in the study of these attacks under different categories. Richa and Priti [2] listed in detail the solutions to alleviate some of these attack points on iris recognition system. The existing methods to handle different attack points concentrate solely on considering one of them at a time. The combined approach to mitigate these attacks simultaneously has not been studied yet. In this paper, we propose a solution to handle replay attack and database attack simultaneously, achieving an acceptable performance of the system.

Replay attack is the "illegal interception of message on the communication channel between sensor and the system". Its replay to the system at later time may get access to it [3, 4]. Impostor gaining access to templates stored in the database is known as database attack. In either of the cases, the biometric template is at a high risk of being revealed to an impostor. This can permanently reveal the identity of the user. Database attack has been classified under two categories – biometric cryptosystem and cancelable biometrics. Cancelable biometrics aims at distorting the biometric template in such a way that its theft does not reveal much useful information to the impostor [5].

© Springer Nature Switzerland AG 2018
U. S. Tiwary (Ed.): IHCI 2018, LNCS 11278, pp. 239–250, 2018.
https://doi.org/10.1007/978-3-030-04021-5_22

The two important properties for a technique under this category are unlinkability and irreversibility [5, 6]. Unlinkability means it should be possible to generate different biometric templates from same original template yet allowing diversity, that is, no cross-matching. Irreversibility means it should not be possible to recover original template from the distorted one [7].

We propose the use of robust iris regions [4] to allay replay attack and a non-invertible cancelable transform of these regions to generate a new biometric template. The request of randomized subset of robust iris regions and its response allays replay attack. This has been shown in our previous research [4]. The non-invertible transform, using application specific 'seed', to a transformed subset of these robust regions, achieves irreversibility. The selection and randomization of a subset of robust iris regions, helps to achieve unlinkability. This has been experimentally proven in the following sections.

2 Literature Survey

Replay attack poses a serious threat to iris based authentication system. Despite this, it has been rarely studied. One of the latest contributions can be found in [4] where we propose a non-deterministic approach to find robust iris regions. The random sequence of these selective regions is used to mitigate this attack. The system achieves equal error rate (EER) to be 1.24%, which is comparable to other techniques. Shelton et al. [8] propose the use of genetic algorithm to extract features from iris and mitigating this attack. Richa and Priti [3] suggest use of reversible watermarking having timestamp and sensor ID as watermark. This technique was used to avoid the performance degradation due to watermark and yet achieving the purpose of mitigating replay attack. In another approach, Hämmerle-Uhl et al. [9] also suggest use of watermarking to mitigate this attack. Another contribution by Smith et al. [10] has been made in the area of face recognition. They suggest the use of watermarking the face images based on reflections on the screen and mitigate replay attack on videos.

Another separate category, cancelable biometrics, has also been widely studied as an approach to handle template-based attacks. Gomez et al. [11] propose the use of bloom filters on local binary pattern histograms. They apply different gabor filters to each block and derive the local binary pattern (LBP) histograms from each. They achieve EER of approximately 5.5% on the system. Rathgeb et al. [7] also propose use of bloom filters with application specific key to mitigate this attack. They achieve system performance of 97.95% with EER as 1.14%. Syarif et al. [12] propose use of different LBP histograms based on key. They used two keys: first key is used to decide the number of histogram bins for each block from the image and second is used to permute the histograms from each block, which is used for authentication. They achieve EER of 0.0001 and 0.0003 on two different face databases but with only 38 and 12 subjects respectively. Dwivedi et al. [6] propose use of look up table and decimal encoding of iris images for generation of cancelable template. They achieve EER of 0.43 on CASIA Iris-v3-Interval DB.

Most of these techniques, found in literature, focus on one point of attack. In the proposed technique we aim to mitigate replay attack together with template-based attack, which has not been studied yet.

3 Proposed System

The working of the system is divided into two broad phases – training and verification and is summarized in Fig. 1.

3.1 Training Phase

The three random images are picked from the database for each subject and used to train the system. They are used to determine the robust iris regions. The rest of the images are used for user authentication. This phase involves image processing, normalization, feature extraction, robust region determination and non-invertible feature transform as discussed in the following sub-sections.

Image Processing and Normalization. This step pre-processes the eye image and performs segmentation to identify the pupil and iris from it. Unrolling the iris to polar coordinates further normalizes the segmented iris image. The segmentation and normalization has been performed using OSIRIS Iris software version 4.1 [13]. The incorrectly segmented images are discarded, as they are not fit for experiments.

Feature Extraction. The normalized iris region is averaged around the center pixel using Eq. (1) and divided into 64 regions (4 × 16) of size 64 × 32.

$$g_c' = c_{x,y} = \sum_{u=x-1}^{x+1} c_{u,y} + \sum_{v=y-1}^{y+1} c_{x,v} - c_{x,y} \tag{1}$$

where, g_c' and $c_{x,y}$ is the intensity of center pixel.

$c_{u,y}$, $c_{x,v}$ are the intensities of its neighboring pixels.

Texture information from each of the region is extracted using Average Local Binary Pattern (ALBP) codes. The $ALBP_{P,R}^{u2}$ operator denoting Local Binary Pattern (LBP) codes with P neighbors at radius R, used is presented by Eq. (2).

$$ALBP_{P,R}^{u2} = \sum_{p=0}^{P-1} s\left(g_p - g_c'\right)2^p, \qquad s(x) = \begin{cases} 1, & x \geq 0 \\ 0, & x < 0 \end{cases} \tag{2}$$

where, g_c' is as defined by Eq. (1).

g_p is the gray value of neighboring pixels whose co-ordinates are given by $\left(x_c + R\cos\frac{2\Pi p}{P}, y_c - R\sin\frac{2\Pi p}{P}\right)$.

The feature vectors are further extracted from this texture information by creating histograms. The ALBP configuration used in the proposed approach has P = 16 and

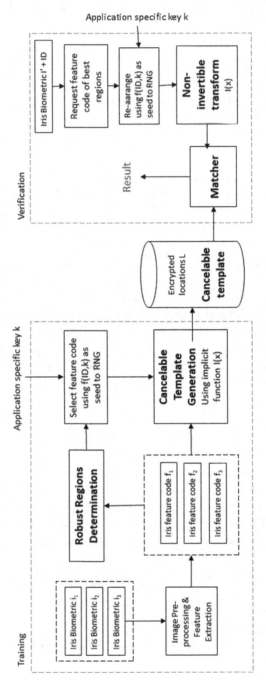

Fig. 1. Working of proposed approach

R = 4, which corresponds to n = 243 bins for uniform patterns [4]. A single feature template is formed by combining all these feature vectors, which is further used for authentication.

Robust Region Determination. The feature vectors are used to determine the robust iris regions that are found to be stable across the training set of images. A region is considered a candidate for stability if its distance metric (Chi-Square distance) with other corresponding regions from all the training images for that subject is minimum. These regions have found to be sufficient enough for authentication, with an acceptable performance. Our previous paper [4] elaborates the technique to generate robust iris regions and its application to allay replay attack on iris recognition system.

Non-invertible Transform. A random subset of robust iris regions is selected and their corresponding feature templates are collated to form new template X. The seed used for this random generation is derived from the User ID and system specific key K represented as follows in Eq. (3).

$$F(ID, \ k) \ = \ ID + k^2 \tag{3}$$

This feature template is transformed using non-invertible transform [14] given by Eq. (4).

$$I(X) = round(\sqrt[k]{X} + X) \tag{4}$$

3.2   Verification

The typical iris recognition methods follow a deterministic approach. The information flow in these systems, if intercepted, is easy to comprehend. This can revel many important user characteristics and leave that biometric useless for any other application. In the proposed approach, we propose a non-deterministic system, which overcomes this limitation. The information flow is tailored according to each user and mitigates replay attack and template-based attack to the system. This has been shown in Fig. 2 and detailed here.

The user authentication involves following steps-

Step 1: The user presents his claimed identity (ID).
Step 2: The system validates the user's identity, extracts and decrypts the robust iris locations (L) for the claimed user from the database.
Step 3 – The fetched iris locations are permuted and their corresponding feature code is requested from the sensor by sending a feature extractor FE (Eq. 5). The locations in feature extractor are encrypted using public key RSA cryptography. This overcomes the limitation to our previous approach [springer paper], where the interception of these messages was still a threat to the security of the system.

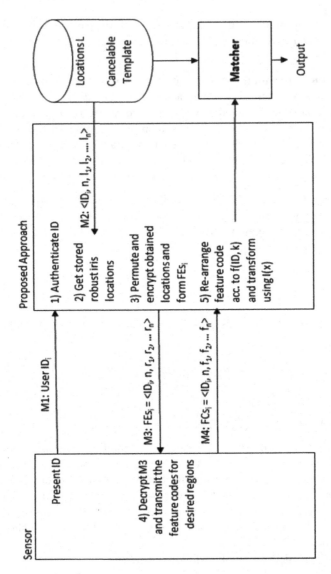

Fig. 2. Information flow of the proposed system

$$FEs_i = \ <ID_i, n, r_1, r_2, \ldots r_n>\ \tag{5}$$

where, ID is the unique user ID.

n is the count of regions.

$r_1, r_2, \ldots r_n$ are the encrypted region numbers chosen for authentication.

Step 4 - The FE received is decrypted using private key and feature codes are sent back.

$$FC_{S_i} = <ID_i, n, f_1, f_2, \cdots f_n> \tag{6}$$

where, ID is the unique user ID.

n is the count of regions.

$f_1, f_2, \ldots f_n$ are the feature codes for the corresponding regions as specified by r_i.

Step 5 - The obtained feature codes are re-arranged according to the system defined function (Eq. 3), transformed using implicit function (Eq. 4) and sent to the matcher for verification.

Step 6 - Matcher authenticates the user by comparing the transformed template with the one found in database using Chi-Square distance as given by Eq. (7).

$$\chi^2\left(FV_a^i, FV_b^j\right) = \sum_{k=1}^{n} \frac{\left(FV_{a,k}^i - FV_{b,k}^j\right)^2}{2 * \left(FV_{a,k}^i + FV_{b,k}^j\right)}, n = 243 \tag{7}$$

where, FV_a^i and FV_b^j represent feature vector of ith region of iris sample 'a' and j^{th} region of iris sample 'b' respectively.

n is the total number of histogram bins.

The match score between host template 'a' and query template 'b', over 'r' regions is calculated using Eq. (8), [4, 15].

$$Match_{score(a,b)} = \sum_{x \in r} sum(f(x)) \, where, f(x)$$
$$= \begin{cases} 1, & if \; x = y \, and \, \min\left[\chi^2\left(FV_a^x, FV_b^y\right)\right] \\ 0, & otherwise \end{cases} \tag{8}$$

where, y = [1,2,...64].

If the obtained score attains a certain thresh old the user is considered to be an authentic user otherwise is barred the access. This is detailed in our previous paper [4].

4   Experimental Results

To assess the working of the proposed approach, CASIA-Iris-Interval v3 [16] is used. This is the most widely used database for testing the iris-based system, that makes it easy to evaluate and compare the system performance. This database is rich in iris texture and is freely available. The database consists of 249 subjects, with a total of 2639 images of 320*280 resolution. We consider left and right eye of a subject to be different and thus the database is considered to have 395 subjects for comparisons. After evaluating the system and excluding the incorrectly segmented images, the database is reduced to 373 subjects with 2376 images. In this section we experimentally prove the effectiveness of the proposed approach in mitigating replay attack and template-based attack. The comparison with other existing techniques has also been shown here.

4.1 Performance Related to Replay Attack

Replay attack is interception and replay of the intercepted message to breakthrough the system. This can be termed as interception of message M4 (Fig. 2), and its replay to the system. The ability to mitigate this attack is detailed here, keeping in mind all the possible interceptions.

Case 1:   Interception of M1
Impact: No impact on biometric authentication
Case 2:   Interception of M2
Impact: Some encrypted message known but useless without key
Case 3:   Interception of M4
Impact: ·Iris feature code for random regions known but not useful for replay attack as a new different ordering of regions is chosen on each authentication. This has been experimentally proven in our previous paper [4].
Case 4:   Interception of M1 and M2
Impact: User identity known no access to actual iris data nor the key to decrypt M2
Case 5:   Interception of M2 and M4
Impact: An encrypted message and feature codes are known. The region ordering is reset after each attempt and the new feature extractor is issued only on successful user authentication (message M1). This information is useless without a valid ID of the targeted user.
Case 6:   Interception of M1 and M4
Impact: Feature codes for some random regions is known. A different region ordering makes it useless alone. The probability of getting the same ordering of regions over next authentication is 1/40! only, which is quite small.
Case 7:   Interception of M1, M2 and M3
Impact: All the elements of the communication is known. In case, modification of intercepted message is not possible, the system is highly secured. Otherwise, where modifications are possible, it still requires decoding M2 correctly so as to know the possible arrangement of iris feature codes. The performance of the system while authentication with incorrect ordering of the regions has already been shown in our previous approach [4].

The limitation of our previous approach [4] was, when the impostor knows all three messages M1, M2 and M4, it reveals useful information. We overcome the drawback here by using public key encryption algorithm RSA to encode M2 and allay man-in-the-middle attack [17].

4.2 Performance Relaed to Cancelable Template

The three important properties for cancelable template are – irreversibility, unlinkability and renewability.

(1) Irreversibility – It should not be possible to get the original biometric template (B'), which is close to original template (B)s, so that illegal authentication is involved.

(2) Unlinkability - The cancelable templates from more than one application, should be unlinkable, that is, there should be no cross matching.
(3) Renewability – In case of stolen template (B'), new template may be generated based on same biometric.

The proof to these properties is based on two important features of the proposed approach – randomized robust iris region and invertible transform as explained in following subsections.

Irreversibility Analysis. The system maintains a list of robust/best regions for each subject, which is randomized using function F(ID, k) as given by Eq. (6). The histograms corresponding to these randomized regions are transformed (using Eq. (3)) and saved to the database. The inbuilt property of histograms being irreversible, ensures the irreversibility of the cancelable template. The added randomization to it, further makes it robust against irreversibility.

Table 1. Performance with different keys @FAR = 0.01%

Key	1-FRR (%)	Accuracy (%)	EER (%)
2	91.84	95.91	2.01
4	94.11	97.04	2.02
6	95.19	97.57	1.93
8	94.98	97.47	1.89
10	**95.05**	**97.5**	**1.75**
12	95.31	97.63	1.85
14	95.18	97.56	1.82

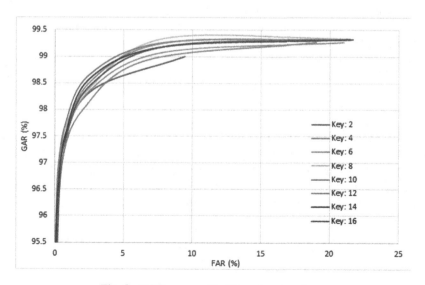

Fig. 3. ROC curve with different system keys

Unlinkability Analysis. The selection of best regions (40 best regions) and their randomization is application dependent. Each application shall use a different key k, which in conjunction with user ID, decides the randomized order of these regions. These regions are further transformed using key k, which changes the properties of template. The properties of these templates (feature vector containing histograms) are so alike that one cannot determine the correct order from several cancelable templates as well. The system performance on random order of these regions has been experimentally proven in our previous paper [4]. The detection of correct order of feature vectors is made difficult in the proposed approach with the knowledge of key. This shows that any authentic user trying to access a system without the permission is discarded and the system does not allow any impostor to authenticate.

Renewability Analysis. Using a different system key k, and a different set and order of best regions, new cancelable template can be generated from the original template (B). This new template can replace the old template and the biometric is ready for authentication.

Table 2. Comparison with existing approaches

	Rathgeb [7]	Richa [4]	Proposed
GAR	97.95	96.31	95.05
EER	1.14	1.24	1.75
Attack support	Database Attack	Replay Attack	Database Attack + Replay Attack

4.3 Performance Evaluation

The performance of the system has been shown with different key values, using a step size of 2. Table 1 shows the performance with varying key at False Accept Rate (FAR). The table shows results of False Reject Rate (FRR), Accuracy and Equal Error Rate (EER) at FAR = 0.01%. The Receiver Operating Characteristic (ROC) curve in Fig. 3 shows a rise in accuracy for initial keys from 2 to 10, after that the accuracy becomes stagnant. This is due the reason that the contribution of values with larger keys becomes insignificant and hence no further rise in the performance. This helps to determine a desirable range for key k as 2 to 10, where key is real-valued.

The comparison of the approach with other existing approaches on the same database is shown in Table 2. The table compares the system performance at FAR = 0.01% on CASIA Iris v3 Interval DB. The comparison shows a minor decline in the system performance but this at the cost of increased security. The existing methods are capable of handling single point of attack only, whereas the proposed approach is mitigating replay attack and database attack simultaneously.

5 Conclusion

In this paper, we extend the work of our previous work of using non-deterministic approach to allay replay attack and template-based attack. This is an important achievement as to the best of our knowledge; no work could be found in literature that focuses on more than attack simultaneously. The effectiveness of our approach can be seen with the help of Genuine Accept Rate (GAR) which is 95.05% @ FAR = 0.01%. We prove the robustness of our approach with respect to various properties of cancelable biometrics (Sect. 4.2) and also compare with other existing approaches (Table 2).

Acknowledgement. Thanks to Dr. Arpana Sharma, Mathematics Department from Delhi University who assisted to understand the concept of linear transformations.

References

1. Ratha, N.K., Connell, J.H., Bolle, R.M.: Enhancing security and privacy in biometrics-based authentication systems. IBM Syst. J. **40**, 614–634 (2001)
2. Gupta, R., Sehgal, P.: A survey of attacks on iris biometric systems. Int. J. Biometrics **8**, 145–178 (2016)
3. Gupta, R., Sehgal, P.: Mitigating iris based replay attack using cuckoo optimized reversible watermarking. In: Seventh International Conference on Advances in Computing, Control, and Telecommunication Technologies - ACT 2016 (2016)
4. Gupta, R., Sehgal, P.: Non-deterministic approach to allay replay attack on iris biometric. Pattern Anal. Appl. 1–13 (2018)
5. Gomez-Barrero, M., Rathgeb, C., Galbally, J., Busch, C., Fierrez, J.: Unlinkable and irreversible biometric template protection based on bloom filters. Inf. Sci. (Ny) **370**, 18–32 (2016)
6. Dwivedi, R., Dey, S., Singh, R., Prasad, A.: A privacy-preserving cancelable iris template generation scheme using decimal encoding and look-up table mapping. Comput. Secur. **65**, 373–386 (2017)
7. Rathgeb, C., Breitinger, F., Busch, C.: Alignment free cancelable iris biometric templates based on adaptive bloom filters. In: International Conference on Biometrics (ICB) 2013, pp. 1–8. IEEE (2013)
8. Shelton, J., Roy, K., O'Connor, B., Dozier, G.V.: Mitigating iris-based replay attacks. Int. J. Mach. Learn. Comput. **4**, 204–209 (2014)
9. Hämmerle-Uhl, J., Raab, K., Uhl, A.: Robust watermarking in iris recognition: application scenarios and impact on recognition performance. ACM SIGAPP Appl. Comput. Rev. **11**, 6–18 (2011)
10. Smith, D.F., Wiliem, A., Lovell, B.C.: Face Recognition on consumer devices: reflections on replay attack. IEEE Trans. Inf. Forensics Secur. **10**, 736–745 (2015)
11. Gomez-Barrero, M., Rathgeb, C., Galbally, J., Fierrez, J., Busch, C.: Protected facial biometric templates based on local gabor patterns and adaptive bloom filters. In: 22nd International Conference on Pattern Recognition (ICPR) 2014, pp. 4483–4488 (2014)
12. Syarif, M.A., Leslie Ching Ow Tiong, A.G., Nen, L.M., Lee, K.W.: Cancelability for LBP biometric authentication. In: 2015 Asia-Pacific Signal and Information Processing Association Annual Summit and Conference (APSIPA), pp. 612–618 (2015)

13. Sutra, G., Dorizzi, B., Garcia-Salicetti, S., Othman, N.: A biometric reference system for iris, OSIRIS version 4.1. Telecom Sud Paris, Fr. Technical report (2012)
14. Lang, S.: Introduction to Linear Algebra. Springer, New York (2012). https://doi.org/10.1007/978-1-4612-1070-2
15. Sun, Z., Tan, T., Qiu, X.: Graph matching iris image blocks with local binary pattern. In: Zhang, D., Jain, Anil K. (eds.) ICB 2006. LNCS, vol. 3832, pp. 366–372. Springer, Heidelberg (2005). https://doi.org/10.1007/11608288_49
16. CASIA-Iris version 3 interval database. http://biometrics.idealtest.org/dbDetailForUser.do?id=3. Accessed 20 June 2018
17. Man-in-the-middle-attack. https://en.wikipedia.org/wiki/Man-in-the-middle_attack. Accessed 20 June 2018

Liveness Detection in Finger Vein Imaging Device Using Plethysmographic Signals

Arya Krishnan$^{(\boxtimes)}$ ⓘ, Tony Thomas ⓘ, Gayathri R. Nayar ⓘ,
and Sarath Sasilekha Mohan ⓘ

Research Centre of Cochin University of Science and Technology, India, Indian
Institute of Information Technology and Management-Kerala (IIITM-K),
Thiruvananthapuram, Kerala, India
{aryakrishnan.res15,tony.thomas,gayathri.nayar,sarath.sm}@iiitmk.ac.in

Abstract. Finger vein modality is a relatively new area in biometrics
that overcomes the limitations of biometric systems based on external
features. Despite the fact that finger veins are invisible to naked eye and
latent print doesn't exist, presentation attack on finger veins is possible
if stored samples are stolen or compromised. To counter these attacks,
liveness was ascertained using learning based methods. However, these
methods are designed to detect only finger vein artefact generated using
specific materials. Hardware based liveness detection methods make use
of intrinsic characteristics of a live body to differentiate living tissues
from artificially created materials resembling it. Thus hardware based
liveness detection methods appear to be more robust to a wider class of
spoofing attacks. In this paper, we propose a finger vein biometric device
with a switchblade model sensor plate to ascertain the presence of a live
finger. The blood flow pattern obtained from the sensor is hard to repli-
cate and the presence of a physiological signal inherently implies liveness
of the subject. The results after comparing quality of the vein images
acquired from the proposed device and images from open databases show
that the proposed device produces good quality images. The experimental results demonstrate that the developed prototype device with presentation attack detection (PAD) can successfully avert spoof attacks.

Keywords: PAD · Finger vein · Switchblade model

1 Introduction

Biometrics is an emerging technology that has garnered interest within the
research community. Finger vein biometrics is a relatively new branch of biometrics which identifies a person using the unique vein patterns inside his or her
finger. Biometric systems are prone to attacks which might affect its reliability.
Attacks on a biometric system can be classified into two main groups [1]: direct
attacks and indirect attacks.

© Springer Nature Switzerland AG 2018
U. S. Tiwary (Ed.): IHCI 2018, LNCS 11278, pp. 251–260, 2018.
https://doi.org/10.1007/978-3-030-04021-5_23

A direct attack is launched on the sensor using synthetic biometric samples whereas, the indirect attack requires information about the internal working of the system. Direct attack or presentation attack is of higher interest as it merely involves presenting a fake biometric sample to fool the sensor.

Recently finger vein has shown itself to be vulnerable to spoofing by IDIAP researchers. They have reported in [2] that finger vein biometric system can be fooled using finger vein image printed on a paper. This kick-started the research on the presentation attack detection (PAD) on finger vein biometric systems. The presentation attack on finger vein includes printed paper and smartphone display based ones. The printed paper attack is carried out by presenting a finger vein image printed on a paper (using laser and inkjet printers) to the sensor [2]. The smartphone based attack is performed by loading a real finger vein image to a smartphone and presenting the same to the sensor [3]. Most of the existing anti-spoofing techniques are constructed on learning based schemes that are designed to detect finger vein artefact generated using specific materials. So, if a new presentation attack arises the whole system needs to undergo a relearning phase.

There is little literature on hardware based presentation attack detection for finger vein biometrics. Hence, in this paper, we propose a novel scheme for finger vein PAD at the sensor level. The proposed finger vein imaging device eliminates the need for quality enhancing preprocessing steps as it uses a focus adjusted raspberry pi camera. The sensor plate attached to the finger vein scanning module decides whether the presented finger is real or fake.

The main contributions of this paper can be summarized as:

1. Development of a finger vein acquisition device with improved image quality using a raspberry pi NoIR camera and near infrared LEDs;
2. Integration of a PAD module onto the finger vein acquisition device.

The rest of the paper is structured as follows. In Sect. 2, a review of related works on the finger vein biometric device and PAD methods are given. In Sect. 3, a description of the lab made finger vein image acquisition device is discussed. In Sect. 4, the proposed PAD mechanism is elaborated. The experimental results are given in Sect. 5. Conclusions and future directions for research are given in Sect. 6.

2   Literature Review

This section discusses the state of the art research in finger vein biometric device development and PAD techniques.

In [1], a multi modal biometric sensor using near infrared and visible light sources is given. Unlike the state of the art works that incorporate two dedicated sensors to capture finger vein and fingerprint, they employ a single camera for capturing both. Bram Ton et al. [4] introduced a customized finger vein acquisition device and finger vascular pattern dataset containing 1440 finger vein images from 60 volunteers. Several papers found in the literature [1–4] have used web-cams with IR filter removed for finger vein imaging. Even though these devices qualify as low cost solutions, the quality of the images obtained is low.

Presentation attack detection techniques can be broadly classified into two: hardware based and software based ones. There is no literature available on hardware based solutions for finger vein spoofing attacks to the best of our knowledge. Several researches are being performed in the direction of developing software based solutions for PAD. In [5,6], an SVM based classifier was used to discriminate between real accesses and spoofing attempts. Kannala et al. [6] extracted binarized statistical image features from finger vein images, fed them into a SVM classifier and the final score was calculated using sum fusion rule. The B-Lab team [5] took advantage of monogenic scale space based global descriptors. It captures the local energy and local orientation at the coarse level in order to differentiate between the actual vein image and the spoofed one. A deep learning based approach was proposed in [7] to counter the spoofing attacks on finger veins in which convolutional neural network was used to classify presented finger vein images into fake or genuine. Raghavendra et al. [8] proposed a Euler video magnification technique to identify spoofing of a finger vein biometric system. This work uses the magnified blood motion in the finger vein and optical flow to compute the motion features.

Although the aforementioned works have demonstrated to be efficient in presentation attack detection in finger vein images, they have several limitations. The feature extractors in these works were designed by observing the differences in real and spoofing images. As a result, they reflect the characteristics that are specific to real and fake images. The problem with the learning based techniques is that it needs a re-learning phase in the event of any new attacks. For qualifying as a low cost solution, the image level or software based liveness is preferred over sensor level check. However, it is possible to incorporate sensor level liveness check at a comparatively low cost and reduce the computational overhead for learning or processing the captured image.

3   Proposed Finger Vein Acquisition Device

This section discusses the development of our in-house finger vein image acquisition device with liveness detection technique incorporated into it.

3.1   Finger Vein Imaging Device

The mechanism used by the device to capture finger vein image is based on transmission or light penetration. Here, LED light source is placed on the back side of the finger and the image is captured using sensor placed on the palm side. Figure 1 illustrates the schematic representation of our in-house finger vein imaging device. The device consists of four integral units: (i) NIR LED array, (ii) physical structure with a slit, (iii) switchblade model sensor plate for liveness detection, (iv) raspberry pi camera. A slit is aligned in the middle of the finger,

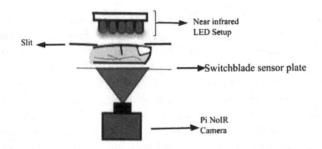

Fig. 1. Layout of finger vein imaging device

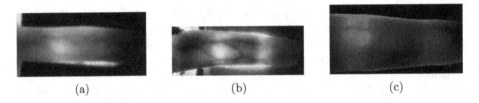

(a)   (b)   (c)

Fig. 2. (a) Images from the lab-made device before focus tuning (b) After focus tuning (c) Image from SDUMLA [10]

as shown in Fig. 1, for uniform distribution of light through it. In pursuance of high quality vein image, we used Pi NoIR (no IR filter) camera that has extended spectral range and the ability to capture images under low lighting conditions [9].

The image captured using our device was of good quality. However, the vessel pattern was not clearly visible as shown in Fig. 2a. When the focus of the camera was adjusted, the contrast of the image improved significantly and the vessel pattern became clearer as seen from Fig. 2b. The finger vein sample image (104/right/index.bmp) taken from an open source database [10] is shown in Fig. 2c. This image from SDUMLA database suffers from non-uniform illumination, low quality and poor visibility of veins when compared to the focus adjusted finger vein image (refer Fig. 2b) obtained using our proposed device.

3.2   Switchblade Model Sensor Plate

The region of interest for finger vein recognition is the region between first and last knuckles of the finger. Hence, it is necessary to verify the authenticity of the presented sample at these regions. We designated these regions as Zone II(region between first and second knuckles) and Zone III(region between second and third knuckles) as represented using black lines in the Fig. 3. The sensor plate is designed so as to hold three sensors at locations corresponding to three finger zones. The physiological signals from fingertip(Zone I) are used in vascular diagnostics [11]. Thus the signals taken from Zone I can be used as a reference for evaluating the signals from Zone II and III.

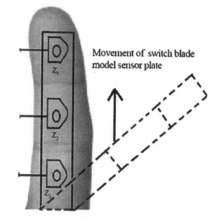

Fig. 3. Finger zones for signal capture

Fig. 4. Schematic of switchblade model sensor plate and its movement

Figure 4 illustrates the schematic representation of the proposed sensor plate. When a finger is placed on the sensor plate, the sensors detect the blood flow in the presented finger. The APG signals, representing the blood flow, are measured from the three finger zones simultaneously. The presentation attack detection is performed by observing the peaks of these signals. The sensors are placed corresponding to the three zones in finger. After ascertaining the liveness of the presented finger, the switch blade model sensor plate retracts making way for finger vein image acquisition.

4   Proposed Liveness Detection Method

In this section, we discuss the proposed liveness detection mechanism using the proposed finger vein imaging device described in Sect. 4. Our novel idea is to monitor the blood flow in the finger for vitality detection with the help of APG signals.

When a finger is presented to the system, the signals from three zones of the finger are simultaneously acquired by the sensor plate. The signals thus acquired helps in determining whether the presented finger is real or fake. If it is real then the finger vein image will be captured. An alarm will be generated if the presented object is not a live finger. The flow of blood inherently implies liveness of the subject and it is hard to mimic. No prior work that implements a hardware-based technique for finger vein liveness detection has been reported yet.

4.1   Presentation Attack Detection (PAD) Module

In this subsection, the underlying idea and working of the proposed PAD module is discussed. The significant part of the proposed PAD module is the tracing of the APG signal peaks collected from the sensor plate. It exploits the observation that the signal peaks from the three zones occur almost simultaneously.

When the sensor plate is not in contact with the finger, the analog signal hovers around the mid-point of the supply voltage which acts as the reference signal. As the sensor plate comes in contact with a finger the change in reflected light caused by blood flowing through the tissues causes the signal. Microcontroller watches the signal from the sensor plate and decides on the presence of a signal when the input rises above the mid point. This is when blood surges into the capillaries. As soon as the signal goes below the reference line, microcontroller senses this and gets ready to find a new signal peak.

The signal peak detection consists of two steps: initialisation and peak tracing.

1. Initialisation: In the initialisation stage the users are required to place their fingers on the sensor plate with hands stretched to facilitate the smooth flow of blood. The signals from the sensor plate will be sent to the microcontroller during this stage.
2. Peak tracing: The microcontroller always listens to the output from the sensor plate. Once the signal from Zone I crosses zero voltage, tracing process is initiated.

Algorithm 1. Presentation Attack Detection Algorithm

   Input: signals from three zones z_1, z_2 and z_3
1 $T = SignalStartTime$
2 $t_1 = t_2 = t_3 = 0$
3 **while** z_1 *changes from zero voltage condition* **do**
4   **while** $T \leq 3sec$ **do**
5   **if** s_{peak} *is detected at* z_1 **then**
6              $t_1 = t_{peak1}$;
7   **if** s_{peak} *is detected at* z_2 **then**
8                  $t_2 = t_{peak2}$;
9   **if** s_{peak} *is detected at* z_3 **then**
10                     $t_3 = t_{peak3}$;
11   **else** generate alarm(Attack detected);
12   **else** go to step 13;
13 Wait till a change from reference occurs

The algorithm for PAD is given in Algorithm 1. The inputs to Algorithm 1 are the three signals delivered by the sensor plate, namely z_1, z_2 and z_3. The variable $SignalStartTime$ denotes the time at which the micro controller starts reading the signal and s_{peak} denotes the peak of the signal. The algorithm iterates through the signal peaks in order to verify the genuineness of the presented finger. Initially, the microcontroller checks for occurrence of a peak in the signal from

Zone I. If a change is detected, then the peak tracing process begins. The time at which the peak of signal(t_{peak1}) from Zone I occurs is saved to t_1. After saving t_1, it checks for occurrence of a peak in the signal from Zone II. The signal from Zone I is used a reference for signals obtained from Zone II and Zone III. The time at which the peak of signal(t_{peak2}) from Zone II occurs is saved to t_2. Since all the peaks occur simultaneously, after s_{peak} from Zone II is obtained, the microcontroller checks for signal peak from Zone III and saves its time of occurrence as t_3. If an artefact is present in place of Zone II and Zone III, no signals will be obtained from these regions and an alarm will be generated to indicate a potential attack. If the input z_1 was a mere noise signal, then the controller would exit the whole loop and wait till the signal changes from the reference line. The iteration continues till a total time of 3 s. The time window of 3 s was fixed empirically as discussed in Sect. 6.

5   Results and Discussion

This section discusses the experimental results obtained while evaluating the performance of the proposed finger vein acquisition device and the liveness detection module. The ability of the proposed PAD module to detect spoofing attempts are evaluated through experimentations using already existing presentation attacks on vein biometrics [12].

5.1   Image Quality Evaluation

In this subsection, the quality of finger vein images obtained using lab-made device is evaluated against images from open databases [10,13,14]. Evaluation is carried out using two statistical measures: entropy and standard deviation.

1. Entropy: Entropy is a statistical measure to characterize the texture of an image. Low entropy values indicate that the image has very little contrast. For an image which is focused the entropy is usually large, whereas the entropy of an unfocused image is usually smaller [15].
2. Standard deviation: It is a statistical measure of variability or dispersion. It shows how much variation exists from the mean value. Low standard deviation of finger vein image indicates that the background of the image is uniform, thus making the vein in the image easily recognizable.

For each open source database, the total number of users and images per user was different. Hence, we have chosen only the first 50 finger vein images from every database for calculating the average entropy and standard deviation. From Table 1, it can be noted that the average entropy of our database is the highest when compared to other three database images. The standard deviation of the vein images from our device is the lowest among other three public database images. These results affirm the quality of the vein images obtained from our in-house vein capturing device.

Table 1. Comparison of entropy and standard deviation of several databases

Sl. No:	Database	Entropy	Standard deviation
1	SDUMLA-HMT [10]	6.93	38.95
2	VERA [14]	7.52	53.57
3	PKU [13]	6.59	64.80
4	Our database	7.71	34.93

5.2   Time Window Computation

Figure 5 shows the output from the sensor plate viewed using an oscilloscope.

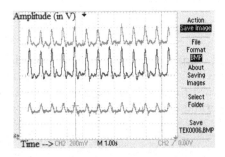

Fig. 5. Sample APG signal obtained from three zones of a subject using an oscilloscope.

Since the blood flow is from the palm to the finger, first APG signal will be obtained from Zone III, as indicated by the signal in green colour in Fig. 5. Due to lower capillarization at Zone III, the signal obtained there is of low amplitude. As the blood reaches the tip, the amplitude of the APG signal also gets higher since the tip is densely capillarised. From the figure, it can be observed that the time/division in oscilloscope is set to 1 s. It can be inferred that within 1 s time interval, signal peaks from three zones appear almost simultaneously. Experimentation results from several users also showed such a pattern. In order to check whether the signal obtained is real, 3 consecutive cycles of the signals are to be checked. As can be observed from the Fig. 5, 3 consecutive cycles occur within 3 s. Thus, we fix the time window for checking occurrence of the signal peaks to be 3 s.

5.3   Spoofing Attack Detection

This subsection demonstrates ability of our proposed mechanism to thwart existing and other possible spoofing attacks. In Table 2 the presentation attack scenarios with three different fake samples fabricated using printed paper, prosthetic finger and rubber cap are shown. In print paper attack, a finger vein image from the database was printed on a paper using an inkjet printer and was pasted on the finger before presenting to the sensor plate as shown in Table 2. Similarly, a prosthetic finger and a thin rubber cap with print paper pasted into them was presented to the proposed sensor plate for liveness detection. The output from the sensor plate demonstrated using an oscilloscope showed only a noisy signal for all these attack scenarios which affirms that the presented samples were fake.

Table 2. Response of our system in the wake of different attacks

Sl.No:	Existing or possible attacks on finger vein modality	Artefacts	Experimental Setup	Output from sensor plate demonstrated using an oscilloscope
1.	Printed paper attack [12]			
2.	Prosthetic finger with finger vein image pasted onto it [16].			
3.	Thin rubber cap with paper artefact pasted into it [11].			

6   Conclusion and Future Work

In this paper, a novel hardware based technique for finger vein identification systems has been proposed and implemented. The images acquired using the proposed device is of high quality and better contrast. The proposed liveness detection technique is based on the signals obtained from finger using the sensor plate at three valid locations. This liveness detection module is integrated with the finger vein device at the sensor level itself. The liveness detection module was able to avoid all the existing finger vein spoofing attacks successfully. The future work aims to expand the number of users and evaluate the scalability and reliability of the proposed PAD module. More research is required for evaluating the proposed hardware based solution for spoofing attack detection for finger vein biometrics.

Acknowledgement. This work is done as a part of Centre of Excellence in Pattern and Image Analysis project (CEPIA 2017-18), which is funded by Kerala state planning board.

References

1. Raghavendra, R., Raja, K.B., Surbiryala, J., Busch, C.: A low-cost multimodal biometric sensor to capture finger vein and fingerprint. In: 2014 IEEE International Joint Conference on Biometrics (IJCB), pp. 1–7. IEEE (2014)
2. Liu, Z., Song, S.: An embedded real-time finger-vein recognition system for mobile devices. IEEE Trans. Consumer Electron. **58**(2), 522–527 (2012)
3. Prasad, N.V.V., Mohan, K.V.M.: A real time embedded finger vein recognition system for authentication on mobile devices. Int. J. Eng. Trends Technol. **2**, 105–108 (2014)
4. Ton, B.T., Veldhuis, R.N.: A high quality finger vascular pattern dataset collected using a custom designed capturing device. In: 2013 International Conference on Biometrics (ICB), pp. 1–5. IEEE (2013)
5. Tome, P., Raghavendra, R., Busch, C., Tirunagari, S., Poh, N., Shekar, B., Gragnaniello, D., Sansone, C., Verdoliva, L., Marcel, S.: The 1st competition on counter measures to finger vein spoofing attacks. In: 2015 International Conference on Biometrics (ICB), pp. 513–518. IEEE (2015)
6. Kannala, J., Rahtu, E.: BSIF: binarized statistical image features. In: 2012 21st International Conference on Pattern Recognition (ICPR), pp. 1363–1366. IEEE (2012)
7. Nguyen, D.T., Yoon, H.S., Pham, T.D., Park, K.R.: Spoof detection for finger-vein recognition system using NIR camera. Sensors **17**(10), 2261 (2017)
8. Raghavendra, R., Avinash, M., Marcel, S., Busch, C.: Finger vein liveness detection using motion magnification. In: 2015 IEEE 7th International Conference on Biometrics Theory, Applications and Systems (BTAS), pp. 1–7. IEEE (2015)
9. Back, A., Deady, C.: Introducing the PI NoIR camera. MagPi **18**, 16–18 (2013)
10. Homologous Multi-modal Traits Database (SDUMLA-HMT). http://mla.sdu.edu.cn/sdumla-hmt.html. Accessed 22 May 2018
11. Wang, Y., Zhao, Z.: Liveness detection of dorsal hand vein based on the analysis of fourier spectral. In: Sun, Z., Shan, S., Yang, G., Zhou, J., Wang, Y., Yin, Y.L. (eds.) CCBR 2013. LNCS, vol. 8232, pp. 322–329. Springer, Cham (2013). https://doi.org/10.1007/978-3-319-02961-0_40
12. Tome, P., Vanoni, M., Marcel, S.: On the vulnerability of finger vein recognition to spoofing. In: 2014 International Conference of the Biometrics Special Interest Group (BIOSIG), pp. 1–10. IEEE (2014)
13. PKU Finger Vein Database. http://rate.pku.edu.cn/. Accessed 22 May 2018
14. VERA Finger Vein Database. http://www.idiap.ch/dataset/vera-fingervein. Accessed 22 May 2018
15. Thum, C.: Measurement of the entropy of an image with application to image focusing. Optica Acta Int. J. Optics **31**(2), 203–211 (1984)
16. Kang, H., Lee, B., Kim, H., Shin, D., Kim, J.: A study on performance evaluation of the liveness detection for various fingerprint sensor modules. In: Palade, V., Howlett, R.J., Jain, L. (eds.) KES 2003. LNCS (LNAI), vol. 2774, pp. 1245–1253. Springer, Heidelberg (2003). https://doi.org/10.1007/978-3-540-45226-3_169

Applications of HCI

Gesture Aided Voice for Voiceless

Dipti Jadhav[✉], Tejaswini Koilakuntla, Sonam M. Mutalik Desai,
and Ramya Ramakrishnan

Department of Computer Engineering, Don Bosco Institute of Technology,
Kurla, Mumbai 70, India
dipti_jadhav13@yahoo.com, k.trivani@yahoo.in,
sonam.mutalikdesai1996@gmail.com,
ramya.rk20596@gmail.com

Abstract. Language is used to express to our thoughts and to communicate with others. It is not limited to speech and sound. A sign language uses gestures which are a combination of hand movements and shapes, orientation, body movements and facial expressions instead of using sound. Sign language is the primary communication medium for the differently abled who have been given the title of "Divyang". But the inability of common people to comprehend it poses as a problem for efficient communication between the specially abled and others. The idea is to solve the problem by building an wireless and efficient two way communication system to bridge the gap between sign and speech and also vice versa. The system makes use of gloves fitted with flex sensors along the fingers and wrists of both hands to record the bend and corresponding change in resistance while performing Indian Sign Language (ISL) gestures. Microcontroller would be used for mapping the voltage values and its corresponding identifier i.e. the word as it is fast and is effective in a real-time communication scenario. This is then sent to a mobile app using a Bluetooth module where the text is displayed and converted to speech which the normal person can understand. The proposed system would help the hearing and speech impaired community in their daily lives as well as to enhance their employability.

Keywords: Human machine interaction · Indian Sign Language
Hand gesture interpretation · Microcontroller · Natural language processing

1 Introduction

Sign language has been an essential aspect of communication among people from ages. Simple sign language was used by humans to express basic ideas when they did not know any common language to communicate with each other. Sign language is an integral form of communication for hearing impaired community. Common people have used facial and hand gestures to represent communication idea, even when vocal communication was commonly used. This marked the origin of sign language.

In order to communicate efficiently and seamlessly with common people, sign language is used by deaf and mute people. A combination of facial expressions, physical movements, posture and gestures is used in sign language [16].

© Springer Nature Switzerland AG 2018
U. S. Tiwary (Ed.): IHCI 2018, LNCS 11278, pp. 263–271, 2018.
https://doi.org/10.1007/978-3-030-04021-5_24

There are many spoken languages in different countries and similarly there are different sign languages all over the world. Thus, sign language is not a universal language. Some countries may have more than one sign language [17].

The difference in the same sign language mainly arises due to varied culture. India is a vast country having many languages and varied culture. Since, the sign language hugely depends on culture, there is a huge variation in sign language used by all areas in India. So, it is necessary to establish a particular standard to enable smooth communication for hearing and speech impaired people.

There are many systems available in American Sign Language (ASL) standard to bridge communication gap between common and Divyang people by providing gesture aided speech. But, in India very less such systems are existing which provide a common standard for such people. So the project is to provide digital assistance to Divyang people using ISL.

The major problem is that normal people do not understand sign language. Thus, a more suitable solution should be devised in a manner that not only makes language used by speech impaired people understandable by the other people but also the reverse.

Thus, the proposed work focuses on building a compact system which enables two way communication for Divyang people. Firstly, the gestures performed by speech impaired people must be recognized properly and turned into a form that the others can understand i.e. translation of gestures made by hearing and speech impaired people into speech/text for common people. The second phase focuses on other way of communication i.e. translation of the speech input from a person to produce text output. Using the system, Divyang people can not only talk efficiently to the normal people but also comprehend their reply.

2 Literature Review

The research work was done taking into consideration different aspects such as the difficulties faced by the speech impaired people, efficient implementation approaches, commercial products available in market for them. The difficulties faced by the Divyang is that, in India not many commercial products are available in ISL standard. So the research work was done on standard sign language used in India. Also, efficient technology that needs to be built was reviewed.

Tripathy et al. (2013) proposed a system, where the gestures are captured using webcam and converted into text using Image processing in [1]. Only alphabets were captured in this method, but for efficient communication, speech in form of words and sentences are required, which is not implemented in this image processing based approach.

In [2], architecture of hand glove was developed in application. The motivation to implement a wireless glove in the proposed idea was taken from this hardware system. The glove used is bulkier and not compact, thus it is not easily portable.

In [3], hand gestures along with the facial expressions and the body language are used to convey the intended message. The smart glove has been used as hardware which is also a part of this proposed idea. But ASL is used and also only single way communication is enabled in this glove based system.

The motivation to implement a two way communication software application was received from [4]. But, video processing has been used in this software to convert gesture to speech, which is not an efficient approach because it requires pixel mapping.

In [5], a low cost wired interactive glove has been implemented. The glove maps the orientation of the hand and fingers with the help of bend sensors, which is also used in the proposed idea. But the device is bulky due to wired connections, which is taken care of in the proposed idea. Accelerometer glove has been used in [6]. In gesture acquisition system, Parallel Hidden Markov Model has been used for sensor-fusion modelling for reducing the equal error rate. But the hardware used is not cost efficient due to use of expensive sensors.

Wireless glove hardware controller in [7] allows the user to control a hardware device using natural gestures. For this purpose, flex, force, gyroscopic sensors with hand gestures has been used. But a major constraint is cost in sensor based devices.

In [8], image processing based approach is used. Natural Voice processing and Digital Image Processing algorithms were used to take necessary precautions to combat a noisy environment. But pixel mapping is always required in image processing and also static gestures are captured in this approach, which should be replaced by some efficient approach.

In [9] concept of hand-glove controlled wheel chair was studied, in which the wheelchair has been operated using the gloves instead of traditional joystick. This is done by the transmitting circuit present on the hand-glove, which can be implemented in parallel lines in the proposed idea. But since sensors along with wired gloves are used, the cost for implementation has been a constraint in such systems.

Micro controller based approach has been used for gesture recognition in [10]. The design of the ADC0808, ADC0809 has been optimized by incorporating the most desirable aspects of several A/D conversion techniques, which was a motivation for the proposed system to optimize the micro controller.

In [11], Electronic Hand Glove Gesture has been used. The CyberGlove and the hand tracking system were used to collect a dataset ISL signs. The proposed system also uses ISL for its implementation. Electronic approach requires wired connections which leads to bulkiness of hand glove, thus reducing its portability.

In [12], Gestures have been recognized using wrist watch. 2-d image has been captured and inputted in the web cam. Then watch has been detected in the image followed by its preprocessing. The image is matched using pattern recognition. To reduce time complexity and unnecessary matching, tree technique is used. This is actually an efficient approach. Thus, the proposed idea also uses wrist for gesture mapping.

Tripathi et al. (2015) implemented a video processing approach is used in Gradient based key frame extraction method, which are helpful for splitting continuous sign language gestures into sequence of signs as well as for removing uninformative frames. The results obtained from Correlation and Euclidean distance gives better accuracy compared to other distance classifiers for recognising sign language gestures. Better approaches for mapping sentences are compared in this report [13].

The Glove based method in [14] uses sensor devices for digitizing finger motions. The basic idea and motivation for the proposed system was taken from this report. However, the devices used are extremely bulky and compact devices can be used. So an improved approach needs to be implemented.

3   Proposed Methodology

The method to be implemented involves the hand gesture recognition using gloves consisting hardware. The system has three modules namely data acquisition, processing, wireless communication setup. The system architecture is given in Fig. 1.

3.1   Data Acquisition

The data here is the signals generated from the flex sensors, the resistance of the flex sensor increases as the body of the component bends, the data is generated whenever the flex sensor is bent. In the system the differently abled person can make signs by wearing glove, having all the circuit mounted. The entire flex arrangement follows a voltage divider network. The bend amount is recorded and it is mapped to a particular voltage. The data stream obtained is in analog form which is fed to the Analog to Digital converter (ADC) which produces digital signal.

3.2   Processing

Arduino reads various combination values of sensor signals from two hands. Depending on the output voltage from the Flex sensors, processor checks the ADC response with the pre coded values and if there is a particular identifier gesture which corresponds to the ADC response, then the output is fetched and given to the wireless communication module.

3.3   Wireless Communication Setup

The wireless communication consists of a Bluetooth module that promotes successful exchange of data between the android phone and the hardware. The data is the text which will be fetched as output from the processing module. This module also will be consisting an android phone which would display the data received in textual form and also will give an audio output of the received data. Thus the normal person can interpret what the speech impaired person is trying to express.

The phases of this project are based on Design thinking stages. In First stage the problems faced by Divyang Community were emphasized, where visits were made to a school and a professional workplace to find out the sign language standards used in India and their way of communication.

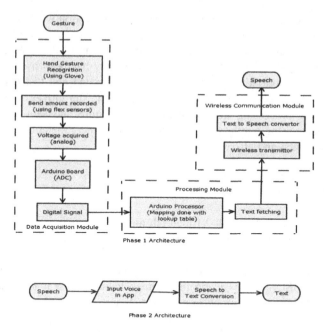

Fig. 1. System architecture

4 Materials and Methods

It was found that Indian Sign language was used in both the places. Also, fast interaction is required in workplaces like bank, malls, etc. But, the Divyang Community face difficulties while interacting at a faster pace in such workplaces. So to enable faster interaction, a Keyword based approach can be used at workplaces, where most frequently used words like Cash, Card, etc. Payment can be represented using particular sign for that starting letter of the alphabet.

In second stage, the problems were defined clearly. In third stage, different methods to detect sign language were reviewed upon and final method was selected. In fourth stage, a prototype design was made for the method selected. The main stages of the project are divided in two phases. First phase includes acquisition of signs, processing the sign, detecting the sign, sending the detected sign to app via Bluetooth, text output and voice output. Second phase includes voice input, text output.

The Gloves were first set up with sensors fitted above fingers and wrist of both hands. The glove connections were secured and tested for connectivity. The voltage divider circuit was made and connected to the Arduino.

As a part of the data processing, Arduino coding was done by recording the voltage values obtained while making various sign language gestures using both the hands involving movements of finger joints and wrist. These values were coded into the Arduino along with a comparison logic for recognising gestures.

In android application, two phases for 2 way communication were integrated. In 1st phase the sign received from the Bluetooth module in form of text when connected to the microcontroller, the text was converted to speech using text to speech conversion libraries. In 2nd phase, speech to text conversion library has been used.

All the modules individually developed were integrated and tested together as a whole system. The input gestures were performed using the gloves. Using the comparison logic, the processing module mapped the gesture and sent the data to the mobile application using wireless transmission module where the conversion from text to speech takes place and also vice versa.

5   Observation and Results

Gloves have been connected with 2 Bluetooth modules; so before making gesture, the connection between 2 Bluetooth modules and application should be turned on in the mobile application.

The certain selected gestures have been pre coded with their respective signs. When selected 2 hands ISL gestures made the voltage values are sent to Arduino Actual mapping of gesture to text is done in precoded Arduino which results the text of the particular gesture. Figure 2: Making gestures.

The text result is transmitted to the mobile application from both the hands wirelessly via Bluetooth modules.

Here the 2 hands text is received by Bluetooth, the mobile application has been pre coded for the 2 hands gestures corresponding to a single sign/gesture. Thus the respective sign is recognized with text and speech as output.

The recorder must first be selected to start the capturing of speech. The when user speaks the speech is captured.

Using the speech to text converter library embedded in the mobile application after capturing of speech the text is generated as output.

Fig. 2. Making gestures

The signs recognized by the proposed method are given below. The words can be customized as sentences as well. Table 1 shows Gesture Mapping with left and right hand.

Table 1. Gesture mapping

Left hand gesture	Right hand gesture	Final gesture interpreted	Supported by the system (Yes/No)	Further Requirement
Plate	Plate	Plate	Yes	-
L	Food	Food	Yes	
L	Dinner	Dinner	Yes	
Hat	Hat	Hat	Yes	
Payment	Payment	Payment	Yes	
-	Water	Water	Yes	
-	Fork	Fork	Yes	
-	Vegetarian	Vegetarian	Yes	
Chicken	Food	Non-Veg	No	Accelerometer
-	Food		Yes	-
OFF	OFF	OFF	Yes	-
ON	ON	ON		
Work	Work	Work	No	Contact Sensors
Computer	Computer	Computer	No	Accelerometer

6 Conclusion and Further Work

This work was mainly done on the Indian Sign Language standard and the architecture of the system. A background survey was done by visiting a deaf and mute school to observe the sign language used in both areas. It was found that Indian sign language standard was used in both places. Then various architectures for system were reviewed upon such as Image processing based, sensor based and hardware based approaches. But, it was found that hardware based approach was more efficient and gave accurate results compared to other approaches. To minimize the architecture of hardware, a design thinking approach was used for the project stages to make the system more compact and portable.

Gloves were designed for both hands gestures made were sent to the android app via Blue tooth module. The use of Arduino made the system compact. This project implemented an optimal system for efficient communication between Divyang and common people. Thus, two way communication system for Divyang has been successfully completed.

References

1. Tripathy, A.K., Jadhav, D., Barreto, S.A., Rasquinha, D., Mathew, S.S.: Voice for the mute. In: International Conference on Technologies for Sustainable Development (ICTSD), Mumbai, pp. 1–6 (2015)
2. Bajpai, D., Porov, U., Srivastav, G., Sachan, N.: Two way wireless data communication and american sign language translator glove for images text and speech display on mobile phone. In: Fifth International Conference on Communication Systems and Network Technologies (CSNT), Gwalior, pp. 578–585 (2015)
3. Praveen, N., Karanth, N., Megha, M.S.: Sign language interpreter using a smart glove. In: International Conference on Advances in Electronics, Computers and Communications (ICAECC), Bangalore, pp. 1–5 (2014)
4. Ahire, P.G., Tilekar, K.B., Jawake, T.A., Warale, P.B.: Two way communicator between deaf and dumb people and normal people. In: International Conference on Computing Communication Control and Automation (ICCUBEA), Pune, pp. 641–644 (2015)
5. Chouhan, T., Panse, A., Voona, A.K., Sameer, S.M.: Smart glove with gesture recognition ability for the hearing and speech impaired. In: IEEE 2014 Global Humanitarian Technology Conference - South Asia Satellite (GHTC-SAS), Trivandrum, pp. 105–110 (2014)
6. Gałka, J., Mąsior, M., Zaborski, M., Barczewska, K.: Inertial motion sensing glove for sign language gesture acquisition and recognition. IEEE Sens. J. 16(16), 6310–6316 (2016)
7. Dekate, A., Kamal, A., Surekha, K.S.: Magic glove - wireless hand gesture hardware controller. In: International Conference on Electronics and Communication Systems (ICECS), Coimbatore, pp. 1–4 (2014)
8. Suresh, P., Vasudevan, N., Ananthanarayanan, N.: Computer-aided interpreter for hearing and speech impaired. In: Fourth International Conference on Computational Intelligence Communication Systems and Networks (CICSyN), Phuket, pp. 248–253 (2012)
9. Meeravali, S., Aparna, M.: Design and development of a hand-glove controlled wheel chair based on MEMS. Int. J. Eng. Trends Technol. (IJETT) 4(8), 3706–3712 (2013). Fig 5: Gestures recognition

10. Patel, B., Shah, V., Kshirsagar, R.: Microcontroller based gesture recognition system for the handicap people. J. Eng. Res. Stud. (JERS) **II**(IV), 113–115 (2011)
11. Rajalakshmi, V., Vasudevan, N., Rajinigrinath, D., Kumar, S.P.: Electronic hand glove gesture to voice recognization using physically challenged persons. Int. J. Innovative Res. Comput. Commun. Eng **3**(8), 90–94 (2015)
12. Singh, S., Tripathi, A.: Gesture recognition using wrist watch. Int. J. Sci. Eng. Res. **4**(6), 984–986 (2013)
13. Tripathi, K., Baranwal, N., Nandi, G.C.: Continuous indian sign language gesture recognition and sentence formation. In: Eleventh International Multi-Conference on Information Processing-2015 (IMCIP- 2015), Procedia Computer Science, vol. 54, pp. 523–531 (2015)
14. Jadhav, D., Tripathy, A.K., Jose, C., Fernandes, R., Joy, J.: Gesture aided speech-framework, unpublished
15. Cho, I.-Y., Sunwoo, J., Son, Y.-K., Oh, M.-H., Lee, C.-H.: Development of a Single 3-axis Accelerometer Sensor Based Wearable Gesture Recognition Band, unpublished
16. Sign language history. http://www.deafwebsites.com/sign-language/history-sign-language.html. Accessed 30 Oct
17. Sign language Introduction. https://wfdeaf.org/our-work/focus-areas/sign-language. Accessed 30 Oct
18. http://ai2.appinventor.mit.edu/?locale=en#4735656302215168. Accessed 5 Jan
19. https://www.Arduino.cc/en/Tutorial/ReadAnalogVoltage. Accessed 6 Jan
20. https://create.Arduino.cc/projecthub/user206876468/Arduino-Bluetooth-basic-tutorial-d8b737. Accessed 12 Jan
21. http://www.instructables.com/id/LED-Control-using-Arduino-Bluetooth-and-Android-Pa/. Accessed 13 Jan

Towards Evaluating Architectural Design of Ancient Pilgrimage Site Using Agent Based Modelling and Simulation

Abha Trivedi[1]([⊠]) and Mayank Pandey[2]

[1] GIS Cell, Motilal Nehru National Institute of Technology,
Allahabad 211004, Uttar Pradesh, India
abhson1711@gmail.com
[2] Computer Science and Engineering Department, Motilal Nehru National
Institute of Technology, Allahabad 211004, Uttar Pradesh, India
mayankpandey@mnnit.ac.in

Abstract. In India, there are many ancient pilgrimage sites with high religious significance. These sites experience a huge surge of crowd on auspicious occasions. The old infrastructure of these pilgrimage sites is not capable to accommodate present crowded situations. Nowadays, these sites are getting congested due to the encroachment on the nearby areas. These conditions make them vulnerable to tragic incidents. Modelling and simulation technology provides a platform to do the comprehensive assessment of architectural designs on different crowded situations. In this paper, we have created near to real virtual environment of an ancient pilgrimage site in an Agent Based Modelling tool. We have created intelligent agents that act, react and interact within this virtual environment. The crowd of intelligent agents are simulated for three different emergency evacuation scenarios and two different dimensions of gates. Subsequently, we explored the effect on emergency evacuation time with respect to dimensions of gates, location of gates and population size inside the temple. The simulation results establish the applicability of our methodology.

Keywords: Agent Based Modelling · Emergency evacuation
Design evaluation · NetLogo

1 Introduction

There are different types of occasions such as political rallies, sports, religious festivals, etc. that attract a large gathering of people. The places of large gatherings must have a good architectural design. The architectural design should have sufficient carrying capacity and ways to handle emergency situations. Generally, in mass gatherings, possibility of emergency situations is higher. The consequences of the emergency situation may be hazardous. There are different

© Springer Nature Switzerland AG 2018
U. S. Tiwary (Ed.): IHCI 2018, LNCS 11278, pp. 272–284, 2018.
https://doi.org/10.1007/978-3-030-04021-5_25

reasons and circumstances of these situations like fire, rumour, natural calamities, etc. In other words we can say that, all those factors that comprise the event are equally responsible for tragic incidents. Location and infrastructure of the site, people attending the occasion, authorities in charge, crowd management and planning schemes are some of the factors among many others. It is necessary to view and analyze all the factors collectively for the successful accomplishment of a crowded event. There is a history of incidents at the places of large gatherings around the world. Among the several incidents, many are from India specially at the pilgrimage sites [20]. Design issues such as narrow entry/exit points, old fragile boundary wall, etc. are the main reason of all these incidents. At the time of emergency egress, number of people increases near the exit points. If the exit points are narrow, then there may be congestion and long halts creating huge pressure between individuals. Due to this sudden rush and pressure, people may feel asphyxiation and get trampled to death.

India is the land of religious people of different cultures and beliefs. In India, there exist many ancient pilgrimage sites [17] that have high religious significance. Because of their significance they experiences huge surge of crowd on auspicious occasions. These ancient sites are now the part of congested areas of developing cities. The old infrastructure of these pilgrimage sites is not capable to accommodate present crowded situations. In such circumstances there is a need to perform comprehensive investigation of management schemes in terms of carrying capacities, emergency planning, required architectural adjustments and so on. Generally, investigation to understand the requirements is performed by discussing past experiences, making speculations based on discussions and planning based on speculations. To implement the speculated plans directly without prior testing may be ineffective and inefficient. Moreover, empirical implementation of speculated plans is infeasible for prior testing. An innovative way to test such plans is making use of Modelling and Simulation technique. With the help of this technique, critical parameters related to crowd or architectural designs can be efficiently tested and analyzed. Critical parameters can be capacity bottlenecks, safety, emergency planning, management and control strategies, etc.

Modelling and Simulation technique has gained lot of attention by the wide range of discipline such as social sciences, military, engineering and others. This technique is generally cheaper, safer and faster than conducting real world experiments. Among the various problems being modelled and simulated from different domains one is Crowd Modelling and Simulation [27]. It has attracted researchers to study dynamic crowd behaviours [9,20]. Mainly, three approaches are used to model crowd behaviour that are macroscopic, mesoscopic and microscopic [12]. Among them, microscopic approach is used to analyze individual-individual and individual-environment interactions. In precise terms, this approach describes crowd behaviour in a fine grained manner. Microscopic modelling approach includes Social Force Model, Cellular Automata Model and Agent Based Model [23]. Agent Based Model (ABM) [3] describes the action and interaction of intelligent autonomous agent on a simulation platform. It is an elegant technique to create virtual environment and model the intelligent agents with different characteristics and dynamic capabilities. The intelligent agents have the ability to act, make decisions, interact with other agents, perceive and learn from their environment. Significant research have utilized ABM to investigate the crowd flow behaviour under emergency evacuation scenarios [15] in different public infrastructures such as buildings, malls and stadiums. However, these studies lack the evaluation of architectural design of religious sites to investigate the evacuation time during emergency situation, especially in an Indian context.

In this paper, we have created the virtual environment of a pilgrimage site and modelled intelligent agents with dynamic capabilities to generate different crowd gathering scenarios. This pilgrimage is famous as Alopi Devi temple in the name of goddess Durga, one of the shakti peethas [22]. It is situated in the middle and congested area of Allahabad city, India. We have used Agent Based Modelling technique to evaluate two different dimensions of temple gates in terms of evacuation time under emergency situations. We have applied theories of crowd dynamics [9,20] to define the procedures of our model. We have mainly worked on exit designs in terms of dimensions, location and number of exit gates. To create our model, we have used NetLogo, a well-designed Agent Based Modelling platform [26]. Our contributions in this work are listed as below:

- Create the infrastructure of Alopi Devi Temple as the virtual environment of our model based on the actual measurement of geographical parameters.
- Simulate normal procedures of crowd gathering inside temple premises. Individual agent shows specific behaviour in different situations.
- Simulate emergency evacuation on different exit design of the temple.
- Compare and evaluate evacuation time in different designs of exit points.

The rest of the paper is organized as follows: The relevant related works are discussed in Sect. 2. Section 3 describes of our Agent Based Model which is followed by simulation experiments and results in Sect. 4. Section 5 provides conclusion and future directions of this work.

2   Related Work

There have been research surveys [10,14] on crowd related disasters in mass gatherings of people on different occasions at different places around the world. They have featured possible reasons and circumstances which triggered the panic situations. Possible measures are also suggested for their rectification. There are studies [5,7,13] that have analyzed the impact of complex designs of public infrastructures on pedestrian movement and flow behaviour under normal and emergency evacuation scenarios. Some of the studies [16,18] have created small laboratory setup consisting of human participants to experiment their behaviour under normal walking, blocked vision and slow running situations. But, to use human beings as part of empirical setup for understanding complex crowd behaviour can expose them to risk. Therefore, crowd modelling and simulation approaches are preferred to analyze the impact of complex designs and to understand dynamic behaviour of crowd during emergency evacuation.

In [5], an agent based model named as "Nomad" is utilized to assess pedestrian behaviour around emergency doors with respect to their design and capacity. Agent-based simulation is performed in [4] to investigate the relative effectiveness of staged and simultaneous evacuation strategies in the City of San Marcos, Texas. In [13] a deep insight on the design issues of buildings is examined for safe evacuation. They explained that space dimension is one of the important factors to be considered by the planner of any event. Adjustments in the architectural designs of a large room are examined in [7] to improve crowd flow out of that room. In [11], the effects of adjustments in the exit design of Dutch train station is assessed which is based on the levels of service defined by Fruin. The impact of complex architectural configurations such as crossings, turning and merging points is investigated in [6] to assure safety under high density and emergency scenarios.

The aforementioned works performed evaluation of existing designs of buildings, large single rooms or stations to understand crowd flow and evacuation scenarios. We have utilized these concepts to explore the exit designs of an ancient pilgrimage site in terms of their dimensions and locations. Pilgrims arrive from different parts of the country to visit this temple. The assessment of architectural designs of pilgrimage sites is significant because this would help the authorities to enhance their crowd management and control strategies.

3 Our Agent Based Model

In this section, we have presented the description of our Agent Based Model which is created to simulate emergency evacuation scenarios in terms of exit dimensions and exit locations of Alopi Devi Temple. We have evaluated the impact of these scenarios on total evacuation time. Agent Based Modelling is an elegant approach to model individuals as agents with the incorporation of physiological and psychological factors [2,19].

3.1 Virtual Environment of Alopi Devi Temple

In the field survey, we used a GPS unit of trimble series [25] to measure the geographical parameters of temple premises. Also, we had several meetings with temple authoritatives to understand their crowd management strategies. This temple experiences huge surge of crowd during Kumbh Mela and Navratri (festival of nine days occurs two times in a year). On the basis of our survey we have created virtual environment of the temple. Virtual environment includes two adjacent roads, all the inner pathways, three different walls (boundary wall, temple building and sanctum sanctorum), three gates and nine sliding channels. Figure 1 depicts the virtual environment of our model which is created in a scale of 171cells × 191cells of the simulation tool. Size of each cell is assumed to be equal to 1m^2.

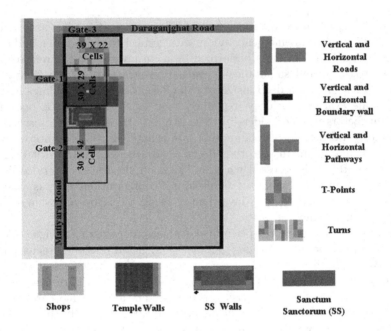

Fig. 1. Snapshot of simulation environment

3.2   Pilgrims as Intelligent Agents

We have modelled pilgrims as intelligent agents that have the capability to act and react according to situation. Psychological abilities defined in [24] are incorporated in them. This ability help them to take decisions such as choice of route at intersections, choice of gates for ingress/egress, choice of nearest gate in emergency evacuation, etc. The pilgrim agents have certain velocity with which they move. We have assigned moving speed to the pilgrims based on two parameters namely age and gender [21]. Pilgrim agents also have the ability to sense presence of obstacle and type of obstacle on their way. According to the type of obstacle, they decide their next action like change in speed or direction. If pilgrim agents sense presence of another pilgrim agent then they slow down their speed to avoid collision. If the agent sense wall like obstacles they take turns according to the availability of space. Besides these abilities, Pilgrim agents have the ability to interact with the environment on which they are moving. They exhibit interaction with the spatial environment when they try to occupy empty cell or try to move in a cell that have less number of pilgrim agents. This maintains the accommodation threshold of each cell which is set as 4agents/m² [20] for normal density situation. If cells under $5\,m^2$ has more than 20 pilgrims over it then this is alarmed as overcrowded situation. We have defined many procedures with stochasticity to incorporate natural variance in the behaviour of pilgrim agents. For example, movement procedure is implemented with stochastic variable "speed", route selection procedure is implemented with stochastic variable "direction" and so on.

In normal situation, pilgrim agents exhibit 'indirect objective-seeking' behaviour. This behaviour can be defined in six steps. The steps are as follows: they enters inside the temple, may or may not purchase offerings, move to sanctum sanctorum, stay for a while to perform rituals, come out of the sanctum sanctorum and exit from the temple. While in emergency situation they exhibit 'direct objective-seeking' behaviour. This shows their adaptation capability in which, they change their calm movement behaviour and adapt the anomalous behaviour. This directs the pilgrim agents to evacuate with improved velocity. Further, we have applied basic concepts of social forces model described in [9] and crowd density factor in terms of space utilization discussed in [8,20] to define physiological features of crowd dynamics in our model. Some of the features of crowd which we have incorporated are overcrowding, exertion of forces, pressure creation and reduction in physical energy of individuals. The state of these agents changes according to the change in their action and behaviour. Figure 2 shows the possible states and actions of pilgrim agents.

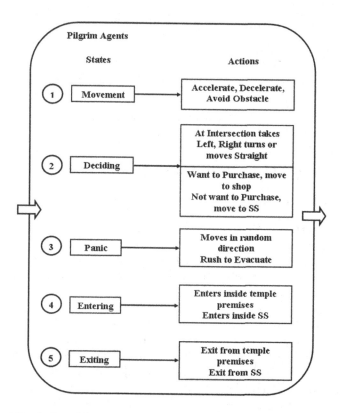

Fig. 2. Possible states and different actions of pilgrim agent

3.3   Modules of Our Model

The modules of our model are divided into two different categories. In first category we have defined procedures to create infrastructure of Alopi Devi temple as the simulation environment. In second category we have defined different actions of pilgrim agents. Figure 3 depicts the scheduling of all the processes executed during the simulation.

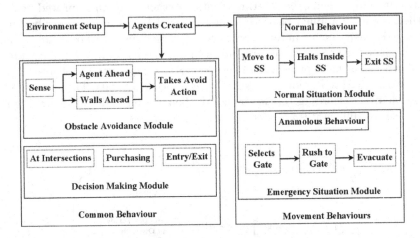

Fig. 3. Different modules of our model

4   Simulation Setup, Experiments and Results

4.1   Simulation Setup

We have used NetLogo [26], to create our virtual environment which is an Agent Based Modelling tool. The simple programming style, excellent GUI support, rich helping resources and many other features made NetLogo an elegant choice for the modelers to model different type of agents and their behaviours. The interface of our model includes controls such as buttons, sliding-bar, switches, etc. to set various parameters. These parameters are arrival rate, arriving direction, inter arrival timings, acceleration, deceleration and widths of gates. A button control is available in the interface of the tool which we have named as "Set Environment" to setup our virtual environment. It is linked with a background procedure in which we have defined different variables of this environment. Figure 4(a) and (b) depicts the parameter controls used in our model. In our simulation temporal scaling includes model time step (ticks) which is assumed as one-tick = one-second and simulation run time is set for one day which is 86400 ticks.

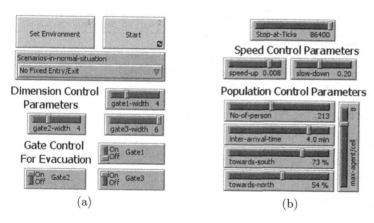

(a)   (b)

Fig. 4. Parameter controls of our model

4.2 Experiments

We have conducted simulation experiments for three different emergency evacuation scenarios on two different dimensions of temple gates. We did this experiment to analyze a suitable case for the fast evacuation of pilgrims at emergency. The two dimensions are 4 m and 6 m wide gates. The three different emergency evacuation scenarios are based on the location of temple gates. The three evacuation scenarios are as follows: (1) Gate-1 and Gate-2 are kept open, (2) Gate-1 and Gate-3 are kept open, & (3) Gate-2 and Gate-3 kept open. Figure 5(a), (b) and (c) depicts the simulation snapshots of emergency evacuation by the pilgrim agents.

We have implemented two different situations in our model namely normal-situation and emergency-situation. As explained in Sect. 3, pilgrim agents do normal activities like entering inside premises, may or may not purchase offerings, move to sanctum sanctorum and so on under normal-situation. While, in emergency-situation, instead of doing normal activities they rush towards the exit gates that are set "open". We have utilized the concepts of [1] to implement selection of gate for emergency evacuation. Following Algorithm presents the pseudocode for emergency evacuation module. In Algorithm 1, abbreviation "ap", "nc", "tp-cells" and "ma/c" are used to denote actual position of agent, neighbouring cells, cells of temple premises and max-agent/cell, respectively.

4.3 Results and Design Analysis

We have simulated each experiment multiple times and evaluated average of all the simulation results. On the basis of comparisons between these results, we have suggested the best scenario which can be used for evacuation during emergency. We have analysed total time taken by the pilgrim agents to evacuate the temple premises. Equation 1 is utilized to evaluate Total Evacuation time TE_t:

$$TE_t = LE_t - FE_t \tag{1}$$

Algorithm 1. Algorithm to implement selection of gate for evacuation

---
1: **procedure emergency − evacuation**
2:      *initialization: give meaning to cells as g1, g2 and g3 to represent gate*
3:      ▷ *check which combination of gates is set to open*
4:      **if** selection = Gate1 and Gate2 **then**
5:          *exit-cell ∈ g1-cells ∨ exit-cell ∈ g2-cells)]*
6:      **else if** selection = Gate1 and Gate3 **then**
7:          *exit-cell ∈ g1-cells ∨ exit-cell ∈ g3-cells]*
8:      **else**
9:          *exit-cell ∈ g2-cells ∨ exit-cell ∈ g3-cells]*
10:      **end if**
11:      *dt = distance(ap, exit-cell)*
12:      **for** *nc* = 1 → 8 **do**
13:          **if** ∃ nc : nc ∈ tp-cells and ($\sum_{nc}$ agents) ≤ ma/c and distance(ap, exit-cell) < dt **then**
14:              *move forward to nc*
15:          **end if**
16:      **end for**
17: **end procedure**

Here, LE_t denotes the time when last agent evacuated and FE_t denotes the time when first agent evacuated. Table 1 shows the simulation results for all scenarios. In Table 1, Evacuation Time, Gate-1, Gate-2 and Gate-3 are abbreviated as ET, G1, G2 and G3, respectively. Equation 2 shows all the factors that affect Total Evacuation time:

$$TE_t = f(N_a + N_{aa} \sum_{i=1}^{N_{aa}} (S * D))/((W_g * P_{ua}) + N_g) \qquad (2)$$

Here, N_a is the number of agents already present near the exit gates (refer Fig. 1 to understand the areas considered near each gate), N_{aa} denotes number of agents arriving with speed S covering distance D towards the same exit area, W_g is the width of each exit gate, N_g denotes number of exit gates and P_{ua} denotes number of agents per unit area. There are more than 7 agents per unit area (unit area = 1m^2) during emergency situations in the simulation of our model. The results significantly vary for different evacuation scenarios. This happens because we have incorporated stochasticity to show natural variance in the behaviour of pilgrim agents.

Figure 6 is a clustered histogram plot for the simulation results in both dimensions of gates. This graph plots average population and total evacuation time against each evacuation scenario. The x-axis represents two different clusters and y-axis indicates the count for population and evacuation time. Size of population inside temple premises depends on the width of gates. Therefore, it may be observed that number of evacuees is higher in 6 m wide design of gates than in 4 m. More precisely, we can state that "if the gates of temple are wide then ingress is more". Further, it may also be observed that evacuation time is minimum when pilgrim agents are guided to evacuate from those gates that are located at a distance far enough from each other. This distance forms an angle of no less than 45° to the pilgrim agent observing both gates. On the basis of these results, we can suggest that Gate-1 and Gate-2 should be utilized for fast evacuation in emergency situation.

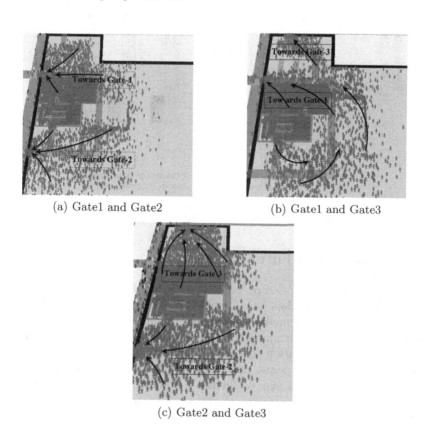

(a) Gate1 and Gate2   (b) Gate1 and Gate3

(c) Gate2 and Gate3

Fig. 5. Snapshots of three emergency evacuation scenarios

Table 1. Average population and average evacuation time

No. of gates open	4 m		6 m	
	Population	Total ET (minutes)	Population	Total ET (minutes)
G1 and G2	2556	445	2608	455
G1 and G3	1718	803	1801	774
G2 and G3	2394	429	2512	457

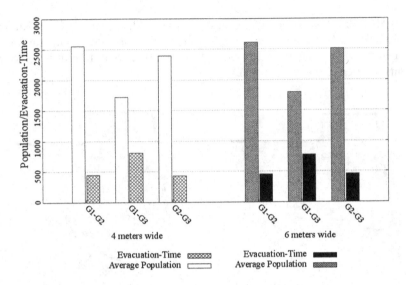

Fig. 6. Average population and total evacuation time

5   Conclusion and Future Works

In this paper, we have presented our Agent Based Model which implements virtual infrastructure of Alopi Devi Temple and different behaviours of pilgrim agents. We have used this model to evaluate evacuation time over two different dimensions of gates. We then have compared the evacuation time between three types of emergency evacuation scenarios. The evaluation results supported the selection of exit points for better and fast evacuation scenario. These outcomes of our Agent Based Model may be further communicated to the authorities of the pilgrimage site for application in real-time scenarios. At present, we are attempting to create an Agent Based Model which can be utilized to assess and compare the existing and modified architectural designs of this pilgrimage site. Further, we wish to utilize this approach for larger religious gatherings in open areas.

References

1. Almeida, J.E., Kokkinogenis, Z., Rossetti, R. J.: Netlogo implementation of an evacuation scenario. In: WISA 2012 (Fourth Workshop on Intelligent Systems and Applications), Madrid, Spain, 20–23 June 2012 (2012)
2. Axelrod, R.: Agent-based modeling as a bridge between disciplines. Handb. Comput. Econ. **2**, 1565–1584 (2006)
3. Bandini, S., Manzoni, S., Vizzari, G.: Agent based modeling and simulation: an informatics perspective. J. Artif. Soc. Soc. Simul. **12**(4), 4 (2009)
4. Chen, X., Zhan, F.B.: Agent-based modelling and simulation of urban evacuation: relative effectiveness of simultaneous and staged evacuation strategies. J. Oper. Res. Soc. **59**(1), 25–33 (2008)

5. Daamen, W., Hoogendoorn, S.: Calibration of pedestrian simulation model for emergency doors by pedestrian type. Transp. Res. Rec. J. Transp. Res. Board **2316**, 69–75 (2012)
6. Dias, C., Sarvi, M., Shiwakoti, N., Ejtemai, O., Burd, M.: Investigating collective escape behaviours in complex situations. Saf. Sci. **60**, 87–94 (2013)
7. Escobar, R., De La Rosa, A.: Architectural design for the survival optimization of panicking fleeing victims. In: Banzhaf, W., Ziegler, J., Christaller, T., Dittrich, P., Kim, J.T. (eds.) ECAL 2003. LNCS (LNAI), vol. 2801, pp. 97–106. Springer, Heidelberg (2003). https://doi.org/10.1007/978-3-540-39432-7_11
8. Fruin, J.: Designing for Pedestrians. Public Transportation United States (1992)
9. Helbing, D., Molnar, P.: Social force model for pedestrian dynamics. Phys. Rev. E **51**(5), 4282 (1995)
10. Helbing, D., Mukerji, P.: Crowd disasters as systemic failures: analysis of the love parade disaster. EPJ Data Sci. **1**(1), 7 (2012)
11. Hoogendoorn, S., Daamen, W., Boer, A., Vaatstra, I.: Assessing passenger comfort and capacity bottlenecks in Dutch train stations. Transp. Res. Rec. J. Transp. Res. Board **2002**, 107–116 (2007)
12. Ijaz, K., Sohail, S., Hashish, S.: A survey of latest approaches for crowd simulation and modeling using hybrid techniques. In: 17th UKSIMAMSS International Conference on Modelling and Simulation, pp. 111–116 (2015)
13. Illera, C., et al.: NO_PANIC. "Escape and Panic in Buildings"–architectural basic research in the context of security and safety research. In: Klingsch, W., Rogsch, C., Schadschneider, A., Schreckenberg, M. (eds.) Pedestrian and Evacuation Dynamics. Springer, Heidelberg (2008). https://doi.org/10.1007/978-3-642-04504-2_71
14. Kasthala, S., Lakra, H.S.: Disaster preparedness for mass religious gatherings in India-learning from case studies. In: Second World Congress on Disaster Management (2015)
15. Santos, G., Aguirre, B.E.: A Critical Review of Emergency Evacuation Simulation Models (2004)
16. Shi, X., Ye, Z., Shiwakoti, N., Tang, D., Wang, C., Wang, W.: Empirical investigation on safety constraints of merging pedestrian crowd through macroscopic and microscopic analysis. Accid. Anal. Prev. **95**, 405–416 (2016)
17. Shinde, K.: Religious Tourism and Religious Tolerance: Insights from Pilgrimage Sites in India, vol. 70 (2015)
18. Shiwakoti, N., Shi, X., Ye, Z., Liu, Y., Lin, J.: A comparative study of pedestrian crowd flow at middle and corner exits. In: The 38th Australasian Transport Research Forum (ATRF 2016), pp. 1–10. Australasian Transport Research Forum (2016)
19. Smith, E.R., Conrey, F.R.: Agent-based modeling: a new approach for theory building in social psychology. Pers. Soc. Psychol. Rev. **11**(1), 87–104 (2007)
20. Still, G.K.: Introduction to Crowd Science. CRC Press, Boca Raton (2014)
21. Tolea, M.I., et al.: Sex-specific correlates of walking speed in a wide age-ranged population. J. Gerontol. Ser. B Psychol. Sci. Soc. Sci.**65**(2), 174–184 (2010)
22. Trivedi, A., Pandey, M.: Agent-based modelling and simulation of religious crowd gatherings in India. In: Bhattacharyya, S., Chaki, N., Konar, D., Chakraborty, U.K., Singh, C.T. (eds.) Advanced Computational and Communication Paradigms. AISC, vol. 706, pp. 465–472. Springer, Singapore (2018). https://doi.org/10.1007/978-981-10-8237-5_45
23. Wang, X., Li, J.: Study on the simulation models for pedestrian evacuation movement. Int. J. Digit. Content Technol. Appl. **7**(8), 503 (2013)

24. Was, J., Lubaa, R.: Towards realistic and effective agent-based models of crowd dynamics. Neurocomputing **146**, 199–209 (2014)
25. Westminister: Trimble juno series handhelds: Juno 3B and juno 3D, user guide (2012). https://gis14.uwec.edu/GeoSpatialResources/Manuals.htm
26. Wilensky, U.: Netlogo 5.2 (1999). https://ccl.northwestern.edu/netlogo/
27. Zhou, S., Chen, D., Cai, W., Luo, L., Low, M.Y.H., Tian, F., Tay, V.S.H., Ong, D.W.S., Hamilton, B.D.: Crowd modeling and simulation technologies. ACM Trans. Model. Comput. Simul. (TOMACS) **20**(4), 20 (2010)

Content-Based Music Classification Using Ensemble of Classifiers

Manikanta Durga Srinivas Anisetty[1]([⊠]), Gagan K Shetty[1]([⊠]),
Srinidhi Hiriyannaiah[1], Siddesh Gaddadevara Matt[1], K. G. Srinivasa[2],
and Anita Kanavalli[1]

[1] Ramaiah Institute of Technology, Bengaluru, India
amd.srinivas@gmail.com, gagankshetty@gmail.com,
srinidhi.hiriyannaiah@gmail.com, siddeshgm@gmail.com,
anita.kanavalli@gmail.com
[2] Ch. Brahm Prakash Government Engineering College, Delhi, India
kgsrinivasa@gmail.com

Abstract. This paper presents an application of Ensemble learning in the field of audio data analytics. We propose a system using Hierarchical ensemble model to classify the genre of a music track based on the contents of the track. The hierarchical ensemble comprised of 7 classifiers trained on different sections of the dataset that can co-relate the output of each other for classifying the data. Using this hierarchical ensemble model, we achieved an accuracy boost of 15% over machine learning models. This hierarchical ensemble has been proven better than an ensemble model with hard voting logic in term of accuracy. This work describes the comparison of basic models with hierarchical model and its characteristics.

Keywords: Music classification · Machine learning
Ensemble learning · Free music archive

1 Introduction

In the rising world of technology and intelligent systems, audio sensing and voice commands can be a vital interaction means that can help in improving the user interaction with a system. Building accurate systems to work with audio data helps in achieving this.

Classification corresponds to the task of training a system to identify different types of entities in the data. This involves probabilistic inference that a data point belongs to certain class based on the training data provided to the system. These trained systems are called classifiers or estimators. There are various applications for this process in the fields of medical imaging, image recognition, sentiment analysis and many more. One such application is classifying music into different genres.

Ensemble learning corresponds to training multiple classifiers and co-relating each other to achieve a collaborative output. In this technique, we use multiple

© Springer Nature Switzerland AG 2018
U. S. Tiwary (Ed.): IHCI 2018, LNCS 11278, pp. 285–292, 2018.
https://doi.org/10.1007/978-3-030-04021-5_26

classifiers that are trained on different sections of the dataset and combined using an ensemble logic, that defines the behaviour of the ensemble model. This method helps in increasing the performance of the system by narrowing down the problem solved by each classifier, eventually solving the entire problem through ensemble.

In this work, we propose an ensemble model that is trained to classify the genre of a music track. As discussed in further sections, the ensemble approach helped in increasing the accuracy over standalone systems.

2   Related Works

Transfer learning is a very promising technique in machine learning. It involves using a pre-trained model's parameters for a task different than the one it has been trained for. This method is very helpful for problems with limited data available. The authors of this paper [1,2] suggest using deep learning techniques for feature extraction. The concept of a deep neural network is that as the data goes through the forward phase, where the lower level features are learnt in the first few layers, for example the edges of objects in case of image classification tasks, then the later layers build upon the lower features and learn the higher features, for example the objects themselves. A similar logic exists when this is applied to a music classification task, hence the idea for the transfer learning task for the classification of music. The final list of features generated are not just the output of the network, but also the activations of the intermediate layers, which are concatenated to the features list. Kapre provides on-GPU preprocessing layers for music data which can aid in feature extraction tasks [3]. Kapre is built specifically for audio data using keras. It provides easy-to-use classes for Spectogram and Melspectrogram that are used for audio pre-processing tasks.

In computer vision tasks, there are several well established datasets for bench marking, such as the MNIST [4], CIFAR [5], ImageNet [6]. The Free music archive (FMA) [7] intends to provide a dataset for bench marking for music classification tasks, as the lack of standardised datasets hinders the research in music information retrieval systems.

This work [9] proposes a new technique called 'DWCHs', which captures the information of the music files based on the wavelet histogram. Wavelets has many applications in the fields of data mining [10], which makes it a promising technique in this field.

A huge set of features is a burden on classifiers and they generally end up overfitting. A novel method was proposed for dimensionality reduction called "Locality Preserving Non-Negative Tensor Factorization (LPNTF)" [11]. Using this technique, they were able to beat the state of the art models on the GTZAN and ISMIR2004 datasets. Dimensionality reduction also reduces the effects of the outliers, noise and missing data.

Support vector machine is a very effective algorithm. The authors of this paper [12] have described the advantages of a support vector machine for the task of music classification. Since we work on classifying multiple genres, typically a Multi-class Support Vector Machine is suitable. One way is to use the

One against the rest method [13] which is widely used in Multi-class classification problems. The features extracted for the music files are not linearly separable [8] and hence a linear classification algorithm will fail to classify the music accurately. SVMs can learn non-linear functions using a kernel trick [14].

The authors of the paper [15] proposed a novel ensemble-based approach based on a segmentation strategy presented. Several representations of the digital audio signal were used since each segment generates a different feature vector. When using this segmentation strategy, it is possible to train a specific classifier for each one of the segments, and to compute the final decision about the class from the ensemble of the results provided by each classifier. The output of each classifier is taken and a combination of the results is achieved through the majority voting rule, max rule, sum rule and product rule.

The papers [16–18] discuss the applications of hierarchical ensemble in the fields of biology and computer vision. The authors have reported significant improvement in tasks such as solving protein function prediction and image classification problems using this technique.

3   Dataset

We used Free Music Archive dataset for the training purpose. This dataset comprised of 106,574 tracks arranged in 161 hierarchical genres. We used a small subset of the dataset which comprised of 8000 tracks from 8 genres. Each music track in the dataset is of 30 s duration.

4   System Developed

The system is built as 2 blocks:

– Feature Extraction
– Classification

The feature extraction module is used to extract the features from the given music files. The extracted features are fed to the classifier for prediction of the genre. The system design is shown in Fig. 1.

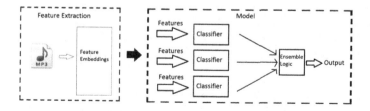

Fig. 1. System design

4.1   Feature Extraction

We used the kapre audio processing library for the feature extraction. Kapre is an audio processing module built over Keras to accelerate the deep learning tasks involved in audio processing tasks. We used a 5 layer convolutional neural network trained using Theano and Kapre by the authors of this paper [1]. The network outputs a 160 dimensional vector on the input file which serves as the extracted feature vector.

4.2   Classification

The vital step in a classification task is to choose an estimator that is suitable for the dataset used. The dataset used is inseparable with linear models due to the overlap of the data points across multiple genres. This resulted in poor accuracy with linear models. In order to achieve better accuracy, Support Vector Machines are used to learn the non-linearity in the data. Since we are working with a hierarchical ensemble model, we train a series of binary SVM estimators.

SVM classifies the data into classes by using a maximum margin separator. Kernel trick is used for non-linear fitting by allowing to fit the separator in a higher dimensional transformed space. The non linear function used for the purpose of this experiment is the Gaussian radial basis function.

4.3   Ensemble of Classifiers

Ensemble methods use multiple learning algorithms to obtain better predictive performance than could be obtained from any of the individual learning algorithms alone. This enables the system to intelligently decide the appropriate classifier suitable for the data point to be classified.

Hierarchical Ensemble. Hierarchical ensemble is an ensemble method which involves multiple classifiers with each classifier trying to predict a subset of the classes. Subsets that are highly separable are at higher levels in the hierarchy and as we go down the hierarchy, the genres get difficult to separate. Initially, we have a root classifier that segregates the classes into subsets of classes. The lower level classifiers are then trained on these subsets to either predict a final class or further divide the class into subsets of classes. This segregation of the further possible classes at each level results in reaching the final result with a better confidence even if the final result is inaccurate. This allows for backtracking of the classification result along with the performance boost.

Algorithm. The decision-making path will be based on the output of the classifiers, i.e., the sub-tree of the predicted class will be considered. For example, if root class predicts Class-A, then the Class-A classifier's result will be considered, and Class-B classifier's result will be ignored. The algorithm developed is as described in Algorithm 1.

Data: *Features*
Result: Genre of the music file
PrimaryPrediction ← *RootClassifier(Features)*;
if *PrimaryPrediction* = *ClassA* **then**
    SecondaryPrediction ← *ClassAClassifier(Features)*;
    if *SecondaryPrediction* = *ClassAA* **then**
        | *FinalPrediction* ← *ClassAAClassifier(Features)*;
    else
        | *FinalPrediction* ← *ClassABClassifier(Features)*;
    end
else
    SecondaryPrediction ← *ClassBClassifier(Features)*;
    if *SecondaryPrediction* = *ClassBA* **then**
        | *FinalPrediction* ← *ClassBAClassifier(Features)*;
    else
        | *FinalPrediction* ← *ClassBBClassifier(Features)*;
    end
end
return *FinalPrediction*;

Algorithm 1. Hierarchical ensemble algorithm

5 Experiment

The dataset was randomly split with 70–30 basis into training and testing sets, resulting in 5,600 tracks for training and 2,400 tracks for testing.

For the implementation of the classifiers, we used the Sklearn [19] library of Python to generate the individual machine learning models. For the ensemble classifier, we used 7 of such machine learning models, each trained individually on its own special handcrafted dataset. To achieve this, we modified the labels of the original dataset as described below:

1. For the root classifier, the genres Folk, International, Pop, Rock were treated as Class A and the genres Electronic, Experimental, Hip-Hop, Instrumental as Class B. The root classifier was hence trained on 8000 tracks, with two labels: Class A and Class B.
2. For the next level, the subset of the genres were considered. For example, Class A classifier only dealt with the genres Folk, International, Pop, Rock and the Class B classifier dealt with the remaining 4. The genres Folk and International were treated as ClassAA and the genres Pop and Rock were treated as ClassAB. Hence, the Class A classifier was trained on 4000 tracks, with the two labels: ClassAA and ClassAB. Class B follows the same logic.
3. For the third level, again a subset of the genres were considered. For example, Class AA classifier only dealt with the genres Folk and International and Class AB classifier the remaining 2, and similarly the Class BA and Class BB classifier. The split of the genres is illustrated in the Fig. 2.

Split of Genres

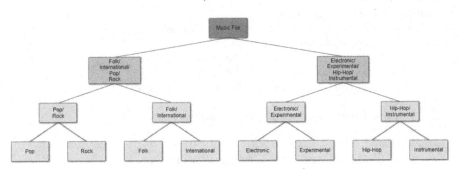

Fig. 2. Genre split

In this way 7 classifiers were trained and the decision making path is decided by the ensemble algorithm. The masking of the genres, i.e, choosing the correct tracks at each step was done using the Pandas [20] library in python.

6   Results

6.1   Ensemble Evaluation

The system achieved an accuracy of 75% over the testing set. The confusion matrix for the testing dataset is as shown in Table 1. The time taken for training the models on the dataset is 43 s (after feature extraction). The average time taken by the system to classify a music file of 30 s duration is 15 s (feature extraction + prediction).

Table 1. Confusion matrix

Predicted	Electronic	Experimental	Folk	Hip-Hop	Instrumental	International	Pop	Rock
Actual								
Electronic	243	22	4	8	13	2	4	4
Experimental	38	176	17	7	17	12	9	24
Folk	0	4	250	1	18	12	4	11
Hip-Hop	23	6	2	251	8	1	7	2
Instrumental	19	14	9	6	233	2	1	16
International	16	2	16	5	1	245	4	11
Pop	16	9	33	11	7	21	146	57
Rock	4	8	11	4	5	5	14	249

6.2   Comparison with Different Models

Along with evaluating the model developed, a comparative study was conducted to understand the improvement in performance of the ensemble model in terms

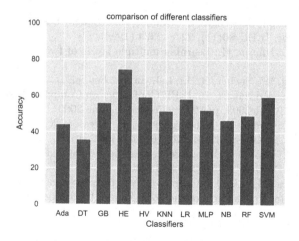

Fig. 3. Comparison of the models

of accuracy is shown in Fig. 3. We considered 10 existing estimators along with the hierarchical ensemble (HE). They are Naive Bayes classifier (NB), Logistic Regression model (LR), SVM with rbf kernel (SVM), Decision tree classifier (DT), Decision tree classifier (DT), K-nearest neighbours estimator (KNN), Multi-Layer Perceptron (MLP), Random forest classifier (RF), AdaBoost Classifier (Ada) [21], Gradient Boost Classifier (GB), Hard-voting ensemble model (HV) [a combined model of previously mentioned models]. Each of these models were trained with a 3 fold cross validation, and the average is taken as the final accuracy in order to reduce the bias effect.

7   Conclusion

Using a hierarchical ensemble has evidently improved the accuracy of the classification. Using more intelligent ensemble algorithms can lead to more accurate ensemble models. This approach can be extended to various other audio analytic tasks to arrive at accurate and improved ensemble algorithms.

References

1. Choi, K., Fazekas, G., Sandler, M., Cho, K.: Transfer learning for music classification and regression tasks. arXiv preprint arXiv:1703.09179 (2017)
2. Zeiler, M.D., Fergus, R.: Visualizing and understanding convolutional networks. In: Fleet, D., Pajdla, T., Schiele, B., Tuytelaars, T. (eds.) ECCV 2014. LNCS, vol. 8689, pp. 818–833. Springer, Cham (2014). https://doi.org/10.1007/978-3-319-10590-1_53
3. Choi, K., Joo, D., Kim, J.: Kapre: On-GPU audio preprocessing layers for a quick implementation of deep neural network models with keras. arXiv preprint arXiv:1706.05781 (2017)

4. LeCun, Y., Bottou, L., Bengio, Y., Haffner, P.: Gradient-based learning applied to document. Proc. IEEE **86**(11), 2278–2324 (1998)
5. Krizhevsky, A., Hinton, G.: Learning multiple layers of features from tiny images (2009)
6. Deng, J., Dong, W., Socher, R., Li, L.J., Li, K., Fei-Fei, L.: Imagenet: a large-scale hierarchical image database. In: IEEE Conference on Computer Vision and Pattern Recognition, CVPR 2009, pp. 248–255. IEEE, June 2009
7. Defferrard, M., Benzi, K., Vandergheynst, P., Bresson, X.: FMA: A dataset for music analysis. arXiv preprint arXiv:1612.01840 (2016)
8. Tzanetakis, G., Cook, P.: Musical genre classification of audio signals. IEEE Trans. Speech Audio Process. **10**(5), 293–302 (2002)
9. Li, T., Ogihara, M., Li, Q.: A comparative study on content-based music genre classification. In: Proceedings of the 26th Annual International ACM SIGIR Conference on Research and Development in Information Retrieval, pp. 282–289. ACM, July 2003
10. Li, T., Li, Q., Zhu, S., Ogihara, M.: A survey on wavelet applications in data mining. ACM SIGKDD Explor. Newsl. **4**(2), 49–68 (2002)
11. Panagakis, Y., Kotropoulos, C., Arce, G.R.: Music genre classification using locality preserving non-negative tensor factorization and sparse representations. In: ISMIR, vol. 14, no. 1, pp. 249–254, October 2009
12. Mandel, M.I., Ellis, D.: Song-level features and support vector machines for music classification. In: ISMIR, vol. 2005, pp. 594–599, September 2005
13. Weston, J., Watkins, C.: Multi-class support vector machines. Technical report CSD-TR-98-04, Department of Computer Science, Royal Holloway, University of London, May 1998
14. Suykens, J.A.: Nonlinear modelling and support vector machines. In: Proceedings of the 18th IEEE Instrumentation and Measurement Technology Conference, IMTC 2001, vol. 1, pp. 287–294. IEEE, May 2001
15. Silla Jr., C.N., Kaestner, C.A., Koerich, A.L.: Automatic music genre classification using ensemble of classifiers. In: IEEE International Conference on Systems, Man and Cybernetics, 2007, ISIC, pp. 1687–1692. IEEE, October 2007
16. Valentini, G.: Hierarchical ensemble methods for protein function prediction. ISRN Bioinform. **2014** (2014). https://doi.org/10.1155/2014/901419
17. Kim, B.S., Park, J.Y., Gilbert, A.C., Savarese, S.: Hierarchical classification of images by sparse approximation. Image Vis. Comput. **31**(12), 982–991 (2013)
18. Huang, J., Kumar, S.R., Zabih, R.: An automatic hierarchical image classification scheme. In: Proceedings of the Sixth ACM International Conference on Multimedia, pp. 219–228. ACM, September 1998
19. Pedregosa, F., et al.: Scikit-learn: machine learning in Python. J. Mach. Learn. Res. **12**, 2825–2830 (2011)
20. McKinney, W.: Pandas: a foundational Python library for data analysis and statistics. Python High Perform. Sci. Comput., 1–9 (2011)
21. Hastie, T., Rosset, S., Zhu, J., Zou, H.: Multi-class adaboost. Stat. Interface **2**(3), 349–360 (2009)

A Decision Tree Based Context-Aware Recommender System

Sonal Linda[✉] and K. K. Bharadwaj

School of Computer and Systems Sciences, Jawaharlal Nehru University,
New Delhi, India
lindasonal@gmail.com, kbharadwaj@gmail.com

Abstract. Context-aware recommender systems (CARSs) have emerged from traditional recommender systems (RSs) that provide several different opportunities in the area of personalized recommendations for online users. CARSs promote incorporation of additional contextual information such as time, day, season, user's personality along with users and items related information into recommendation process that makes market based e-commerce sites more attractive to users. Content-based filtering (CBF) and collaborative filtering (CF) are two well-known and most implemented recommendation techniques that offer various hybridization approaches for producing quality recommendations. Moreover, contextual pre-filtering, contextual post-filtering and contextual modeling are some paradigms through which CARSs take advantages of user's contextual preferences in recommendation process. In this paper, we introduce a decision tree based CARS framework that exploits the benefits of both CBF and CF techniques using contextual pre-filtering paradigm. We apply ID3 algorithm for learning a user model to exploit the user's contextual preferences and utilizing rules extracted from decision tree to neighborhood formation. Experimental results using two real-world benchmark datasets clearly validate the effectiveness of our proposed scheme in comparison to traditional scheme.

Keywords: Decision tree · Content-based filtering · Collaborative filtering
Context-aware recommender system

1 Introduction

Emerging intelligent techniques for recommender systems (RSs) constitute a path for online users to interact with digital world and provide web-based services to them. Some applications based on traditional RSs are still heavily rely on users and items related information and not formulating contextual information into recommendation process may fail to provide personalized and useful recommendations. Personalization dynamically adapts context-based user's profile that consists of related ideas, situations, events or information in order to enhance the quality of user interactions with the system and provides support to satisfy the needs, preferences of each individual [1]. Day, time, companion, price, time, user's personality, etc. are some contextual features required to incorporate into RSs that yield context-aware recommender systems

© Springer Nature Switzerland AG 2018
U. S. Tiwary (Ed.): IHCI 2018, LNCS 11278, pp. 293–305, 2018.
https://doi.org/10.1007/978-3-030-04021-5_27

(CARSs) for providing personalized and useful recommendations. CARSs can act smartly with the changes in the user's contextual situations and produce quality recommendations that pertinent to the user in order to offer suitable and acceptable suggestions. For example, a list of recommended movies for watching at afternoon on a weekday with colleagues will be different from watching at night on a weekend with spouse. Similarly, a list of recommended restaurants for lunch at low price for hardworker will not be same as a list of restaurants for dinner at high price for hunter ostentation. The adaptation of appropriate contextual features highly depends which application domain generates what recommendations and for whom. Movie based CARS generates a recommended list of movies that considers some essential contextual features such as day, time and companion whereas Restaurant oriented CARS provides a recommended list of restaurants that takes into account some other contextual features for instance price, time and user's personality, etc.

CARSs have various paradigms for integrating contextual features with existing recommendation process. These paradigms are broadly classified as: contextual pre-filtering, contextual post-filtering and contextual modeling which utilize one of the most popular traditional recommendation techniques: content-based filtering (CBF) and collaborative filtering (CF) to provide personalized context-aware services to users [2, 3]. All recommendation techniques have strengths and weakness. CF faces the problem of data sparsity which can reduce the dimensionality of space needed for neighborhood formation whereas CBF have a start-up problem in which it requires enough ratings to build a relative user model/classifier. Despite of that, hybridization of both techniques can achieve better performance with less drawbacks of any individual technique [4]. Since CARSs have emerged from RSs and offer several different opportunities, it will be beneficial to employ hybridized approaches to provide quality recommendations [3].

Extensive literature is available to explore the domain of CARSs to establish an intelligent system that fulfill the user's satisfaction about the recommended products. For providing context-aware services to mobile users, a modified CF-based model LARMU [5] is designed that exploits classification rules to understand user's needs. A rule based RS uses advance neighborhood formation approach to find similar users with similar characteristics [6]. Moreover, a newly invented language ECA-DL [7] facilitates a rule-based engine component that has capability to process the behaviors of context-aware applications to adjust with context sensing, discovery, extraction, interpretation and manipulation. Furthermore, AMAYA [8] is built to provide contextual recommendations by adapting user's situation that successfully implemented to provide web based news service on user's demand.

In this paper, we proposed a decision tree based CARS framework to build a user model/classifier in which contextual features are embedded with the system using contextual pre-filtering paradigm. The main contributions of our work are summarized below:

- Build decision tree classifier [9] for each user using content-based filtering (CBF) approach.
- Extract classification rules from decision tree and utilize rules in neighborhood formation.
- Predict unknown ratings using collaborative filtering (CF) approach [10].

The remainder of the paper is structured as follows: Sect. 2 discusses about work related to this paper. Our proposed decision tree based CARS framework is presented in Sect. 3. Experimental evaluation and results are demonstrated in Sect. 4. Finally, Sect. 5 concludes our work with some future directions.

2 Related Work

A substantial amount of challenges have been attempted in the field of CARSs that covers user modeling and unknown rating prediction depending on user's tastes and preferences [3]. Recent research in user modeling recognized the need to keep track and adapt a user profile continuously for every user in the ubiquitous computing environment [11]. The ubiquitous computing offers the personalized recommendations that match the individual's current context, preferences, knowledge, goals and needs. The process of personalization leads to offline learning in which collection and processing of acquired data may vary according to application domain. Moreover, a system may face the challenge of drifting user's interest that may raise difficulties for learning user profile and building a perfect model.

2.1 Recommendation Techniques

Some recommendation techniques require users to input data explicitly for interacting with the system and can be categorized into two-dimensional and multi-dimensional recommendation techniques [2, 3].

2.1.1 Two-Dimensional (2D) Recommendation Techniques

Traditional RSs are based on 2D recommendation techniques that completely rely on two dimensions users and items, to model a user profile that can be categorized as follows [2]:

- Content-based filtering (CBF): A recommended list of items is generated by exploiting users past preferred similar choices.
- Collaborative filtering (CF): A recommended list of items is generated by aggregating past ratings of a user's like-minded neighbors with similar tastes and similar preferences.
- Hybrid approaches: A recommended list of items is generated by hybridizing the both CBF and CF techniques.

2.1.2 Multi-dimensional (MD) Recommendation Technique

Context-aware recommender systems (CARSs) based on MD recommendation techniques rely on multiple dimensions such as users, items and multiple contextual features to make 2D recommendation techniques more advance, successful and relevant to broader range of real-life applications. There are various ways to extend the capabilities of traditional recommendation techniques [3]:

- Contextual pre-filtering: Current contextual preferences are initially used for acquiring relevant set of data and then any traditional 2D recommendation technique can be applied on the selected data to generate recommended list of items for each user.
- Contextual post-filtering: Any traditional 2D recommendation technique can be applied initially on entire data and then current contextual preferences are used to adjust recommended list of items for each user.
- Contextual modeling: Current contextual preferences are used directly in the recommendation function and give rise to truly MD recommendation function to generate recommended list of items for each user.

2.2   Classification by Decision Tree Induction

Decision trees (DTs) are widely used learning techniques to build classification models that closely resemble human cognition [12, 13]. The utilization of DTs offers efficiency, interpretability and flexibility in handling demographic and contextual features for various recommendation models [9]. Moreover, a rule-based hybrid approach can be effective for handling uncertainties due to missing data that may cause ambiguities in selecting appropriate model for mobile CARSs [14]. The model also called classifier used for classification that is constructed by analyzing training samples where each sample is described by some features and belong to a predefined class label. DT represents knowledge in a flexible way so that it can be easily implemented for building high performance systems, such as medical diagnosis systems, intrusion detection systems, decision support systems, etc. [15]. ID3 is an iterative and simplest algorithm to construct decision trees. Empirical studies suggest that an exact decision tree is constructed more quickly by ID3 algorithm than by building a tree directly from the entire training samples [16]. The algorithm follows the concept of information gain that works on entropy-based measure.

The learning process starts with selection of features that will split the samples into individual classes. Features will become the test features at the node of DT and a branch is formed for each known value of the test feature. The procedure repeats recursively to build a DT for the samples at each split. It terminates only when any one of the following conditions is met:

- For a given node all training samples associated with the same class.
- For further partitioning of training samples there is no feature left.
- For adding a new branch there is no sample remains.

The prediction process starts using classification rules extracted from DT and represented in the form of "IF-THEN" rules [16].

3   Proposed Decision Tree Based CARS Framework

We propose a decision tree classifier using ID3 algorithm based on content-based filtering (CBF) technique to build separate decision tree for each user and apply collaborative filtering (CF) based recommendation process into CARS framework.

The idea of this hybridization is to combine the two well-known recommendation techniques, CBF and CF to produce quality recommendations. The tree is similar to the CBF approach where contextual features under which active user rated some items in past are used to build a classifier that explains the user's liking/disliking of a certain item. Following contextual pre-filtering paradigm, the feedback provided by the dedicated decision tree for the target item is considered to be the decision (like/dislike) needed to generate neighborhood set of active user. Finally, CF approach is used to predict rating for target item by computing ratings collected from neighborhood set of the active user.

The classifier acquires data in the form of $\langle User \times Item \times Contextual\ Features \rightarrow Rating \rangle$. More formally, we assume that $U = \{u_a : 1 \leq a \leq m\}$ be a set of m users, $I = \{i_t : 1 \leq t \leq n\}$ be a set of n items, $C = \{c_f : 1 \leq f \leq r\}$ be a set of r contextual features and $I_a^{(u)} \subseteq I$ be the set of items rated by the active user u_a. The goal is to recommend new item i_t to the active user u_a associated with contextual features vector C, where $i_t \in I \bigwedge i_t \notin I_a^{(u)}$.

3.1 Decision Tree Based Classifier

We employ the decision tree based classifier into CF method in which the target item i_t associated with contextual feature values is considered as a test sample which is to be classified and other items previously rated by the active user associated with contextual feature values are considered as training samples. For example, an active user u_a takes like and dislike as decision classes on the basis of contextual feature values associated with his/her previously rated list of items $I_a^{(u)}$. To determine the most likely class for the target item i_t, we adapt decision tree based classifier [16]. The decision tree is composed of two major steps: Induction and Inference [15]. In the first step, building of decision tree using training samples starts with a tree has empty nodes and selecting contextual features for each class label (like/dislike). We use ID3 algorithm for building decision trees. The information gain of every contextual feature is used as the splitting criteria. The same procedure of splitting contextual features continues for each sub tree until reaching leaves and allocating their corresponding class labels (like/dislike). For tree generation, let D constitutes of d. training samples and each sample belongs to one of the predefined classes $Cl_j (for j = 1, 2, \ldots, k)$. The information gain $Info_{gain}(D)$ for classification is computed using Eq. (1).

$$Info_{gain}(D) = - \sum_{j=1}^{k} P_j log_2 (P_j) \tag{1}$$

where P_j is the probability of class values that belong to class Cl_j and is estimated by $d_j / |D|$. Let a contextual feature c_f has v distinct values $c_{f1}, c_{f2}, \ldots, c_{fv}$ are used to partition D into v subsets. For contextual feature c_f, the information gain $E(c_f)$ is computed using Eq. (2).

$$E(c_f) = \sum_{j=1}^{k} P_j Info_{gain}\left(D_{c_{f1},c_{f2},...,c_{fv}}\right) \tag{2}$$

Figure 1 illustrates a decision tree based user's profile using two different application domains. In the second step, the test sample with all the contextual feature values is selected for classification. Then, it tracks the path from root to the internal node having same contextual feature values until the leaf is found. Finally, we use the path associated with class label (like/dislike) to predict class for the given test sample.

3.2   Neighborhood Formation

The target item is finally labeled with like/dislike class using decision tree based classifier which helps to generate neighbors $N_a^{(u)}$ for active user u_a. Suppose the target item i_t for active user u_a is labeled as 'like' then only those users are selected as neighbors whose given ratings associated with contextual feature values also belongs to the 'like' class for target item i_t. The classification rules are generated from decision tree by tracking the path from the root node to each leaf node in the tree. Some extracted sample rules from DT (see Fig. 1) that used to classify the target item i_t and predict the class label like/dislike are shown in Tables 1 and 2 respectively.

$$N_a^{(u)} = \left\{u_b : u_b \in U \bigwedge u_b \neq u_a \wedge PClass(u_a, i_t) = AClass(u_b, i_t)\right\} \tag{3}$$

where $N_a^{(u)}$ is the neighborhood set of active user u_a, $PClass(u_a, i_t)$ is the predicted class of active user u_a for target item i_t and $AClass(u_b, i_t)$ is the actual class of neighbor u_b who already rated the target item i_t.

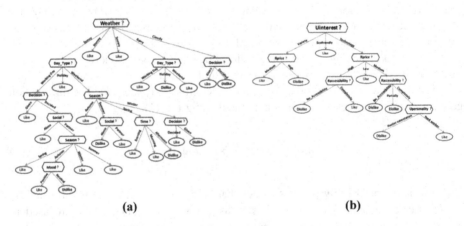

(a)   (b)

Fig. 1. Decision Tree for **(a)** User 1 for LDOS-CoMoDa dataset **(b)** User 2 for Restaurant & consumer dataset.

Table 1. Extracted sample rules from decision tree for User 1.

Rule #		Rules		
R1:	IF	Weather = 'sunny' AND Day_Type = 'working day' AND Decision = 'given'	THEN	Class = 'like'
R2:	IF	Weather = 'sunny' AND Day_Type = 'working day' AND Decision = 'decided' AND Social = 'alone'	THEN	Class = 'like'
R3:	IF	Weather = 'sunny' AND Day_Type = 'working day' AND Decision = 'decided' AND Social = 'partner' AND Season = 'spring'	THEN	Class = 'like'
R22:	IF	Weather = 'cloudy' AND Decision = 'given'	THEN	Class = 'like'
R23:	IF	Weather = 'cloudy' AND Decision = 'decided'	THEN	Class = 'dislike'

Table 2. Extracted sample rules from decision tree for User 2.

Rule #		Rules		
R1:	IF	Uinterest = 'variety' AND Rprice = 'medium'	THEN	Class = **'like'**
R2:	IF	Uinterest = 'variety' AND Rprice = 'high'	THEN	Class = **'dislike'**
R3:	IF	Uinterest = 'ecofriendly'	THEN	Class = **'like'**
R9:	IF	Uinterest = 'technology' AND Rprice = 'medium' AND Raccessibility = 'completely' AND Upersonality = 'hunter ostentation'	THEN	Class = **'dislike'**
R10:	IF	Uinterest = 'technology' AND Rprice = 'medium' AND Raccessibility = 'completely' AND Upersonality = 'hard worker'	THEN	Class = **'like'**

3.3 Prediction and Recommendation

Based on similar liking/disliking behavior with targeted item the neighborhood set is generated using Eq. (3) and then further utilize the rating pattern of neighbors to predict the rating for the active user which is similar to CF method. To provide context-aware recommendations by taking contextual information into consideration with CF, we use cosine similarity measure for computing similarity score between two contextual feature vectors C_a and C_b using Eq. (4). The adapted Pearson Correlation similarity measure is utilized to compute similarity between two users u_a and u_b using Eq. (5). Afterward, the context feature similarity and user similarity scores are utilized to predict rating for u_a to i_t along with contextual features vector C_a using Eq. (6).

$$cosineSim(C_a, C_b) = \frac{\sum_{j=1}^{r} c_{a,j} \times c_{b,j}}{\sqrt{\sum_{j=1}^{r} (c_{a,j})^2} \times \sqrt{\sum_{j=1}^{r} (c_{b,j})^2}} \qquad (4)$$

$$userSim(u_a, u_b) = \frac{\sum_{i_x \in I_a^{(u)} \cap I_b^{(u)}} (r_{u_a}(i_x) - \bar{r}_{u_a})(r_{u_b}(i_x) - \bar{r}_{u_b})}{\sqrt{\sum_{i_x \in I_a^{(u)} \cap I_b^{(u)}} (r_{u_a}(i_x) - \bar{r}_{u_a})^2} \sqrt{\sum_{i_x \in I_a^{(u)} \cap I_b^{(u)}} (r_{u_b}(i_x) - \bar{r}_{u_b})^2}} \tag{5}$$

$$Pred(r_{u_a,i_t,C_a}) = \bar{r}_{u_a} + \frac{\sum_{u_b \in N_a^{(u)}} userSim(u_a, u_b) \times cosineSim(C_a, C_b) \times (r_{u_b}(i_t) - \bar{r}_{u_b})}{\sum_{u_b \in N_a^{(u)}} |userSim(u_a, u_b) \times cosineSim(C_a, C_b)|}$$

$$\tag{6}$$

where $\bar{r}_{u_a}$ represents the average rating of user u_a, $r_{u_b}(i_t)$ s the rating for i_t given by user u_b and $N_a^{(u)}$ is the neighborhood set of u_a. Finally, the predicted ratings $Pred(r_{u_a,i_t,C_a})$ are used to create the Top-N recommended list of items for an active user u_a.

The main steps of our proposed framework are summarized below:

Step 1: Utilizing the contextual features into DT classifier to construct the user model.

Step 2: Forming Neighborhood set for active user by exploiting similar liking/disliking behavior for target item.

Step 3: Computing predicted rating for active user to target item associated with contextual features value using similarity measures $userSim(u_a, u_b)$ and $cosineSim(C_a, C_b)$.

Step 4: Generating Top-N. recommended list for active user.

4 Experiments and Results

To evaluate the effectiveness of our proposed scheme, we have conducted experiments on real-world multidimensional datasets which belong to two different application domains: LDOS-CoMoDa[1] and Restaurant & consumer data[2]. LDOS-CoMoDa contains 2098 ratings given by 112 users to 1189 movies along with 12 contextual features that are explicitly acquired from the users. Restaurant & consumer data comprises 1089 ratings given by 130 users to 129 restaurants accumulated with 46 contextual features. For experiments, we have chosen 10 contextual features from each domain to build generic model for CARS framework.

We employ holdout method in which two-third of the dataset are allocated for training the model/classifier and remaining one-third is allocated for testing the model's accuracy. We assign class label 'like' to those samples consist ratings in range [3–5] and 'dislike' to those samples consist rating 1 or 2 since class label for each sample must be provided to build user model.

---

[1] http://www.lucami.org/index.php/research/ldos-comoda-datasetlang=en.

[2] https://archive.ics.uci.edu/ml/datasets/Restaurant+%26+consumer+ta.

4.1 Performance Evaluation Metrics

In order to evaluate the effectiveness our proposed scheme DT based context-aware CF (CACF-DT), we compare its performance with CACF scheme and conduct experiments using the following performance metrics:

- Coverage of a rule R. is defined as the ratio of the number of training samples covered by R to the number of samples in training set T_r

$$Coverage(R) = \frac{N_{cover}(R)}{|T_r|} \tag{7}$$

- Accuracy of a rule R. is defined as the ratio of the number of training samples correctly classified by R to the number of training samples covered by R.

$$Accuracy(R) = \frac{N_{correct}(R)}{N_{cover}(R)} \tag{8}$$

- Mean Absolute Error (MAE) is defined as the average absolute difference between the predicted rating $Pred(r_{u_a i_t})$ and actu rating $Act(r_{u_a i_t})$ from test set T_s. set.

$$MAE = \frac{1}{T_s} \sum_{j=1}^{|T_s|} |Act(r_{u_a i_t C_a}) - Pred(r_{u_a i_t C_a})| \tag{9}$$

- Precision is defined as the ratio of relevant number of items recommended to the number of recommended items.

$$Precision = \frac{N_{rec} + N_{rel}}{N_{rec}}. \tag{10}$$

- Recall is defined as the ratio of relevant number of items recommended to the number of relevant items:

$$Recall = \frac{N_{rec} + N_{rel}}{N_{rel}} \tag{11}$$

- F1 score is computed using Eqs. (10) and (11) as follows:

$$F1\ score = \frac{2 \times Precision \times Recall}{Precision + Recall} \tag{12}$$

4.2 Experiments

Initially, we examine the quality of classification rules extracted from DT built for each user in terms of coverage and accuracy using Eqs. (7) and (8). The coverage and accuracy of rules for two random sample users *User* 1 and *User* 2 belong to different application domains movie and restaurant respectively, is depicted in Fig. 2.

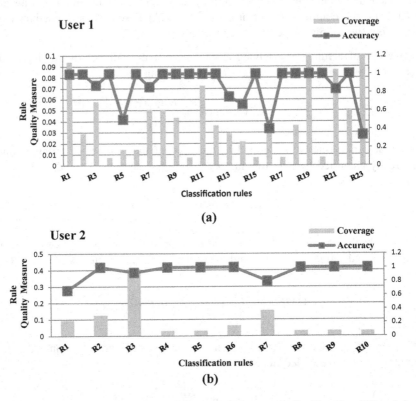

(a)

(b)

Fig. 2. Rule Quality Measure in terms of accuracy and coverage for User 1 and User 2 for **(a)** LDOS-CoMoDa dataset **(b)** Restaurant & consumer dataset.

Next, we compare the prediction capability of proposed scheme CACF-DT with CACF scheme in terms of mean absolute error (MAE) using Eq. (9). It is evident from the Fig. 3 that proposed scheme CACF-DT outperforms CACF scheme.

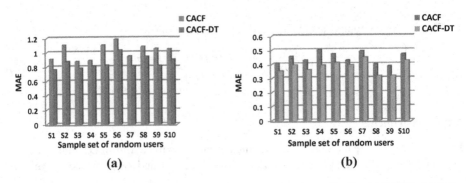

(a)   **(b)**

Fig. 3. Comparison of MAE for two schemes CACF and CACF-DT using **(a)** LDOS-CoMoDa dataset **(b)** Restaurant & consumer dataset.

Finally, experiment for evaluating the system's recommendation accuracy at Top-15 recommendations using two schemes CACF-DT and CACF is conducted via precision, recall and F1 score using Eqs. (10), (11) and (12) respectively.

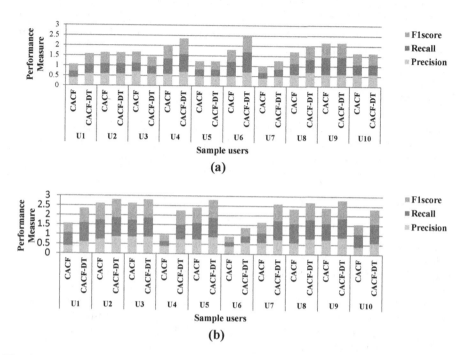

Fig. 4. Comparison of two schemes CACF and CACF-DT in terms of precision, recall and F1score using (**a**) LDOS-CoMoDa dataset (**b**) Restaurant & consumer dataset

The results depicted in Fig. 4 shows the relative performance of CACF with our proposed scheme CACF-DT. It is clear that proposed scheme CACF-DT considerably performed better than CACF scheme in terms of MAE, precision, recall and F1 score.

5   Conclusions and Future Directions

In this paper, we developed a decision tree (DT) based CARS framework using ID3 algorithm. By following the contextual pre-filtering paradigm, contextual features are incorporated before applying any 2D recommendation technique for recommendations. Our proposed recommendation scheme is twofold: initially, a DT user model is built by learning appropriate contextual preferences for active user using content based filtering (CBF) approach and then utilize the extracted classification rules to generate an effective neighborhood set so that it makes feasible to predict unknown ratings for active user through collaborative filtering (CF) approach. We conducted various experiments using two real-world benchmark multi-dimensional datasets belonging to different application domains in which the performance of proposed scheme CACF-DT is compared with CACF scheme via MAE, precision, recall and F1 score. Results clearly demonstrate that CACF-DT consistently outperforms CACF. As future work, we plan to upgrade the current predictive model using other inductive learning approach ILA [17] to handle large datasets and enhance it with other techniques used for neighborhood formation [10].

References

1. Stewart, A., Niederée, C., Mehta, B.: State of the Art in user modeling for personalization in content, service and interaction. NSF/DELOS Report on Personalization, pp. 1–6 (2004)
2. Adomavicius, G., Tuzhilin, A.: Toward the next generation of recommender systems: a survey of the State-of-the-Art and possible extensions. IEEE Trans. Knowl. Data Eng. **17**(6), 734–749 (2005)
3. Adomavicius, G., Tuzhilin, A.: Context-aware recommender systems. In: Ricci, F., Rokach, L., Shapira, B., Kantor, P. (eds.) Recommender Systems Handbook, pp. 217–253. Springer, Boston (2011). https://doi.org/10.1007/978-0-387-85820-3_7
4. Burke, R.: Hybrid recommender systems: survey and experiments. User Model. User-Adap. Inter. **12**(4), 331–370 (2002)
5. Kim, K., Ahn, H., Jeong, S.: Context-aware recommender systems using data mining techniques. World Acad. Sci., Eng. Technol. Int. J. Ind. Manuf. Eng. **4**(4), 381–386 (2010)
6. Imran, H., Belghis-Zadeh, M., Chang, T.W., Kinshuk, G.S.: A rule-based recommender system to suggest learning tasks. In: Trausan-Matu, S., Boyer, K.E., Crosby, M., Panourgia, K. (eds.) Intelligent Tutoring Systems. ITS 2014. LNCS, vol. 8474, pp. 672–673. Springer, Cham (2014). https://doi.org/10.1007/978-3-319-07221-0_102
7. Daniele, L., Dockhorn Costa, P., Ferreira Pires, L.: Towards a rule-based approach for context-aware applications. In: Pras, A., van Sinderen, M. (eds.) EUNICE 2007. LNCS, vol. 4606, pp. 33–43. Springer, Heidelberg (2007). https://doi.org/10.1007/978-3-540-73530-4_5
8. Rack, C., Arbanowski, S., Steglich, S.: A generic multipurpose recommender system for contextual recommendations. In: 8th International Symposium Proceedings on Autonomous Decentralized Systems (ISADS'07), pp. 445–450. IEEE, USA (2007)
9. Gershman, A., Meisels, A., Lüke, K.H., Rokach, L., Schclar, A., Sturm, A.: A decision tree based recommender system. In: 10th International Conference Proceedings on Innovative Internet Community Services, Bangkok, pp. 170–179 (2010)
10. Agarwal, V., Bharadwaj, K.K.: A collaborative filtering framework for friends recommendation in social networks based on interaction intensity and adaptive user similarity. Soc. Netw. Anal. Min. **3**(3), 359–379 (2012)
11. Kuflik, T., Kay, J., Kummerfeld, B.: Challenges and solutions of ubiquitous user modeling. In: Krüger, A., Kuflik, T. (eds.) Ubiquitous Display Environments. Cognitive Technologies, pp. 7–30. Springer, Heidelberg (2012). https://doi.org/10.1007/978-3-642-27663-7_2
12. Patidar, A., Agarwal, V., Bharadwaj, K.K.: Predicting friends and foes in signed networks using inductive inference and social balance theory. In: IEEE/ACM International Conference Proceedings on Advances in Social Networks Analysis and Mining, pp. 384–388. IEEE, Turkey (2012)
13. Bobek, S., Nalepa, G.J.: Uncertainty handling in rule-based mobile context-aware systems. Pervasive Mob. Comput. **39**, 159–179 (2017)

14. Bobek, S., Misiak, P.: Uncertain decision tree classifier for mobile context-aware computing. In: Rutkowski, L., Scherer, R., Korytkowski, M., Pedrycz, W., Tadeusiewicz, R., Zurada, Jacek M. (eds.) ICAISC 2018. LNCS (LNAI), vol. 10842, pp. 276–287. Springer, Cham (2018). https://doi.org/10.1007/978-3-319-91262-2_25

15. Jenhani, I., Amor, N.B., Elouedi, Z.: Decision trees as possibilistic classifiers. Int. J. Approximate Reasoning **48**, 784–807 (2008)

16. Han, J., Kamber, M., Pei, J.: Data Mining. Concepts and Techniques, 3rd edn. Morgan Kaufmann, Burlington (2011)

17. Tolun, M.R., Sever, H., Uludag, M., Abu-Soud, S.M.: ILA-2: an inductive learning algorithm for knowledge discovery. Cybern. Syst. **30**(7), 609–628 (1999)

Mining of Influencers in Signed Social Networks: A Memetic Approach

Nancy Girdhar[(✉)] and K. K. Bharadwaj

School of Computer and Systems Sciences, Jawaharlal Nehru University,
New Delhi 110067, India
nancy.grl991@gmail.com, kbharadwaj@gmail.com

Abstract. The tenacious unfurl of social networks and its unfathomable influence into the daily lives of users is overwhelming that tempts researchers to explore and analyze the domain of social influence mining. To date, most of the research tends to focus only on positive influence for discovering influencers however, in signed social networks (SSNs) where besides positive links there are negative links that ascertain the presence of negative influence also. Thus, it is essential to consider both positive and negative influences to mine influential nodes in SSNs. In this work, we propose a novel approach based on memetic algorithm (MA) for finding set of influential users in a SSN. Our contribution is twofold. First, we formulate a new fitness function termed as *Status Influential Strength (SIS)* grounded on status theory and strength of links between users. Next, we propose a new approach for *Mining Influencers based on Memetic Algorithm (MIMA)* in signed social networks. The performance of proposed approach is validated through various experiments conducted on real-world Epinions dataset and the results clearly establish the efficacy of our proposed approach.

Keywords: Signed social networks · Memetic algorithm
Social influence mining · Discovering influencers · Status theory

1 Introduction

Social media sites owe their phenomenal success and popularity largely to the billions of users of these sites that grabbed the attention of many researchers to examine social media phenomenon and its role in contemporary society. Sharing information (photos, videos, texts) on social networks has become a trend now, making these social networks common venue of crowdsourcing, folksonomy and user-generated content [9]. Despite the users' friendly kinship, the fingerprints of users' antagonistic behavior cannot be denied in social networks, thereby social networks are not untouched with hostile relations shown by users towards other users in the form of dislike, poor ratings and negative comments etc. These positive and negative interactions among users of these networks directed to the advent of Signed Social Networks (SSNs) comprised of both types of relationships: friendly and hostile [9, 15]. Friendly (positive) and hostile (negative) relations are symbolized with $+1$ and -1 respectively, annotated on the links between users in the network. These networks now-a-days are far more than just

© Springer Nature Switzerland AG 2018
U. S. Tiwary (Ed.): IHCI 2018, LNCS 11278, pp. 306–316, 2018.
https://doi.org/10.1007/978-3-030-04021-5_28

platforms rather they have gradually been integrated into people's daily life. The study of signed links between users provides a window to understand users' preferences, their requirements and the influence propagation in the networks based on their activities and past topic related conversations and interactions.

Due to rapid dissemination, amplification of content and the potential to impact large number of people both positively and negatively, signed social influence mining finds their applicability in many disparate businesses. Providing social media touch to a business brand not only creates more business but also associates with customers better and assists them on a higher level. This led to the phenomenon of viral marketing widely used by small businesses in order to gain publicity by reaching out to these social networks [6, 11, 13], benefiting these businesses to get exposure and increase their brand awareness through self-replicating viral processes. Early examples of research into influence mining include diffusion process i.e. "word-of-mouth" for viral marketing applications [4, 6, 17], greedy algorithms to mine influencers [6, 7], influence propagation models [5, 10, 12] and identification of influential users [2, 3]. Although, ample of published studies is available to address the problem of social influence mining but most research takes into account only positive influence amid the users thus, unveiling this phenomenon in the view of both positive and negative influence (signed social influence mining) have not been adequately focused on. Therefore, to contemplate this aspect, we framed our approach to consider both positive and negative influences based on the status theory developed by Leskovec et al. [15]. To this end, we propose a naïve memetic approach to discover set of influencers with maximal status influential strength in signed social networks.

Precisely, the main contributions of our work towards developing *MIMA* are as follows:

- To discover set of influencers in the network, computation of status of users in the network based on the *Theory of Status* [15], considering the fact that higher the status of a user more influential it will be. Moreover, this theory is well suitable for directed SSNs, thus, it takes into consideration the direction of link information besides the sign and the links itself.
- Next, we have assimilated the concept of strength of ties between users in the network based on the notion that more a user has links; less will be its tie strength with these links [1]. This asserts more importance to the user-to-user interaction.
- Finally, a novel approach based on memetic algorithm is proposed named as Mining Influencers based on Memetic Algorithm (*MIMA*) to mine the influencers in SSNs. For this, a new fitness function Status Influential Strength (**SIS**) of a user is formulated, which is product of the status of the user and his/her average tie strength with other users in the network.
- To elucidate the effectiveness of the proposed model, experiments are conducted on real-world Epinions dataset.

The rest of the article is structured as: Sect. 2 presents the brief of related work on SSNs. Section 3 gives the details of the proposed model. Section 4 elaborates the datasets and evaluation metrics with experiments and results. Finally, Sect. 5 summarizes our work with future challenges.

2 Related Work

Enthralled by the popularity of social networks and its usage in various business applications such as viral marketing applications, advertisements industries and government services, garnered the attention of many researchers to explore the domain of influence mining in social networks. Thus, the problem of social influence mining has been addressed by the research community in different perspectives. In a survey on influence analysis in social networks various aspects of social media content are explored to develop new methods for analyzing social influence in large-scale social networks [16]. A great deal of work in social influence mining has focused on the influence propagation methods [5, 10, 12]. This strategy inspires users to swap, spread or share the information to disparate users which can lead to multi-fold growth of the network.

Most researchers investigated the concepts of diffusion of innovations based on node specific thresholds such as centrality, betweenness in social networks [8, 10, 11]. Bonchi [5] studied influence propagation in social network considering data mining perspective. Bharathi et al. [4] proposed a mathematical tractable model to diffuse multiple innovations in the network. A number of authors have also considered influence spread by improving the efficiency of greedy algorithms [6, 7].

Some researchers also emphasized on social influence mining as influence strength and influence maximization problem [3, 4, 6, 7, 11, 13]. Most recent attention has focused on the provision of mining influential users [1–3, 11]. The idea behind finding influencers is that they are *worthy targets* well capable of influencing large number of users by activating an influence chain reaction induced by *word-of-mouth*. This phenomenon of shift from broadcast mechanism to many is the key idea behind the viral marketing in which with a very small marketing cost user can actually ingress a huge segment of the network. A markov random field model proposed Domingos and Richardson [8] to discover influential users for viral marketing. Xu et al. [17] proposed to find target groups to maximize the joint influence power (JIP) of influential nodes, where weights on the link between users represent strength of the ties. All these approaches considers social network as a trust network with only positive influence without taking into account the negative influence generated due to antagonistic behavior patterns of the users.

There is relatively small body of literature that is concerned with both positive and negative influences based on the positive and negative relationships among users of the networks. Ahmed et al. [2] proposed mineSeedLS model based on trust network of users to discover influential nodes. Awal et al. [3] proposed an evolutionary approach to discover the set of influential users in SSNs. As evolutionary approaches (EAs) perform good at *discovering* the search space but find it tough to *dig-in* good solutions. Further, EAs can fail as they could converge to a sub-optimal solution. Moreover, MAs have been shown to be orders of magnitude more precise and agile than EAs for many problems [14], thus, we have proposed a novel approach based on memetic algorithm for social influencers mining (*MIMA*) in signed social networks.

3 Mining Influencers in Signed Social Networks: A Memetic Approach

Memetic algorithms (MAs) are popularly known as *hybridized genetic algorithms* which are amalgamation of *genetic algorithm* and *local search mechanism*. MAs and hyper-heuristics are good algorithmic templates that aid in the *balancing act* of successfully and cheaply using general, of-the-shelf, reusable solvers (EAs) with adds-on instance specific features [14]. The following section presents the details of the steps followed by the proposed approach *MIMA* to mine set of influencers in SSNs.

Step 1: **Chromosome Representation and Population Initialization:** We have randomly generated N chromosomes to maintain the diversity in the solutions, represented as a vector of size k, where k is the number of influential users to be mined as shown in Fig. 1.

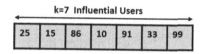

Fig. 1. Chromosome representation

Step 2: **Genetic Operators:** Performance of genetic algorithm is highly dependent on the genetic operators chosen and their parameter values. For selection of chromosomes that undergoes crossover and mutation to produce offsprings *roulette wheel selection* operator is used. For crossover, we have used *two-point crossover operator* to generate new offspring to avoid the premature convergence of the algorithm as shown in Fig. 2. To introduce diversity in the solutions and to avoid the local optima of solutions, *mutation* is employed by randomly replacing a gene with a new gene in the solution, shown in Fig. 3.

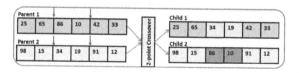

Fig. 2. Two-point crossover operator

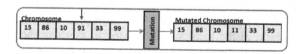

Fig. 3. Mutation operator

Step 3: **Fitness Function** is used to quantify the quality of solutions produced by genetic algorithm and to direct its focus to produce optimal solutions. For computation of influential strength of a user in the network, we have formulated a new fitness function called *Status Influential Strength (SIS)* that aims to optimize the following two objectives to mine set of influencers in a signed social network.

Objective Function1: **Status of a node** in the network can be defined as the sum of degrees of positive incoming links deg_{in}^+ and negative outgoing links deg_{out}^- of the node minus the sum of degrees of positive outgoing links deg_{out}^+ and negative incoming links deg_{in}^- of the node [9], given by Eq. (1).

$$Status(i) = \left(deg(i)_{in}^+ + deg(i)_{out}^-\right) - \left(\deg(i)_{out}^+ + \deg(i)_{in}^-\right) \tag{1}$$

Objective Function2: **Strength of tie** (*Str*) between two nodes in the network can be computed as the ratio of one to the sum of degrees of the nodes minus one [1]. Strength of tie between two nodes node i and node j with degrees $deg(i)$ and $deg(j)$ respectively, computed as:

$$Str(i,j) = \frac{1}{\deg(i) + \deg(j) - 1} \tag{2}$$

Thus, **Average tie strength** (*Avg_Str*) of a node i can be calculated as:

$$Avg\_Str(i) = \frac{1}{n}\sum_{j=1}^{n} \frac{1}{\deg(i) + \deg(j) - 1} \tag{3}$$

Fitness Function: The measure articulated by us termed as **Status Influential Strength (SIS)** to mine influencers in the network is bound to optimize two objectives: *Status* and *Avg_Str* concurrently. This measure will compute the strength of influence a user can apply over other users in terms of his/her status and average link strength on rest of the users in the network. *SIS* of a user i is formulated as the product of user i status and his/her average link strength value given by Eq. (4).

$$\text{Maximize:} \qquad SIS(i) = Status(i) * Avg\_Str(i) \tag{4}$$

It is to be noted that larger the value of strength of influence of a user, more influential the users is.

Step 4: **Local search** is employed in order to improve and refine the next generation population composition. Local search acting on offspring offers systematic search in the proximity of good solutions thus, speed up the *endgame* of an EA. In our work, we have opted hill climbing technique so as to inject appropriate individuals in the mating pool. *FindNeighbors(x)* in the local search is used to generate the neighbors of the current chromosome by randomly selecting a gene from the current chromosome and replacing it with a gene that results in higher fitness value and thus, a new chromosome is produced. The procedures followed for local search and proposed memetic approach *MIMA* for finding set of influential users are given as follows:

Procedure Local Search (x)

---

begin

    repeat until (Stopping criteria is met)

        new ← FindNeighbors(x)

        if f(new) > f(x) then   /* $f(x)$ = fitness of x chromosome */

           x ← new;

        endif

      return x;

  end

Procedure Memetic Algorithm

---

begin

  t=0;

  Randomly generate an initial population Pop(t) $\in \{p_1, p_2,...,p_N\}$;

  for i=1: popSize

    p ← GenerateSolution ( );

    p ← LocalSearch (p);

    Add individual p to Pop(t);

  endfor

  repeat until (Stopping criteria is met) **Do**

    Compute fitness Fit (p) $\forall$ p$\in$ Pop(t) and choose a subset of Pop(t), store them in Q(t) ;

    Recombine and variate individuals in Q(t), store result in Q'(t);

    for   i = 1 : P_c

      Randomly select two parents $P_a, P_b \in$ Q(t);

      P_{child} ← Crossover (P_a, P_b);

      P_{child} ← LocalSearch (P_{child});

      Add individual P_{child} to Q'(t);

    endfor

    for i = 1 : P_m

      Randomly select an individual $P_d \in$ Q(t);

      P_{off} ← Mutation (P_d);

      P_{off} ← LocalSearch (P_{off});

      Add individual P_{off} to Q'(t);

    endfor

    Select individuals from Pop(t) and Q'(t) to generate Pop(t+1);

    t ← t+1;

  endDo

 return best p $\in$ Pop (t-1);

end

---

4 Experimental Setup and Results

4.1 Dataset and Evaluation Metrics

For experimental set up we have used real-world dataset of Epinions [9]. Due to memory constraints we have taken multiple different partitions of 5000 nodes each of this dataset to perform experiments. To nullify the effects of random error we ran the algorithm 10 times on different partitions using the same settings. Details of parameters used to run proposed memetic approach MIMA is given in Table 1.

Table 1. Memetic algorithm parameters

Parameter	Meaning	Value
popSize	Population size	100
pool	Mating pool size	*popSize*/2
P_c	Crossover probability	0.9
P_m	Mutation probability	0.1
tour	Tournament selection	2
Local_Search	Local search	*HillClimbing*
maxGen	No. of iterations	50

To show the performance and validate the effectiveness of proposed approach we have evaluated following metrics:

- **Enhanced Joint Influential Power (EJIP)** is recalled from [3, 17] and reformed as the sum of total effective influence of k influential users let say, G on rest of the users in the network without cogitating inter-influence between them. Thus, from the mined set of k influencers from the network *EJIP* can be computed as follows:

$$EJIP(G) = \sum_{\substack{i \in G, \\ j \in G'}} SIS(i) \tag{5}$$

where, $SIS(i)$ is the status influential strength of user i in the network, $|G| = k$, G' is the complement of G consisting rest of the users in the network.

- **Influence Spread (IS)** is the sum of number of triggered users i.e. *influenced users* (*IU*) by the mined k influencers [3], given by Eq. (6)

$$IS(G) = |IU| = \sum_{i \in G}^{k} IU(i) \tag{6}$$

where, $|IU(i)|$ is the number of users influenced in the network by the user i.

- **Joint Influential Power (JIP)** of the set of mined influencers G is harmonic mean of *Enhanced Influential Power (EJIP)* of G and *Influence Spread (IS)* by G [3] computed as:

$$JIP(G) = \frac{2 * EJIP(G) * IS(G)}{EJIP(G) + IS(G)} \qquad (7)$$

4.2 Experiments and Results

To validate the effectiveness of MIMA, we have compared our proposed approach with state-of the-art: evolutionary genetic approach to mine users in SSNs (MIEA), joint influential power (JIP) [17] and random approach in which influential users are randomly selected (Random) based on the aforementioned described metrics of *Influence Spread* and *Joint Influential Power* for varying k (group size).

It is apparent from the Fig. 4 that MIMA achieved significantly better results for *Influential Spread* compared to MIEA, JIP and Random approach for different k hence, MIMA outperforms the compared existing state-of the-art.

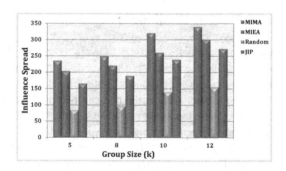

Fig. 4. Influential Spread of MIMA versus existing approaches

Figure 5 shows the results obtained for Joint Influential Power by MIMA and other compared approaches of MIEA, JIP and Random. It can be clearly seen that our proposed approach MIMA compares favorably to the existing approaches and was able to improve the *Joint Influential Power* on consistent basis even for the varying k.

In summary, we can conclude that our proposed approach MIMA is competitive with the state-of-the-art and was able to improve the performance on consistent basis compared to the existing approaches based on evolutionary genetic algorithm, joint influential power (JIP) approach and random approach.

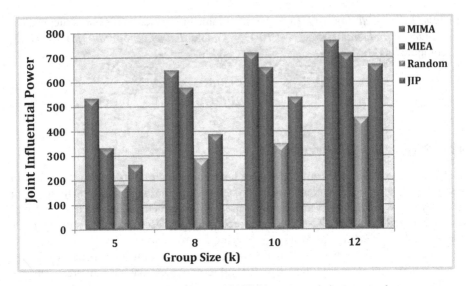

Fig. 5. Joint Influential Power of MIMA versus existing approaches

5 Conclusion and Future Challenges

Social networking sites provide venues not only to users to express their opinions and swap information but also helps businesses as they serve as a platform of an abundant source of information about users' preferences, requirements and the way they get influenced by other users in the network. Influence can be both positive and negative, understanding which can benefit businesses to take action for their future business online strategy. Thus, social influence mining domain is widely studied in both the contexts quantitatively and qualitatively. The purpose of the current work was to determine set of k influential users from SSN that can yield maximum influence on the rest of the users in the network. For this we have proposed a novel model Mining Influencers based on Memetic Algorithm (MIMA) based on our formulated fitness function termed as Status Influential Strength (SIS). The contribution of this work is confirmed through experimental study conducted on real-world Epinions dataset, our proposed approach MIMA compares favorably to the state-of the-art and was able to improve the performance significantly.

This approach will serve as a base for future studies for further exploration of dynamic and temporal aspects of SSNs [9]. Further research would usefully focus on discovering influential nodes based on trust-distrust and demographic features of the users in the network [2, 10]. It would also be interesting to assess the effect of influence maximization [11, 17] and influence propagation [12, 13] in heterogeneous social networks.

References

1. Agarwal, V., Bharadwaj, K.K.: Predicting the dynamics of social circles in ego networks using pattern analysis and GA K-means clustering. Wiley Interdiscip. Rev. Data Min. Knowl. Discov. **5**(3), 113–141 (2015)
2. Ahmed, S., Ezeife, C.I.: Discovering influential nodes from trust network. In: Proceedings of the 28th Annual ACM Symposium on Applied Computing, pp. 121–128 (2013)
3. Awal, G.K., Bharadwaj, K.K.: Mining set of influencers in signed social networks with maximal collective influential power: a genetic algorithm approach. In: Satapathy, S.C., Joshi, A. (eds.) ICTIS 2017. SIST, vol. 84, pp. 263–274. Springer, Cham (2018). https://doi.org/10.1007/978-3-319-63645-0_29
4. Bharathi, S., Kempe, D., Salek, M.: Competitive influence maximization in social networks. In: Deng, X., Graham, F.C. (eds.) WINE 2007. LNCS, vol. 4858, pp. 306–311. Springer, Heidelberg (2007). https://doi.org/10.1007/978-3-540-77105-0_31
5. Bonchi, F.: Influence propagation in social networks: a data mining perspective. IEEE Intell. Inform. Bull. **12**(1), 8–16 (2011)
6. Chen, W., Wang, C., Wang, Y.: Scalable influence maximization for prevalent viral marketing in large-scale social networks. In: Proceedings of the 16th International Conference on Knowledge Discovery and Data Mining, pp. 1029–1038 (2010)
7. Chen, W., Wang, Y., Yang, S.: Efficient influence maximization in social networks. In: Proceedings of the 15th International Conference on Knowledge Discovery and Data Mining, pp. 199–208 (2009)
8. Domingos, P., Richardson, M.: Mining the network value of customers. In: Proceedings of the 7th International Conference on Knowledge Discovery and Data Mining, pp. 57–66 (2001)
9. Girdhar, N., Bharadwaj, K.K.: Signed social networks: a survey. In: Singh, M., Gupta, P., Tyagi, V., Sharma, A., Ören, T., Grosky, W. (eds.) ICACDS 2016. CCIS, vol. 721, pp. 326–335. Springer, Singapore (2017). https://doi.org/10.1007/978-981-10-5427-3_35
10. Golbeck, J., Hendler, J.: Inferring binary trust relationships in web-based social networks. ACM Trans. Internet Technol. (TOIT) **6**(4), 497–529 (2006)
11. Goyal, A., Bonchi, F., Lakshmanan, L.V.: Learning influence probabilities in social networks. In: Proceedings of the 3rd International Conference on Knowledge Discovery and Data Mining, pp. 241–250 (2010)
12. Guha, R., Kumar, R., Raghavan, P., Tomkins, A.: Propagation of trust and distrust. In: Proceedings of the 13th International Conference on World Wide Web, pp. 403–412 (2004)
13. Kempe, D., Kleinberg, J., Tardos, É.: Maximizing the spread of influence through a social network. In: Proceedings of the 9th International Conference on Knowledge Discovery and Data Mining, pp. 137–146 (2003)
14. Krasnogor, N., Aragón, A., Pacheco, J.: Memetic algorithms. In: Alba, E., Martí, R. (eds.) Metaheuristic Procedures for Training Neutral Networks. Operations Research/Computer Science Interfaces Series, vol. 36, pp. 225–248. Springer, Boston (2006). https://doi.org/10.1007/0-387-33416-5_11
15. Leskovec, J., Huttenlocher, D., Kleinberg, J.: Signed networks in social media. In: Proceedings of the SIGCHI Conference on Human Factors in Computing Systems, pp. 1361–1370 (2010)

16. Tang, J., Sun, J., Wang, C., Yang, Z.: Social influence analysis in large-scale networks. In: Proceedings of the 15th International Conference on Knowledge Discovery and Data Mining, pp. 807–816 (2009)
17. Xu, K., Guo, X., Li, J., Lau, R.Y., Liao, S.S.: Discovering target groups in social networking sites: an effective method for maximizing joint influential power. Electron. Commer. Res. Appl. **11**(4), 318–334 (2012)

Author Index

Printed in the United States
By Bookmasters